I0759659
BACKYARD BASH
AT THE GROOVE
PRESENTED BY BLOODSHOT & PANDORA
1103 CALVIN AVE IN NASHVILLE
LYDIA LOVELESS
ROBBIE FULKS
CORY BRANAN
THE BOTTLE ROCKETS
FRIDAY SEPTEMBER 23 5-8 PM
GIVEAWAYS, BEER, FOOD TRUCKS & MORE! FREE TO THE PUBLIC!
BLOODSHOT RECORDS PRESENTS
WRECK YOUR LIFE
RECORD RELEASE
BLOODSHOT RECORDS
SXSW 2017
CHICAGO, IL
DOG PARTY
9PM ROBBIE FULKS
BOBBY BARE JR
BLOODSHOT RECORDS
ROLLING ROCK
70 YEARS
B ★ B ★ Q
12
CHICAGO
THE HIDEOUT
DONATION
AN EVENING OF
~ Spit Roasted Rock n' Roll ~
STARRING
ALEJANDRO ESCOVEDO
WACO BROTHERS WITH RICO BELL
BOBBY BARE JR
DEADSTRING BROTHERS
THE BLACKS REUNITED
SCOTLAND YARD GOSPEL CHOIR
SCOTT H BIRAM
MOONSHINE WILLY
JON LANGFORD
BLOODSHOT RECORDS CHICAGO ILLINOIS USA

Praise for *The Hours are Long, But the Pay is Low*

"Do you possess that perfect combination of idealism and insanity that it takes to evade the minefields evergreen to independent labels—dyspeptic musicians, low budgets, chronic overwork, and blasé audiences? The foolhardy soul contemplating whether indie label life is for them would be wise to pick up Rob Miller's *The Hours Are Long, But the Pay Is Low*, detailing the heady highs and subterranean lows of co-owning Chicago's Bloodshot Records for twenty-five years. The through line is Miller's singular devotion to discovering and propagating great music, learning the hard way that the only way to do it, is to do it."

—**Lisa Fancher,** founder and owner of Frontier Records

"Rob Miller's pseudo-bio of his years with Bloodshot Records covers much musical ground that no foot has yet set upon. He does it with both wisdom and positive enthusiasm for the real and authentic music he played a guiding role in launching. A real treat to read!"

—**Peter Greenberg,** Barrence Whitfield and the Savages

I don't think anyone could have done a truer job of describing the times we all had in the Chicago music scene as Rob does here. He is gifted with such a sincere and un-jaded (no matter how hard he pretends) appreciation of what music and community can do and where it can take you. He has never forced the wide-eyed music fan inside him to 'grow up.' Thank goodness!"

—**Neko Case,** musician, author, and producer

"A gritty, authentic stroll through Chicago's indie music scene told through the eyes of a fan who loved the music so much he built his life on it. For anyone who wants a glimpse into the scene, the time, the music, or Chicago itself, this book is written for you."

—**Kenn Goodman,** CEO and co-founder of Pravda Records

"I very much enjoyed reading this book. The tone was entertaining, and I loved the storyline. The writing is emphatic, authentic, and brainy. Miller's story is one of an outsider—someone who was really struggling, and then slowly becomes enlightened to a whole world that was already there to accept them."

—**Rose Marshack,** author of *Play Like a Man: My Life in Poster Children*

"Wow, what a great read/ride. I found Rob Miller's journey through the music industry fascinating and fun, and when not giggling I was laughing out loud. While obvious in hindsight, the marriage of punk and country was anything but. Yet Miller and his cohorts identified with the punk attitude coursing through many of their favorite bands in Chicago's underground country scene and thought they could help introduce their music to a wider audience. With instinctual grassroots marketing and a commitment to treat their bands fairly, they outmaneuvered the corporate vultures circling overhead. The musical husbandry of Bloodshot Records produced many musical masterpieces over the next twenty-five years. Bloodshot made the world a better place, and Miller was at the center of it all."

—**Jeff Nelson,** Minor Threat and co-founder of Dischord Records

"Back in the day, I used to own a hot dog stand. More importantly, I used to trade hot dogs for Bloodshot CDs. I easily won those deals. Being introduced to Bloodshot's stable of artists was an incredible gift—it was like having the coolest record store delivering its stock direct to my hands every month."

—**Doug Sohn,** former owner of Hot Doug's

"A vibrant, informative, and often hilarious look at a crucial—if undervalued—slice of the music industry. Rob Miller's book also serves as a moving coming-of-age story and a richly detailed description of life in Chicago during the 1990s, a time of upstart artistic explosions and the last vestiges of venerable institutions. *The Hours Are Long, But the Pay Is Low* stands above the slew of books by bigger-name record company founders. While those entrepreneurs seem driven by egos and cash flows, Miller sharply focuses on what the music is all about."

—**Aaron Cohen,** author of *Move on Up: Chicago Soul Music and Black Cultural Power*

"I've always been so proud to be involved with the Bloodshot Records movement and to witness the impact that Rob Miller has had on the arts community in Chicago and ultimately the world. Everyone who shares his love for the moment and his heart-first perspective will delight in this musical journey!"

—**Mike Miller,** owner of Delilah's

THE HOURS ARE LONG BUT THE PAY IS LOW

A CURIOUS LIFE IN INDEPENDENT MUSIC

ROB MILLER

3 Fields Books is an imprint of
the University of Illinois Press.

Manufactured in the United States of America
P 5 4 3 2 1
♾ This book is printed on acid-free paper.

Library of Congress Cataloging-in-Publication Data

Names: Miller, Rob (Co-founder of Bloodshot Records) author
Title: The hours are long, but the pay is low : a curious life in independent music / Rob Miller.
Description: Urbana : 3 Fields Books, an imprint of University of Illinois Press, 2025. | Includes index.
Identifiers: LCCN 2025015716 (print) | LCCN 2025015717 (ebook) | ISBN 9780252088964 paperback | ISBN 9780252048401 ebook
Subjects: LCSH: Miller, Rob (Co-founder of Bloodshot Records) | Bloodshot Records (Firm) | Sound recording industry—Illinois—Chicago | Alternative rock music—United States—History and criticism | Alternative country music—History and criticism | Americana (Music)—History and criticism
Classification: LCC ML3792.B46 M55 2025 (print) | LCC ML3792.B46 (ebook) | DDC 781.640973—dc23/eng/20250617
LC record available at https://lccn.loc.gov/2025015716
LC ebook record available at https://lccn.loc.gov/2025015717

Dedicated to the memories of:

Dex Romweber: A musical idol who became a treasured part of the Bloodshot story and, eventually, a friend. He left this world before he could read what his music meant to me.

Balvinder Mudan: Her unwavering friendship, kindness, loyalty, and astonishing strength and spirit pushed me to get this project over the finish line.

The best music says: you're immortal. But immortal means today, maybe tomorrow. A year from now, with crazy luck.
—Richard Powers, *Orfeo*

Reality comes into being through an interaction.
—Emily Levine

Why do you hate music everybody loves?
—Diana Maldonado

Contents

SIDE B

Prelude

1980. Junior high. I was at the funeral of a friend of my mother's. After the service, I sat alone in the back of the somber, softly lit parlor. I was wearing clunky dress shoes and an ill-fitting, drab, young gentleman's suit—bought for school pictures only to be quickly outgrown—with my gawky wrists dangling beyond the cuffs. An adult friend of the family sat down next to me.

"How's school?" he asked with his gregarious, used-car salesman gusto.

Fine.

"Learning a lot?"

I guess.

He was that guy who always had a saucy *double entendre* for the ladies and an old-school racist joke in the company of men. He was an arm puncher and a backslapper, with a manner that made me as uncomfortable as my Thom McAns.

"I bet you got lots of giiiirlfriends," he leered.

"Well, enjoy," he continued before I could answer. "These are the best years of your life." He smacked my bony knee and was on his way.

I remember that intended-to-be-pep talk with the clarity of a thunderclap. It filled me less with the horror of Gregor Samsa's uneasy dreams than with the droopy-eared discouragement of Eeyore, tied up with a strangling black ribbon of isolation.

This was as good as it was gonna get?

Shit.

Bloodshot
giveashi*t
SUPPORT UNPOPULAR MUSIC
BLOODSHOT RECORDS
KEEP MUSIC EVIL
REVOLT
vinyl.
THIS MACHINE KILLS FASCISTS
VANDOLIERS
do it on vinyl!

INTRODUCTION

Hoist the Black Flag

> There comes a time when every man feels the urge to spit on his hands, hoist the black flag, and start slitting throats.
>
> —H. L. Mencken

I love music: it's a tough thing to say without sounding cheap and sentimental.

But what does it mean?

I love music . . .

It can be a throwaway line, like "Have a nice day" or "Sure, I'll have fries with that."

I *love* music. It's what kids tell their guidance counselors when they say they want to be on *America's Got Talent* someday. It's what adults trot out during the doldrums of the second hour of a first date, after the rundown of siblings and anti-vaxx uncles, but before the anecdotes about that passive-aggressive shrew Janet in accounting.

It's what people yell to their bestie after four Harvey Wallbangers as they karaoke Pat Benatar's "We Belong."

Some *love* music as a distraction, jazz-lite alto sax solos that pass the time while they wait for a prescription or arrival on the seventeenth floor. Some *love* uncomplicated, wallpapery, non-music music whose sole purpose is to avoid the squirminess of silence. Some love it as a nostalgic marker, a catered soundtrack freezing time in a better place when they got the girl and/or the guy, before the rude intrusions of high cholesterol and kids' soccer practices that never end.

For many of us, though, when we say *I love music*, we are speaking of something that impacts us on a level both profound and spontaneous. Through it, we not only discover other worlds, but the paths to maneuver through them. We learn to fight for others, as well as care for ourselves. It offers a leg up or a hand held out, and insights into our past, present, and, often, the future. We hear *us* in it.

Facing page: Photo by Anthony Nguyen, used with permission.

There are as many ways to say *I love music* as there are songs, and there is a story behind each one of them. This is one such story.

And I love music.

Since I was first exposed to what was dismissed as the underground or condemned as punk rock, independent music and the communities surrounding it have been an invaluable instruction manual and companion for, if not standing up against, at least enduring, the confounding world around me and the small minds that said I didn't belong in it. Music was escape, not escapism.

In 1993, I cofounded the independent label Bloodshot Records and devoted the next twenty-eight years to championing music that lurked between genres and under the radar. Alternately accused of and praised for being at the forefront of "insurgent country," Bloodshot was drawn to the good stuff nestled in the dark, nebulous spaces where punk, country, and indie rock mingled and mutated, created by artists who appreciated that music was most innovative and interesting when chances were taken and instincts followed. Sharing a resolutely DIY ethic with most of our artists, we delighted in working over American roots forms with little regard for formality or protocol to take music into strange and exciting new places.

And this happened in, of all places, Chicago.

What compels a music lover to do something as outlandish as starting a record label? Why make the leap from listening to music to getting in the trenches and helping make it happen? I like beer, but I never felt the need to brew my own. I like food, but I never wanted to go on the other side of that door with the porthole window into the kitchen. I like *Big Top Pee-wee,* but I didn't join the circus.

What was the allure? I mean, going to concerts is pretty weird when you think about it. You stand around in a room with strangers. It's dark. It's hot. It's crowded. What time is it? That dumbass spilled a drink on me. What's on the floor and why is it so sticky? God, that first band sucked, and now the tallest dude in the room is standing right in front of me.

But then something mysterious and unpredictable happens. Rising in the sound, lights, heat, conviction, tension, and release is connection and community, a chaotic swirl of new experiences and familiar comforts. Time crystalizes and falls to the floor. I am in a crowd sharing a moment, but also away from the crowd, experiencing my own panoramic view. It is an unruly dynamic where the more we—the audience, the artists—put in, the more we get back. It isn't nostalgia, it isn't self-conscious. It is intensely personal, and fully communal, both transporting and transforming.

For decades, music has grabbed me by the lapels, kicked me in the seat of the pants, and kept me from falling into, or pulled me out of, some deep, lonely pits. It has been a constant companion—a source of encouragement, discovery, and insight—as I stumbled through this life thing. At some point I found I couldn't just go home after a show and think, that was fun . . . *good night*. The question I asked myself wasn't *Why get involved?* but rather *How could I not?*

On the face of it, embarking on a life in music—writing, recording, performing, and certainly being idiotic enough to start a label—is a mad premise. The music business is not a meritocracy: it is a crapshoot taking place in a septic tank balanced on the prow of the *Titanic* while 1,001 snarky know-it-alls pound on the bulkheads with baseball bats and keyboards, a venal snake pit where innovation, creativity, and honest business practices are actively discouraged in favor of get-rich-quick schemes. Being fortunate to make something of a living at it is nothing short of remarkable.

Every independent label is different, but any of them worth their salt and vinyl are, I believe, the same in some foundational ways. To run a label—or any indie endeavor in a creative, localized environment—requires dogged optimism, thick skin, and a balance of dedication and daydream. We all, to a degree, tilt at windmills and chase the joy in hearing something new or different, or hearing something old anew and differently.

Over the years, I had been approached several times to write about my experience with Bloodshot. But how?

Should it be a breezy *Indie Labels for Dummies* handbook to navigate the peripheries of the music world? Perhaps I could pass along pearls of hard-fought wisdom such as:

- The easiest way to get through the crowd and closer to the stage is to follow the waitress with the tray full of drinks as she effortlessly parts the crowd like Chuck Heston did the Red Sea.
- The best sound is, predictably, near the soundboard.
- Never leave home without earplugs.
- When at a crowded show, don't vex the bartender with complicated orders. The name of your drink should have the ingredients in it. Gin and tonic. Vodka and soda. Whiskey and water. Sex on the beach? Sure, but let me finish my drink first . . . *hey now*!
- The person who prefaces something with "I don't mean to be a bother" will be precisely that.
- Never, *ever* stiff the bar and waitstaff, no matter how bad the night.

Many suggested an "I bet you've got some stories, *wink wink*" angle, eager for tales of bands too wasted to play or gossipy revelations of their bad, stupid, or embarrassing private moments. And sure, I have seen—and been in—fights offstage, onstage, backstage, in the studio, in the office, in a van, *on* a van, and outside of Hot Doug's. I've had front row seats to artists' frailties and faults, but tickling prurient interests with tiresome recitations of who threw up on who, who punched who, or who slept with who didn't interest me. I've participated in a few such histories, and they leave me cold, rarely providing insight into the music, the process, or the connection between audience and artist that drove what I did. Besides, many readers have not likely even heard of Bloodshot or given a thought about what insurgent country was. Some of our artists you may have heard of but most you haven't; some were kind of well known in a few circles, but none of them headlined Budokan or had trashy documentaries made about them. It is easy to find label stories with bigger personalities and better drugs. Names aren't named, grievances aren't aired, grudges aren't settled. Read a Mötley Crüe book if that's what you are looking for.

To keep from sinking in a quagmire of sad during the summer of the 2020 COVID-19 lockdown, I read and listened to over a quarter century of interviews, and I noticed I had been asked the same handful of questions hundreds of times:

> *What was your motivation to start a label? How is punk rock an influence in your formation? What's involved in running a label? How has Chicago factored into the Bloodshot Records story? What gets you interested in a band? Etc., etc., etc.*

However, interviewers often weren't (or couldn't be) interested in space-consuming, elaborate answers; they needed crisp quotations. Lengthy tirades, philosophical tangents, or contextual subtleties were usually savagely edited down into something bearing scant resemblance to what I meant. So, as time went on, I polished and refined my responses—and then I polished and refined them some more. I slept-spoke in epigrams that, while true, were only a sliver of the story, *Moby Dick* summed up as a book about a big fish.

Since the topics remained constant, despite the years, albums, and artists changing, I wondered about their persistence. Shaking off the years of soundbites, I realized they boiled down to variations on two questions: *Why?* and *How?* And while the world is unruly and messy—just like music—one thing became unmistakable: The *How* always flowed from the *Why*. They were inseparable.

Telling this story of *How* and *Why* is absurdly simple and endlessly complex. I could flippantly say that Bloodshot Records was started with a frothy blend of boredom, arrogance, ignorance, and innocence, or grandly suggest cherished musical idioms needed "saving" and we had a plan to do it. I could be as glib as "some naïfs ponied up some dough and *presto,* we were a label" or engage in pointy-headed ruminations on the nature of independence and ethics. None of it is true, even though it all sort of is. There's history, but this is not *a* history. I offer suggestions, insights, warnings, and I also glide over or ignore critical norms to suit my whims. In exploring this trip through independent music, the highs, the lows, and the long in-betweens, there may be tall tales and hyperbole, and events might be misremembered, conflated, or condensed, sometimes even on purpose, but they *feel* true—and isn't that what matters these days? This is a book about beliefs, ethics, and motivations, and I can only vouch for my own. It is objectively, unapologetically subjective. This is a story of how I got to where I did.

The more I wrote and explored the questions of *Why?* and *How?*, however, the more I realized that, while Bloodshot might not have been planned, it wasn't an accident.

That might not make sense, but neither did writing down the idea to start a label on a soggy bar napkin in a Chicago tavern one gloomy winter's evening.

SIDE A

1

Don't Conform, Be Like Us

1993. It had been another demoralizing day at Mike's compound in the Old Town neighborhood of Chicago. He had an uncanny ability to anticipate precisely when I needed money and would take any home improvement job he had to offer, so I had hang-doggedly returned his call and agreed to spend the day wire-brushing spray paint off the sewerage covers in his parking lot. It was a raw early December afternoon, raw in that way that Chicagoans learn to sourly endure with hunched stoicism. Wire-brushing paint off cold metal under a dishwater-gray sky was exactly as much fun as it sounded. My fingers were cracked and bleeding. My back hurt, my nose ran, and my soul groaned. I stood up and stretched out the knots and kinks when Mike came out to pay me.

"You've gotten taller."

"Maybe it's the heels on my winter work boots."

"You in heels. Now *there's* something I'd like to see," he winked.

The first time I'd met Mike, a doughy, lecherous man in his sixties—he had responded to my R&B Painting and Carpentry classified ad in the free alternative weekly *Chicago Reader* a couple years earlier—he answered the door in his underwear. I was invited into the baroque kitsch living room that occupied a decorative spectrum between Charles Foster Kane and Liberace and directed to sit on a snow-white sectional opposite his no-longer snow-white comfy chair. We discussed the estimate for the project—minor, nettlesome tasks my work partner referred to as "squeaky cat door jobs"—but it was autumn, we had recently moved to town, and work was scarce. He was watching Anita Hill's testimony during the Clarence Thomas confirmation hearing and asked abruptly, but almost wistfully, "Don't you miss fuck films?" and then took me on a creepy trip down his neon-lit memory lane to a time when Old Town was much seedier, when Wells Avenue wasn't full of sushi bars and improv clubs, but peep shows and adult bookstores.

Um . . .

Turning his attention back to the hearings, he asked me in (mock?) disbelief, "Have *you* ever left a pubic hair on a Coke?"

What . . .?

In the end, I took the job. I had to. Rent, food, etc. He paid well. It's an old story.

Two years later, after pocketing my shredded knuckle wages, I sullenly waited for the 72 North Avenue bus. An express plastered with WCIU-TV Channel 26 ads for their new lineup of syndicated fare, including *Cops* and *The People's Choice,* slopped past me through brown slush the consistency of a shitty diner's mashed potatoes. The local pulled up quickly and soaked me knees to boots. I got on and fishtailed my way to a seat as the driver jerked away from the curb. I put on my paint- and stain-spattered Walkman and Nirvana's "Territorial Pissings" jumped into my ears. I turned it up to cleanse my brain and thought, *I had to find a way, a better way.*

* * *

By 1993, many of the bands I had seen in scruddy punk clubs a few years before in my hometown of Detroit were playing auditoriums. I never could have foreseen that when I was buying their singles or albums out of a rusting Econoline van after shows with four crumpled, sweaty dollar bills, their music would go to influence almost everything coming after it. Back then, the possibilities of broad recognition seemed laughable, but then Nirvana broke a wave that had been cresting slowly in the shadows for years. No one was laughing anymore.

Overnight, music industry scouts threw away their company-issued "How to Tell the Difference between Poison and Whitesnake" and "Ten Hip-Hop Terms Everyone Should Know" pamphlets in order to quickly ascertain the commercial appeal of the Fastbacks and TAD. Major label speculators tossed around contracts to anyone who could name-check two Stooges songs, and underground oddities like Daniel Johnston and Flipper started getting deals. Music nerds were hired fresh from college DJ gigs for A&R positions and tasked with finding the next subsidiary of Grunge, Inc. These underground underdogs, the not-yet-cool kids who got sound thrashings for their "Slack Motherfucker" and Bikini Kill T-shirts, were storming the gates! It was time to let the world know how great the Fall and the Feelies were and put the heads of Van Hagar on pikes by the drawbridge. *Now people will hear these artists . . .*

Idealism ran high. Perhaps, some of us thought, "we" had "won."

The dirty little secret, though, was that the majors weren't buying, they were—now and forever—selling; it was the music *business.* They signed bands like a carnival barker lured the rubes into the snake oil tent, *Step right up, yes YOU in the CBGB T-shirt, YOU could have a hit record, sign right here,* looking for another jackpot. They offered sums that made an indie musician's head dance with visions of luxury and decadence but probably didn't cover the CFO's shoe budget. For every ten failures, they might get a one million-selling success, making the whole undertaking profitable. Little risk, big potential rewards.

I watched with a sinking feeling in my gut as my adopted hometown swooned at the mirages of fortunes made and streets easy as industry forces sensed money in the waters of our miraculously reversed river and decided that Chicago was *next*. I thought of the Clash singing many years before, "Huh, you think it's funny, turning rebellion into money" in *(White Man) In Hammersmith Palais*. When a few local bands clawed their way to a degree of popular consciousness after years of general indifference, the August 21, 1993, issue of *Billboard*, the weekly bible of the Industry, declared it "the new capital of the cutting edge." The article helpfully included a map of Wicker Park, the neighborhood at the center of the city's buzz, and lauded the city's dirty-fingernails work ethic, its rust belt candor and pugnacity. Art from industrial decay mixed with middle American genuineness! "What's Hot" think pieces distilled the notion further to "Chicago: The Next Seattle." This was a splashier story to tell—and sell—than one of diligent work, and nurturing, interwoven circles of artists and friends that had evolved to make Chicago a dynamic sanctuary for the creatively inclined, and passed over the diversity, weirdness, and uniqueness that blossomed here, far from the usual hunting grounds of talent. A vibrantly diverse ecosystem that encouraged musicians to embrace distinctive voices—plus the network of indie clubs, record stores, labels, studios, and *people* who supported them—was ignored as *The Scene* was exalted. Urge Overkill, Liz Phair, the Smashing Pumpkins, Veruca Salt, and many others were lumped together as the *Chicago Sound* solely based on driver's license addresses. It was as reductive as saying a plate of truffle cream rigatoni and currywurst were both "European food": both are fabulous but hardly interchangeable. Just being *from* here was enough. Who had time for nuance? It was time for business, dammit, not critical hair-splitting. Chicago, the popular narratives advanced, was more real than the last thing the industry told us was real. And realer still than that which had been declared real before that. *Death to the phonies from other places!*

Warming in the dirty light streaming through the tall windows of Urbus Orbis, the Wicker Park coffee shop that was the Ground Zero of the Ground Zero of the scene, one could look out and watch as the sharks circled, the vultures descended, and the crocodiles smiled.*

---

* Music industry/animal kingdom comparisons never evoke meerkats or baby otters.

Fresh-faced guitarists carrying Big Muff effects pedals—still in their Guitar Center bags—were chased down the fashionably gritty street, past junkies and third-shifters sheltering in doorways from the vicious lake winds, by tar-hearted mercenaries promising magic beans and tour buses. It fed a frenzy that became a self-fulfilling prophecy: this was going to be big because it *had* to be big, the tenets of rapacious capitalism commanded it to be so. Senior VPs flew in from the coasts for the weekend, set up their sluice boxes on the balconies of their Magnificent Mile hotel suites, and looked to strike it rich. Bands had scouts in the audience for their second-ever show at Thurston's, and getting signed had become the answer, though people had forgotten what the question was. *Consequences, schmonsequences, as long as I'm rich.*

The bands that took the bait were often thrown into a regimen of ham-fisted meddling in the guise of sage advice: *We love what you do, you're hot, you're original . . . but can you play it a bit more like Mudhoney?* And if the record wasn't the next *Nevermind,* or even the next *Every Good Boy Deserves Fudge,* the band might be cast into the morale-eroding quicksand of disinterest, hammier-fisted meddling, "reallocated" resources going in a "fresh" direction, and their label champion getting reassigned or disappeared. If the band managed to survive this sausage grinder, well then, *let's go have some Ketel One martinis and talk about the next record, we've got some ideas . . . don't worry, it's totally recoupable.**

Indie music was becoming another shitty job for another shitty boss.

That alternative turned into "Alternative" shouldn't have caught me by surprise. I wasn't an idiot. This was America and music was big business, and success bred imitation. It was, as the old saying goes, the sincerest form of cashing in. Copying and diluting was easier, and more profitable, than creating. Initially, I wasn't too concerned. My refuge in the underground, a place where I had found solace and inspiration for so long, seemed removed from these craven machinations; it was *different.* When middle-of-the-dial radio stations and teen video shows were clogged with *get the money and run* acts in the burgeoning hip-hop scene, so be it: give the kiddies in their parachute pants and Vanilla Ice fades what they wanted. If hard rock fans wanted the "heavy" in heavy metal to refer as much to pancake makeup applied and hair product sprayed as the music, what did I care? New Girls on the Spice Block? *Mmmmbop* all the way to the galleria, my friends. And that Boomer canon I'd been told for decades *really* mattered, that culture-defining soundtrack to the Summer of Love and the protests that ended the Vietnam War . . . er . . . *eventually* and had been reduced to The Who doddering through "Won't Get Fooled Again" at the Super Bowl and the Beatles' "Revolution" selling Nikes? I never drank that electric Kool-Aid.

* *Recoupable?* thinks the guileless band. *What's that mean?*

But as this imperative to find the Next Big Thing™ turned sharply *toward* the underground, it became personal. Economic and cultural forces that had spurned unpopular music and the dorky curmudgeons like me who listened to it now smelled a quick buck; the previously scorned and marginalized were now hip and profitable. "Alternative" went from vague descriptor indicating *no money to be made here, folks, move along* to a rallying cry during 3Q growth PowerPoints, a marketing buzzword as neutered as "New & Improved" and "Now with Marshmallows!" Community transformed into commodity, and it wasn't sitting well with me.

The smart bands kept the money and kept their autonomy, conscious they would likely never fit in, no matter what the superfan who'd been at the label for eight months told them over $250 bottles of expense account wine. Others put out records beneath their talents—pleasing simulacrums of what had made them compelling in the first place—some made records that got shelved or forgotten, some grabbed moments in the limelight with a few weeks of airplay on MTV's *120 Minutes*, and some crumpled in the face of unreasonable industry expectations. And when the accountants reckoned that Daniel Johnston's fragile warble wouldn't fill arenas with heartbroken teenaged girls carrying cash-filled purses, or Flipper's knuckle-dragging squall wouldn't put the Benjamins into the coffers, no amount of soft-soaping them as "prestige" artists would placate their shadowy overlords. They were no more interested in developing mid-level, sustainable careers for gifted artists than the auto industry was in building safe, fuel-efficient cars in the 1970s.*

When the streams were played out, when the mules had been eaten by the end of a hard winter, it was the musicians, and the indie subcultures that buoyed them, that suffered. The majors pulled up stakes and merrily moved on to the next potential payoff—maybe combining the bone-headiest elements of rap and rock into something that would be known as rap rock—leaving behind a pillaged community that had been ill-prepared for a bottom-line boom and bust mentality to wash over it. As Bugs Bunny said after working over Elmer Fudd with a straight razor in "The Rabbit of Seville": "Next!"

In retrospect, it was laughable for me to think that Nirvana's triumph heralded the remaking of anything. That raw emotion with such tectonic heft could become the norm. That the music industry or, for that matter, the wider culture, would be ushered into an era of imagination and openness. The rock does not command the quarry, and the harsh, age-old reality was that the power would remain where it always had been. Equilibrium would

---

* FLIPPER?! I mean, their half-witted masterpiece "Sex Bomb" has brought me incalculable joy through the years, but they had little place in decent society. That anyone ever expected anything resembling a profitable major label relationship with *Flipper* was a collective fantasy of the highest order.

return. Not even Kurt Cobain's earth-cracking screams could change that. Seeing a Sub Pop or Touch and Go sticker on a rusty Mazda had once meant something; now one had to ask oneself what it was all about. "Alternative" was everywhere, which begged the question, alternative to *what*?

1993. Martha Stewart was telling the morning TV crowd how to throw grunge-themed parties, billboards and bus signs featured attentively scruffed models adorned in the latest all-the-rage flannel wear, and the Great Alternative Revolution flag was being flown by 100,000 Day-Glo Lollapalooza revelers chanting, "Don't conform, be like us!"

In such dark and confusing times, the idea of Bloodshot Records was hatched.

2

My Cleanest Dirty Shirt

The common assumption made of someone who starts a record label is that they must have grown up in a house surrounded by a cornucopia of vibrant sounds, monomaniacally driven to it from an early age. But my earliest memories of music are . . . unsubstantial.

The mid-1970s hi-fi in my parents' house, rarely used, was limited to Mom's Roger Whittaker and Broadway show cast albums that might get played on pinochle night. Dad's favorite music was the growl of a big block 440-V8 in a '71 Plymouth Barracuda, the march of whatever football team's band was playing while he dozed on the couch on weekend afternoons, and, later, the Weather Channel theme. Radio meant WJR 760 AM, 50,000 watts broadcast from the "golden towers of the Fisher Building," Detroit's Albert Kahn–designed art deco skyscraper that was also the headquarters of General Motors. It was the genial, lite-news talk of J. P. McCarthy in the morning and Detroit Tiger baseball with the greatest broadcast duo in history—don't argue with me on this one—Ernie Harwell and Paul Carey at night. I didn't have a cool older sibling, or friends with cool older siblings, to shepherd me into music—conspiratorially letting me steal listens of their new Grand Funk Railroad or Flamin' Groovies LPs, decode the *Sgt. Pepper* cover, explain whatever Golden Earring meant about "red-eye love," or tell me what "wrapped up like a douche/deuce/doosh" could possibly mean. My younger sister stacked her Close 'N Play record player with Shaun Cassidy, and the *Xanadu* and *Grease* soundtracks. It was, as she remembers, "a musical wasteland."

In elementary school, I had no inkling that music could be current and meaningful to one's existence. Foisted on my tender little ears was an amber-crusted book of songs about manifest destiny, mules, and the Erie Canal that Calvin Coolidge would have liked. Some being from another planet listening in on the music classes would have been forgiven for thinking that John

Philip Sousa and George M. Cohan were the hot acts of the day, the meat and liberty potatoes of any ten-year-old's sonic diet. For impenetrable reasons, patriotic Civil War and World War I songs were drummed into us. (With the benefit of hindsight—the Vietnam War was in the process of grinding to its ignominious conclusion—the reasons for the forced patriotism are, perhaps, less impenetrable to me now.) The teacher would roll out the clunky, gray Audiotronics record player and Cohan's "You're A Grand Old Flag" and "Over There" creaked to life, the needle skipping over the dust of doughboys. As we dutifully tweedled songs sixty years removed from the events opaquely referenced in the lyrics, the line *Send the word that the Yanks are coming* had me, a Tigers fan, wondering if the song might have something to do with baseball. The rest of the lyrics were as incomprehensible as the *wah-wah-wahing* of Charlie Brown's teacher.

Fully ignorant of the tenets of separation of church and state, we marched in place and sang the "Battle Hymn of the Republic": *Glory, glory, hallelujah / His truth is marching on . . .* His? Who's he? Sousa's "The U.S. Field Artillery March" was watered down on our chemical-smelling mimeographed lyric sheets as "When the Caissons Go Rolling Along." What *was* a caisson, anyway? Regardless, why were we, with Crunch Berries still stuck in our teeth from breakfast and grass stains from recess on the knees of our indestructible Sears Toughskin jeans, enjoined to sing *Then it's hi! hi! hee! / In the field artillery* in the first place? Yet I shouldn't watch Tex Avery and Daffy Duck cartoons because of the violence? Watching Wile E. Coyote get flattened by an ACME anvil was somehow more ruinous than glorifying the period that gave us the horrors of Verdun and trench warfare?*

The one "contemporary" number I remember was "This Land Is Your Land." As I learned it, it was a jaunty travelogue about skyways, highways, redwood forests, and Gulf Stream waters. America patting itself on its back for a job well done and being so gosh darn lovely. It wasn't until college that I learned they had clipped out all the naughty Commie bits. For my own good, no doubt.

The few albums I could call my own were a handful of *Country Bear Jamboree* and Disney soundtrack LPs. Louis "King Louie" Prima's "I Wanna Be Like You" from *The Jungle Book* still holds up. As Baloo the Bear says, "Man, what a beat." The treacly *Frozen* or *The Lion King* can't touch it.

Other than that, the only "music"—as I fuzzily understood it—that I had any connection to was via my constant companion: television. And I didn't mean when performers like Dean Martin, Eydie Gormé, or Conway Twitty

---

* For a disturbing and illuminating history of many other cornerstones of the Great American Songbook, I strongly recommend Nick Tosches' *Where Dead Voices Gather.*

interrupted the comedy skits on the *Sonny & Cher Comedy Hour* or *Hee Haw* with their adult songs, wide lapels, and chiffon getups. Donny and Marie Osmond's good-natured call for cross-genre understanding, "A Little Bit Country—A Little Bit Rock 'n Roll" left me a whole lot bored. I'd go to the kitchen for a Fla-Vor-Ice when that shit came on. No, the music that I grooved along with were the theme songs. *The Beverly Hillbillies, Green Acres,* and *The Addams Family* told me everything I needed to know about the shows. No complicated, arcing storylines to follow, no real-world intrusions; they were hermetically sealed universes laid at my feet in 103 seconds for easy digestion every half hour. To this day, when I hear *fresh air,* in any context for any reason, my brain doesn't conjure Terry Gross nerding out about Stephen Sondheim, it snaps, in milliseconds, to Eddie Albert pounding his vested chest and Eva Gabor singing "Times Square." Who among us hasn't reflexively filled in "movie stars" after hearing "swimming pools" or said *scre-um* to rhyme with *museum*? And with the quasi-surfing spy hook of the *Batman* theme, *Sanford and Son*'s wild Quincy Jones funk, and the titillating exoticism of *Hawaii Five-O,* who, really, even needed words?*

When I stayed at Grandma's house on Friday nights, I was allowed, beyond the jurisdiction of my parents, to stay up past Official Bedtime and watch *The Rockford Files.* I'd sit cross-legged in front of the hulking Magnavox and eat my Pow-Wow Popcorn (with its unfortunate grinning "Indian princess" logo) out of my green, space-age metallic bowl while she smoked without break. From the opening close-ups of the telephone answering machine—an unimaginably far-out gadget—to the quick-edit montage of all things dangerous and gritty in the realm of an LA private eye, I got a tantalizing peak into the world of adults. And the soundtrack was the distorted harmonica, kettle drums, and whatever the hell that lead instrument was. Hearing two seconds of that song now and I'm right back in that room inhaling second-hand Pall Malls and feeling like I'm getting away with something.

Out of curiosity, I awkwardly tried to engage with what I thought "real" music was. I conned my other grandma into letting me stay up to watch the great technical feat of Elvis Presley's *Aloha From Hawaii via Satellite.* I'd seen some of his movies during Elvis Week, which was never as good as Godzilla Week, James Bond Week, or Raquel Welch Week, on Channel 7's *Four O'Clock Movie.* But this was Prime Time, it involved satellites, it was on the cover of *TV Guide,* it was an Event; it had to be good, right? Instead, what I saw that night was a tubby, glassy-eyed guy pickled in barbiturates wearing a sequined jumpsuit taking leis from hysterical women in the audience. I wondered what the fuss was about and went to bed after a few songs. My sister and I had

---

* Surfboards! Hula dancers! Fish-eye lens views of jet engines! It still makes the blood race!

a stoner babysitter, who wore clunky glasses, a poncho, and sandals—real counterculture stuff at the time—who let me stay up to see Black Sabbath on *Don Kirshner's Rock Concert*. I thought they might be related to the Boris Karloff horror flick of the same name I'd seen on Sir Graves Ghastly's Saturday afternoon TV show. It was not. Instead, it was a few dudes playing what seemed like the same song for an hour in front of a crowd that looked like the older kids with Robitussin sweats I avoided on the playground. Yawn. And the Doobie Brothers on *What's Happening!!* What *was* happening . . .?

I withdrew to my comforting musical funhouse of TV themes, classical music filtered through "What's Opera, Doc?" and composer Carl Stalling's recontextualizations of '30s and '40s popular tunes, whose only deeper meanings to me were "Daffy gets his bill blown off by a shotgun" or "Bugs goes full transvestite to woo Elmer." To this day, people are astounded that I know less about the basics of rock and roll than almost anyone. Other kids had Plant and Page, I had Tigers' double-play tandem of Trammell and Whitaker. Music, as such, didn't yet exist for me.

As I entered junior high school in suburban Detroit, the prospects for this bookish, timid-to-the-point-of-paralysis kid, neither egg man nor walrus, felt bleak. For those possessing little in the way of physical or convivial distinction, help was not offered, and mercy not shown. The weak and weird were tormented in the name of that uniquely adolescent capacity for cruelty. My books or homework might get knocked off my desk or go flying into the bathroom or a trash can. Maybe I'd get a snot-covered hand wiped on my shirt or in my hair. Socks pulled up too high, grounds for a beating by the swim team mesomorphs. Socks not pulled up high enough? Same. Getting an A on a test or paper, grounds for a swirlie. Comb in wrong back pocket, grounds for having it pissed on and run through my hair. Just *existing*, grounds for letting me know what was wrong with me: too short, too ugly, ears too big, hair stupid, T-shirt gay, tennis shoes lame, and no one likes me so why don't I fuck off and die.

Lunch period meant the crucible of the cafeteria. Opportunities to swipe my fries, squirt ketchup on my shirt, dump leftover vegetable "medleys" on my head, or pour milk over my sandwich abounded. During *Animal House*–inspired food fights, I was an acceptable target for any clique. I hung toward the back of the chow line. I gauged that having fewer choices, the last lion to the wildebeest carcass, as it were, was worth it because by the time I found a seat, everyone should be fully engaged in their own meals and might not be bothered to notice me. If I was lucky, I could sneak out and eat in an empty classroom. Beyond the cafeteria was the daunting courtyard, domain of the burnouts: scary chicks with big asses crammed in tight jeans with feathered roach clips in their long, parted-in-the-middle hair, and surly dudes with no asses in saggy jeans with bandanas in their long, parted-in-the-middle hair. It was a gauntlet of eight D-cell battery jam boxes blasting . . . something alien and fearsome, intimidating *fuck yeahs,* clouds of Oakland County ditchweed, and the prospect of a swift pummeling. I was always on the alert. I never knew what was coming, or why, and I got conditioned to dozens of snap calculations every day that bent toward *not standing out.*

Not having the common currency of music didn't help. In a metro area collapsing under the inertial weight of its dying industrial might, the stamping plant fodder distilled their mantra to *Let's get wasted.* It was a workin' for the weekend culture of midnight viewings of *Quadrophenia*, concerts at Cobo Hall, jungle-patching lawns, war wagons—junky cars bought to be graffitied, driven around, and eventually trashed—and the casual teenage vandalism of the privileged, the desperate, and the bored. It was *De*-troit Rock City, a party town, and I had not gotten an invitation.

When faced with the choice of "theater" or "band," I chose band, as standing on a stage and speaking was a hard pass. Because I thought *The Tonight Show* theme was kind of cool, *dah, dunt dunt dah dah,* I chose the trumpet. I'd go through the fingerings and puff out my cheeks like I'd seen Dizzy Gillespie do on the *Dinah Shore Show,* but I had no ear for it. The other trumpet players didn't like me sucking up our section, and spit valves were "accidentally" emptied on me when the teacher wasn't looking. Unsurprisingly, that didn't encourage me to get better. Halfway through the semester, Mr. Franklin, with his pointy black beard and horn-rimmed glasses, told us a French horn player was needed. Volunteers were sought. No hands went up. (Perhaps in hierarchy of brass, the French horn had effete, foreign connotations, and the trombone, trumpet, and flugelhorn players were not interested.) He told us that it would take a lot of study to reach the level of proficiency to join the orchestra, so the French Hornist-to-be would be afforded as much private time as they needed in the practice room next door.

He had me at *private time,* and I became, at that moment, first and only chair French Horn. I spent the remainder of that semester blissfully alone in a cinder block room painted the color of a rotting lemon, reading Jack London and doing my homework. Hauling around the thoroughly uncool-shaped plastic hard case was a trifling price to pay for an hour of solitude and spit valve–free serenity. When I heard the orchestra in the other room coming to the end of a piece, I would loudly stagger through scales, and maybe throw in a couple of wobbly bars of *Stars and Stripes Forever* to suggest effort and progress. Mr. Franklin never checked in on me and I never played a recital or concert, yet I got a B. At the time, I thought I had gotten away with the perfect crime, but I now suspect he had taken mercy on me and didn't even need a French horn.

In my room at home, I spent hours listening to the radio, trying to divine the appeal of the bands whose black, three-quarter-length-sleeve concert tees I saw every Monday in the halls after the big show, to find some portal to, perhaps, connection and acceptance. At the time, Detroit airwaves were saturated with Tull, Floyd, Van Halen, Queen, and, of course, the Zep. One station, WLLZ, was nicknamed "Whole Lotta Led Zeppelin" without a whiff of irony or derision, and the gravelly basso profundo *BABY!* of Arthur "The Poobah" Penhallow on WRIF *ray-day-diddio* was the rallying cry of every kegger and drag race in the 313 area code. (The one program that I *did* like was the syndicated Dr. Demento Show on Sunday nights, which specialized in novelty and comedy recordings. That was sure as shit not something someone looking to avoid sound thrashings mentioned out loud.)

Most of the songs were about partying all night and *ev-er-y day*, wango tangos, and fairies in the land of ice and snow. The operatic horseshit, proggy round-abouting, and spaced-out riding on the storms was so monotonous. "Layla" and "Free Bird" seemed like they would never end. Have they yet? "Stairway to Heaven" made we wonder why people liked music at all. Bustle in my hedgerow? What? And then there were those songs about girls who would never, ever talk to me. If one had—even to tell me to get out of her goddamn way—I would have sputtered away like an untied balloon.* For me, music was just . . . there. Like math, stress hives, and bologna sandwiches on Wonder bread.

In the frightening shop class, while ancient, eight-and-a-half-fingered Mr. Phillips upbraided people for making *mary-ju-wanna pipes* on the drill presses, I kept to myself. A big room with power tools, large racks of lumber blocking the teacher's view of punchings and wedgies, and loud noises drowning out insults was uncomfortable territory. I had nearly completed my term project, a balsa wood scale model of an A-frame house, on October 21, 1977. One of the dudes I reflexively cowered from came into the shop late and relayed the news to the class that a plane crash killed Lynyrd Skynyrd. Judging by everyone's reactions, it seemed like a big deal. I faintly asked my work-tablemate, "Who's Leonard Skinner?" And before I could process the commotion around me, an oversized C-clamp landed on my project, crushing it like Godzilla's foot on a Japanese fishing village in a slapdash burst of mourning and malice. *Are you a fucking idiot?*

I got the only D of my life in that class.

---

* As for the other popular music of the day, disco, its biggest impact on me was the Tigers winning by forfeit the second game of a doubleheader thanks to Disco Demolition Night at Comiskey Park. Chicago DJ Steve Dahl had the bright idea to let fans in for 98 cents if they brought a disco record. Between games, they put them in a pile on the field and blew them up. That anyone was surprised by the ensuing mayhem astounds me to this day.

If I did hear something I kind of liked, the paranoid power pop of "Dream Police," say, and asked what it was, it was treated as the dumbest utterance ever, further proof of my unworthiness. *Fucking asshole, it's Cheap Trick. Rick Nielsen Rules!* At a school dance my mother forced me out of the house to go to, the DJ played Led Zeppelin's "Misty Mountain Hop," and I asked him, "Who's this?" He gaped at me, and the nearby burnouts who overheard me laughed and laughed. When I left the gym, someone had stuck their penknife into my bike tires. *You fucking idiot.*

So I'd slink back to my room and marinate in a dull dread, sighing the sigh of the cast out and get lost in the Richard Pryor and Monty Python LPs checked out from the public library. Why couldn't I just *like* something? I thought Steve Martin's "King Tut" was a jam. Why didn't that count? The music swirling around me about alienation and angst was the soundtrack for the very people causing my alienation and angst. I went to school, week after soul-deadening week, wondering what was wrong with me—because, obviously, it *had* to be my fault—the bullying almost a prosaic symptom of a bigger, more unknowable problem.

What was your first concert?

In 1980, I mustered the nerve to dip a toe into the realm of "the show" and, with some luck, uncover the elusive appeal of music, to do something regular kids did. I bought a ticket in the nosebleed section for Alice Cooper's *Flush the Fashion* tour—with Aerosmith's Joe Perry Project, *Let the Music Do the Talkin'*-era opening—at Joe Louis Arena.

I liked, as much as I liked anything on the radio at that point, the single "Clones," a cool-sounding song about alienation and conformity that felt substantially more relatable and biting than the turgid "Another Brick in the Wall." It is a lesser-known star in *le firmament du Cooper,* already underappreciated, but I still stand by it. I researched his earlier work via the public library as well, especially "School's Out"; "School's been blown to pieces" felt like a potential happy resolution to many of my headaches.

The smells of stale, warm beer, sweaty, smoky air, and reefer in the rafters of the arena were strange and unsettling. During the opener's set, the previously inert burnout behind me sat up and let forth a torrent of puke. I took the brunt of it, chunky wet and pungently sweet and sour. I had to spend all the money I had with me for a concert T-shirt. By the time I got back to my seat, he was out cold again, head between his knees.

When Alice Cooper came out, way, *way* down on that stage, half a mile away it seemed, there wasn't the usual gore and theatrics or whatever people were expecting. This current iteration of his act was, apparently, too "new-wavey" or something and S&M for the denizens of Detroit Rock City. Lots of "you suck" rained down from the cheap seats. By his second act, after a wardrobe change and warhorses like "Under My Wheels" and "Billion Dollar Babies" were unharnessed, Alice had them back in his corner. All was apparently forgiven, or at least forgotten, in the purplish haze swirling around us. When the show finished and the house lights came on, the crowd roared. Puke Guy came to, jolted up, raised his fist, and yelled an ecstatic "YEEEAAHHHHHH!" and that was it. Let's hear it for the transformative power of Rock and Roll!

I wasn't any closer to a kinship with this alien, cabalistic world.

3

Jams, Kicked Out

Every Monday morning in homeroom, I'd sit mute, hopefully invisible, and listen in on the postmortems of the weekend's *Saturday Night Live* musical guests. I watched it for the comedian guest hosts like Eric Idle and Buck Henry, but when the soporific noodling of Eddie Money, the Grateful Dead, or James Taylor came on, I'd go get a snack. It was Eydie Gormé dropping in on the *Sonny and Cher* show all over again. But given that there were so few opportunities to actually *see* bands on TV, maybe I could sponge up some insight. Who rocked. Who was lame. Who ruled. Who drooled.

Nothing clicked.

Then, one February Saturday night, the musical guest was a band called the Talking Heads. Holy shit, *what was this*? Their performance of "Take Me To The River" pulsed with a subdued, jittery menace. There was no bombast, no drum solos, no guitar posturing. The band didn't have capes, sequins, feathered boas, or shaggy Ron Wood haircuts. They looked and dressed and stood awkwardly. Like I did. They looked past the camera, past the audience, with a *like us or don't* bemusement—not a defiance—as if others' judgements were irrelevant. In my memory, singer David Byrne didn't blink the entire song; his was a crazy, unsettling stare and a knowing smirk—like he was in on a joke we didn't even know was being told. His ungainly, barbaric yawps at the end came from a place I could feel but couldn't yet name or access. It was the exultation of *otherness* I didn't understand or know how to uncork. This clicked.*

---

* Adding to their appeal was the decidedly unglamorous bassist Tina Weymouth at a time when women were largely relegated to tambourines, eye candy, and the background. This was in and of itself (sadly) revolutionary. Of course, I fell immediately in love.

The following Monday arrived with something other than my standard nagging apprehension. I suppose it was akin to hope. There existed the possibility to share, a chance to bond. I had *liked* this. The morning conclave assembled, and I tentatively squeaked that I thought the band was pretty good. The blowback was instant and irreversible. *Those punk faggots? You liked that shit? You a faggot too?* Cue laughter and disdain. So much for trying to fit in. Apparently, I had violated some impenetrable taboo against Punk Rock, whatever that was.

How was I to know that in the Detroit rock scene, punk was nothing more than papered-over showbills from long-forsaken downtown dumps like the Grande Ballroom frequented by hippies and commies, an inept and contemptible sideshow for losers, freaks, queers, and pussies? Detroit's musical heritage had been winnowed down to local heroes Bob Seger, the Nuge, and every mondo-partier *swearing* they could hear themselves cheering on the KISS *Alive* album recorded at Cobo Hall. The legacies of hometown *ur*-punks the Stooges and the MC5 had been forgotten and hastily buried in shallow graves at the back of the Dodge Main parking lot to await rediscovery and canonization at some later date. The cranked-up snarls of "Loose" and "Kick out the Jams, Motherfucker" faded into the Stroh's smooth "Night Moves" and aspirational arena rock appeals to move your feet and leave your seat. Acceptable, commodified rebellion.

If kids wanted a laugh, they spray-painted their hair blue, wore a skinny tie, dumb sunglasses, and a tux jacket held together with safety pins and went as "punkers" for Halloween. The *Detroit Free Press*, the daily print media presence in our house, took a high-hatted view in gossip column items about characters unfathomably named Rotten and Hell. The murder of Nancy Spungen and her boyfriend Sid Vicious's subsequent trial played out as more comic than tragic, the bumbling and inevitable punchline for societal nose-thumbers. Why, the gall of that mohawked Wendy O. Williams and the Plasmatics, blowing up cars with her boobies hanging out and calling it "entertainment"! And Jesus Christ, why can't that Patti Smith shave her armpits? Why does she make herself ugly like that? While dads buried themselves in the auto sections, mothers clucked at the tales in the entertainment section about Joe Strummer's dental woes, Bowie's silly androgyny, and concerts filled with violence, spit, and vomit. *How can they walk around looking like that?*

Hell, this was news to me. All I knew was I had heard and seen something that grabbed me, and I was petrified it might not happen again.

* * *

In Metro Detroit at the time, practically everybody built cars, worked on the machines that built cars, worked on the tools that made the machines that built cars, or supplied the machines that built the tools that made the machines that built cars. Others designed cars, sold cars, advertised cars, shipped cars, and most facets of life—social and personal—were seen through these lenses. They were as inescapable as gravity and my stomachaches. Birmingham, where I was at the time, in the days before a tidal wave of Reagan wealth and convenient prosperity theology washed over it, was just another suburban rung on the way up the automotive industry ladder. It was above the UAW Rivetheads and Shoprats between 8 Mile and 12 Mile Roads, but below the inter-generational industrial royalty and stately manors of the Fords and Chevrolets, and the "car guy" star power of Iacocca, Shelby, and DeLorean that stretched north beyond 15 Mile or east to the Grosse Pointes. It was an un-melting pot of Lutherans, Methodists, and Episcopalians with an acceptable smattering of Presbyterians, united in a mutual desire to keep the troubles of the world out of their narrow minds and off their broad lawns. The lack of an inherent culture had petrified into a culture unto itself, and a bunker mentality inculcated a wide-ranging antipathy toward an equally wide-ranging Other. Conformity was commended, but not applauded: why applaud what should be done as a matter of course? This was a nice, safe, clean place with good people who raised good kids to go to good colleges and go on to do good things.

Grooming us for this inevitability was a coterie of dedicated, professional educators. Pillars of the community. My homeroom teacher—all pit stains, sour bourbon aftershave, and poorly concealed nicotine fits—set us on our course of academic achievement and social decorum every morning. Whenever he left the room for a smoke during any PA announcement, the room quickly devolved into a Docksides and Lacoste reboot of *Lord of the Flies*. A pervy gym teacher made us jump for towels in the shower while he watched, encouraging us to really *go* for the next one; being among the meek, I got whatever sodden ones were left on the floor. Another culled the "wussies" in order to keep us out of the way of the "real" athletes during dodgeball or flag football games. (Which, to be honest, suited me fine, even though the "wussy" designation carried far beyond the confines of the gym.) My cross-country coach, a drill-instructor hard-ass type built like a fireplug, led us on training runs past Brother Rice, the Catholic high school rival. If their track team was out training, he'd bark to us, "What comes out of a Chinaman's ass?" and we were to dutifully respond, "RICE! RICE!" I couldn't quite put my finger on it, but that felt . . . wrong.

My Social Studies teacher with Coke-bottle glasses and a toothy grin regularly got the room roaring during "comparative religion" sections. He'd pepper lessons with enlightening cultural tidbits like "What sound does an Italian tire make when it goes flat?" *Dago wop wop wop*. "What does it mean when the Pope does this [making the sign of the cross]?" *Hey, all you wops, get off the grass*. Italian jokes? What were Italians? What was a wop? Will this be on the test? When he "taught" us about China or Buddhism, he'd buck his teeth, squint his eyes, and throw in *me likeys* or *ching chongs* that kept the laughs coming. Islam was summed up with jokes about "Mohammedists" and camels. He helpfully explained how well looked after slaves were before the Civil War, and, since they didn't have to worry about earning money, that was why they got so good at singing and dancing. My introduction to the vast scope of the humanities and millennia of distinct traditions and religions was a TED talk given by Archie Bunker, and sanctioned, apparently, by the powers that be.

Most teachers condoned or looked away from the terrorizing happening right under their well-veined noses. "You gotta toughen up," one told me after, to the great hilarity of the class, a football goon punched me full force in the chest and called me a smartass for answering the teacher's question correctly after he had missed it. If the torments were fomented by jocks, that was one thing, their campus entitlement almost to be expected as they pounded on the occasional sissy for a valuable lesson in the application of raw force. But when it came via the hands of "student leaders"—the smug teacher's pets and preppy classists leading the school spirit assemblies, the model citizens, the ones my parents wanted me to be like—coolly and cruelly doling out or denying social approbation without reason or appeal, it felt more sinister. It left me with a lifelong suspicion of power, popularity, and hypocrisy that later served me well in the music business trenches.

This was my place in the world. This *was* the world. This was what I was supposed to unquestioningly lap up: lessons to be well learned for a lifetime of promulgating the status quo and deciding who and what to keep out of it. My sadness and isolation deepened into something closer to despondence.

It was imperative I find this other world where something like the Talking Heads could exist. If it was out there, I had to be ready wherever or whenever it might jump from the ether again. Over the next few months—staying at home on weekends, naturally—I caught the B-52's, Gary Numan, and the Specials on *Saturday Night Live*, the Clash—that was the guy with the bad teeth, right?—the Jam, and Devo on *Fridays*. I still had to weather episodes featuring Chicago, Boz Scaggs, and Bette Midler, but it looked like there *was* another world out there. There was that tense, edgy spark again, a toughness, style, and immediacy in the Clash and the Specials and a sawtooth cynicism in the Jam's "Private Hell" that I felt in my core. How did a *trio* make such a gripping racket, and there wasn't a gong or double-neck Gibson in sight? I had no context for the guitar tone or the uninhibited gawkiness of the B-52's, or the static electricity of Devo's "Uncontrollable Urge." I wasn't trying to be contrarian, I just *liked* what I was hearing, but anything I did dig on those shows was swept aside Monday mornings. *Hey, whip it, fuckface*, and *rock lobster, you fucking homo*. I was like a spacecraft missing its angle of reentry and being bounced back into space, over and over, forever circling a planet on which I could never land.

* * *

On my sixteenth birthday, I was handed a driver's license. In the Motor City, that was a given, as public transportation was for freedom-haters and derelicts, as well as an affront to the automotive golden calf. It was our birthright to barrel down the Lodge Freeway at 75 mph in a three-ton steel and chrome missile with a mushy suspension and no seat belts one minute after we came of age. Drivers' ed classes consisted of doing circles in a parking lot and watching gory "documentaries" (in black and white, but blood garishly tinted red) like "Death on the Highway." I spent the bulk of my road test waiting in the parking lot of a strip mall while my instructor picked up his dry cleaning.

So off I went. But where to go, what to do? As the man once said, freedom's just another word for nothing left to lose. I didn't have any interest in the mall, where I might be seen and ignored by classmates or, worse, seen and *not* ignored, and their record stores didn't traffic in any of the music I wanted to explore; display walls were literally covered by *The Wall.* Going to the cineplex to see all-the-rage teen comedies depressed me, as I hadn't yet turned up much that was funny about being a teen.

Looking through the newspaper, I saw listings for long neglected movie palaces with a couple of screens struggling to survive by charging two or three bucks for horror and comedy flicks more to my liking. At the Royal Oak, the Main, and the Bloomfield, I saw *Young Frankenstein, Night of the Living Dead, Monty Python and the Holy Grail,* and *Richard Pryor: Live in Concert.* At the Punch and Judy on the far east side, I caught *Harold and Maude, A Clockwork Orange,* and *Eraserhead.* There were Dirty Harry, Pam Grier, and kung fu double features at the Madison on Grand Circus Park, and Marx Brothers festivals at the Redford. I felt welcomed in the faded-glory surroundings as I laughed out loud with people who were laughing at the same things I was. The unfamiliar solace of a communal event. I didn't feel outside of it, I was part of it. What an indescribable fucking joy.

In the ratty lobbies of these theaters were stacks of the *Metro Times*, the free alternative—whatever that meant—weekly. The price was right, so I would take copies home. Record store ads hyped "the latest from the Clash," and "B-52's on Sale." Stores boasted of "records from NYC and London" along with T-shirts, pins, posters, and "more." There were cult comic book, memorabilia, and vintage stores. And so many music venues. An entire ecosystem hiding in plain sight.

Most of the stores were in semi-deserted inner-ring suburban retail districts, near army/navy surplus showrooms, coney islands, and wig shops—the

detritus that had been left behind as grand shopping complexes sprouted out of the fields near off-ramps in the outer suburbs—spirit and ingenuity sacrificed in the name of chain stores, ample parking, and food courts. Walking into Car City Records, Dearborn Music, or Discount Records, wide-eyed and tentative, I found chaos and clutter, an anathema to the world I knew. Posters of the Ramones, Kraftwerk, and not-fat, not-old Elvis were tacked up helter-skelter on every available wall space. Counters were stacked with 45s, buttons, badges, and patches in wild colors and fonts of, I don't know, I guessed they were bands. Instead of uniform, off-white racks made of space-age-smooth materials, records were in milk crates, fruit crates, packing crates, and pilfered, mismatched shelving units, suggesting something more than mere "commerce." The contrast was stark, and it hit me hard. Here was the thrill of bedlam, of discovery, of the unknown.

At Sam's Jams in not-yet-fashionable Ferndale, barely on the "right" side of the 8 Mile Road bridge to Detroit, I wandered through the stacks and racks without purpose or plan. So many categories and styles and names I'd never heard, never heard *of*. There were, it was becoming evident, vast worlds of music beyond the measly purview of the comfortable and manageable boundaries of the Top 40 and rock radio. I didn't know where to begin. I didn't know *how* to begin, the choice both exhilarating and paralyzing. In what was likely an offhand exchange or an expression of simple courtesy, the clerk didn't give me shit when I mustered the courage to ask which Devo album had "Uncontrollable Urge" on it. I had been conditioned to expect scorn, so I mentally clenched. None came. *Are We Not Men?* he answered matter-of-factly. I was so . . . *not* ill at ease . . . *not* anxious . . . *relieved*? I didn't move and must have looked a bit dense because he added, without a hint of impatience, *it's over there*. (I wish that wherever that guy is now, he's had a good life; his sliver of humanity in that moment made a substantive difference to me.)

After playing the record about seventy-eight times that week, I went back eager for more, but also still petrified I might ask the wrong question and sound like a moron. The homeroom rebukes I had gotten used to hung like toxic weights in my brain. I looked for the clerk who'd helped me before, but he wasn't there. *Eep*. My impulse was to skulk out the door and try again another day. Instead, I coolly (I hoped) approached another guy and—using the classic tactic of deflective engagement—asked which was *his* favorite Ramones album. (I didn't think it important to tell him I'd never heard of them before I'd seen their poster in the store the previous week.) "*Rocket to Russia* or *Road to Ruin*," he replied. And, again, the most remarkable thing happened: when answering, he talked *to* me, not at me or down to me. It was like I mattered. Like I was there. He told me how awesome they both were, which songs were his favorites, but, in his opinion, *Road to Ruin* sounded tougher. The guitars crunched more, or something, and the drums *something something*, the production reminded him of *something something something*. I didn't follow, but I was transfixed, both by the covert-feeling intel he was sharing and the easygoing way he was sharing it. Not wanting to disappoint him, and probably favoring the album's cartoon cover, *Road to Ruin* it was.*

With two records to listen to seventy-eight times a week, my anxiety unspooled. There *were* others who didn't think that the bands I had seen on *SNL* and *Fridays* were for pussies and losers. Maybe there *were* others who heard Journey and winced. I was almost afraid to contemplate such prospects. Giving up hope felt worse than never having had it.

To find whatever Talking Heads album had "Take Me to the River," I went somewhere else with ads in the *Metro Times*: Off The Record in Royal Oak. The store had the same approachable and weird energy, a place to be unself-consciously *curious*, in both senses of the word. Toward the back of the store was an enormous, arresting poster, six feet to a side, as my brain wants to remember. *Never Mind the Bollocks Here's The Sex Pistols*. That was the band with the guys from the gossip columns, Vicious and Rotten, right? The exemplars of blockheaded punk rockiness sniggered at between the Jumble and

---

* As a sidenote, the lines "Hanging out on Second Avenue / eating chicken vindaloo" from "I Just Want to Have Something to Do" was my first exposure to Indian cuisine, though I didn't know it at the time. For years I thought they were singing "Chicken Vin da Lou," which I took to be some sort of tough guy New York City/Little Italy delicacy.

the Word Search? But that cover . . . I had no conception of what a *bollocks* might be, but the simple design and brutish color scheme were striking counterpoints to the dense, baroque Bostons, Styxes, and Loafs of Meat covers that I was used to seeing, and that were better suited to being airbrushed on murder vans. Album covers like Skynyrd's *Street Survivors* were nightmare visions of the burnouts chasing me across parking lots. And what the hell is even going on with *Led Zeppelin IV*?

I bought it.

On a different wall was another poster that grabbed me by the eyeballs: The Clash, *London Calling*. That was the song they did on *Fridays*, yeah? And the grainy intensity of that cover image . . . it may be the greatest album cover ever.

I bought that, too.

What I heard when I got home demolished the foppery of the "Stairway to Heavens" of the world. From the opening martial notes of the Pistols' "Holiday in the Sun," I recognized their anger and disgust—even if I hadn't yet figured out that it was anger and disgust I was feeling. "Anarchy in the UK" hit like rocket fuel, from the opening rolling R's in "*rrrrrright* . . . NOW . . ." to the maniacal laugh that followed. The references to UDA, MPLA, and council tenancies went right over my head, and what did I know of anarchy? But I had no trouble with the invitation to "get pissed, de-*stroy*" that registered as a salvation, not a negation. It was a *cri de coeur* for change, to not fall to one's knees. Johnny Rotten menacingly repeating "No future" at the end of "God Save the Queen" was my "We Will Rock You." It didn't cross my mind to be threatened by it. *No Future* wasn't scary: the future, as I saw it being laid out before me and that most were sleepwalking toward, *that* was scary. And when they told me in "EMI"—and it did feel, finally, like music might have the capacity to speak to *me—Blind acceptance is a sign of stupid fools who stand in line*, my nascent distrust of authority clanged into this signpost, a musical expression of ideas I had been absorbing from George Carlin LPs. I came to know every word and cymbal crash on that album. It soaked into my skinny little bones.

As *Bollocks* was Howard Beale shouting "I'm mad as hell and I'm not going to take it anymore" in *Network*, a Molotov cocktail lighting up the night, *London Calling* was the smoky sunrise. The Clash were also mad as hell, but they offered optimism and beliefs in justice as they pilfered a rich treasure chest of jazz, rockabilly, and reggae. They jammed their spades into the weeded-over earth of rock's graveyard to dig up music's still vital relics and mythology, and fused them to their themes of apathy, consumerism, and keeping ideals intact. I was oblivious of the antecedents they were cribbing—to me rockabilly was Fat Elvis, jazz was Chuck Mangione, and I hadn't the faintest idea what reggae was—but their embrace of such a broad range of influences left a long-lasting impression. The audacity of the record never flags, and I still find startling things in its grooves. These two records, more than any others, led to the dawning of my record collection, a manifestation of *self*, and albums by *bands* started to outnumber LPs by Bob Newhart and Bill Cosby.*

It was a giant step on a long, unexpected adventure into strange circles. I would never know if I was the egg man or if I was the walrus, but it no longer mattered, I was not going back.

---

* Oops . . . those latter ones didn't age very well.

4

Everybody's Heard about the Bird

On the counters of the record stops I was frequenting more and more, I kept seeing mimeographed playlists of a late-night show called *Radios in Motion*. It was on WDET, the public radio station—whatever that was—far to the left of the dial where I thought only faint, staticky stations that read the news in Polish or Arabic existed. While I didn't recognize 99 percent of the bands on the playlist, I *didn't* see 100 percent of the bands I *had* heard of and didn't get. Why *not* give it a listen?

The DJ, Michael Halloran, genre-hopped without judgement. If he liked it, he played it. New wave, no-wave, funk, punk, post-punk, proto-punk, goth, hardcore, ska—whatever those terms meant—spilled out of the speakers, and I was a sponge, unburdened of pre-conceptions and prejudices. That weekly playlist started to read like a shopping list. For me, the radio hits of that summer weren't "Don't Stop Believin'" and "Bette Davis Eyes," they were songs by XTC, Was (Not Was), and Bow Wow Wow. While others were getting caught in the Blizzard of Ozz, I was enveloped by the Adolescents, the Slits, and Pete Shelley. Pere Ubu's ominous "Final Solution" was my "Jessie's Girl," capturing the noises in my head with teeth-grinding intensity:

The girls won't touch me 'cause I got a misdirection
And livin' at night isn't helpin' my complexion . . .
Mom threw me out 'til I get some pants that fit
She just don't approve of my strange kind of wit . . .
I don't need a cure/Don't need a cure
Don't need a cure
Need a final solution.

Jesus, that was spot on. What was this stuff? And it had been out there the whole time? And no one in school was talking about it? And no one was going to these shows (did these bands even have shows?) or wearing their T-shirts on Monday morning?

During afterschool UHF reruns of Bugs Bunny or *The Addams Family*, there was a low-rent commercial for AM 560 Honey Radio, an "oldies" station; the hype music was the Troggs' "Wild Thing" and Del Shannon's "Runaway." Thumbing through the records in Mom's hi-fi rack, which included the theme from *A Summer Place* and Pat Boone's "Tutti Frutti," I wasn't inclined to believe that oldies would be any more likely to plug into my brain than "Layla." From what I'd heard on other such stations, the Righteous Brothers, "La Bamba," and "Build Me Up Buttercup" played every hour as oldies stations blandly excreted the same hit after tepid hit. It was ancient history, a rosy faraway land where everyone had *yummy, yummy, yummy love in their tummy*. But "Wild Thing" didn't sound anything like Pat Boone, so I checked it out.

What I heard kicked in a hidden door to rock and roll. Honey Radio played the hits without any regard for how they may have fallen from favor with the current arbiters of taste. It was a fascinating entrée for a musical novice like me. I got hipped to dozens of artists who went on to have a spiderwebbing impact on my growing curiosity and understanding of history. Sam & Dave and the Mar-Keys tracks revealed the whole Memphis sound and Stax Records domain. Jerry Lee Lewis led to Charlie Rich to Carl Perkins to Sun Records to the whole idea of blues and country morphing into rock 'n' roll. The ravings of Screamin' Jay Hawkins led to the feral R & B of Don & Dewey, Esquerita, and the Sonics—a lot of this sounded pretty punk rock to me, but what did I know? I marveled that Clarence "Frogman" Henry could sing like a girl, and he could sing like a frog. Through instrumentals by Santo & Johnny ("Sleepwalk"), the Ventures ("Walk, Don't Run"), and Duane Eddy ("Rebel Rouser"), I learned that songs could be better without words, especially if those words were "Tradin' in his Chevy for a Cadillac-ac-ac-ac" or "Today's Tom Sawyer, mean, mean pride."

Forgotten or marginalized giants like Jackie Wilson, Gene Vincent, and Etta James shared airtime with cast-to-the-wilderness loonies and *what the fucks* like Nervus Norvus ("Transfusion," #13 in 1956), Napoleon XIV ("They're Coming to Take Me Away, Ha-Haa!" #3 in 1966), and Johnny Cymbal (Mr. Bass Man, #16 in 1963). Bo Diddley was a pawn broker in the Blues Brothers movie with one hit as far as I knew, more a symbol of a time gone by than an actual musician of import. Then I had the top of my skull screwed off and the *tombstone hand and graveyard mind* of "Who Do You Love" poured in. I had heard of Peggy Lee (from Disney's *Lady and the Tramp*, her saucy cat character making me feel funny in my short pants), Charlie Daniels (that Devil fiddling song) and the Dixie Cups' gooey "Chapel of Love," but there was more to them than cozy consensus songs masquerading as the entirety of their legacies. When Honey Radio played Daniels's anti-establishment bluegrass meander, "Uneasy Rider," and the Dixie Cups' improbable Mardi Gras gang patois hit, "Iko Iko," I ruminated on what else I might be missing. And I am still unpacking the cavalier world-weariness of Miss Lee's "Is That All There Is?" "Oh no, I'm not ready for that final disappointment" was the Eiffel Tower of existential camp, Joy Division in pump heels and a sequined ballgown, the smell of lady cigarettes and gin oozing out of the speakers.

When I heard Little Richard's "Tutti Frutti," I thought, with disbelief and confusion, who, or *what*, was this covering Pat Boone? I recognized the song from my mother's records, but this inconceivably concussive attack was out of this world. I quickly bought one of his records on my next trip to a record store. I looked at the writing credits. *Who is R. Penniman?* Little Richard's real name? *He* wrote this? In Pat Boone's hands, "Wop Bop a Loo Bop A wop bam boom" came across as Four Freshman "23 Skidoo" gibberish to get a giggle out of the gals in taffeta hovering near the spiked punch bowl at a Sigma Chi mixer. Erupting out of R. "Little Richard" Penniman, "Wop Bop a Loo Bop a wop bam BOOM" was a lustful provocation to hop in the car and head to that side of town you'd been warned about and carried far more philosophical heft than "All we are is dust in the wind." You would be hard-pressed to convince me that the spirit of punk wasn't born right in that song, rather than years later in the Lower East Side, the UK, or a Stooges show.

Until Honey Radio, I couldn't understand why parents feared rock and roll in the '50s. Elvis's wiggling hips? Bill Haley's spit curl? The salacious "Splish splash I was taking a bath?" Now I knew. Little Richard's bare-knuckled "Keep A-Knockin' (But You Can't Come In)" sounds dangerous *now*; I can't imagine the nameless terror the *Leave It to Beaver* set felt back then. I didn't yet grasp that revisionist "Oldies" programmers had spent years spaying and neutering—or discreetly erasing—the weird and the wild and polished the rest into a non-threatening Whitman's Sampler of The Good Old Days™, perfect for any church social, or department store background music. I had been hearing music as filtered through promotions interests hyping *The Big Chill* soundtrack or shilling for the California Raisins. True titans of rock and roll like Johnny Burnette, the Coasters, or the Shangri-Las were forsaken as curators opted for mawkish triggers we've all heard four thousand times too many. This inoffensive canon would have us believe that James Brown, Aretha Franklin, and Ike & Tina Turner were one-hit wonders, and that it was better to hear the Temptations' "My Girl" and Marvin Gaye's "How Sweet It Is" yet again and not get all riled up by the politically charged "Ball of Confusion" and "What's Going On." I couldn't believe these songs were "old." They felt very relevant. And subversive.

What *else* was covered up by this plainly artificial construct of "oldies?" Why had I heard Pat Boone but not Little Richard? And the same could be, should be, asked, obviously, of rock, pop, country, of any format, or any art form.

I quickly added used record stores and flea markets to my buying rounds and spent hours thumbing through miles of singles, grabbing anything by people I'd heard on Honey Radio. At two, three, or five for a buck, I could take chances. The joy of such map-less voyages was that for every artist or song I was specifically seeking, I found things I didn't realize I'd been looking for. There was such a wealth of weirdness and passion and I had been exposed to so little of it. After finding Honey Radio, I never lost interest in sifting through the artifacts of what had come before, no matter how deep they were buried. They revealed what we were really made of.

* * *

I bought Kraftwerk's *Computer World* album the week after *Radios in Motion* played a track off it.

Something about the desolate, dystopian man machine music spoke to me. Go figure. The clerk, after telling me how awesome the album was (*score!*), asked how I'd heard about it.

"The radio," I said, not unproudly. *I know what's up*, thought I.

"On Mojo's show?

Mojo? What's a Mojo?

"He played a whole side last week." The old fear of sounding like an idiot rose, uninvited. My mind raced with questions.

What show? When's it on?

Nonchalantly (I hoped), I said, "Yeah, Mojo's show."

Straightaway, I checked the radio listings in that week's *Metro Times*. There it was: *The Electrifying Mojo*, "the show that "takes the J off Jazz and kicks azz." WGPR, 10 p.m. to 3 a.m. on 107.5 FM, all the way to the right of the dial—did the numbers go that high? Mojo, so legend (his own, mostly) had it, came from outer space and landed his mothership in Detroit. In between his mystical, meandering raps that invited the listener to join him as he soared over the city—*I see you over there on the east side . . . hey, you on Jefferson Avenue, flash your lights*—Mojo preached a transcendental range of music so far ahead of its time we're still trying to catch up. If the music had a direct line to the universal groove, he didn't care where it came from, and he obliterated the airwave apartheid that ruled rock stations. I heard Tom Tom Club, Art of Noise, Prince, Grace Jones, and the Sugarhill Gang for the first time. New favorites like the B-52's were shuffled among unheard of (by me) mindblowers like Parliament-Funkadelic, and the Clash's "This Is Radio Clash" was in heavy rotation alongside The Time's "Get It Up." I mean, without someone dictating some genre, marketing, or race rules to the contrary, why *wouldn't* you play Devo's "Freedom of Choice" back-to-back with the Gap Band's "You Dropped a Bomb On Me"? It was a helluva party, and that summer I became a proud acolyte in Mojo's MFA: the Midnight Funk Association. As with *Radios in Motion*, as with these mutinous record stores, there was no canon to adhere to or code to enforce, only an openness carrying a hint of the evangelical that made it feel like music spoke to something greater in the galaxy.

Increasingly, I regarded commercial radio not in terms of what I was hearing, but what I was *not* hearing. The stations I had been familiar with offered a version of music that I thought was all the world had to offer. The independent stations exposed this as blindness or, worse, a contented ignorance. There was a lot of music out there and I had a lot to learn.

Similarly, discovering independent movies had a profound impact on my understanding of the power of music. In this era of instantaneous access to every video of every performance of every band, to be able to watch an infinite number of times for free at our fingertips, it is hard to overstate how significant seeing bands on film was. We might have seen pictures of them in magazines or on album covers, but unless they were popular enough to be on TV, or we knew someone who had cable so we could watch that MTV thing, they were, in a very real way, a mystery. The worlds they traveled and performed in were a complete unknown. The big screen was all we had, and when the movie was gone, that was it. We had our memory, or we had nothing.

Watching matinees of *Tommy* and *The Song Remains the Same* left me with the same sense of boredom and psychic terror that commercial radio and the school cafeteria did. I saw a numbing double feature of *Woodstock* and *Monterey Pop*, landmark documents, I was told, of the '60s counterculture. I failed to get keyed by the romance of the mud, the blood, and the weed. Fifteen years on, the movies played like wistful monuments for misty-eyed hedge fund managers who, during their Maoist-dabbling rebellion, tripped their brains out and may or may not have gotten laid during Canned Heat. *Crazy times, man, hard to remember*. Hard pass.

But . . . these movies also had mind-blowing performances by Sly and the Family Stone, Jimi Hendrix, and Janis Joplin. *And* Otis Redding backed by Booker T. and the M.G.'s. Nothing came close to that set. "Shake" was revival-level joy, and a note Otis hits in "I've Been Loving You Too Long" still shoots straight into my hypothalamus. I couldn't take my eyes off that tight band in their shiny lime-green suits. No flashy stage moves, no breaking or burning guitars, just cool confidence, and taut, economical muscle shaking it like a bowl of soup.* I had no reference points for this. Maybe the Electrifying Mojo was right, maybe some music *did* drop out of the cosmos.

At the Punch and Judy theater, I saw *D.O.A.*, the grainy, hand-held camera documentary about the Sex Pistols' first US tour that also featured several

---

* I didn't even know at the time that the guitar and bass players were in the Blues Brothers band! Steve Cropper and Donald "Duck" Dunn. R-E-S-P-E-C-T!

other early UK punk bands. I was knocked sideways by two bands I had never heard of: Sham 69 and X-Ray Spex. Like the Talking Heads, the bands looked like they shopped at the same thrift stores I did, and there wasn't a "show" per se but a gripping reciprocity with the audience, one battery charging another. The sweaty people pressed up against the stage were an essential element of the intensity caroming back and forth between audience and performers. They were *in it*. The sum greater than its parts. When Sham 69 played the pile-driving "Borstal Breakout," I didn't have any idea what a Borstal was or why I needed to break out of it, but, goddammit, I was going to find out.

Urgh! A Music War was a riot of concert footage, one band after another, one song after another, playing right *up there* on the screen. It was my first visual exposure to eccentrics and now-icons like Wall of Voodoo, the Dead Kennedys, the Cramps, 999, X, and so many others. And nobody who has ever seen Klaus Nomi's performance of "Total Eclipse of the Sun" has ever forgotten it. These performances had the effect of thousand-watt flashbulbs going off right in front of me, and comparatively speaking, the nodding-out audience at the Joe Louis Arena Alice Cooper show may as well have been at the DMV waiting for their number to be called.

During *The Harder They Come*, featuring the Jimmy Cliff title track I'd been turned onto by *Radios in Motion* and rocksteady/ska superstars the Maytals and Desmond Dekker, people danced in the movie theater aisles. Though I understood about half of the Jamaican dialog, the uplifting power of music was unmissable. The spirituality and street-level urgency were an extension of what I was beginning to understand as "punk rock." There were outsiders everywhere, and there was an uphill search for affirmation everywhere.

When I saw *The Decline of Western Civilization*, the free-floating static in my head every waking and not-able-to-sleep moment crashed onto the screen. This documentary of the LA hardcore scene unveiled a place I couldn't have imagined back when I trembled in the corner of that school dance or gym class. I had heard some bits of the Circle Jerks, X, and FEAR but had never seen them. I did not know what to expect, but then, there they were, in front of me in this nice theater in a nice neighborhood full of nice people who made the existence of these bands very, *very* necessary.*

---

* Like anyone documenting an "exotic" scene, director Penelope Spheeris gravitated to the outrageous at times. Hair and makeup excesses ginned up the shock value, and the leather-pantsed and studded dog-collar looks haven't aged well—though they were pretty ill-advised to begin with, if we're being honest here. People made mean faces and spit and fought for the camera, and no one would mistake interview nuggets like "Sure, man, punk's the scene, man" and "I swear to god I hate cops" with an Algonquin Round Table discussion on bohemian estrangement and nihilist uprisings among the youth.

The venues were condemned churches and crummy civic halls with spray-painted bedsheets as banners. The shows were bare bones and bare bulbs, no distractions, total adrenaline, and the songs were without ornamentation—fast, raw, loud spasms of dark humor and crude rage. There was a radical demolition of the delineation between band and audience: band members came out of the audience to play or jumped into the audience while playing, audience members jumped onstage and sang or jumped back off. It was a seething, organic whole. I was bug-eyed through most of it. I thought I saw myself. Black Flag, with their end-of-the-world-energy attack and anti-rock star guitar player sporting a button-down shirt and Supercuts hairstyle, played "Depression:"

I ain't got no friends to call my own
I just sit here all alone
There's no girls that want to touch me
I don't need your fucking sympathy,

It bulldozed into my brain. I got it. I hadn't been responding to songs about having a broken heart or partying with friends because I didn't know that I was even *allowed* to have a heart to break or friends to party with. I hadn't felt like I had a place in the world, let alone a voice.

They say things
are gonna get better
All I know is
they fuckin' better

Now I knew I had a say in the matter. I had *agency*. What a revelation.

5

"A Serious Matter"

When I was young, our family road-tripped Up North, a generic term Michiganders use to refer to anywhere north of where they live, be it thirteen or three hundred miles away. We stopped in Petoskey, known (in Michigan, at least) for its namesake fossilized coral found along the lakeshore. Polished up, these stones have a distinctive hexagonal pattern that everyone in the state is congenitally predisposed to get weak-kneed over. Many a vacation hour has been spent by beachcombers trying to find the little bastards. That day, I was intent on finding one of my own. I walked the waterline, I stopped, I stared, I stared some more. All I saw was an indistinguishable blur of rocks and pebbles.

Then my mother picked up a stone that looked like any other stone, rinsed it off, and there it was: a Petoskey stone, in its full, ancient, mottled glory. I started looking closer, and I found one too, then another, then I couldn't stop finding them. How could I have missed them before?

I just had to look down and *see*.

What I was seeing now were previously imperceptible possibilities. It was dawning on me that all the spandex, banks of keyboards, flying V-neck guitars, pyrotechnics, giant inflatable pigs, spaceships landing on stage, and their assurances of normality and popularity were pure hokum. Absolute farce.

* * *

By the time junior year of high school started, I was looking at my world through a very different lens. I had a new curiosity to look up and out at the world, to explore rather than glumly accept, and to do so without looking over my shoulder for permission or, worse, approval. I noticed the kid with a black trench coat and pointy shoes, or the girl with a blood-red miniskirt and streak of purple hair, or the skinny weirdo with bleached hair, Bermuda shorts, and hand-drawn Agent Orange T-shirt. Maybe now it doesn't seem like much, but this was a time and a place where a *Gabba Gabba Hey* button no bigger than a bottle cap or hair cut shorter than Bo or Luke Duke's would invite all manner of harassment, get you labeled an untouchable by classmates, a troublemaker by staff, and the possible recipient of abrupt violence. With quick *hey, how's it going* nods in the cafeteria, or an easygoing *see you later* in the hall, I felt an implicit tolerance. Nobody had to answer for their outsider status. It just *was*. I started to get invited to movies, small parties, and basements to listen to records. I could hang out with people and not wonder if a random pounding was forthcoming. I felt like I could breathe. Finally.

Devo was coming to town, and it was time to reappraise the whole live music thing, hoping for the connections I had found in the theaters and record stores, and, of late, daily life. It had to be better than that stultifying arena rock vibe.

It was.

Here, the band wasn't a speck on a distant stage, they were twenty or thirty feet away. I could feel the heat of the lights and the drums in my chest and see the spray of their spit and sweat in the stage lights. I was surrounded by people who, in that moment, were into the same thing I was; the elation of the shared experience and the *aha* of discovery put a buzz in my brain. When guitarist Bob 2 climbed the PA stack during "Gut Feeling" and soloed until every one of his strings were broken? Man, I haven't wanted to be anywhere but smaller venues since.

After that, I was impatient for more. From smudgy, mimeographed, hand-drawn, hand-stapled samizdat sources where I was getting my actionable music intel, ads in the *Metro Times*, and flyers on telephone poles and abandoned storefronts, I saw there was music happening all around me. These shows weren't advertised on the radio stations or written about in the daily newspapers. There weren't ticket giveaways or life-sized cardboard cutouts of the bands in the mall store across from the Orange Julius stand. But they were right there, all I had to do was see them.

At the once-stately Grand Circus Theater, across from a park occupied by bums, pigeons, and statues of long-forgotten robber barons and mayors, I saw the Plasmatics. (I hadn't been so much intrigued by the prurient press coverage of their "antics" as I was by them going "hunting" with John Candy—aka Gil "The Fishin' Musician" Fisher—on *SCTV* and finding a gorilla in a mine shaft. An incontrovertible classic of punk rock comedy.) The Ramones followed a couple of weeks later and I felt the rush of standing next to a passing train as they played without pause. While the strangeness of the Alice Cooper show felt abstract, this strangeness was direct and personal; I was drawn in, not pushed away. And, while bodies and bottles in brown paper bags may have been flying around, I never got barfed on.

From there, it was a blitz. In a blurry span of four or five months, I saw unknown and now-famous bands like Black Flag, Minutemen, the Gun Club, Hüsker Dü, Minor Threat, Circle Jerks, Misfits, Beastie Boys, Bad Brains, King Sunny Ade, Pigbag, Shockabilly, Necros, Negative Approach, Naked Raygun, X, the Flesh Eaters, U.K. Subs, Government Issue, L-Seven, Kraftwerk, Chuck Berry, Meat Puppets, Effigies, Dead Kennedys, and the Cramps. Punk, funk, hardcore, roots, world, and weird.

Many of the shows were at Clutch Cargo's, a converted 1920s women's club with the capacity of a few hundred in a disintegrating part of downtown.* As soon as the music started, I'd be pushed to the front, pushed up on stage, pushed off the stage, tossed around, and I never felt in danger or out of place. It was great. Before a Black Flag show, I passed a table in back and bassist Chuck Dukowski was writing out the set list. Right *there*. Quietly, *because who the hell was I to interrupt*, I asked if they were playing "Depression" tonight. He looked up at me, grinned, and wrote DEPRESSION on the list. Just like that. And they played it. A couple of months before, I had seen this band in a *moving picture*, and now I was talking to one of them, asking for a song, and getting it. It was so unreal, immediate, and personal. Did Aerosmith fans ever feel this way?

Another club was the Freezer "Theater," a dilapidated storefront in the heart of the Cass Corridor,

* When I was sixteen, I looked twelve—maybe a hard thirteen. I was five foot nothing and weighed 110 pounds if my pockets were full of wet nickels, but the club paid no mind to the fake ID I got from the shabby office above the Lindell AC, a notorious sports bar where long ago Tigers' manager Billy Martin would get into drunken fistfights.

a notoriously shitty neighborhood full of dope dealers, dope stealers, hookers, and other cast-outs and casualties. The Freezer was a venue in only the broadest sense of the term and not much bigger than the record stores and bookstores I was going to. It held maybe one hundred, more if they could be wedged in—which they often were. Who was gonna stop them? There couldn't have been a single legal thing about the whole setup. They likely pirated the power, wires hung indiscriminately from the ceiling, and to get in, you stepped through a pilfered freezer door. There were no bathrooms or stage lights. There were low risers in the back for the audience and a nothing stage in front with space on ledges for band gear behind that. Every surface was graffitied. During sets, there wasn't so much a gathering of individual audience members as a pulsing cauldron. In between sets, everyone went out to the street to cool off, skateboard, drink 64-ounce bottles of Big Jug beer (sold to anyone who looked older than fourteen by any self-respecting Chaldean party store owner), piss in an alley, or make a quick Burger King run.*

And then we'd go back in for the next band that would pop out of the crowd and plug in and play. That guy I was standing next to? In the band. Hanging

* For non-Michiganders: A "party store" sells beer, wine, Funyuns, Faygo, lotto tickets, air fresheners, cigarettes, and the like—as in "let's go to the party store for a case of Stroh's and some King Dons." They have nothing to do with cakes, costumes, or streamers. When we are outside the state and reflexively say "party store," we are met with confused looks and responses like "Party store? Do you need balloons?"

out. These weren't Rock Godheads deigning to favor us mortals with their presence upon our lowly plane of existence. It was so egalitarian, so egoless, *it could be me*. The music itself was pure speed and pent-up aggression, young lifetimes of fears and anxieties venting in a sustained howl in the face of a stifling system that didn't seem to have a place for us.

Us.

Not just *me*.

* * *

While I thought I was merely finding a way, my way, my *tribe*, as it were—*and wasn't that what everyone tried to do*?—punk was getting cast in an increasingly villainous light in the eyes of the mainstream. The condescending wisecracks about purple hair and singers named Johnny Vomit morphed into something more mistrustful. The hair and safety pins could be treated as a joke, but the giggles hid an uneasiness, an unconscious (perhaps) awareness of how flimsy and easily rattled the snug order really was. The ominous something people felt about this *thing* manifested itself in baffling ways.

I had been friends with Bill for a few years. My folks loved his starched-white cheeriness and outgoing nature, and crossed their fingers that some might rub off on me. Sometimes we played pool in his rec room and listened to records. He'd sing along to Supertramp and Toto. I'd bring along convulsive blurts, like Jodie Foster's Army's "Cokes and Snickers" ("Cokes and Snickers is all I eat/ Cokes and Snickers is all I need"), that summed up my spleen in forty-five seconds more germanely than six-minute epics about scaramouches and fandangos ever could. I think I lost him for good when I played Public Image Ltd's *The Flowers of Romance*. Something in those droning, alien sounds—were those Middle Eastern influences?—branded me as irredeemably strange, and, if word about these inclinations of mine got around, he might be presumed guilty by association. I was harmless when I was a mere nothing—it was almost quaint for someone popular to have a "loser" friend—but he could no longer afford the hit our friendship might cause his social rank. After that, we'd see each other in the halls and desultorily half-wave, but the pool games dried up entirely. A year before, I would have been devastated, but now it barely registered. I was bewildered as much as anything.

At a high school Battle of the Bands in Berkley—a notorious suburban redoubt for burnouts where flared jeans and biker wallets reigned supreme—my friends and I were treated like degenerate interlopers. After a buddy's band had the temerity to do a New York Dolls cover, the teacher/judges cut the power, disqualified them, and we were chased out to our car. For good measure, a cement block was thrown through our windshield as we sped away.

My chemistry teacher blindsided me one morning by kicking me out of class for wearing a Dead Kennedys "Holiday in Cambodia" T-shirt, screaming *get out of here with that* as he shoved me into the hall. I got good grades, I was quiet, I never talked back or disturbed class. I wasn't trying to be provocative; I was wearing a shirt of a band I was into. Everyone did that, right? The teacher's response was reasonable and proportional, said the principal. This was a serious matter, said my advisor. *What?* The hallways were thick with goons wearing shirts with Iron Maiden's Eddie the Head Number of the Beast mascot and chesty vixens being ravaged by Vikings. Give Pot a Chance? The Rolling Stones' tongue? Rape, Satan worship, and drugs were A-OK, but this shirt was a problem? It stank of something other than a stupid t-shirt.

At a time when Detroit wore the Murder Capital USA crown, when presumably there were more pressing matters at hand, the police found time to surveil "violent" shows, break up parties, and badger stores for selling "obscene" records. With the city being hollowed out from the bottom by $24 heroin deals going bad and rotting from the top by DeLorean getting caught with $24 million of cocaine in a hotel room, they still had the manpower to hassle kids wearing Bad Brains T-shirts and checkerboard Vans. Why was I getting run in for disorderly conduct and suspicion of vandalism for walking down the street? Why did I get my ID checked and get accused of shoplifting every time I was in a mall or department store?*

TV, my trusty, lifelong companion, hopped on the bandwagon, too. Daytime talk shows paraded mohawked, dog-collared, dress-up thugs and their apoplectic parents into klieg-lit colosseums for old-fashioned public shamings. Once-open-minded Baby Boomers suddenly became "disturbed parents" and formed groups like "Parents Against Punkers" to go on TV and *tsk-tsk* this violent and drugged-out degradation of rock and roll, as if Altamont, Spahn Ranch, or Vanilla Fudge never happened. As if pogoing was less dignified than the Frug or whatever they were doing while up to their knees in piss and empty cans of beans at Woodstock. As if their good kids weren't puking and passing out at Joe Louis Arena every weekend.

Prime Time scared parents and school administrators witless with *cinema verité* chair-grabbers involving "those kids" and "that music." Self-righteous episodes of *Quincy* and *CHiPs* did punk the way *Dragnet* did hippies: with all the subtlety of a Rocky Balboa training montage, and all the legitimacy of Dan Quayle rapping Grandmaster Flash's "The Message." While dialogue like "mosh pits are like soldiers fighting an insane war," "punkers are into an angry thing," and "why would anyone want to listen to music that makes you hate?" was 24 karat comedy gold to those in on the joke, it did the job of making calls for curfews and police involvement easier. And when Ponch

* *Cry me a fucking river*, says, rightfully, every person of color reading this.

bested Pain (singing their hit "I Dig Pain") at the Battle of the Bands with a diabetes-inducing rendition of "Celebrate," Mom and Dad and little sister on the sofa could rest assured that good would triumph over evil, the storm would pass, and proper order would be restored. Provocative stuff with comforting moralizing conclusions.

Thus, "Punk Rock" became the shorthand for a wide range of societal ills, and "punk rockers" the *enfants terribles* mucking up the Shining City on a Hill with their boot prints. What could once be dismissed as a harmless and incomprehensible fad, as if kids were swallowing goldfish or squeezing into a Volkswagen Beetle—*oh those zany new wavers with their flowerpot hats, what'll they try next*—was harder to ignore when there were thinly veiled intimidations like the hype sticker on Black Flag's *Damaged* LP with a quotation by a record executive whose company refused to distribute the record:

> *"As a parent, I found it an anti-parent record."*

Could this have explained the berserk reaction to what I thought was reasonable self-expression? Know thine true enemy.

My history teacher, Ms. Taras, a lefty firebrand in an otherwise conservative faculty, showed our class a documentary on the civil rights movement. The kids started laughing at the black-and-white footage of a raucous church service full of the sort of dancing, singing, and overt faith and joy not likely found at the First Presbyterian up the road. One of the good kids from a good family, who was going to go to a good school and one day do good things, cracked wise *look at those monkeys* and got laughs from the class. Ms. Taras, who brooked no bullying or bullshit, shut the projector off in a flash. Up and down the classroom in an accusatory stalk, she railed about privilege, ignorance, bold-faced racism—as well as polite, subtle Main Street racism—and how repugnant their reaction was. She wrapped it up with a scalding diatribe regarding the slavery-era etymology of a term she hated hearing, *motherfucker*, flippantly tossed around by these scions of automotive royalty. It was a righteous smackdown that revealed to me that not only could the bromide "that's the way things are" be incomplete, covering up inconvenient truths, simply wrong . . . or a lie, but that the enforcers of standards of behavior and their followers might be irrefutably full of shit.

What was your first job in the music business?

In 1982, I had been recently canned, mid-round, from a caddying gig. The old, rich hacker I was carrying for noticed my shirt. Caddies were required to wear a white polo shirt. I did not have one. I did, however, have a polo-styled shirt with the *National Lampoon* double amputee frog logo. I had worn it for almost two years without anyone noticing (the better I did my job, the more inconspicuous I was, not unlike, I would find out later, being a production manager or label owner). I wasn't being a wise guy or a boat rocker, it was the only shirt I had that approached the dress code.

"That's not a polo pony," he said.

Not fully understanding the swift and immutable retributions that can be meted out by people with an inflated sense of importance and a deflated sense of humor, I answered flatly, "No, it's the *National Lampoon* double amputee frog." I was replaced after the ninth hole, not paid, and told to never darken the doorway of the caddy shack again.

I took a job at Marty's Records in Birmingham. Minimum wage. $3.35 an hour.

Since music was beginning to take hold in my life, why not?

Marty's was a literal mom-and-pop neighborhood shop that leaned toward the Hot 100 and had better-than-average jazz and classical sections. If a parent came in and asked for something *punk, but not, you know, crazy* for their kid, we had the Go-Go's and, as an antidote to mosh pits, "The Safety Dance"; if they apprehensively asked for something for their teen to *break and pop to, but, you know, not dirty or violent,* we could set them up with the *Beat Street* soundtrack; if they were looking for some metal, but, *you know, not satanic,* we had all the Night Ranger they needed; if they sought R&B, we had Motown; if they wanted country, other than Dolly's *9 to 5,* they were SOL. We carried the whole Chipmunks catalog, and at Halloween brought out the haunted house spooky sound effects albums. It wasn't a store looking to change the world.

At Marty's, I saw how the sausage was sold. I learned about hits, and we couldn't sell Huey Lewis & the News, Michael Jackson, or *Flashdance* soundtrack LPs fast enough, or keep the "Do They Know It's Christmas" single in stock. *Born in the U.S.A.*? Let me take your name and we'll call you when we get more. Taco's "Puttin' on the Ritz" 45? Expecting more on Tuesday. Awful, great, flash-in-the-pan, novelty, it mattered not, they gave the people what they wanted. I learned that many—if not most—people didn't come into the store to explore, they came to buy the thing they came to buy. End of story.

I found out about promotional records and in-store play copies: what to play, how often to play, and how they were part of a system of favors, understandings, insider back-slappings, and deals. When the Clash's *Combat Rock* album arrived, I got grudging permission, since they were at the height of their popularity (i.e., moving units), to play the promo copy. It went well until "Straight to Hell," the hypnotic dub-bossa nova about, perhaps—I was a kid, what did I know?—the Vietnam War and decline of empire, came on at the end of side one. Mrs. Marty bolted out of the office and whispered to me *this isn't appropriate* and replaced it with the new Lionel Ritchie chart-topper. We weren't there to convert, we were there to reassure . . . and make the sale.

I discovered that girls, real live girls, would come into the record store to hang out and talk to me. They might even wait for my lunch break so we could go next door to Olga's for a souvlaki on Olga bread (the hometown take on a pita—*it's not a sandwich, it's an Olga!*)

Creem, a magazine I picked up occasionally, as it seemed less concerned with the doings of REO Speedwagon and Rush than most others and covered some of the bands I was getting into, had their offices upstairs. One day, a screw-loose-looking woman—black leather, silver bangles, scarves, shag hair, somewhere on the sartorial spectrum between Suzi Quatro and Morticia Addams—wandered in looking lost and asked me in a high-tar, Boston-thick rasp, *Where are the Creem people?* It was Joe Perry. Yes, the selfsame Joe Perry I had seen a couple years before opening for Alice Cooper. I pointed him to the right door.

My duties were simple: rearrange the Top 40 singles rack every week, restock the LP bins, make note of when we got low on big sellers, and answer customers' questions, more of a *where can I find . . .* variety than a *what do you suggest*? I was even occasionally consulted about what to stock—nothing radical, think Split Enz not the Descendents—but it was my first participation, however low-level, in evangelizing for music. I started to recognize the type of person who lingered in the store, who looked thoughtfully at an album cover, who, just maybe, might be persuaded to try a Romeo Void or Gang of Four release. They acted like me.

It felt like I was part of something. It was a start, and I didn't even know it. Maybe that makes for the best kind of start.

By senior year, I was all in. Punk was the refuge for those whom others ignored, feared, loathed, or didn't care to understand, where suppressed ideas and outlooks could be embraced. And it was all around me. More than just the music, it was a place, a mindset. Daffy Duck was punk. Groucho Marx was punk. George Carlin was punk. Used record and book stores, indie radio and theaters, and unconventional neighborhood enterprises were punk. It wasn't the normal place, but I was okay with that being my place. I did not see inherent wisdom in institutions, I saw mechanisms of control. I no longer paid attention to *sotto voce* discussions in homeroom about what MTV videos were cool or what rad concerts were coming next weekend. I didn't bother to chime in about what I liked, nor did I flinch when they gabbled over my homemade T-shirts. I didn't lean in to suck up divinations that might steer me through the linoleumed morass of hallways and malls or allow me to understand the teenage condition.

Sample offering of the back-row Aristotelian discourse re: the pronunciation of the title of an album by the Rockets—a Detroit hard rock band frustratingly one power riff away from broader popularity:

> *Dude, it's Rockets Live, cuz it's with an audience.*
> *Yeah, but it's Rockets Live, cuz they rule.*
> *Yeah but . . .*
> [Continues back and forth for . . . well . . . it might still be going on.]

Knowing another world existed apart from this, having seen it, heard it, and been uplifted by it, I knew the *short "i" versus long "i"* conundrum need not concern me. These dolts weren't tuned into something valuable or imbued with material insights, and their opinions were not worth seeking nor acknowledging. The *fag* and *pussy* taunts and random bursts of punching and spitting continued, but more so out of habit than an active malevolence.*

An oft-seen T-shirt in the halls was a picture of Hendrix and JIMI LIVES above it in block letters. One day, without giving it much thought other than it made me and a friend laugh, I drew JIMI DIED and a peace symbol with an X through it on a T-shirt. When I got to school, some goggled at me like *was this guy fucking crazy?* The burnouts and jocks were spooked by this straight-up apostasy. Threats were made but never acted on. They withered when their vacant outlooks were questioned. It was a potent lesson in empowerment.

---

* There was even something of a *rapprochement* between the tiny clutches of punks and the metalheads. They hated the jocks and preppy ruling class as much as we did and there were musical commonalities in the Venn diagram of our tastes. Motorhead. AC/DC. Judas Priest. Some thought punk was gnarly, and they dug the Ramones and the Misfits. Peace prevailed among us.

That spring, I was mindlessly slapping along on the dashboard of fellow music nerd/outcast Phil's car to a cassette playing the Cramps' "Human Fly." I'd heard the song on *Radios in Motion* a few months before and I became obsessed with it. Fellow music nerd/outcast Brad in the backseat took notice and said, "Wanna be in our band?" *Sure, how hard could it be?* That was my audition. The next day, we convened in Brad's basement. I sat behind a well-used Rogers sunburst red four-piece kit, originally belonging to early Midwest hardcore band the Necros, and picked up drumsticks for the first time. We clanged through "Human Fly" and the Ventures' "Pipeline," and we were on our way. We talked our tall, skinny, and fearless friend Mike into singing, and when he quit, we talked our equally tall, skinny, and fearless friend Nate into singing. We hadn't the faintest idea what would happen. It was magnificent.

We gravitated toward . . . whatever we liked, cribbing from records we'd bought that week as we vacuumed up music around us. Over 99-cent Whoppers, we wrote hardcore songs that made fun of hardcore, metal songs that made fun of metalheads, and a *hyuk-hyuk* song based on our infantile perception of country music. We played covers of "London Dungeon" and the "Inspector" theme from *The Pink Panther*, not seeing any reason why someone couldn't love both the Misfits *and* Henry Mancini. I learned everything I could about drumming from hundreds of spins of the Gun Club, the Cramps, and Sham 69 records. (I learned nothing from X, Dead Kennedys, or Black Flag records because I wasn't good enough to figure out what they were playing.)

We took our name from a nylon bowling shirt with Olde English lettering bought for 85 cents at the Highland Park Value Village on Woodward Avenue: The Wood Butchers. (In the days before computer modeling and 3-D printing, Wood Butchers made scale models of prototype vehicles out of wood—a reminder that the car world was never far away.) For our logo, we shamelessly repurposed the Warner Brothers' WB we had seen a million times before every weekday afternoon Bugs Bunny and Daffy Duck cartoon.

So, we thought, *we're a band, what's next*? Play shows. We put up flyers on the social media milieu of the time: flag poles, utility poles, mailboxes, dumpsters, and abandoned storefronts (no shortage of those in the Detroit area), and left them in the record stores, bookstores, and movie lobbies. Without a shred of self-consciousness of how primitive we were, without knowing how to tune, work cannibalized PA systems, or do anything other than run though our miniscule repertoire as quickly as possible, we played: house parties, friends' basements, strangers' basements, abandoned storefronts, pool parties, and wherever we could plug in and get out before the police came. We had our gear confiscated on the way to a gig across the Detroit River in Windsor, Canada, because the border guards didn't like the look of us, and we played a UAW picnic for $50 and a pony keg of Goebel. The one stipulation to receive this king's payday: We had to learn Billy Idol's "White Wedding" and play it whenever requested. Seems that our presence was something of a joke, to, *hahaha*, have a "punk band" at their annual picnic. We must have done it ten times. Our singer leaned into it every time with the fist pumps and sneers. Let the lesson be learned: give the people what they want.

We got a taste of the music biz when we booked a show at a "real" club, the venerable Paycheck's Lounge in Hamtramck, the then-Polish enclave within the city of Detroit where I'd seen the Gun Club, on that very same stage, several months before. A doorman. A soundman. A PA. Monitors. Lights a color other than "harsh, confession white." Semi-functioning bathrooms. A *bar*. And even though none of us, or our fans, were eighteen, let alone twenty-one, Detroit was lax about such things in those days and the subject never came up.

Then people *paid money* to hear us. We played with moderate competency, and they clapped and yelled. So much for a high bar of entry to this mysterious world. We ended our set with an eight-minute cover of Flipper's "Sex Bomb," a song so simple-minded even we could learn it. Joining us for the song on saxophone was our friend Jeremy, who maniacally jammed in the lane between Lounge Lizards' John Lurie post-bop squawk and feral tomcats falling into a garbage disposal. Settling up with Mr. Paycheck at the end of the night (*he was going to pay us?—this is brilliant!!!*), he counted out $75 in fives and sweaty singles, and told me in his thick Polish accent, "You boys did good tonight. Lots of people, lots of beer. But that last song. Mrs. Paycheck no like that. You boys never play here again." Oops. Let another lesson be learned: don't piss off the club owner's wife.

Before a couple band members started college that fall, we recorded our least unpolished songs in Phil's living room on his dad's four track. None of us knew what we were doing, and we played until it sounded good. We dubbed cassettes, one by one in real time, and hand-drew the covers and a ridiculous booklet, one by one. We took them to the weirdo record stores we had spent incalculable time and money in and said, "Hey, would you sell these?" Yes, they would. And did. Making our wares, selling our wares, it never dawned on us that this wasn't "the way it was done." It was a directness, a hustle, an indifference to the indifference of the "system." *Just*, as some company would later say, *do it.*

Twenty years later, I started getting asked in interviews, "Do you think music saved your life?" That was both melodramatic and reductive. It characterized an intensely personal—and *ongoing*—quest of discovery as if it were a made-for-TV movie, a parable with a tidy, maudlin ending—maybe a freeze-frame of me laughing, head back, in a circle of accepting friends as the credits roll.*

Before the blazing revelation of music, life was a pitch-black, locked, and airless room. Music broadly, and punk specifically, was a flashlight and a coat hanger. I used the flashlight to find the door and the coat hanger to pick the lock and get the hell out, to find other paths to travel where I wasn't told where to go or what to think. Not fitting in wasn't my problem, it was someone else's. Not only was it OK, but I'd be the better for it. The days of feeling bad or awkward or wrong about it were *over*. The lessons I learned through music at that time resonate still. These weren't trifles stuffed in the back of a closet in a forgotten shoebox marked "high school stuff" along with a Question Authority button, a twelve-page, A-minus paper on the three branches of government, and a still-unsolved Rubik's cube. These were commandments for navigating the world. I finally understood that knowing grin I had seen on David Byrne's face three years and a hundred lifetimes ago. The joke was being told and most people around me weren't even trying to hear it. *I* could do it, whatever *it* was. Music was liberation. Thinking back to that guy's "pep talk" at that funeral home, he couldn't have been more wrong. The best was ahead.

In the UK anarchist collective Crass's *"Big A Little A"* single from 1982, I heard a statement of principle that eventually manifested itself in my approach to running a label, something I've repeated to myself hundreds of times:

> *If you don't like the rules they make*
> *refuse to play their game.*

---

* For the record, I'd like to be played by Oscar Isaac or Idris Elba. Clive Owen will do in a pinch.

6

Knocking Off Hats

Beware the melancholic gray of Chicago, it can lead to ill-advised contemplations. In the winter of 1993, in between going to shows at Lounge Ax or Phyllis' Musical Inn, three music fans pleasantly in their cups were often found on the bar rails of the Ten Cat, the Crash Palace, or Lottie's—where sympathetic bartenders poured heavy, extended freebie shots, and rounded tabs to the low side—discussing the latest album by so-and-so and pondering why it wasn't more popular.

We were captivated by—one couldn't call it a scene really—the wellsprings of roots-oriented music percolating around the city. It was inventive, raw, unschooled, and unconstrained by rules or expectations of profitability. The artists were developing organically, delving into an electrifying world of sounds and themes and filtering them through their own tangled perspectives.

Many of these bands were stumbling around in blissful isolation and didn't have much of an idea there were others in town doing the same. Their own album collections guided them; haunting the same record stores as I did sharpened them; their ideas of independence and creativity centered them. They arrived at a similar spot via a hundred different routes. Time and place serendipitously synched up, and the more I *listened*—tuning out the balkanizing propensities of genre—the more I heard country and rock and punk intertwining all around me. The closer I looked, the lines between them got blurrier and in those blurry areas was promise and potency. It was honest and straightforward in a way I hadn't heard and felt in years, and few were paying attention to it. It was impossible to predict, ludicrous to explain, and blindingly obvious when thinking back, but Chicago was fertile ground for something completely unexpected like this. Maybe there was a scene, after all.

Meanwhile, a perverted manifestation of "success" settled like a February fog over the city's indie music landscape. Horse-racey articles reported the inside skinny on who was seen with what scout at what bar/club/trendy restaurant, who was signing with whom for what $$$, who was hot and who was not hot. There were gossipy columns about feuds, drugs, and backstabbings. Who walked out of whose show! Bickering over whether X was indier than Y, who moved south of North Avenue before the other and who was a regular first at Club Dreamerz. Few talked about the music. I felt like I was reading *Crain's Business Chicago* and *Us Weekly* instead of *UR Chicago* or the *Chicago Reader*. So much a-feudin' and a-fussin' to make it in a system the underground had consciously turned away from. The industry gatekeepers were being restored to their powerful perches.

As this was happening, music and artists tarred with the "country" brush were unceremoniously consigned to the *Not Interested* piles at most indie labels. And, really, why shouldn't they have been? America was in the grip of Achy Breaky Fever: Billy Ray Cyrus, boot-scooting, and "You Might Be a Redneck If" jokes the primary symptoms. Former rock producers had the brilliant/heinous idea to combine the worst impulses of arena lite-rock like Def Leppard with soft-gloss, sanitized paeons to pickup trucks and cold beer at mama's farm to achieve a melodious gruel that made the cash registers sing (with a tasteful twang). Brink's trucks lined up along Nashville's Music Row to spirit away the filthy lucre earned from this aural scourge.

But taking refuge in the bars and clubs where local artists were dipping their country-curious toes into overlooked waters, we thought we were hearing music deserving of some sort of documentation.

What if, our last-call cogitations went, we brought artists no one else was showing an interest in, together under one umbrella? *What if*—our eyes gleamed, in and out of focus, Old Styles in our hands—we put them on a CD and released it *ourselves*? On our *own label*? It was a brilliant plan. Well, it was a plan, anyway. If nothing else, it might be a good way to cadge some guest-list spots and free drinks around town.

Besides, it was a golden era of indie labels. You couldn't swing a dead cat in 1990s Chicago without hitting one that was defined by idiosyncratic interests and personalities, all dogged enough to make them viable. Touch and Go, Delmark, Alligator, Wax Trax!, Thrill Jockey, Drag City, Minty Fresh, Carrot Top, Johann's Face, Atavistic, Pravda, Feel Good All Over, kranky, and others were supporting original music. Some had stars in their eyes and future stars on their rosters. Others liked their buddy's band and thought a few hundred others might as well. They followed their ears and their hearts; if their brains, some luck, and enough fans followed, so much the better. Whatever they were doing, they *did* it. The pioneering spirit was everywhere. Anyone, we thought, could do it. We grabbed a napkin and quickly made a list of fifteen or twenty names. It really was that simple, the motivation that genuine. Besides, someone had to put a stop to Stone Temple Pilots.

So it came to pass, in this setting, in this city, in this time, that Eric Babcock, Nan Warshaw, and I started a record label. We each ponied up $2,000 from our wretched day jobs or savings accounts and *POOF* we were a label. As the idea of "alternative" was gelded, punk had taught me that I could act, so I *should* act. Thinking about the consequences would only slow us down. When one doesn't have hazy expectations of profit or longevity, naiveté is a powerful substitute for common sense. The whole idea tickled my Melvillian itch to walk into the street and knock off people's hats. The underground—and the dispositions it fostered for me as a kid—was experiencing a damp, drizzly November in its soul. Since we weren't talking about deep-sea welding or vascular surgery, not really knowing what we were doing didn't feel like an impediment, and calculations of risk or failure never crossed my mind. The worst that might happen was we'd be left with a pallet of unsold CDs and I'd go back to repairing squeaky cat doors and painting over bloodstains in cruddy apartments. Perhaps, in the end, I would crawl into an office cube to do things I didn't believe in for a boss I hated until I retired and got my pension or threw myself into traffic in quiet desperation. (Oh wait, that *did* sound pretty bad.)

With unearned and unreasonable confidence, we did it because we weren't smart enough to think of a good reason not to. In the early days of punk, there was a poster and T-shirt picturing three guitar chord charts and the caption "This is a chord, this is a chord, this is a chord. Now form a band." With Bloodshot, it was: "This is a cool band, this is a cool band, this is a cool band, now form a label." Starting was, to paraphrase music critic Lester Bangs, a glorious mistake, an unplanned leap into the unknown.

It was an unexpected turn of events, considering I had moved to Chicago a couple years prior to get away from music after a decade of finding in it kinship and identity, excitement and growth, and culminating in burnout and dismay. But music will always surprise you like that if you let it.

I took the bar napkin with the list of names home.

Were you aware of the rich history of country music in Chicago when Bloodshot started?

Country music coming out of Chicago was an inversion of expectations for most people, myself included. I knew Chicago punk heroes like Hound Dog Taylor and the Effigies. I knew the aggro-mechanical pummeling of Big Black and many of the Touch and Go bands, the experimental post-rock, un-jazz of Tortoise, early Chicago house music, and the tedious industrial scene, with their black fingernails, bad breath, and smack habits. I knew I hated the band named after the city.

And, like so many, I knew that Chicago equaled blues. When I moved to town, I had one address committed to memory: 2120 S. Michigan Ave, the Chess Records studio and office. I had become a Chess devotee in college. Making my record store rounds one freshman-year Saturday, I picked up the compilation LP *Wizards from the Southside* for $4.95 at Ann Arbor's Schoolkids Records. The album was a thirty-six-minute Chicago Blues 101 tutorial that has proven more essential to me than any Intro to Poli Sci or History of Astronomy class I dozed through. On it were names I'd heard of—Muddy Waters, John Lee Hooker, Bo Diddley—and a few others that were completely new to me, like Little Walter, Sonny Boy Williamson, and Howlin' Wolf. The album's lead track, Wolf's "Down in the Bottom," from 1961, stopped me cold; it was country blues that came to the city, plugged in, and blasted off, resulting in weapons-grade proto-punk. Hubert Sumlin's distorted, angular electric guitar, Willie Dixon keeping up on galloping bass, and Wolf's larger-than-life gravel-truck voice and *almost* out of control, *almost* violent acoustic slide guitar work were as intense as anything on early hardcore records. There was a ferocity, a *snap*, that I honestly couldn't get my head around. That song unlocked the stellar Chess catalog and drew a mainline in the red dirt straight to the primordial soup of Robert Johnson and Son House Delta blues and thus the beginnings of rock and roll. You don't ever hear someone say something *sounds like Howlin' Wolf*. Because it don't. It can't. *Wolf* sounds like Wolf. There aren't many artists like that.

Sadly, though, by the time I got to Chicago, the scene had largely been reduced to the tourist-friendly "blues" of the *Here's yet another version of "Sweet Home Chicago" for you* variety, providing a *low-down* soundtrack for a $35 plate of mojo redfish at the House of Blues.

But did I know country music's rich history in Chicago? Did I know about the National Barn Dance on WLS-AM, a radio show that predated the Grand Ole Opry and launched the careers of Gene Autry, Patsy Montana, Rex Allen, and dozens more? That there was a string of Madison Street honky-tonks in the Loop, like Wagon Wheel and the Casanova Club? Was I aware of the legacy of the Old Town School of Folk Music and its connection to Pete Seeger, Big Bill Broonzy, John Prine, Steve Goodman, and generations of roots music luminaries?

No, no, and no.

7

Journey to Chore

How did I get burned out on music by my mid-twenties? What led to a disillusionment so acute that I turned my back on something that had meant so much to me for so long, that had saved my ass so often before, and that made me flee my hometown? What about it could be worse than my repugnant job interview during that Clarence Thomas hearing?

After college in Ann Arbor, Michigan, in 1989, I washed up a few miles southeast via Washtenaw Avenue in Ypsilanti. I subleased a room for a hundred dollars a month, cash, from a guy with a fondness for the freebase. I hid anything of value behind the furnace because he'd show up at two or three in the morning raving about rent money. Fortunately, his taste in music was pretty shitty. He swiped rat-assed copies of *Toys in the Attic* and *Are You Experienced?* that I had picked up for a buck at flea markets but left the Minor Threat EPs and Ray Charles 45s. One housemate was in the "swinger" scene, and fragrant, unmarked packages of videotapes and lotions appeared on the front porch every month. Another housemate did "Purging Fridays," drinking a 48-ounce bottle of prune juice and spending the night in the bathroom. One night I came home, and he was feeding the Bible into the woodstove a page at a time. The other tenant was so boring as to be virtually nonexistent. It was not an environment conducive to mental well-being.

I took low-paying, mind-killing jobs with long and irregular hours. At a junk mail distribution warehouse, I stuffed, sealed, and bundled promotional envelopes, watching Ed McMahon's avuncular grin shoot past me on a conveyor belt 10,000 times a day. Others on the line told me, *You work too fast, slow down.* After a few weeks, I was threatened with a promotion for my competence. I quit in terror.

I worked the third shift at a plastics factory in the shadow of an I-94 off-ramp. They gave me oyster-shucking gloves, a lethally sharp cutting tool, and a workstation next to a bus-sized injection molding machine spewing automotive parts and toxic gasses. I stood in one spot the entire night trimming excess plastic off the extruded components and tossing them into a bin, trying not to sever a thumb or pass out from the heat, noise, and fumes. At the end of the shift, I'd go to the parking lot, the sun wanly rising over the interstate—*drear, thy name is Ypsilanti in March*—and have a drink. Whatever I was breathing during my shift gave me a powerful thirst. One of my line-mates, someone who had already been there four or five years and may still be there now, filled the trunk of his Chevy Nova SS with ice and beer so we could gargle the powdery, chemical taste out of our mouths. One wasn't enough, three was too many, five was just about right. We'd drink that cheap watery beer like it was water in the chill, dead morning and toast the next crew coming in.

After breakfast at Abe's Coney Island, I'd head to WCBN-FM, the University of Michigan radio station. They had let me keep the shows I had done when I was in school: the Rockabilly Show, the Friday Night Fish Fry (blues, R&B, soul), and a four-hour freeform show. None of them had required playlists, so I was able to go sonic spelunking with the audience in real time. Off air, I'd spend hours poking around the vast shelves of LPs and listening to them in studio B. I'd look at the names on spines I had only heard of—Coltrane, Williams, Cline, Nelson, Hopkins, Piazzolla, Holiday, and soak them in—and let their music guide me to the music of others. Some shows I'd focus on a specific label—Stiff, Chess, Twin/Tone, Vee-Jay—and listen to what made them sound like *them* and no one else. I was Burgess Meredith in that *Twilight Zone* episode, piling up stacks of books to read before he broke his glasses. The music kept me from slipping off to somewhere best left alone. Anything to forget everything else. The world of extruders and junk mail melted away.

Every week, a group of DJs met to review releases for general airplay. We would reach into a pile of albums, grab five, take them home to listen for profanities, write reviews for the other DJs, pick favorite tracks, and discuss them at the next meeting. These were glorious afternoons sitting in a room with other music nerds ragging on or praising new albums by Digital Underground, N.W.A., the Long Ryders, Ofra Haza, Flaco Jimenez, Art Ensemble of Chicago, Eleventh Dream Day, Fishbone, Afrika Bambaataa, and regional odd ducks like Couch Flambeau.* It was a valuable exercise

* We also had to put up with a budding William F. Buckley Jr. wannabe, who talked as if he was choking on a thesaurus. He postulated philosophical dorm room inanities such as a concern that the station's programming was, swear to God, too "anthropocentric." *We know dolphins are sentient. What if,* he said slowly drawing on his clove ciggie for dramatic effect, *the station was on at one of the science building's laboratories and there was a dolphin in a tank in that laboratory. Do we have any shows that would appeal to that dolphin's interests?*

on how to approach music I had never heard, didn't have a context for, and might not even like.

At that time, college radio was a powerful force in underground music, part of a subversive and righteous cause. Through the station, I connected with the local circle of club owners, promoters, and media. There was a steady schedule of concerts to publicize with nonexistent budgets: flyering, ticket giveaways, writing ad copy, and conducting on-air interviews. I learned to interview people whose music I wasn't yet familiar with (Run Westy Run, Bullet LaVolta, Poi Dog Pondering, Steel Pole Bathtub, etc.), and some whose music I already loved (X's John Doe, Phil Alvin of the Blasters, Texas guitar madman Evan Johns and the H-Bombs, and Detroit's low-fi houserockers the Gories). Even icons like John Lee Hooker, Janis "the Female Elvis" Martin, and the towering figure of musical time, space, and dimension, Willie Dixon, stopped by. By way of explaining how every rock 'n' roll song came from the blues, John Lee Hooker sang, a capella, Chuck Berry's raver "Nadine" at a slow, mournful tempo. The thought of it still gives me chills.

When Mr. Dixon came to the station, wearing an immaculate suit and a blinding-white homburg, he shook my hand—his hands were the size of freaking dinner plates—and I honestly tried not to faint. What did a timorous twenty-four-year-old dork in a Magic Sam T-shirt ask the writer, producer, and performer of countless linchpins of popular culture? The music he had his giant paws in left Chicago, went around the world, and came back at us dressed in frills, 'fros, and ruffles with the British Invasion, and seeped into the gutter of the Lower East Side to be reborn as punk. What templates were Johnny Thunders and his crew cribbing from? Berry and Diddley sides he played on or produced. Were Mick Jagger and Jimmy Page even imaginable without his Chess Records masterpieces? Perhaps, but not in any form we would recognize now. While it might be a clickbait argument or late-night, rambling parlor game to name *one* person most responsible for rock and roll, if you said Willie Dixon, I wouldn't dispute it. I took the journalistic tack of "how was recording with . . ." a few times and let the man tell stories, praying I didn't sound like Peter in the voice-cracking episode of *The Brady Bunch*.

At some point, my enthusiasm for music led to a production agency offering me a job as a stagehand. Considering that I had spent a previous weekend in the basement of the Ypsilanti house batting away with a pool cue beer bottles a housemate was throwing at me, and my plastics job was siphoning my life force, I didn't see any downsides that were any downer than the sides I already had. I had reviewed the Mekons' album *Rock and Roll* not long before for the station, and a line from the song "Memphis, Egypt" about destroying my safe and happy life before it was too late rattled around in my head. My life was neither safe nor happy, but it definitely needed destroying before it was too late; stagehanding seemed as good an idea as any.

And so I blundered into live music production. The venues I worked around Southeast Michigan were little clubs like the Blind Pig, Rick's, the Ark, Sully's, and Alvin's, bigger rooms such as the Nectarine Ballroom, Saint Andrew's Hall, and the Majestic, and auditoriums like Hill, the Michigan Theater, State Theater, and the Latin Quarter. The crowds ranged from eight paid at a Smashing Pumpkins Blind Pig show to 20,000 at a cornball heavy metal festival in Flint. Over the next couple of years, I went from being part of a crew emptying forty-four-foot semitrucks of gear, coiling cables, humping monitors, stacking PAs, and flying lights, to stage and production managing. Along the way I learned the soup-to-nuts process of The Show: three-phase power, sound, lights, security, catering, merchandise, force majeure, setup, breakdown, payouts, tickets, the local crew, the road crew, and from which Eastern Market butcher I could get enough pigs' blood for a GWAR show. I was often the first one in the building and the last one out. It was an insane amount of responsibility, and a fascinating classroom.

I had become a participant in the community of musicians, fans, and indie forces on a crusade. I shared in the experience when artists on the cusp of breaking bigger grabbed an unsuspecting room and made their mark. Working for Nirvana, k.d. lang, Screaming Trees, Stereo MC's, Dinosaur Jr., and the exquisitely punishing Bob Mould's Sugar in rooms barely large enough to contain their energy and potential, it was impossible *not* to be sucked in. It seemed there might be no limit to what some of these artists, and by extension, the corps that buttressed them, could do.

During a poorly attended gig in Pontiac, Michigan, the duo of Alejandro Escovedo (whom I had first heard in his ahead-of-their-time cowpunk band Rank and File) and violinist Susan Voelz mesmerized me with a set of sparse, gripping storytelling I felt ennobled to have witnessed. At the Latin Quarter, I watched openers L7 slap down the headlining Butthole Surfers and their meathead boys club audience in the most convincing way possible: a devastatingly powerful rock and roll show. The same with Babes in Toyland a few weeks later: by their third song, the headlining Skinny Puppy seemed irrelevant. Hanging over the stages on such nights was the broad sweep of surprise and discovery, of *possibility*. It was faith, in a very pure form, which was often forgotten about on bigger tours catering to, and cashing in on, the transitory tastes of a fickle marketplace.

I had the privilege, the absolute thrill, of working in small clubs for legends that had otherwise been relegated to niche or curiosity status. Doc Watson, Bo Diddley, J.J. Cale, The Five Blind Boys of Alabama, James Cotton, Sleepy LaBeef, Buddy Guy, Mitch Ryder, Charles Brown, Mose Allison, Ruth Brown, Clarence "Gatemouth" Brown, Dirty Dozen Brass Band, Commander Cody, Koko Taylor, Johnny Adams, Etta James, and more: my *job* was to work in a close environment with these titans, hear cornerstones from music's rich history performed, share a backstage drink, and maybe get a story or two about the "old days." This was material more enduring than whatever routinely filled the big rooms, and it was an eye-to-eye—not eye-up-to-stage—intimacy I had felt at punk shows years before in venues like the Freezer Theater and Clutch Cargo's.

I also saw the grace, vulnerability, respect for craft, and shared humanity of artists in unguarded times: bands carefully developing material during soundchecks; the Special Beat (featuring members of The Specials and The English Beat) letting the underage Ann Arbor ska fans in for the soundcheck—a simple, thoughtful, and totally unnecessary gesture that probably made the *year* for those kids; Living Colour's Vernon Reid practicing solos during soundcheck with the skill and free and easy confidence of a master; and singer Corey Glover laying into Sam Cooke's "A Change Is Gonna Come" a capella during soundcheck that stopped the crew where we stood. I piled the distraught

Cowboy Junkies into my car to take them to the hospital when their drummer's appendix burst. After a load-in rife with setbacks and delays that I scrambled a whole day to overcome, the Count Basie Orchestra's elegantly cool bandleader introducing me to his wife, *this is Robert, he's a good cat,* made my day. My week. Hell, it *still* makes me smile. I accompanied Australia's Divinyls to Lafayette Coney Island so I could explain what to order, and Laurie Anderson took me on a pricey tour of French wines at an after-show dinner as my boss and his credit card looked on nervously. When I showed up to a venue with a monstrous cold, the Indigo Girls' Amy Ray took me off the stage, *you look terrible, let's get you some tea and you can lie down in our room. Don't worry, the show will be fine.* I woke a passed-out Townes Van Zandt for his set opening for the Cowboy Junkies only to watch him get booed lustily. Afterward, I took him back to his dressing room and he asked if I could sit with him for a while; the look in his eyes was both a thousand miles away and just beyond my arm's length. We sat there silently as he gazed off to some far-off place I couldn't see. After a couple minutes, it was like he abruptly came back into the room, was surprised to see me again, and said *thanks* with a thin smile.

As she was being introduced for her first performance in almost a decade at Ann Arbor's way-over-capacity Nectarine Ballroom's closing show featuring Fred "Sonic" Smith of the MC5, Lenny Kaye, the Stooges' Asheton Brothers, and more, Patti Smith hesitated at the edge of the stage and grabbed my arm. *I don't know if I can do this, it's been so long*. The moment was calling for *me* to buoy up one of *the* bad-asses of rock and roll? *What the . . . ?*

I awkwardly backslapped a *you'll do great, everybody wants you here* pep talk out of somewhere, and she went out and killed "Piss Factory." When she finished and the crowd's roar washed over her, she had a smile of joy and relief that lit an eight-foot halo around her that the fans, the crew, and the *room* shared. I was deeply grateful in those moments, when music was a dialog, a greater whole, and I was able to play a humble part in it.

Ah, my friends thought enviously, *so much glamour! So much music and excitement!* At times, but mostly the work was hard and monotonous, the money bad, and the hours long—a foreshadowing, it turned out, of label-owner life—and I generally didn't see much of the concerts. There were constant worries, conflicts, and complications to attend to, a spare E string or grocery that carried a preferred brand of herbal tea to find, and *fast*. I had to MacGyver plumbing, flat tires, scrims, stands, stages, mirrors, and hotplates. I had to find a suitable rocking chair for Johnny Winter's "old lady" to watch the show from onstage right and make sure he had two cases of Dr Pepper for the bus afterwards. I rousted band members from the bus/van/bathroom/dressing room/merch table/bar/Popeye's Chicken down the street when they went AWOL. If no one else was available, I ran monitor sound, took tickets, stamped hands, checked IDs, and threw stalkers out of backstage. I made casual inquiries regarding female companionship for artists on Cass Avenue, and I endured new pop sensations who shall remain nameless phoning in performances and behaving as if their gravy trains would never end. Since Detroit was often the first stop before or after a border-crossing Toronto date, many tours also needed help disposing of or replenishing contraband.* One night at the Latin Quarter, there was some sort of bullshit power struggle between the club owner and the promoter, and the police were called at the end of the night. I came to the front of the house just in time to watch both being led away in handcuffs. An officer came up to me and said, "We're looking for Rob Miller, the production manager." I calmly said, "I'll go find him," quick-stepped backstage, told the crew they were on their own, and drove home.

Most of my memories of the shows themselves are strobe-light flashes disassociated from any thrill of the music or performance. Killing Joke insisting on at least 140dB at the mix point to "pummel" the audience. The Sisters of Mercy demanding enough smoke machines to make it impossible for the audience to see them. Signing a nondisclosure agreement that I would not reveal any description of the Residents out of costume. Ministry's Al Jourgensen's fart spray, which he found hilarious to soak the crew with. Blues Traveler's mellow-mannered tour manager flipping out when I wouldn't let them have a three-hour set in the middle of a festival. A now-icon of industrial music

---

* There was a house sound guy nicknamed Booger because he was often high on his own supply and his personal grooming habits needed refining, stagehands who *knew a guy, let me make a call*, and several artists who had their own skeezy connections already waiting for them when the bus pulled up. Many ends of nights saw road crews and bands selling off or giving away anything they were carrying to the eager local crew—*$50 for the day plus an ounce of good weed, three unknown pills, and a leftover sub sandwich? This is the best job in the world!*

The Graystone International Jazz Museum relies upon your support to spread the good news to a new generation of young musicians, and a new generation of hearts that need the love that this music gives to all of us to whom it is given. Your financial and moral support of Graystone is what keeps it alive, and with it, the love of Jazz!

The Board of Directors

James T. Jenkins - President
M. A. Lahab - Vice President
Ann Campau - Treasurer

Thomas H. Bowles, Sr.
Jack L. Campau
Nathaniel Clover
Calvin Euseary II
Wesley Norris
James Ruffner
Eugene White
Jimmy Wilkins
Linda Yohn

GRAYSTONE
Hall of Fame
International Jazz Museum, Inc.
3000 E. Grand Boulevard, Detroit, MI 48202
PRESENTS:

The
Count Basie
Orchestra

Plus the
Jimmy Wilkins Kansas City 7
at THE NEW LATIN QUARTER

from Ohio speaking with an English accent that, weirdly, he didn't have the last time through town, needing a ride *now* . . . so he could be driven across the parking lot to his bus. The quick birthday dinner with my girlfriend during the break before doors opening that was interrupted by the artist in the middle of a coke bender in his motel room: *I'm not playing tonight if I don't get more. I'm serious.* A Too Live Crew show cancelled because of death threats. Teutonic industrialists Front 242's unrelentingly humorless crew, who reminded me of the *Die Hard* villains. The jury-rigged lighting tower swaying nauseatingly over the audience at an oversold Jesus Jones show. My crew being instructed not to speak to Black Francis of Pixies, and that I should refer to him as *Mr. Francis.* Following Shane MacGowan's Brobdingnagian trail of puke after he left the stage, not to return, during the second song of a Pogues show. The veritable torture of the Sonic Youth *and* Living Colour crews soundchecking the PA all afternoon using a Steely Dan CD—the soundmen insisting it was the "perfect" album to test a room. My absolute terror when the Flaming Lips set off pyrotechnic cannons in the low-ceilinged Blind Pig and balls of spark shot into the crowd, off the ceiling, and down the pit of the darkest fears a stage manager can have: fire, panic . . . and worse.

As I made mid-show rounds at an LL Cool J show, I checked in with security at the entrance. Inside the front doors was a heavy cardboard barrel half filled with handguns. My eyes saucered. The three-times-wider, one-and-a-half-times-taller-than-me bouncer shrugged. *Yeah, we're frisking and confiscating. Everyone's being cool. They'll pick them up after the show. If he's not worried,* I lied to myself, *then, OK, I'm not worried.* When the door of

Danzig's equipment semitrailer rolled up, the first thing the local crew and I saw was a twelve-foot-tall stage prop of Satan's head or Prince of Darkness or something squeezed in the back. The beefy, seen-it-all Eastside metalheads I'd hired to do heavy lifting burst out laughing. Standing next to the tour manager, I gave him my best Nigel Tufnel wonderment: "And oh, how the people of Stonehenge danced . . ." He quickly whispered, "Do *not* make any *Spinal Tap* jokes. I'm serious. He will fucking flip."

If everything was going smoothly, I might be lucky enough to catch a nap. I rang in the New Year of 1991 at a Nine Inch Nails show, fast asleep on a sticky road case backstage. *For auld lang syne, my dear. For auld lang syne . . .*

I also saw up close a full menu of scams by promoters, tours, venues, agents, unions, and inspectors: arguments about undercounting ticket sales, overcounting merch, stealing booze, understocking booze, cheap meals, no meals, fake number of road crew members to get more meals, not hiring agreed number of local crew, blowjobs for backstage passes, phony guest lists, phony receipts for promotion expenses, permits needed, permits not needed, permits needed and ignored, permits needed and ignored *but we'll let it slide if . . .*

One old-school tour manager patiently listened to my boss tick off reasons why he couldn't pay the agreed amount: low ticket sales, print advertising price hikes, etc. *The show really didn't make any money*, he explained earnestly. The tour manager nodded along cordially. He opened his briefcase and indifferently shuffled some papers around, not drawing attention to, but certainly not hiding, his pistol. (I saw others make their pistol's presence known right away. It minimized the double-talk.) The man got paid in full. Actions and counteractions. The curtain had been peeled back to reveal a game of cutthroat chess, and everyone at this level was playing their part.

The minute a show was over, the band, fans, promoters, and hangers-on began their post-show revelries, *that was great, what a night, you rule, we rule*, and the crew began dismantling everything we had set up half a day ago. When I was done with my night, when I got to sit back and savor another night pulled off without incident, the band long gone and the road crew pulling out, there was scarcely enough juice left for tired handshakes with stagehands, maybe a beer if someone had the foresight to squirrel away a few from backstage. An alleyway of city rats feasting out of a dumpster as the backdrop.

And if a whole night went off without a hitch, no one would have noticed the work that went into making it happen and no one would remember the effort. I inhabited that thankless space of baseball umpires and airline baggage handlers. Invisibility was the mark of victory. (See appendix A.)

* * *

The gigs rolled in relentlessly, one after another, without distinction. Jane's Addiction, Rollins Band, Nick Cave, the Neville Brothers, Pearl Jam, Cocteau Twins, Ian McCulloch, Tony! Toni! Toné!, MC 900 Ft. Jesus, Camper Van Beethoven, Aztec Camera, Violent Femmes, Peter Murphy, George Thorogood, Midnight Oil, Ramones, Dread Zeppelin, KMFDM, Taylor Dayne, The Jesus & Mary Chain, They Might Be Giants, Yo La Tengo, Soul Asylum, Dee-Lite, the Sundays, Happy Mondays, the Sugarcubes, Pet Shop Boys, and on and on. Another week, another slate of shows. I was never home, and, worst of all, I wasn't listening to my records or going to shows I wasn't paid to be at. Music had become what I yelled over while I told the head of security to make sure fire exits were kept clear, or asked the lighting guy if the issue with PAR 56 cans flickering on stage left was getting worse, or got in a tour manager's face about the opening band stopping so we could stay on schedule. Judgements on the day became based on how smooth the load-in went or if soundcheck was on time. Never the music. I was getting *nothing-new-under-the-Vari-Lites* jaded. Concerts became factory work: the same cues, same set list, same banter, same encores, and the same *special* encores, because the fans in [*Name of City*] are awesome! Make the trains run on time, present the product, and move on. Repetition, not creation. I stopped seeing an artistic enterprise; I saw a commercial one. What had been fascinating became empty.

I arrived at the State Theater on Woodward Avenue in downtown Detroit on a *not hot yet but it goddamn will be soon enough* July morning at ten. I had left the State barely seven hours earlier after a fifteen-hour day working for a band I've long since forgotten. This day's show was the Replacements, a band I'd worked for a few times before. Over the course of a few albums, adored by most critics but ignored by most of the marketplace, they had progressed from indie rock anti-heroes playing at the divey Joe's Star Lounge in Ann Arbor to bigger and bigger rooms as they became anointed standard bearers of the indie movement. Even though I was exhausted from the night before, and there had been some tensions at their last show—band members peevish about dressing rooms, separate buses, sound, management, each other—I was looking forward to the show; they were scruffy, *I Hate School* underdogs with whom I felt a kinship.

A guy in a black mesh trucker hat and grimy yellow T-shirt with cutoff sleeves was hosing down the sidewalk in front of the venue. Torn police tape fluttered from a No Parking signpost. *Two guys*, he told me, *left the show last night pissed at each other. They went their separate ways, but later met back up in front of the theater and shot each other. It took a couple hours for them to bleed out. It was a mess.*

And so the day began.

The band played a grimly rote concert with one foot already out the stage door and on the bus. Even the audience could tell that no one was having fun on stage. I thought, *Yeesh. . . . is this what it comes to? Is this what the process, the grind, does to music and musicians?* After it was over, everything packed up and everyone on their way, I left the venue feeling like someone had dumped a bucket of tired on me. With a worn-out stare, I took in haunted Woodward Avenue, well before Comerica Park, Ford Field, or Little Caesar's Arena were there. The moist, garbagey day had given way to a moist, desolate night, a knotted band of the police tape all that was left on the signpost.

I thought of something a tour manager told me earlier that year: the music business is no place for a music fan to be.

Yeah, I'm done, I decided, *this isn't where I want to be with music.*

The Replacements broke up onstage at the Taste of Chicago festival two days later. Two months later I quit my job, pointed the Dodge Omni westward, and moved to Chicago to get far, far away from music.

When did you first visit Chicago?

In 1986, three friends and I were drinking beer on our Ann Arbor porch and the college radio station announced the schedule for the Blues Festival in Grant Park. That sounded fun. We were in the car and on our way within the hour.

We followed signs to Michigan Avenue, bought a couple cases of Old Style at a Loop Walgreens. and humped them to the Petrillo bandshell (such things were, if not expressly permitted, not noticeably discouraged at the time). There we watched the *unreal* lineup of Memphis Slim and Matt "Guitar" Murphy, Otis Rush, Willie Dixon's Big Three, Bo Diddley, and Chuck Berry backed by his original band plus Keith Richards, with a city that hadn't been abandoned like my hometown shining in the background. We slept on benches in Lincoln Park. Over the next two days we caught sets by such musical titans as Bill Doggett, Otis Clay, Pops Staples, and the Staple Singers, Albert King, and John Lee Hooker, and I drove home in a cloud of exhaustion and wonder.

A couple of years later, I made the same drive for Dwight Yoakam and the iconic Buck Owens at the equally iconic Chicago Theater in the Loop. Before the show, my friend and I ate across the street at Soul by the Pound, a fabulous soul food buffet of questionable cleanliness. You piled your plate up and took it to register, where there was a scale: $3.99 a pound, $4.99 if you got ribs. I got the ribs. The peach cobbler made me dizzy with delight.

After the show, which was as incredible as anyone who knows anything about anything might imagine, Buck and Dwight swapping lead vocals all night, my friend wanted to take me to a place nearby she thought I might like. We walked the mostly empty street on that stuffy August night to Randolph Street, turned, and stepped down an unspectacular flight of stairs—and stepped back fifty years. I was in the Double-R Ranch, the last—*there had been others?*—honky-tonk in the Loop. It was dark, it was loud, there were more people dancing than were on the street, and the unknown-to-me Chicago institution the Sundowners were on the stage behind a railing made of wagon wheels. We found a table and watched these three old-timers in cowboy hats and neckerchiefs perform a tight, loose, and utterly sincere set of country music. I soaked it in goggle-eyed and -eared: a menu offering dozens of chili iterations, the giant leather map of Texas, "No Poker Playing in the Kitchen" and "Horses Not Allowed Upstairs" signs, corny jokes, seamless musicianship, and harmonies sung as if they were brothers.

This? In the Loop? Where was I? *When* was I? The past? The future? *Now . . .*?

After watching a couple of sets while having a few beers at a graffiti-carved table surrounded by paneling covered in tack, we walked up and out to the street and the still warm summer air and I distinctly remember thinking, "I think I am going to move here."

8

Holy Cow, Whattasetta . . .

Why Chicago?

For those like me, born and raised in and around Detroit, coming of age in the oil embargo hangover '70s and Reagan hangover of the '80s, our hometown had become a shell of what it once was. It wasn't yet the *cause célèbre* of French tourists fascinated by photogenic industrial decay and seeking to walk the same streets as *Iggy et les Stooges*, or a magnet for urban apiarists, craft distillers, and custom bike fabricators. In the early '90s, there were dead-end jobs at the whim of the car economy and not much else. The bottom hadn't yet been reached; it wasn't even in sight.

Chicago has been a regional hub, a lure, a blank slate, for almost two hundred years. Lakes, rivers, canals, railroads, and interstates brought people here to exchange ideas, to invent something or reinvent themselves, to make and lose fortunes. Now it was the place to come to for those who didn't want to go to the coasts but still felt the gravitational pull of the Midwest.*

So I came to give it a try. Mine was a migration replicated thousands of times in hundreds of beater cars from dozens of cities, towns, and nowheres, from Milwaukee to Saginaw, Kansas City to Carbondale, Dubuque to Dayton, and Louisville to Frankenmuth, all of us drawn by an indefinable sense of potential—or at least a chance—lacking at our starting points.

---

* Michiganders get edgy when we stray too far from the Great Lakes. I can't swim, I don't fish, I've never fancied myself a member of the boating set, and I can count the number of times I've gone out of view of the shore on one hand and still have enough panicky fingers to pull the trigger on a 12-gauge flare gun/distress signal, but it is a source of comfort to know they are nearby. Salt- and shark-free. Hands off, Vegas and Phoenix. You chose to live in deserts.

* * *

When I arrived on Labor Day 1991, my roommate and I rented a $600-a-month apartment with no heat in the two bedrooms in an ordinary brick six-flat. It was at Belmont and Leavitt, on the edge of Roscoe Village, a *not quite gone enough to come back yet* neighborhood, and across the alley from a boarded-up dry cleaners and Miska's Liquors.

Across the street was the dividing line between Latin Kings and the Black Disciples turf—a tidbit the landlord neglected to mention when we signed the lease over beers at Cody's Tavern. While we waited for the bus at that corner on our first weekend in the city, a kid slowly pedaled by on a Schwinn with an extended fork, flashed a gang sign at another kid standing nearby, and started shooting. The other kid went down, shot in the neck. I stood there incredulously, not thinking *duck and cover*, but *wait, this is where I moved?* My roommate jerked me into the safety of a doorway. The next weekend we were drinking beer on the back porch when a Buick Regal raced up the street, and on the hood, straight out of an episode of *Starsky & Hutch*, was a guy holding onto a wiper and beating the windshield with a baseball bat. We wordlessly looked at each other and got back to our beer. Such was the neighborhood.

Still, the area had a spirit that had mostly vanished from my hometown. Four blocks up, Roscoe Street, with its wilted German/Polish charms, reminded me of my grandma's neighborhood in Detroit before it began to look like postwar Dresden. There were three butcher shops, a bakery, a thrift store, a barber shop, and a couple of dark, smoky bars—*eingang* and *ausgang* signs on the doors—frequented by old men with eggplant noses and perpetual scowls. Within weeks, we were on a first-name basis at Edith's Diner. Edith, holding forth over her six stools and eight tables, had a face whittled out of a two-hundred-year-old oak stump. She shuffled around in her house slippers, rightfully bragged about her homemade breakfast sausage, and merrily gave us shit—especially if she sensed we were hungover. A block over was the Village Tap, a cozy tavern with outstanding bar food, a tent in the back, Battleship and Scrabble games on the shelf, and something local called "Goose Island Honker's Ale" on tap. East of the apartment on Belmont was a row of junk stores, a 24-hour diner run by a Kentuckian who whipped up a $2.99 plate of eggs, ham on the bone, and homemade gravy that could cure any self-inflicted ailment, a newly opened music club, the Beat Kitchen, and Man-Jo-Vin's Pizza.*

Cardena's, the neighborhood grocery whose bilious yellow linoleum was accentuated by harsh, OG fluorescent lighting, had seen better days. But the shelves and coolers were brimming with tortillas (There was more than one

---

* Named for brothers Manny, Joey, and Vinnie, of course.

kind? More than one size? What else had Taco Bell, my sole Mexican food reference point, hidden from me?), chorizos, a rainbow of dangerous-looking peppers, and the alluring smell of rotisserie chickens. On our first visit, customers were walking around with plastic cups of beer—the store had tapped a free keg of Modelo back by the meat counter. The decision to leave behind that world of music in Michigan was looking better and better.

Two fellow Michigan defectors and I started drumming up painting and carpentry jobs all over Chicago. We didn't have any idea of the neighborhoods or the history, where was hip and where wasn't. The city was a blank slate. As much as anything, we got to know it through cheap, never-encountered-before lunch counter fare. Italian beef—what, is that some sort of mob argument? Dipped? Why not?! Čevapčiči? I'll take three. Rib tibs? Too cheap *not* to eat. Supertacos, aggressively seasoned "taco meat" overstuffed into a pita? Sounds super. What's that being hawked out of the pushcarts with the bugle horns? Elotes, you say? Sure, slather on some of that glistening whatever-it-is sauce out of the tub and finish it off with lime and chili, *por favor*. Pizza puff? What is this sorcery? I'm in! Pierogi at Sophie's Busy Bee, biscuits and gravy at Leo's Lunchroom in Wicker Park, kimchi pancakes at Jim's Grill on Irving Park, hot links at Edna's on Clybourn Ave, pad thai by the pound at Thai Grocery in Uptown, and burritos advertised to be—as if it made them more appealing—as big as body parts (heads, arms, etc.) fueled our ten-hour days. To keep us caffeinated, there was a White Hen—the 7-Eleven of Chicago before 7-Eleven became the 7-Eleven of Chicago—nearby for two-liter bottles of RC Cola and something that approximated coffee.

Off days and rainouts were spent at mysterious establishments known as "tap rooms," half liquor store and half bar, like the Peacock, Cut-Rate, the Save-More, and, under the Addison brown line El stop, Giannini's. Drinks were often served on carpet squares instead of coasters, and glasses of Old Style came with a can of Clamato if you needed to steady the helm. It was where I learned my first (but, sadly, not last) Chicago-centric ethnic slur: the Irish nap.* We could walk in with some oily Serbian cheesebread or dense Guatemalan pupusas during a passing thunderstorm, have a couple of Old Styles, and when the sun showed its sunny face again, walk out with a plastic jug of Popov for after work.

While rolling paint onto endless walls at jobsites, there were plenty of alternatives to whatever Chicago radio's equivalent of *Whole Lotta Led Zeppelin* was. WXRT, despite an unfortunate affinity for Pink Floyd and Steely Dan, had an eclectic and comparatively non-repetitive playlist, a rarity in the world of commercial radio. They occupied a Los Lobos, Patti Smith, Elvis Costello, David Bowie, R.E.M. lane, with occasional WTF head turners like

* Passing out on the bar—typically when it was still daytime.

Muddy Waters, Lene Lovich, and Graham Parker. Q101 had "new music" covered in that prelapsarian time when it *was* new and interesting and, dare I say, alternative, and un/underknown artists like Radiohead, Breeders, Proclaimers, PJ Harvey, and the Cranberries were in rotation. On the far north side, we listened to freeform programming on the low-wattage Northwestern and Loyola college stations. Further south, the days grooved by with the deep voice of Herb Kent the Cool Gent on V103. I stopped bringing cassettes to play on the boombox; radio was creeping back into my life.

For after-work conviviality, the city bustled with establishments that had survived the wave of blight that had obliterated Detroit: neighborhood joints, pure and simple, with a Cherry Master 2000 in the corner, Christmas lights year round, and stories hanging in the air. Ask for a lychee-infused, juniper-forward gin with house-made tonic and you would have been run out of the place. If you wanted snacks other than pickled eggs, sausages, or a toaster-oven frozen pizza, you were SOL. If there was a TV, chances were it was tuned to superstation WGN and their father, son, and holy ghost of omnipresent personalities: Andy Griffith, endlessly ebullient weatherman mainstay Tom Skilling, and half-in-the-bag Cubs' broadcaster Harry Caray. If you wanted the channel changed, the bartender might have to find the vise grip pliers to do it because the knob went missing years ago.

I'd shoot pool or play the damnable vintage baseball pinball game at the Ten Cat, tabletop shuffleboard at the Bluebird, or the addictive duck hunting game at Marie's Riptide Lounge. Over automatic bowls of pretzels, or on special nights, Bugles, the namesake matriarch of Rose's on Lincoln Avenue, sat behind the bar between her TV and dusty Grundig stereo console. She'd sweetly ramble on in her thick (Macedonian?) accent about killing rabbits in her garden with a shovel—*they eat-a my garden*—and how a movie star gave her $10,000 for the 1970 T-Bird that her late husband had bought for only $500.

Next to the typewriter repair shop (!!!), the stairway that Tom Cruise and Paul Newman argued in in *The Color of Money* led to the North Center Bowl. The chain-smoking, solitaire-Yahtzee-playing bartender mixed up $1.25 Sunny Delight screwdrivers while the jukebox played Material Issue and Bobby Darin. Down the block, the cramped and unfussy Augenblick felt like someone had opened a bar in their garage. The neon lights, luscious, serpentine bar, and snug booths gave Ukrainian Village's Rainbo Club an irresistible Rat Packy glow, and Danny's in Bucktown had a couch. A couch! In a bar! What a city!

Bucket O' Suds, a Willy Wonka–ish funhouse of a tavern far west on Cicero just south of Belmont Avenue, had the only license in the city at the time to make its own spirits. Or so the story went. When the owner, Joe, who bore more than a passing resemblance to Larry "Bud" Melman from *Late Night with David Letterman*, buzzed you in, you entered a dark, dusty cathedral of drink with a gorgeous, ornate bar and bowls of salty, salty pretzels served with homemade mustard. The oddly shaped and colored booze bottles were mostly unlabeled. There was no beer or wine: don't ask. "Joe," one might say, dazed and intrigued, "I'm looking for something not too sweet, with a fizz," or, "Joe, I'd like a drink with a bite and hint of fruit," or "Joe, I had a shitty day and I need to forget about it." He'd size the person up through his clunky, black-framed glasses and wander off muttering, leaving them unsure if he had even heard them. Ten minutes later he'd putter back and say, "Here's a Tropic Lush." Or a Helicopter, Boss Rumba, or Elixir Lucifer. He wouldn't say what was in it, the name itself had to suffice. On one quiet night, he showed me a bottle of Chinese whiskey that he said Chiang Kai-shek gave him when he was in China during World War II. It had a mummified frog in it for strength and virility. I looked closely into the murky amber. There was a mummified *something* in it. If it wasn't a Chiang-era amphibian and his story was bullshit, so be it. If it was true, so much the better. Either way, a grade-A bartender yarn.

Bucket O' Suds newsletter. News you could trust.

And if none of these suited the mood, options named simply Old Style, Cerveza Fria, or Zimne Pivo dotted the city; dive bars when they were just dive bars, not slippery markers of authenticity or a Yelp category for urban ironists looking for a night out. The city had so much to discover.

* * *

On weekends, I started prowling the cluttered, welcoming independent record stores of the sort that had provided my escape hatch to the underground in Detroit: Quaker Goes Deaf, Reckless Records, Blackout!, Val's Halla, 2nd Hand Tunes, Shake, Rattle and Read, and the dizzying selection at Jazz Record

Mart. (And I learned to always make time for a stop in at Uncle Fun, a store where Pee-wee Herman, David Lynch, Rip Taylor, and Judy Garland's dog walker might have scavenged the narrow, jumbled aisles for necessities/novelties like rubber vomit, a bag of plastic spiders, rainbow boas, or a *Fall Guy* lunchbox). The thrift stores and flea markets that could be found in every neighborhood held enticing bins of cheap LPs in the back behind shelves of Commodore 64 consoles and impossibly heavy TV sets. Then there was the open-air junk shop of all junk shops: the Maxwell Street market. Sociologists and historians know it as an entryway into the chaos and opportunity of American free market economics for wave after wave of immigrant communities; I knew it as the place John Lee Hooker threw down "Boom Boom" in *The Blues Brothers*. Most Sundays, I'd get there as early as I could—once or twice straight from closing a 5 a.m. bar and fortifying myself with Polish sausage or a pork chop sandwich at nearby Jim's Original. I'd feast upon the wares, foods, petty crime, and hustling parade that existed less than two miles southwest from the Chicago Board of Trade, where the *real* crime and hustling took place. If the Board of Trade's allegory for its rapacity was the three-story art deco statue of Ceres, Roman goddess of agriculture, atop the building, Maxwell Street's symbol of *do anything to get by and get ahead* was the rusted blue Blues bus, with the names of greats like Little Walter, Sonny Boy Williamson, Muddy Waters—some of whom had regularly played at the market—painted in white and yellow on the sides and windows and filled with (often bootlegged) cassettes. Two sides of the same Chicago coin.

With a Styrofoam cup of a magical, restorative elixir called horchata ladled out of giant glass jars, I'd wander past sellers of tube socks, cases of thawing frozen pizzas that had "fallen off a truck," tools, car parts, bike parts, batteries of every size, chili powder sold by the pound, low-grade porn tapes like *Holy Cow, Whattasetta Knockers*, and hot links and ribs glistening in scrap-iron smokers. There was music, from crudely amplified bands to crudely amplified DJs. Dealers with bins of bloodied but unbowed LPs by Wynonie Harris, Eddie "Cleanhead" Vinson, and Koko Taylor played them on shitty stereos powered by car batteries to prove they didn't skip—*naw, man, they just look tired*—$4 each, three for $10.*

---

* Maxwell Street was also the go-to for blank cassettes. Standing at a table one day perusing the selection (some still with Tower or Best Buy price tags), a guy came to the table and stuck a gun in the face of the seller.

"I got these last week from you," he said and threw a package of TDKs at his chest. "These are *fucked up*, they don't work. This is *bullshit*."

Without giving any indication this was out of the ordinary, the seller said, "try these," and tossed him some Maxells.

"Cool." The man with pistol walked away, satisfied.

Author hunting for records, Maxwell Street. Photo by Cathy Noble, used with permission.

And Chicago had food, the likes of which I had never known. When I was growing up, fresh garlic was considered excessively ethnic in our family, and "foreign" foods were limited to Old El Paso hard shell taco night and Chef Boyardee's Beefaroni. But in this city? After work I'd tie a napkin around my neck and wander Argyle Street to try something called pho. Or Jamaican curried goat in Rogers Park. Smothered chicken and greens at Army & Lou's on the Southside. Polish buffets on Milwaukee Avenue. The comforting, pillowy pot stickers the size of plums at Orange Garden. The pear-flavored turpentine served up by the glassy-eyed owner Drago at Little Bucharest. At the most efficiently named establishment in Chicago, *24 Hour Korean Restaurant* on Lawrence Avenue (whose entire menu misspelled "pork" as "dork," much to my juvenile delight), I'd dig into the improv jazz sounding *Bi bim bop*. At the most inappropriately named restaurant, Healthy Food Lithuanian, in Bridgeport, I tried platters of hearty, stick-to-the-ribs, to-the-lungs, to-the-ventricles, fare like sausages, kugelis and eggs, and koldunai—meat dumplings. I swear, there was even bacon in the *water*. Hasenpfeffer at the Oktoberfest-sized Zum Deutschen Eck on Southport. Red-checkered tablecloth trattorias in Heart of

Italy, where middle linebacker-sized guys with dead eyes and full-length camel hair coats loitered out front. The Jewish-owned, mob-frequented Myron and Phil's on the far northwest side for thick steaks and baked potatoes on the table, and signed photos of Walter Jacobson, Bill Buckner, and Charo in the lobby. Marie's Pizza, the only pizzeria I'd ever been to that you had to walk *through* a liquor store to enter. Ribs you didn't need teeth to eat at Biasetti's on Irving Park near Ashland—the loungy piano player sitting beneath a framed newspaper copy of his erroneously printed obituary. Ropa vieja and tostones at Habana Libre in West Town. Luscious oatmeal shakes at the Costa Rican Irazu. Trying to catch the eye of the four-hundred-year-old woman pushing the dim sum cart in Chinatown before the BBQ pork buns were gone and the only dishes left were beaks and mysteries. There was potato sausage in Andersonville, the *Swedish* neighborhood. Who knew Swedes needed their own neighborhood? And what quickly became my favorite Thai restaurant, my favorite restaurant, period, Rosded in Lincoln Square—extended-family run, eight tables, faux wood paneling, jugs of soy sauce and boxes of paper towels stacked in the narrow hallway on the way to the bathrooms, secret menu, and resolutely un-dumbed-down spice and *naam pla* levels for Western tastes. To order several Rosded dishes Thai-style (plates coming out of the kitchen one after another for all to enjoy) with a table full of friends was the haut-iest of haute cuisine for me.

After last call, if I wasn't quite done yet, I could stop at Arturo's, a cantina on Western Avenue at the edge of Bucktown for a stabilizing *milanesa de pollo* torta. "Can I get a beer too?" The waiter with a gunslinger mustache, unruly mullet, and tan cowboy boots would wink and say, "It's after hours, all we have is water, that'll be $4," and a beer in a Styrofoam cup would arrive with the salsas and chips. If my courage was Dutch enough, I closed the night at the diner at Irving Park and Damen with a sign boasting/threatening "The Best Hat Dogs in Tawn." River Kwai on Belmont Avenue opened at 10 p.m.; the whole building precariously leaned to starboard, and the super fantastic *pad kee maow* came with complimentary sides of cheap, second-hand Chinese cigarette smoke courtesy of the owner and cook. For the classics—tuna melt, Monte Cristo, BLT, or early breakfast to ward off the goblins—a golden spectrum of diners that may or may not have been related, Golden Apple, Golden Waffle, Golden Angel, and Golden Nugget, dotted the city: count on wizened waitresses, plastic mother-in-law's tongues by the cash registers, red plastic cups of water, and blessedly fast service.

These were not intimidating tweezer and foam platings at bistros owned by hospitality groups. They did not deal in the emulsion and mirepoix argle-bargle that make mouthfeel-conscious foodies convulse with anticipation. They were delicious expressions of *place*, of bond, not only *in* the neighborhoods, but *of* the neighborhoods, that never left you barking like an uncle grousing about the high price of a new set of whitewalls, or making a sandwich later because you were still hungry. There was real pleasure and adventure in a $4.95 plate of potato pancakes, *gai pat krapow,* or tikka masala cooked in a kitchen not much bigger than my own, by a grandma (also, not much bigger than my own), brought to the table by a son while a granddaughter played in the corner and a TV blared an incomprehensible soap opera. So many choices. It was a lot to take in.

Michigan expats may never fully integrate. We'll never be able say "Chi-*caw*-go" the way natives do (nor do we particularly want to), and we cringe when someone says they're picking up *beeersss* at *da Jewelsss.* We will always think 16-inch softball, putting salads on a hot dog, cutting round pizzas into squares, and piling wheelchairs/stools/broken lawn furniture into a parking space at the first sign of snow is stupid. Nor do we understand the fondness for imperious mayors and aldermen that people abide, like Russian peasants, with an enigmatic mixture of resignation and dignity, grateful to get the alleys plowed in a timely manner as the city is otherwise plundered by the powerful and the connected. And we will never stop pointing to our hand when we explain where someplace is in our home state.

In Chicago, March lasts for three months and the winds blow unimpeded from every direction. From the west, gusts off Colorado's Front Range send us the piquancy and dust of Iowa feedlots in the summer and Laura Ingalls Wilder blizzards in the winter. From the south, with nothing taller than a ten-story *Jesus Saves* cross along I-55 to slow them, winds carrying rivers of Gulf moisture make it feel like Grandpa's sweaty undershirt was draped over my head. From the north, a hard wind off the lake, flowing from Hudson Bay, Alberta, or wherever Nunavut is, will drive joy completely from my soul and make me wonder if that harsh sound was the crunch of an over-salted sidewalk or my bones cracking.

Nonetheless, it was starting to feel like a paradise.

9

Haunting Taverns

I wasn't alone in these feelings about Chicago. As other wayward folks visited and returned home with stories of a place with low rents and mass transit, full of independent bookstores, record shops, movie houses, theaters, and galleries, with more opening every month, word in the Midwest got out. Throw in the abundance of cheap, weird foods and cheap, weird bars and the city had all the ingredients to attract cheap, weird people.

What turned out to be Chicago's *real* superpower, though, what enabled it to evolve into the uniquely creative hotbed it became in that time, was what many mistook as its liability: to many, especially in the established centers of media, it was a backwater, a dirty-fingernailed outsider in the worlds of art and culture. But rather than being discouraging, this off-in-the-hinterlands dismissal nurtured talent with the boldness, or indifference, to respond *If you don't want us, fine, we didn't need you anyway . . .* Where there wasn't much expectation of gain, there wasn't much to lose. So Chicago became a destination and a haven for people willing, or *preferring*, to create on the fringes, unburdened by external interests and judgements. Writers, illustrators, animators, producers, designers, woodworkers, photographers, painters, poster artists, screen printers, comedians, playwrights, and actors came with an entrepreneurial zeal and developed their own self-sustaining ecosystems. The more that came, the more everyone rose, the more that could be built. The dynamic was contagious.

This seemed especially true for musicians. Existing far from the entertainment company towns of New York, Los Angeles, and Nashville, Chicago could be a place to take chances. To channel the inner-Sandburg everyone develops here in due time, it was a city without constraints and artists could look to the horizon.

Chicago was big enough to support diverse artists, ideas, and sounds, but too big for one promoter, one club, one label to control or define it. The City of Neighborhoods kept it manageable, personal, and inclusive. Without a central entertainment district, music was everywhere, every night. It wasn't a "showcase" town, it was a "do-the-work" town. If a band needed a cheap practice space, empty warehouses abounded. Better yet, since there were stages in every neighborhood, do a show on a Monday night and work out the kinks without pressure. The Clearwater Saloon, Schubas Tavern, Déjà Vu, Czar Bar, Phyllis' Musical Inn, Empty Bottle, Quencher's, Beat Kitchen, and the Fireside Bowl were cheap and carried little pretense of a *show*; they were hangouts where people happened to get on stage with instruments and play for a while. Artists had free rein to perform without fear of making jackasses of themselves. To wrestle, refine, or blow up new ideas. To create and fail, switch projects, create and succeed. Because artists were very much *a part* of the community, as opposed to apart from or above it, people were forgiving of the foul balls, giving works in progress a chance to grow and breathe. And since the local indie music scene wasn't built on proximity to, or interest in, business per se, clubs, promoters, and labels could be mutually supportive and non-competitive. As a result of this openness, labels supporting an astounding assortment of musical styles flourished, and artists could record for a half dozen of them if it suited their imaginations. There wasn't a sense of ownership over the artists, and it wasn't rarified or complicated, a far cry from the horseshit promoter and club turf wars I had left behind in Detroit.

And any night felt like it might bring with it adventure. The small west side blues bar Rosa's Lounge—fifty people and it was packed—had luminaries like Sunnyland Slim playing on weeknights. I saw Homesick James on his eighty-eighth birthday perform the best version of "Little Red Rooster" I will ever hear. I couldn't believe it. To me, it was like a rock fan walking into their local bar and catching a $6 set by Pete Townsend. The Elbo Room was across the street from a chicken slaughterhouse, and catching a breather between sets of blues-punk delinquents the Red Devils, the corner became a mix of smoking, black-jeaned hipsters and white-smocked, rubber-booted, hair-netted butchers smeared with feathers and blood. On big band night at the famous post-prohibition jazz shrine the Green Mill in Uptown—complete with a Galaxy 200 jukebox full of Keely Smith and Bill Doggett—I'd put on the shiny suit I got for cheap at George's Resale basement on Clark Street in Andersonville and dive into a martini, wondering who might join the band onstage. At FitzGerald's in nearby Berwyn, I caught, up close, a *who's who* of roots music like Rosie "The Rockabilly Filly" Flores, Dave Alvin, Mavis Staples, Bill Kirchen, Del McCoury, Junior Brown, and Dale Watson. It was the best Texas dance hall outside Texas; it was better than most dance halls *inside* Texas.

After bailing on a pointless alt-rock show at the Metro, I headed to Carol's Pub, an enclave for hard country in the up-from-Appalachia, Uptown neighborhood, past Graceland Cemetery, final resting place of mayors, magnates, robber barons, governors, captains of industry and commerce, and other assorted crooks and larcenists.*

Overseen by namesake Carol and her take-no-shit crew of waitresses and bartenders, the beer was cheap, the house band was rowdy yet polished, and the clientele could fight, fall down, or whoop it up, as occasion dictated. Nick the bartender in *It's a Wonderful Life* could have been talking about Carol's when he told Clarence the wannabee angel, "We serve hard drinks in here for men who want to get drunk fast, and we don't need any characters around to give the joint atmosphere."

From a block away I noticed blue and red police lights swirling around the front of the bar. As I got closer, I saw the yellow DO NOT CROSS police tape tied from the front door, looped around a lamp post and across to a parking meter, the throw-rug-sized puddle of blood to the left of the door hard to miss. Standing among the clot of pear-shaped policemen was Carol herself.

"It's OK, we're still open. Come in, come in. A couple of idiots got into it, and neither would back down, so they stabbed each other. They'll be fine," she explained. I limbo-ed under the tape, gave the puddle wide berth, and went in.

The band was great, the beer was cold.

Taking night classes at DePaul University for a master's degree meant that I was a block away from the Lounge Ax, Sue Miller and Julia Adams's now shuttered Lincoln Park club. While my classmates went straight home after class to thoughtfully consider conflicting theories of source material for Shakespeare's *The Merchant of Venice*, or the difference in the glottal stop and the fricative, going to this crusty and beloved indie club became a post-class reflex for me. It didn't matter who was playing. I filled my ears with the Jon Spencer Blues Explosion, the Gun Club, Royal Trux, the Muffs, Calexico, the Reverend Horton Heat, Shellac, Billy Bragg, New Bomb Turks, Mazzy Star, 7 Year Bitch, Shadowy Men on a Shadowy Planet, Tortoise, Dirty Three, Morphine, Cordell "The Rock 'n' Roll Grandma" Jackson, Los Straitjackets, Nine Pound Hammer, Ronnie "The Blond Bomber" Dawson, Chickasaw Mudd Puppies, Go To Blazes, Guitar Wolf, and dozens of others. I left Uncle Tupelo's last show with bruises mid-thigh from being wedged against the stage.

---

* There are more than historical sonsabitches, though: there are also "Mr. Cub" Ernie Banks, boxer Jack Johnson, and architect geniuses Sullivan, van der Rohe, Khan, Adler, and Root. It's a great place for a summer meander.

Southern Culture On the Skids threw fried chicken at me, my preconceived ideas of bluegrass were blown out by the Bad Livers' covers of "Jailbait" and "Lust For Life," and the Jesus Lizard's David Yow's genitalia grazed me as he crowd-surfed.*

It didn't matter that the bands were often obscured by the thick cigarette smoke, or that the bathrooms were CIA dark-site punishment chambers, or that those structuralist seminars and drywalling gigs came awful damn early the next day. Anything could happen. A show could suck, or it could be revelatory. There might be ten people there, or it might be jammed. Once I got past taciturn Dan the ticket-taking man, implacable as a marble statue, I again felt that sense of camaraderie that does not exist in auditoria or stadia. There was an absence of *process*, and the compelling tension between carefree and drive, of creativity and fun, that I hadn't felt since falling into the punk scene in Detroit over a decade before. After working dull, big rooms for a couple of years, being back in the chaos of little clubs was tickling parts of my brain I'd forgotten about. I was back on the other side, free to plunge into the moment.

There was also the simple matter of geography. Everyone toured through Chicago. That meant that fans, local musicians, writers, and any active participants in Chicago's music scene were constantly exposed to the larger world. On the flipside, these bands went home and told others about Chicago's music, fans, and clubs, and the circle grew. So, while everything for

* Granted, that wasn't particularly noteworthy—probably a quarter of all Chicagoans of a certain age and attitude have had his ballsweat on them at one time or another.

music and *industry* was here, the *music industry* was not, making conditions ripe for a down-to-earth and boundary-stretching setting. One could call it nurturing, but Chicagoans are too flinty for that kind of praise.

Hasil "Haze" Adkins, a demented treasure in the forgotten crate of American music, played Lounge Ax one night. With a backwoods spirit that made Andy Griffith in *A Face in the Crowd* seem like Andy Griffith in *The Andy Griffith Show*, Haze, a one-man band, beat his guitar and strummed his drums on an anarchic ride through his "hits" rescued from oblivion by the renegade indie label Norton Records: "No More Hot Dogs," the Cramps-covered "She Said," and the dance sensation "Do the Hunch." He beseeched us to *turn the White House into the Hunch House!* It wasn't retro. It wasn't ironic. It wasn't hot, hip, or likely to make anyone any money. What the Haze was transmitting to the room was, in a very real sense, a revival meeting. And I was being *revived*.

Coming to the end of a Jerry Lee Lewis raver, Haze preached/threatened "goodness, gracious, great balls of *fire*" and his guitar spastically hurtled into the cymbals, as if someone only he could see and hear commanded *Stop playing now!* The pint glass of vodka he kept on the floor tom was knocked over. He exhaled loudly into the mic, spent. "Show's over." Amen.

After nights like that—to the extent any night was like that—my go-to was the *port in a storm* comfort of Jeri's Grill at Montrose and Western, with its washed-out, chrome-framed *Nighthawks* poster, Elvis and Route 66 trinkets, and a jukebox that no one ever fed but from which George Strait, Madonna, and Ricky Martin popped on randomly. The gentle, rhythmic scraping of the grillman's spatula as he worked the hash browns and tossed off opaque koans like *It ain't toast until I put it in the toaster, know*

what I mean? was the soothing denouement to a night's often raucous festivities. Over my usual of grilled cheese, glistening fries, and pickle slices—not spears—I turned over in my head the strange fact that I had come to Chicago to get away from music. Now I was kicking around this new city, savoring what I had become numb to, re-embracing what had become lost. While consumed by the considerations and pressures of *The Show*, I had neglected the thrill and the fulfillment of *the music*. I had forgotten the simple power of the shared experience.

I began to show up to work and class with a palimpsest of hand stamps from clubs, smelling of smoke, beer, fun, and perhaps a *Hat Dog*, my ears ringing from the new sounds and mind racing at the new prospects around me. For kicks and promo records, I started writing album and show reviews for some of the fanzines I had been picking up at record stores. I rediscovered my record collection, and the impulse to share it, by getting DJ gigs at strange little bars like Sweet Alice, Inner Town Pub, and the Empty Bottle. The punk rock cavern the Crash Palace on Lincoln Avenue had a country night every Wednesday. After relentlessly pestering the DJ with requests for the Mekons, the Knitters, Wanda Jackson, and other artists she hadn't heard of, she suggested I take every other Wednesday. It felt like stealing to get paid as I reconnected to music's capacity to transform and convert. Music was sucking me back in. All I had to do was admit it. And do something about it. How could I help?

10

The Squares Will Rule

The soggy napkin with the list of bands somehow did not get lost, thrown away, or dismissed in the clear-thinking light of day.*

With dewy-eyed zeal, the three of us spent the gloomy early months of 1994 approaching people around town to give us a song for our unnamed, untried idea that existed in a smoky, middle-earth space between abstraction and pipe dream. We sought out the kids left off the other teams, the Bad News Bears of the underground, the outsiders of the outsiders. We hung out at my apartment listening to records and cassette demos and going through the club listings in the *Chicago Reader*. We propositioned bands working the club circuit—the Riptones, the Texas Rubies, first-wave bluegrass/punk/rockabilly outfit Moonshine Willy, and the New Duncan Imperials—that were somewhat established but not part of any identifiable "scene," a few side projects, and a couple of groups that were never heard from again.

One night we listened to an LP by the Sundowners, the cowboy trio I had seen earlier on one of my first trips to Chicago. It had this fantastic song on it, "Cigarette State," a bluegrass-tinged raver with the snarky line of lines: *Alabama's grand / the state, not the band*; there was respect for form, but also totally bent content. Perfect. It was credited to one "Robert William Fulks." We'd seen "Robbie Fulks" listed at clubs like Déjà Vu and Lower Links—it had to be the same guy. We looked up *Fulks, Robert* in the phone book—1993 a time when every apartment, no matter how ill furnished, had one laying around somewhere, even if to hold up the three-legged couch—and cold-called. *Could we use the song? Sure*, he said, *but I've got my own version*. The deal was sealed.

* Late-night bar ideas, obviously, having a historically low success ratio.

The Mekons' Jon Langford, who had moved to the city a few years previous, walked into the original Empty Bottle, where a couple of us were busy at the bar, emptying bottles. We pitched him on participating. With his buccaneer spirit and keen eye for potential mischief, he was in. Within weeks, he delivered "Over the Cliff," featuring Tony Maimone—the bassist of heroes of my youth, Pere Ubu—which etched a sharp line from what we were doing with the label back to what had helped get me there in the first place.

The Handsome Family had given us a four-song demo cassette with a drawing of a raccoon on it and a note with the caveat that they weren't very "good" yet and didn't have a lot of material. But I was floored by "Moving Furniture Around," a song squarely in our sought-for wheelhouse—timeless country pathos updated for an urban environment. With parking tickets and shitty landlords taking the place of coal mines and company stores, a distorted guitar rattling like a cold wind past the semi-abandoned furniture showrooms on Milwaukee Avenue, and a knack for deep-catalog Americana weirdness, they fused the malaise of Kristofferson with the simmering rage of the Pixies. I couldn't wait to see them live. They had a show at Phyllis' Musical Inn, one of Nelson Algren's old Polish Broadway haunts, on an unfashionable stretch of Division Street. Past the well-used bar, with its dusty bottles of DeKuyper schnapps, was a "stage" wedged into the corner. Singer/guitarist Brett Sparks introduced himself and sheepishly told me they were going to suck but, you know, *enjoy the show*.

I sat at the bar next to a red-haired guy who looked vaguely familiar from Lounge Ax shows. Once the Handsomes started, it was obvious that Brett wasn't being self-deprecating; they really weren't very good. Tempos changed mid-song, bass parts wandered off in different directions, and Brett was still learning how to effectively project his dark-as-a-dungeon voice. Ugh. Could I get out of this somehow? Sitting eight feet from the stage, it'd be tough to make a stealthy exit. Worse, the guy next to me, now a bit drunk, loved them and wasn't bashful about expressing it. *What a dummy*, I thought. After the show, I paid vague compliments to the band, thanked them for the tape, and bolted. I'd use the song, but I didn't think they had much of a future as a band.*

I went to the Double Door, when it still had both a street entrance and an entrance from the back of the liquor store, a true double door, to check out

---

* Messed that one up, didn't I? The Handsome Family spent the next twenty-five years putting out some of my favorite albums, exquisitely terrifying and beautiful albums, the way a decaying, mossy log or a half-awake-at-dawn nightmare can be terrifying and beautiful. I'm an idiot, I have thought to myself a thousand times since. Turned out that superfan was the owner of another recently formed local label, Carrot Top Records. I think he signed them that night. I missed it, but at least someone else didn't. It was emblematic of the just do it verve of Chicago at the time.

a potential contributor playing that night. It was a weeknight in November and Wicker Park still had a pre-gentrification desolation to it. I grabbed a barstool and watched a bunch of guys competently run through a few Elvis hits to a handful of people who looked like they began reveling at two in the afternoon twenty-five years ago. Behind the bar was a velvet Elvis painting with what appeared to be bullet holes in his forehead. When the bartender, a slab of dude with a walrus mustache, thick jowls, and a nose that suggested he'd spent a lot of time on the other side of the bar—an archetypal Chicago look—brought me my Old Style, I asked as I pointed at the hole, "Somebody not like Elvis?"

"Yeah, happened last week," and he filled me in. Some guy kept asking a woman at the bar to dance. Her date told the guy to buzz off. After the next song, the guy came back and asked again. Buzz off. He came back again. *Fucking* buzz off.

"Aw man, they're playing Elvis, it's cool, let us dance."

The date stood up, pulled a revolver out of his chest holster, put two holes in the painting, and told the guy, "Fuck Elvis." The bartender, noticing my wide eyes, reassured me, "It's OK, he was an off-duty cop."

Freakwater and the Bottle Rockets were bands that had already released albums, so we regarded them as seasoned giants in this little field, and they said yes as well. It was a stretch to claim the Rockets as Chicagoans since only their bass player lived here, but fuck it—*we* were defining our parameters. Furthermore, they were on indie labels, Thrill Jockey and East Side Digital, that we looked to as role models. Having these "heavy hitters" on board, with their critical acclaim, outside-the-area-code tour histories, and "real" label support might even lend credibility, if only through glancing association, to the project.

Finally, we thought a nod to Chicago's country music history would provide a narrative arc for those who might think Chicago + Country = Absurd. We included two tracks from the Sundowners, who had helped, unwittingly, coax me to Chicago in the first place, and now it was time to pay them back.

The album was mastered on the sly in a studio in Harold Washington Library after days of beery debate over a sequence, to find a flow, to tell a story in the era before shuffling and streaming. Jon Langford lent us a painting depicting ghostly country music figures, skulls, and a protecting angel for a cover that struck a balance between unsettling and classic, unorthodox and yet somehow familiar. For a main title, we cribbed "For a Life of Sin" from "Lost Highway," the Hank Williams honky-tonk hymn I had first heard through a cover by a band of reckless Nashville punks, Jason & the Scorchers.

The bands we had gathered were glad someone, anyone, wanted to document what they were doing at that place in that time. There was no expectation of a career, no one was trying to "make it," and no one, but no one, ran home, kicked open the back door, and dragged their S.O. into the boudoir, yelling victoriously, *prepare for some sweet, sweet lovin' because I'm on my way to the big time, I've been signed by . . .*

Oh right, we needed a name.

Where did the *Bloodshot* name come from?

When asked the origin of "Bloodshot," my go-to answer was that I looked in the mirror one morning and it was yawning back at me. And while a good one-liner is rooted in truth, sometimes miserable, too much cheap beer, too little sleep, and half a pack of second-hand Marlboro Reds truth, there was more to it. We brainstormed on themes inherent to country and punk: hard-living, rebellious streaks, quotidian hassles and humiliations, and the little guy getting screwed over. Listening to Johnny Bond's "Hangover Tavern" one night, I thought "hangover" was a good jumping off point. I thought of my favorite hangover song, "Nausea," by X: *Bloody red eyes go to nausea . . .*

"Blood" felt like ripe terrain.

I was a fan of Wynonie Harris, the '40s and '50s blues shouter with more lascivious roll in him than malt shop rock for the tastes of parents terrified of fledgling teenage culture and race-mixing. His 1951 killer hangover song "Bloodshot Eyes" on King Records rattled around my head: *Don't roll those bloodshot eyes at me / I can tell you've been out on a spree.*

Bloodshot it was. It sounded cowboy, but not hick, more renegade black hat *Magnificent Seven* Yul Brynner than hagiographic white hat John Wayne. It looked *mean* with a quasi-cattle brand font, and it didn't conjure the schmaltzy Nobility of the Rural Class imagery that was the rage at the time. It could be many things. It could be its *own* thing.

Since critical language surrounding the melding of roots and punk was rare, discursive, or dismissive, we wanted to plant our black flag and define our own message before someone else hung a horrendous tag on it. We took it for granted that launching this project into an underground rock environment using "country" as a broad characterization would have been outright idiocy. It was a loaded term that would elicit reflexive derision—like a movie description that began "Starring Pauly Shore"—from the very indie music followers, people like us, we thought would be most interested. The entire genre had been cast by many—for often good reasons—down an elevator shaft. We needed a subheading that both captured people's attention and provided the solace of an easily digestible taxonomy for those more comfortable with sharp lines than chiaroscuro. We wanted a term that tapped into the kindred feelings of rebelliousness and candor that had drawn me to punk rock initially and that I was finding anew in this music. We felt it was wisest to *tell* them what to call us.

At the time, I was living in an asphalt-shingled two-flat under the Brown Line curve between the Addison and Paulina El stops. Pelly's Liquors was a quick walk over the tracks and across the street from Betty's Resale, a junk store *par excellence* that had jumbles of furniture, tools, expired canned goods, and, unbelievably one weekend, live pigs rooting around in the back aisles. Johnny, the owner of the bar on the other side of the vacant lot from Betty, whose frozen-in-1940s establishment one had to be buzzed into, would complain in his indeterminable Old-World accent about what a crazy old bat she was. Then he'd wax nostalgic for the days when the block wasn't full of "fancy hair salons" and was a row of Greek-owned brothels, *front apartments classy girls, back apartments, not so classy*, and pour me another shot of anise-tinged lighter fluid. Around the corner at Wolcott and Roscoe was an establishment with a $2.99 three-egg, hash browns, toast, and "meat" breakfast special, which would close for a few hours and reopen as a charmless, stabby dive bar for the rest of the night. Our next-door neighbors were three generations of Tennesseans who retained their native twang and, like the other longtime residents of the block, stopped talking—mid-sentence—whenever a train passed overhead. They had an above-ground pool filled with radiator-fluid green water, and the grandson had a monster truck named "Nice Package" that he worked on religiously in the yard. He also, through hammering, swearing, and sorcery, kept my Dodge Omni running long past its expiration date.

When a new condo development paved the gravel lot at the end of the street, everyone's basements flooded after the first heavy rain. *That's never happened before*, griped the elders of Newport Street. Solution? Throw a block party fundraiser for the alderman so he'd "fix it," and so that one Saturday afternoon bouncy castles and cameos by fire engines for the kids and an Elvis impersonator for the adults appeared. "Elvis" strutted down the block and sang to everyone on their porches, his assistant pulling a portable PA on a Radio Flyer behind him. He asked my friend sitting next to me her name, gave an Elvis-y *thankyouvurrymuch,* and busted into *Mustang Lisa, guess you better slow your Mustang down.* Toward the end of the day, a bucket was passed from house to house. To fill with cash. To fix the drainage. To give to the alderman? By the end of the month, the issue was resolved.

In other words, it was a block working the naked graft with a *live and let live* vibe, and it wouldn't be troubled much by Eric and I spending hours in my yard drinking, listening to loud music, and crafting our initial press release, our statement of purpose. As recovering English majors, we wanted a good yarn about this quixotic endeavor, but we needed a strong hook to convey the outsider aspect of it, to show that *this* country music wasn't *that* country music.

And while it is a world of uncertainty and chaos, it is a truism that where there are English majors and beer, there will also be a thesaurus and dictionary nearby. We ran through words like rebel, guerrilla, revolution, and malcontent as I dug through the trusty *Roget's* until "insurgent" caught my eye. It had it all: conviction, purpose, and an antisocial, piratical flourish. Thus, a "genre" was coined. A British interviewer once commented that "insurgent country" sounded "something a bit Woody Guthrie and a bit Sex Pistols." I'm good with that.

Compilation compiled, we sent it off for the mysterious and faraway process of manufacturing and I went back to painting two-flats, drywalling a home office, stripping crown moldings, whatever, in Old Town, West Town, Boystown, wherever. And we waited.

What were we looking to accomplish in this city known for blues, industrial, and razory-guitar indie rock? Maybe we'd sell the CDs. Maybe not. Maybe one day an eccentric Japanese or German completist would find a copy at the back of a used record store and be thrilled the same way I was when I found a compilation on Detroit's Fortune Records that had Skeets MacDonald's "Tattooed Lady" plus *Eleven Other SIZZLERS* on it. The question, to the extent it was ever asked by either the artists or us, wasn't "why do this?" but "why not?" I was so excited at the prospect of shining a light on this fluky little scene in Chicago that I doubt anyone could have talked me out of it.

So it came to pass one day in June 1994 that a shipment of BS 001 *For a Life of Sin: A Compilation of Insurgent Chicago Country* CDs arrived at the "office"—the dining room table of one of the partners—and a new independent record label launched its first, and we thought last, album. No champagne was popped, no *we're on our way now* toasts were made. There was a name, a press release, and . . . now what? What *did* a label do? Even though Eric had worked at small, local indie labels before, Nan had done some freelance promotion and publicity, and I had my production writing/reviewing/college DJ experience, the next step was new and unknown. Forty boxes of plastic discs stacked in the corner? It sure didn't feel like the makings of moguldom, but it was something. We had *made* this.

I would love to say there was a grand plan, that foundations were being carefully laid upon which a mighty empire would rise. Or that there was even a minor plan upon which a shed with a leaky roof might teeter. However, that would be a lie.

* * *

The world at large responded to our first release, quite appropriately, by not noticing. Little did I know that getting the damn thing made was the easy part. Now it was time to get to work. With a DIY mentality molded in my earlier days, we made our rounds to the network of neighborhood record stores, this time (trying) to sell rather than buy. Most took a few—*you're local, we're local, we know our customers.* Chain stores responded with the hollow-souled catch-22 of *can't buy it without a sales history, but can't get a sales history without selling it.* I'd gather up the local fanzines, freebie newsletters, and mags like *Tail Spins, Free Fest, Butt Rag, Roctober*, and *Punk Planet* that were available, like pre-internet forum/chat rooms, at the entrance of every indie book and record store, get their mailing addresses, and send them promo copies. Maybe they would be interested in this story, if only as counterpoint, aside, or comic relief from the goings-on in the "real" Chicago scene. Late nights, if I wasn't at shows, I'd be cutting, pasting, and copying postcards and press releases at the Kinko's at Ashland and Clybourn.

Poster for Bloodshot's first showcase. Artwork by Mike Werner.

We held the compilation release party at Delilah's—formerly the Crash Palace—which was quickly becoming the de facto clubhouse for all the punk-meets-country misfits. The food was provided by the Hot Nuts dispenser near the door and drinks by the *you're-having-one-more* owner Mike Miller, whose presence in the room was normally as subtle as Fozzie Bear after a few cans of Monster Energy.*

* Representative exchange one night as I attempted to leave before he considered it prudent, polite, or necessary:

Mike Miller: What are you drinking?

Me: I'm good.

Mike Miller: That's not what I asked.

People showed up. Enthusiastic people. People willing to cross the seemingly un-crossable chasm between punk and country. It was both terrifying and encouraging to encounter others we didn't know were out there who shared our musical thirsts.

We pressed onward. In a matter of a few weeks, we put together showcases at Lounge Ax and the Double Door.

Later that month, I volunteered, or was volunteered, to be the woefully underqualified drummer for compilation contributor Moonshine Willy and off I went to experience the peaks and valleys of touring life. Before playing to three people in Hattiesburg, MS, the club owner suggested a place with a 99-cent all you can eat buffet. *Bingo!* "All you can eat buffet" is the "Eagle has landed" for the touring band, even if it was in a line-dancing club the size of an airplane hangar. During our indecorous feasting, a woman with a headset on the dance floor talked people through the latest shuffles and two-step boogies. We opened for the Old 97's in Dallas's Deep Ellum neighborhood and directly after the show drove fourteen hours to make soundcheck on time in El Paso—for our efforts, the bartender offered us a twelve pack of Zima and pickled sausages that had been there "since the last owner." We played in Phoenix on the Fourth of July, when it was 120 degrees. On the way into town from El Paso, the van's AC had crapped out, and the radio aired news about children getting third degree burns from falling on the sidewalk. In LA, all eyes were glued to the TVs while we played—it was right after the O.J. murders. In Albany, CA, we were greeted by the bouncer in front of the shabby venue. He was in full biker regalia and had profound dental issues that . . . well . . . let's just say he looked like he could handle himself in a barfight, but corn on the cob would bring him to his knees.

"Where you from?"

"Chicago."

"Cool, we love Chicago blues here."

Uh-oh.

Due to a spat between rival rockabilly factions in Salt Lake City (I know, *really* . . .), zero (0) fans came to the show, but the club owner still insisted that we play three sets to get paid. We woke up the next morning forty-five minutes away in Provo at the promoter's house, with four children, seventy-two pictures of Jesus, and what may have been two wives. At a festival gig in Denver, we killed in front of a couple thousand people, and I floated through the crowd afterwards, only to have that high quickly tempered by sleeping with my head next to a kitty litter box at the club's waitress's house—she had taken pity on us and let us crash there after the show.

Along the way, I visited record stores in cities we played. Perhaps, as with the punk compilations I'd grown up with—like Alternative Tentacles' *Let Them Eat Jellybeans* or Dischord's *Flex Your Head*—I might muster some niche interest in a regional release. I would drop off a promo copy, maybe consign a couple of sales, and chat up knowledgeable clerks about cool local clubs, fanzines, and radio stations—anyone who could help us build a database from zero. It was the grassiest of grassroots beginnings.

At last, it was home to a triumphant, sold-out Empty Bottle show with the Riptones, Robbie Fulks, and Jon Langford—according to local legend Wesley Willis's song about the night, we *whipped a mule's ass*—closing Marie's Rip Tide Lounge afterwards, and then, as the sun peeked from the direction of Lake Michigan, finishing the night with a plate of patties and eggs at the Diner Grill, menthol ashes from the grill man's ciggie included free of charge.*

These independent, locally minded clubs around the country opened their doors, without hesitation, and let us stick our foot in; no track record, no pay-to-play, and no *we'll get back to you . . . never.* (I would be remiss, however, if I didn't mention the Double Door whipping up a list of "hidden" expenses at the end of the night, rendering our "near sell-out" a "make zero money." It reminded me of the scams I'd seen run in Detroit. I exacted a measure of revenge when I found several cases of empty beer bottles in the then-unfinished basement and methodically pitched them, one by one, against a wall.) We were the beneficiary of a preexisting, unfenced, fertile landscape where we could quickly and easily sink our untested shovels. It wouldn't be the last time that would happen.

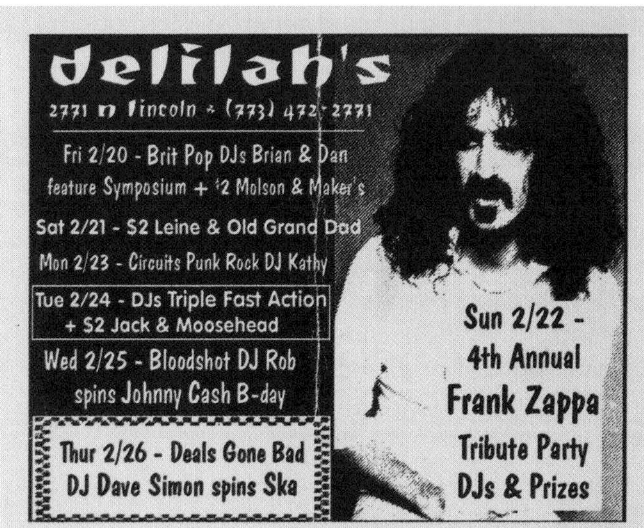

And on we went. I took the El to the Harold Washington Library in the Loop and spent hours in a room with hundreds of municipal telephone books from around the country that in the world before the internet were indispensable

* Shortly after that, I decided my skill set was far more suited to helping other musicians, *real* musicians, and I got back behind the scenes where I belonged. The world was not the least bit poorer for it. I was to drums what a McRib sandwich was to BBQ. As for the drum kit, I gave it to a pretty woman a few months later because she asked nicely.

resources. I compiled numbers and addresses of record stores, music venues, magazines, indie weeklies, and whoever else might be responsive to our curious endeavor. With one eye on the late-night, low-rent TV commercials for Empire Carpet, Eagle Insurance, Moo & Oink, and Victory Auto Wreckers (*aw man, my fuckin' car door fell off*), I had the other eye on piles of mail to be stuffed, stamped, and mailed beyond the 606XX zip code. *More envelope stuffing! Less Ed McMahon!* I had no idea if anyone would care.

By the beginning of autumn, Delilah's was full up every Wednesday for the country night DJs—fans two-stepping between tables when space allowed—as more like-minded outsiders were drawn to the convivial space as a conversation and mutual exploration of the music deepened. It had become a real time laboratory both for those who were put off by the idea of punk and country mixing, and those who knew they could. There would be sing-alongs to the Statler Brothers' "Flowers on the Wall" ("Smokin' cigarettes and watchin' Captain Kan-ga-rooooo"), and I'd slip in Rosie Flores reviving a Janis Martin cover. I'd put Dallas thrashgrash progenitors Killbilly's "Mountain Dew or Die" next to the classic high-lonesome Osborne Brothers' "Rocky Top" and let the connections speak for themselves. Everyone knew Flatt and Scruggs' "Foggy Mountain Breakdown" and Jeannie C. Riley's "Harper Valley PTA," but they likely hadn't heard them nestled among Meat Puppets and Minutemen tracks. *I never saw them as this . . .* (See appendices B and C.)

Every week, more curious folks stopped or staggered into Delilah's on their way from work or to a show. They'd grab a handful of Hot Nuts, do a yoga half forward fold to take a piss in the absurdly configured men's room, and listen to the owner's tall tales of obscure whiskey, *try this one, it was aged in a barrel made from the wood of Emperor Wilhelm I's funeral caisson.* And they'd hear classic music hatched from peculiar sources in a pointedly un-classic environment. "Country" genre constraints were eased for people who didn't even know they were fans: there *were* outlaws, weirdos, and songs about the life's shit sandwiches, it could be pissed off and it could be a laugh. It wasn't stately and pristine, and it didn't have to be boring. "Country" could be many things, just like punk. It seems obvious now, but it wasn't then.

Bloodshot had started with a napkin, but it wouldn't end there. Bands were playing more frequently to growing crowds, and there was a growing sense of *possibility* in this terribly uncool backwater of music. This out-of-the-ozone diversion was snowballing into something. We were, it seemed, off and running. But to where? And how?

11

All Alone and Lost

When probing the formative headwaters of Bloodshot, I was asked how I first became interested in "this kind" of music, "this" being shorthand, I suppose, for "country and roots—influenced." But back then—nor even now, for that matter—I never heard it as *this* kind of music or *that* kind of music; that presumed a level of contextual awareness I did not possess. Or thought existed.

When I heard the Cramps' "Human Fly" for the first time on *Radios in Motion* one night in high school, it wormed into my ears through the headphones and gave me an itch I still scratch. They oozed, I throbbed. The song was rock and roll reduced to its most essential, its DNA laid bare. Physicists say the closer they get to the Big Bang, the more beautiful the universe becomes. The Cramps beckoned me towards rock and roll's Big Bang.

Like many great things, the song started simply: a creepy-crawly, descending run on a single guitar string, like a ghost gliding through an open attic window. An eight count on the ride cymbal. And then . . . a crash that sounded like a world ending and a world beginning.

Nick Knox pounded out the most basic 4/4 beat without any filler—*kick, snare, kick, snare, kick, snare*—as simple and as necessary as a pulse. Then two guitars, no bass, joined in.*

Bryan Gregory's buzzsaw guitar sizzled like a frayed electrical cord snaking through time and place, from Memphis to the Moon, over a thousand shitty stages in a thousand shitty clubs, a fata morgana bleeding from cinder block walls. Poison Ivy Rorschach, who said more with her icy sneer and snap of her gum than she did with virtuosity, dismissed every tenet of guitar heroics.

---

* As urban myth has it, when asked why they didn't have a bass, they answered, in the most exquisite summation of the punk ethos ever, "No one wanted to play bass, so no one did."

Her guitar solo was a paragon of minimalism, an anti-solo that any competent shredder would dismiss as farce—so simple anyone could have played it, but no one else had. And, like a warm, breathy voice growling in your ear from behind in a dark room—alluring and forbidding, one half Elvis and one half Vincent Price, one half hillbilly and one half punk—Lux Interior, the showman, shaman, and rock and roll archeologist sang, or boasted,

Well I'm a Human Fly
I spell F-L-Y

The dumbest, most perfect couplet in rock and roll, incontrovertible nonsense yet undeniably true.

I got 96 tears in 96 eyes

Ninety-six tears. A slick callback to 1960s garage-rock weirdos ? & the Mysterians. A conjuring from the past to let us know the Cramps were trafficking in ignored or never-known treasures like Andre "Mr. Rhythm" Williams, Ronnie Dawson, the Novas, the Phantom, Charlie Feathers, and Ronnie Cook & the Gaylords. These marginal figures possessed age-old wild ideas and thirsts for glory that anyone looking for a way up or a way out needed. Every song the Cramps reanimated—"covered" is too weak a word—was like a mysterious rune. With the Cramps drawing a primitive map on the sides of catacombs with black eyeliner, I was driven to search out these *real* freaks and rebels, oddballs and blackballs, the never-beens and no-hit wonders, to go deep and go down, to explore music's nether regions, to go straight to the unsung architects of rock 'n' roll, as decayed and neglected as they might be. I may not have known then the specific antecedents in "Human Fly," but they were as much a part of my genetic code as Huck Finn, the Creature from the Black Lagoon, Robert Johnson, and dirty magazines. Americans are made up as much from a McDonald's drive-thru window as we are the Declaration of Independence, as much blue-plate special as blue suede shoes.

I got a garbage brain
It's driving me insane

I bought their *Gravest Hits* EP the next weekend at Sam's Jams. I rushed to the house of one of the few friends I had, and we blasted it for hours, letting the fatback reverb, horror show ethos, and campy heresies contained in those grooves crawl over and into me. I was hooked. That my original copy still plays is a miracle, that the cracks and buzzes add to it only natural.

Seeing the Cramps for the first time at Clutch Cargo's later that summer, the club in the shadows of crumbling hotels and theaters in Detroit, helped cement my embryonic love of live music and the communities that flourished

within it. Before the show, I saw the band pile out of their van in front of the venue, and they asked me (ME!!!) where they could buy some wine. I pointed in the direction of a party store down the street and off they went. Later, guitarist Kid Congo Powers was writing out the set list near the same table where I'd seen Black Flag's bassist doing the same thing a few weeks before: again, a demolition of the barrier between performer and audience, a disintegration of the hierarchy.

When the rubber-limbed Lux came onstage, there was no posturing or shoe-gazing, only feral confrontation. With the conviction of a snake-handling preacher, he was going to take the audience on a sweaty ride to unknown lands whether we wanted to go or not. Ivy, in her high heels and skintight leopard print, as hot and as cool as the surface of the sun, was *the* punk rock sex goddess. She rarely moved, so even the tiniest slip of the hip, or sideways swivel, sent a jolt through this kid mystified by cookie-cutter frosted hotties named Heather or Christie. And Nick Knox, with his cadaverous stare, kept the rhythm of the telltale heart. In a punk/hardcore scene where regionalism was celebrated and every flyer hyped bands that were "from DC" or "from LA," one flyer for a Cramps show offered, "From Outer Space." I was not then, nor am I now, inclined to disagree.

Rock and Roll, like most families, I was learning, has roots that burrow indiscriminately through the muck, members who are uncomfortable to have around, and stories it would be convenient to forget. The flashback factories and revisionist musical historians would like us to enjoy—and consume—the past as if it was nothing but Peggy Sues, sock hops, and malt shops. They want uncomplicated memories for everyone to recall while sitting on the slip-covered sofa beside your kindly aunt as she thumbed through a neatly organized photo album. The Cramps were the mysterious distant uncle I secretly wished would come to family reunions. He'd tell stories about knife fights and scoring with showgirls, hand me a shrunken head he bought at a bazaar *somewhere in the East* and then wink, give a boozy, smoky laugh, and let me take a pull off his flask if Mom wasn't looking. And while both sides of the family of rock and roll sang about the virtues of wanting to kiss your sweet lips, the Cramps aimed a little lower, and a little closer, to the truth than most spoke of in decent company.

"Human Fly" was a baptism in the murky waters that course past us unseen, but not unfelt. Thanks to that pulsing, aural equivalent of an opening rusty crypt door, I have taken the road more strange and less popular, and that has made all the difference.

* * *

By the end of high school, the bloom had, as they say, fallen off the rose of much of punk's promise. A friend of mine once remarked that hardcore had the shelf life of unpasteurized buttermilk, and many aspects of a scene that had arisen from a dissatisfaction with conformity quickly slid into the age-old traps of tribalism and self-destruction. One orthodoxy was traded for another; boots and braces became the new IZODS and boat shoes. Hair too short at school was now not short enough at shows. I'd been to this movie before, and I didn't get into punk and hardcore only to feel out of place again.

Government Issue was a band on Dischord Records with a sloppy, jagged sound and a sense of humor that distinguished them from the dour, pedantic, rapid-fire 1-2-3-4 attack of so many others. At their Freezer Theater show, some of the *in-crowd* were really laying into a guy with shaggy ginger-blond hair and a long-sleeved, wild-patterned polyester shirt—blatant violations of . . . *something*. Much to their surprise—as this was before the internet afforded instant access to every image of every musician ever—the guy hopped on stage. He was the singer.

Worse, there was an emerging absolutism regarding the music itself. It was hardcore or it wasn't. There were "right" albums to have, and "wrong" albums to have, "right" shows to go to and "wrong" shows to go to. Wearisome *What is* versus *What is not* arguments of authenticity—which I'd encounter ad nauseum in a different context later with Bloodshot—overtook the conversation with Talmudic gravity. Were the Ramones fast enough, had the Clash sold out, was Jello Biafra too faggy, was Black Flag's hair too long now? Yes!

I mean No! Let us consult the *Book of Darby*! When the Meat Puppets and the Minutemen opened for Black Flag at Clutch Cargo's, and my friend and I had our minds blown by the funky, herky-jerky intensity of the Minutemen and the Meat Puppets' acid- and bluegrass-laced freakouts, many stood back with their arms crossed and deemed it "not hardcore."*

Claustrophobic localism—the need to prove *our* hardcore scene was purer than *your* hardcore scene—and way-to-live-up-to-the-stereotype violence, crept in. At a Minor Threat show at the Freezer Theater, a brawl broke out in the street. I was leaning against a parked car watching it unfold and it seemed to be some dumbasses from Ann Arbor or East Lansing getting into it with suburban kids over favored brands of skateboard casters or decks that quickly escalated into something stupider. A few months later at their show in a Serbian Orthodox Church in downriver Ecorse, tensions remained. What I had once seen as a largely unified band of misfits focused on something bigger was now a room of simmering factions, waiting—perhaps wanting—to set the whole room off in an internecine parody of itself. Some adopted "punk" for a few laughs, copping thrills from petty vandalism, or exalting the nodding-out incoherence of Sid Vicious in a sort of cultural rumspringa before heading off to a college. And some, with an unfocused and indiscriminate anger, wanted to tear it all down for the sake of tearing it all down.

Courtesy of Jeff Nelson and Dischord Records. Used by permission.

---

* Fanboy sidenote: During Bloodshot's twentieth anniversary year, the Minutemen's Mike Watt had me on his podcast "Watt From Pedro." It was one of the singular thrills of my label weasel career. When I brought up that show he said he remembered it and that "yeah, Detroit didn't like us too much."

And then there was the overt racism. Some latched onto a noxious affinity for the far right-wing National Front and the thuggish haikus and distilled nuggets of hatred from *Oi* bands coming out of England. I even heard some affected Cockney accents, as if an East End section of suburban Southfield magically appeared. Skinheads goosestepped across the stage and *Sieg-Heiled* at shows, and colorful terms for African and Arab-Americans—the same terms used by the sclerotic assholes people were purportedly rebelling against—were tossed around freely.

On June 23, 1982, Chinese-American engineer Vincent Chin was beaten to death outside a Detroit bar by a couple of white, laid-off auto workers. They were given probation. It was the culmination of years of smoldering anti-Asian sentiment brought on by the growing dominance of foreign automakers on our turf and a recession decimating our mono-economy. As Japanese cars got torched in parking lots around the city, some members of "my" scene were finding common cause with Reaganite ideologues and scapegoating "foreigners." I saw Asian fans fight their way out of clubs, and "fellow travelers" called my Korean girlfriend "Yoko," asked if I was "Turning Japanese" (and not that it should matter, it was all vile, but nuances like "She's Korean, not Japanese" fell on deaf ears), if my laundry was clean, or if I minded that she was taking "our" jobs. And *then* they got offensive.

The vibe of inclusivity seemed lost. So much for personal liberty, acceptance, creativity, and shared principles. Some might have been cool with it, but it wasn't what I had signed up for. Punk was becoming a handy excuse to be an aggressive, small-minded fuck-up. Way to change the world everybody! My naiveté, in hindsight, was prodigious.

At its best, at its most useful, though, punk did provide outlets for those uncomfortable with their surroundings and what was expected of them. It demystified and decentralized the process of creativity, and chucked veneration, stylistic straitjackets, and decorum out one window and opened others that existed beyond the purview of the culture industries. There was the thrill of discovery, and the thrill of the *possibility* of discovery. Maybe punks *couldn't* play as well as beatified old farts like Clapton, but the animating passion was something new, a threat or a dare. Or both. Punk, as I chose to view it, could be found anywhere and applied to anything in everyday life. At the end of the day, I took those lessons forward and left what went sour behind.

* * *

I've had friends who are teachers tell me that the most effective way students learn is when they are unaware that they are being taught. Undoubtedly, another facet of punk and hardcore's appeal was their scorched-earth ethos. With a jaundiced view of sentimentality and history, *Yeah man, you shoulda been there back then,* was an admission of impotence and failure. *Back then,* they thought, didn't matter; *right now,* mattered. They cleared away the dead trees and junk brush of a stale and tired landscape. But what happens if the only things left are 47-second songs about punching cops and being a self-righteous "other"? There is inertia, and suffocation quickly follows. Nothing grows from nothing. The idea distorted into a dead end.

While the fratricidal inanities of certain elements of punk sucked the oxygen out of the room, I was discovering sounds and ideas percolating at the edges. After coming across the Cramps, it was a swift joyride to the Blasters, the Meat Puppets, the Beat Farmers, Barrence Whitfield & the Savages, Tex & the Horseheads, Jason & the Scorchers, Beasts of Bourbon, Jon Wayne, Michelle Shocked, Camper Van Beethoven, Go To Blazes, Fetchin' Bones, Tav Falco's Panther Burns, Mojo Nixon, the Pontiac Brothers, Nine Pound Hammer, and a host of others who had an excitement and curiosity for what had come before.

Through the tenets of punk rock and its inherent disinterest in restrictions and protocols, these bands were resurrecting our collective, though often shunned, past. They were, perhaps, ahead of their time, out of their time, out of their minds, and providing lessons in a school I was unaware I was attending.

When X played "Johnny Hit and Run Paulene" in *The Decline of Western Civilization,* I was clueless that guitarist Billy Zoom was cribbing riffs from Chuck Berry. When I listened to the Cramps' teetering-on-the-edge-of-an-event-horizon version of "Surfin' Bird," I never would have fathomed it was a cover of the Trashmen, a demented Minneapolis band from decades before. There were hints of what would later be dubbed "Americana" in the Clash's "Brand New Cadillac," and in the Violent Femmes' "Country Death Song," from their *Hallowed Ground* album, which I found hilarious at the time—*hahaha, throwing a little girl down a well, hahaha*—that tapped into the unknown-to-me, centuries-old traditions of the murder ballad. I heard it in the *Cowboy Junkie Au Go Go* EP by Florida's Charlie Pickett & the Eggs, who rode a squall of throat-grabbing feedback, chilling despair, and Stonesy musical middle fingers. "Overtown," their snarling tale of scoring heroin in the Miami projects, was as much Johnny Thunders and Lou Reed as it was people I hadn't yet heard like Son House and David Allan Coe, and "Liked It a Lot" was a love gone really, *really* wrong song that scared the shit out of me. Still does. Hell, you can even hear a pharmaceutical-speed precursor of the Old 97's train drumbeat in the Dead Kennedys' cover of "Rawhide."

And the Gun Club's 1981 album *Fire of Love* hit me like a goddamned thunderbolt. Ward Dotson's guitar and Terry Graham's drumming set benchmarks by which I still measure most others in terms of efficiency and intensity. Covering Delta blues immortal Robert Johnson, Jeffrey Lee Pierce's howling melted time and space into a sinuous continuum from the sweat and dirt of the

Mississippi Delta to the scuzz and dirty needles on the streets of Los Angeles. Lyrics I took as pure punk braggadocio, threats as fresh as the letterman's spit landing on my textbook after a teacher's back was turned, "Gonna buy me a graveyard of my own / And kill everyone who done me wrong," were imagery tangled in the trees of the oldest and remotest forests. Darkness and terror that I was hearing through my prism of dive bars, strange indie labels, and shitty speakers were already deeply embedded in the American musical psyche. It sounds as tortured, and ecstatic, as it did when I first played it.

* * *

After high school, I briefly bolted from Michigan and, in the summer of 1985, was living with a snotty punk rock girlfriend in righteous squalor in Oakland, California. By night, we went to flyblown clubs, semi-abandoned industrial buildings, and house parties to see Fang, Flipper, Fishbone, and Tales of Terror. By day, I had a warehouse gig unloading semitrucks full of small appliances and housewares and bought lunch from a vendor cart selling gingery, toothsome delights I'd never heard of called "pot stickers." The old hands regaled me with bullshit tall tales of late-night drives to Reno to gamble and whore—*Hey man, you gotta come with us, the girls will get a kick out of you*—and hipped me to the best rack spots to steal a couple hours of sleep out of view of our supervisor.

(During my time in the Bay Area, my girlfriend's super-hippie weed connection mentioned friends were looking for a drummer. Good news: $25 every Sunday night plus all the beer I wanted. Bad news: it was a Grateful Dead cover band that played at a seedy bar in the Lower Haight. My only vivid memory of the place was the chalkboard of import beer selections. Two columns: name and country of origin. Grölsch/Holland. Guinness/Ireland, Sapporo/Japan, etc. The last one on the list was Stroh's/DETROIT, as if it wasn't part of the United States. It filled me with a perverse sense of civic pride. The acid-casualty band members twenty years older than me took great pleasure introducing me as their "punk rock drummer." Bottles and feathered roach clips were raised in mock toasts. That I didn't—or care to—know any Dead songs was not an impediment to the gig. They'd start and I'd join in, some basic, loping 4/4 shuffle, and four, ten, or seventy minutes later of drivin' that train, the guitarist would nod my way and . . . *ba da dum ba dump bump* . . . the song ended.)

Listening to the University of California, Berkeley, college radio station KALX one day on my Walkman during my break, I heard a song from a side project of the Blasters and X—the Knitters—that fully upended the *all history is bunk* outlook of punk and made a connection to music with a discernable past. I was smitten.

At the end of my shift, I walked to Rasputin Music on Telegraph Ave., my local Sam's Jams surrogate, and bought their *Poor Little Critter on the Road* LP on Slash Records. There were the faces and names I knew from punk bands: Exene, John Doe, Dave Alvin, drummer DJ Bonebrake. But what was this music? They played mostly acoustic instruments, their touchstones were the Brothers Delmore, not the Brothers Ramone, they sang about broken hearts and getting drunk, not smashing the state and nuclear annihilation. The songs smoldered rather than raged. Much to the dismay of the girlfriend—who quickly derided the record as "that hick shit"—I started seeking out the names in the songwriting credits—the Carters, the Ledbetters, the Haggards—as well as noting curious designations like "public domain" and "traditional," and I have never really stopped. The harbingers of roots had been there in other bands, albeit lurking in the shadows, but I had been too dim to perceive them. The Knitters flipped a switch.

Without knowing it, I had already been hearing echoes of the music that came before punk; they only *seemed* fresh and daring because we had turned our collective back on them.

Roots music ran deep, and it stubbornly survived. To unearth it, to reimagine and repurpose it, took archeologically curious musicians working without a net or a blueprint. They respected their forbearers but didn't revere them; reverence was its own form of murder and monuments were meant to be torn down. As Mark Twain said, "Sacred cows make the best hamburger."

For me, it was a part of a new, far-reaching, inventive fire. I didn't hear these bands and think—pushing up my eyeglasses—*these are compelling and energetic postmodern manifestations of preexisting musical idioms.* I was wholly ignorant of what it was or where it came from. Would that have made a difference? Should it have? All I knew was that I hadn't heard anything like it in the malls, during the Saturday night syndicated hit parade *Solid Gold*, or at the increasingly monochromatic hardcore shows. Since indie record stores simply filed roots-tangent music under "Punk/New Wave," I could be innocently snared by albums from Tav Falco's Panther Burns and Rank & File while searching out records by the Stranglers or the Avengers. Without labels or a critical language to "explain" it, "this music" hadn't been detached from "that music" yet. It was a time when the possibilities seemed as rich and diverse as the traditions and history the artists pilfered. Their underappreciated and under-known works resonated in strange ways, including in what would one day become Bloodshot.

* * *

Being a bone-deep Midwesterner, I drifted back to Michigan for college in Ann Arbor. Every Friday, I'd leave my after-classes job at the Mathematics Library (don't be impressed, I was shelving books and journals and was in no way involved in any brainiac work) and walk to the Beer Depot, an anachronistic and dangerously convenient drive-thru liquor store. They'd cash my paycheck, deduct what I owed for the week, and often comp me a 40-ounce of Goebel's beer: as the ads said, with something of a *whattyagonnadoaboutit* resignation—*Goebel's, You'll Enjoy it!* Then I'd head to the Blind Pig, an off-campus club known for booking blues and "college radio" bands, for happy hour where there was no cover and 2-for-1 pitchers.

And from five to eight, Drivin' Sideways played. A band of thirty- and forty-somethings, featuring a couple line workers from an Ypsilanti auto plant, a hot shot young guitarist, a wicked good pedal steel player with all the stage flair of a pharmacist filling a contact dermatitis prescription, the former drummer of southern rock band Blackfoot (!!!), and Pistol Pete on vocals, Drivin' Sideways were COUNTRY. Unapologetically so.

Until then, I didn't have any conscious connection to country music. To me, it was a bygone and irrelevant combo platter of the lacquered-up and lip-synched Mandrell Sisters TV variety show, cornball yucks like Ray Stevens' "The Streak," and easy listening—with a wan fiddle in the background—like Kenny Rogers or the Oak Ridge Boys. I had as much reason to pay attention to country as I did Foreigner or Air Supply.

I'd heard the distant derivations that filtered through some punk bands. There were country leanings in some of the oldies 45s I was snapping up, like Sun Sessions Elvis and Bobbie Gentry. I swiped a record from a friend's mom's

record collection, *The Golden Hits of Flatt & Scruggs,* with a cover photo of cowboy hats and white suits, hayseed grins and red string ties. Who hadn't done their best *yee-haw* overbite and sung along to the *Beverly Hillbillies* theme? Then I heard "The Randy Lyn Rag" from that album, and, shit, these dudes were *punk*: the dexterity, the musicianship, the *speed*. They played at a level I couldn't comprehend. But I wouldn't have thought to ever acknowledge that I was a *country* fan. When I first heard Jason & the Scorchers' reckless country metal cover of the Hank Williams totemic "Lost Highway," I didn't even know it was a cover.

The crowd, and it was consistently packed, was a mixed bag of other line workers, slow-dancing older couples, ornately coiffed and costumed rockabilly throwbacks, bikers, townies, and the random biz admin grad student. In other words, a gathering of music fans out on a Friday night.*

It was here that I got a crash course in what *country music* was, and how and *why* it needed to be played and heard. And always will. With complete sincerity, Drivin' Sideways played dancing country songs, sad country songs, funny country songs, and fast country songs, set after set. They worked the

---

* Working for the promoter at the Blind Pig a couple of years later, I had to delay opening the doors for the evening show because the happy hour crowd would *not* let Drivin' Sideways stop playing. Nirvana and their fans would just have to wait.

room, got people thirsty, and often coaxed the waitress to the stage to sing Patsy Cline. One regular announced that he was quitting drinking the next day, so the band played Jim Ed Brown's "Pop a Top" while the guy stood on stage and downed a beer at every "*pop a top again . . .*" They tore through Buck Owens, Conway Twitty, Tammy Wynette, and Commander Cody truck-driving, pill-popping music. I laughed at George Jones's "White Lightning," and I was knocked off my stool by the existential bite of his "He Stopped Loving Her Today"—and Pistol Pete had the range to pull them both off. I had heard of Johnny Paycheck thanks to the ubiquity of "Take this Job and Shove it," but his "Barstool Mountain" and "Apartment #9"—during the latter Pete would remove his gimme cap and proclaim it the Country Music National Anthem—gave me the same jolt, the same immediacy as when I first heard punk. I didn't have to listen long before the pathos and truth, the very things that had drawn me to the underground, took hold of me in a whole new way.

Once more, I had stumbled into a place far more alluring and relevant than it appeared when viewed through culture's accepted playlists. The day after Drivin' Sideways shows, I was often rummaging around Wazoo or PJ's, the shabby, disorganized used record stores of choice, for 45s of songs I heard the night before. Sure, there was an ironic component to some of them; alcoholism, hangovers, heartaches, cheating, car wrecks, and tragic death still seemed like faraway problems in college. It was hard *not* to find Ernest Tubb's "Drivin' Nails in My Coffin," Jimmy Dean's "I Won't Go Huntin' with You Jake (But I'll Go Chasin' Women"), or Loretta Lynn's "Fist City" hilarious. But, for every goof like George Jones's "Who Shot Sam?" there was a song bursting with fierce, emotional detail like "She Thinks I Still Care." Paycheck's "Pardon Me, I've Got Someone to Kill" could be taken as a laugher or a literal threat. It carried "Anarchy in the U.K."-level annihilation with sharp pedal steel licks in place of Rotten's raspy howl, with enough switchblade menace to make Bauhaus's "Bela Lugosi's Dead" sound as frightening as an episode of *Scooby-Doo*.

I found there was more to Hank Williams than his song "Hey Good Lookin'," which had recently been blasphemed by the National Dairy Board's commercial: *How's about cooking something up with cheese*. In a body so young came a voice coughing on the cinders of the centuries, singing of timeless torments with an archetypal gravitas that provided the building blocks for an entire genre. If the songs weren't on vinyl, they may as well have been chiseled into stone tablets. When I heard *Hear that lonesome whippoorwill / He sounds too blue to fly* in "I'm So Lonesome I Could Cry," I immediately realized that the *40 Greatest Hits* double LP I picked up one Saturday morning would be one of the five most consequential albums I'd ever own. *Too blue to fly!* I've read many a book about depression, and none have come closer to describing that indescribable pain than those four words. Heartache? "I Can't Help It (If I'm Still in Love with You)" hit with a heaviness that "I Want to Know

What Love Is" couldn't in a thousand years or a thousand laps around the roller rink. And here was the original "Lost Highway." There is an elemental depth to this song. It's in the soil, it's in our bones, it's in the isolated hollows and at the side of every roadway ever walked. It's a song that could be ten thousand years old, but its longing and deep sadness was relatable to each of us at some time or another, maybe even tomorrow.

I remember where I was when I was poleaxed by Johnny Cash's recording of Kris Kristofferson's "Sunday Morning Coming Down" as clearly as I remember my first baseball glove (Detroit Tigers' centerfielder Mickey Stanley model) and my first taste of Thai food. My Wood Butcher buddy Phil—a fellow Drivin' Sideways fan and country music newbie—and I were spending a summer afternoon playing our latest LP hauls, a "Best of Johnny Cash" collection among them. It was impossible not to be attracted to Cash's innate bravado: he had the black attire, drunken, speed-freak bona fides, made live records from prison, flipped off photographers, and had all the cool lines about shooting cocaine and a man in Reno, and being the boy named Sue. The social justice underpinnings of "Wanted Man" fell right into my political/music sweet spot, a natural extension (or, more properly, a precursor) to so much of what I was hearing in punk. He was an emissary for country's long history steeped in populism, from Bob Wills to Loretta Lynn to Merle Haggard, a revelation for someone who still thought country music was largely jingoistic paeans to America's greatness and *Urban Cowboy*. He was The Man in Black.

Phil and I were nursing recent breakups and a bottle of Cuervo—no salt, no limes—passed between us with nonchalant frequency. I had just been dumped for a *bass* player. In a *cover* band. A *Grateful Dead* cover band. There were so many layers to that onion of humiliation, it had hung a real stink on me. I felt like a stone sinking in the deepest, muddiest goddamn lake in a state with over 11,000 goddamn lakes.

From the opening line, "*Well, I woke up Sunday morning with no way to hold my head that didn't hurt*," I was in. After the second, "*And the beer I had for breakfast wasn't bad / So I had one more for dessert*," my cosmic dislocation had been wrapped in a fluffy coat of the blackest humor. Not even the cheesy dubbed-in strings and horns or phony audience applause at the end could dull the impact of that three-minute-and-fifty-something-seconds homily. When the song ended, Phil put the needle back to the beginning. We listened to "Sunday Morning Coming Down" maybe a dozen times in a row. Hearing that yawning lonesomeness so precisely conveyed weirdly unburdened me: I wouldn't be alone on this trip; misery loved company. The song kept the indifference of the cosmos at bay.

As I poked around used country LP bins of my go-to record haunts, I stumbled onto more contemporary artists who hadn't forsaken the classic forms in favor of popular schmaltz. John Hiatt, the Flatlanders, k.d. lang,

Kinky Friedman, and Gram Parsons, among others, were more country than "country" and opened my mind to something of a punk attitude coming from the *country* side of music, as opposed to a country attitude coming from the punk side. I watched Dwight Yoakam on the David Letterman show and quickly snapped up his *Guitars, Cadillacs, Etc., Etc.* LP. In a metal club on the east side of Detroit, I saw Steve Earle with about twenty other people in 1988 on the *Exit 0* album tour. He played *a new song I'm working on* called "Copperhead Road" solo on mandolin and told stories about taking acid and getting beaten up by cowboys. *Hmmm,* as with accepted narratives surrounding oldies and rock and roll, country music's wasn't so simple, either, and those who promoted a company line that *This is Country Music* were curiously avoiding entire chapters of its story. And anybody saying it wholly sucked wasn't looking very hard.

Courtesy of Lisa Fancher and Frontier Records, used with permission.

The more I listened, the more connective tissue I found between country and punk. I felt parallels in the way the two genres confronted the hardships, horrors, and joys of the human condition through stories told from the perspective of those looking up, not punching down. Legendary Nashville songwriter Harlan Howard once summed up country music as "three chords and the truth." Country at its best was as honest and direct as anything the Clash ever did, and vice versa, Acuff/Rose and Strummer/Jones two sides of the same album. This music, full of sadness and hope, muscle and humor, fatalism and idealism, and deeply rooted in a rich history, evoked the punk rock I had connected to earlier. It was like a Magic Eye popping into focus, over and over. I felt the reverberations of George Jones's lament "The Grand Tour" in the baked-in-the-desert psilocybin country of Thin White Rope's "The Ghost" from their *Sack Full of Silver* album. Both are requiems of loss told through common objects, evincing longings for better times lost forever. One was from a giant figure of Nashville royalty and went to number one, a song that casually invites the listener into his home, *"Step right up, come on in, if you'd like to take the grand tour."* Then we are blindsided by a crushing emptiness, *"Of the lonely house that once was home sweet home."*

The other was from Frontier Records, a punk label known mainly for releases by the Circle Jerks, and the Adolescents. Through a feedback tempest that recalled what I had heard in Television and, later, in the Haldol-hazed disquiet of the Handsome Family, the narrator mourns a thrown-away youth: *"I felt like a widower stoned and watching a film of his wedding day."*

When he reckons with his future, *"Well, I was lost, and I was bummed, by the ghost of yet to come,"* it is hard not to feel the descent into similar icy chasms of grief.

In high school, as the cramped world I thought awaited me closed tighter around me, trapped by forces I couldn't control, I found a loud and fast remedy in Black Flag's SST single "American Waste":

> *I see my place in American waste*
> *Faced with choices I can't take*

It was a howl of frustration I was surprised to also find in Hank Williams's "Lost Highway." *"I'm a rollin' stone, all alone and lost"* pulses with enough existential exhaustion to dim the lights at an Edvard Munch exhibit, and the following *"For a life of sin, I have paid the cost"* makes Richard Hell & the Voidoids' nihilistic anthem, "Blank Generation," play like the Go-Go's "We Got the Beat."

Maybe I was alone in drawing lines from Black Flag to Hank Williams, and maybe that was a line best drawn with a crayon in a nice, soft room, but the intensity tugging deep in both was unmistakable to me. Why did people respond to punk? Its immediacy, its simplicity. Why did people respond to country? Its immediacy, its simplicity.

As many of my friends were gravitating towards Midwestern college rock like Soul Asylum and the Afghan Whigs or looking to the Pacific Northwest for what would soon be deemed grunge, I was digging full-on country songs about getting shot in bars and drinking to forget the heartbreak, and flipping through milk crates looking for Willie Nelson, Kitty Wells, and Roger Miller LPs. Peeking behind that well-ironed, immaculately hung curtain of *What This Is* had paid off again. A pattern was definitely emerging.

12

Dig!

A central lesson of punk rock is that legitimacy need not, *should not*, be conferred by existing power structures; that states of affairs were not immutable or sacrosanct; and that effecting change was not only possible by people who, like me, weren't entirely sure of what they were doing, but often necessary. I loved music, yes, but the counterpoint to that was I hated a lot of music, too. Maybe most of it. If I didn't, there wouldn't have been the impetus to start a label. If I was content with a bucket of chicken from the KFC on the corner, why would I bother standing in line at Harold's Chicken #88 all the way in Bronzeville? Punk taught me that I didn't have to wait for someone to "let" me do it.

In a very real way, every indie label owner stood on shoulders they couldn't see, and on wreckage they might not even be aware was there. When asked about my label role models, I pointed to those that had gone before and whose aesthetics, personalities, evangelical fervor, illusions—and delusions—I had soaked up while crate-diving at independent record stores, and which pointed to a better, weirder way.

For most casual music consumers, the very notion of "label identity" sounds strange. How could a brand name mean anything in relation to an artist one heard and liked? When discussing movies with a friend, has anyone said, "It's MGM films or nothing for me"? Has a book club participant bailed because they weren't reading enough Simon & Schuster titles? Nobody identified as a fan of Warner Brothers or had a Sony Music T-shirt, tattoo, or bumper sticker. Exactly no one has drunkenly hit on a woman at a bar with the line "You're into Universal Music Group? Me too!" It'd be like saying "Yeah, man, I'm a *huge* fan of Dow and Monsanto, especially their *early* weedkillers and napalm." When somebody wants a song, they don't consider the history or context of the company that released it. If David Bowie had put out an album on *Halibur-Tone Records*, it would have still sold millions. If people liked the song, the transaction was that straightforward. Labels are a hidden part of the process, and one looks like any other. Who cared about that humdrum corporate info on the back of the packaging?

Well, I did. From the early days of cranks building recording studios in their garages out of purloined gear to the emergence of punk labels' *who says I can't?* mentality, something about "label identity" registered with me as something bigger than "making hits." Finding actual *companies* with strong identities that released out-of-the-ordinary and often impolite music that I loved bolstered my feelings of shared purpose. Legitimate business enterprises were advocating for *us*, for *our* interests! How was I to know that many of them were nothing more than a nerd at a kitchen table with a stack of envelopes, a roll of stamps, and persistent insomnia? It was a *record label*!

Punk and hardcore thrived on this strong bond between bands, fans, and labels. And artists who are viewed today as essential in the history of music—not just underground music but *all* music—circumvented the impenetrable jungles of indifference, or even outright hostility, to release their music using the sole viable path available to them: the independent label. Instead of sitting tight while the hierarchy decided their fates, bands stage-dove right in. Scores of '80s and '90s labels released seminal albums with little expectation of mainstream critical acceptance or success. Dischord, Slash/Ruby, SST, Twin/Tone, Crypt, Stiff, Subterranean, ROIR, Alternative Tentacles, Estrus, Frontier, Sub Pop, K, Matador, Sympathy for the Record Industry, In the Red, Rounder, Merge, Righteous Babe, Homestead, Kill Rock Stars, and Cargo taught me, unwittingly perhaps, that if you wanted to do something, summon the pigheadedness and go for it. There was no reason *not* to, other than that it was crazy. But why let that get in the way?

One label that had an outsized impact on me and, by extension, the way Bloodshot operated, was Brooklyn's Norton Records. Norton reveled in the wild side of rock and roll, past and present, made by kooks who wandered the unlit back streets of the American dream. If you liked your music crisp, expertly played, and immaculately produced, move along, they wouldn't interest you. Billy Miller—no relation, alas, what a gnarly older brother to have—owned the label with his wife Miriam Linna and played together in the killer kool garage band the A-Bones. One could not discern where they began and the label ended, testifying to the amount of *themselves* they put into the label. *And* Miriam was an early member of the Cramps—the circle will be unbroken!

The albums they released (or disentombed and reissued) by Hasil "The Haze" Adkins, Andre Williams and . . . wait for it . . . King Uszniewicz and the Uszniewicztones—the preeminent purveyors of 1970s Detroit bowling-alley surf rock—dazzled me. When I was doing college radio, I got up the gumption to mail them a letter telling them about my show and developing predilection for the strange underbelly of American music. And they sent me a package of records!!! Me! A dumb, nobody DJ in the middle of Michigan! Hot damn, did I feel like a BMOC with that stack of Link Wray, Phantom Surfers, and Esquerita LPs. Sure, none of the popular kids or pretty girls cared, but I felt like I was onto something. Or something was onto me. After that, anything with the Norton name on it meant "I'm buying it!"*

Norton taught me about vision and not being afraid to take chances—to, in a way, not even *think* of them as chances—and to *proudly* embrace music most others would run screaming from. Grab people, let them know they are part of the cause; trust them and they will trust you. Of course, I didn't *know* I was attaining this enlightenment, but having my head pried open and filled with the *Where the Loud Sound that Abounds* Norton vibe took hold like an armlock camel clutch. I submitted. Fully and freely.

While major labels carried themselves like inscrutable entertainment juntas, indies debunked the very *idea* of The Label. As active and approachable participants in their local subcultures, and with a low bar for entry, they were advocates first, businesspeople second (or third, or fourth). And if they liked the music, and *you* liked the music, you shared a connection with that label as well as the artists. Being a fan conferred a measure of outlaw legitimacy.

As the songs I heard on Honey Radio and the names I saw in the songwriting credits of punk albums sucked me deeper into rock and roll's past, used 45 rpm bins revealed labels, dozens of them, that offered three-minute rides to wild, unfamiliar places. They had cool, to-the-point names: Minit, Motown, Aladdin, Dot, Dial, Gusto, Vee-Jay, Bullet, Excello, Ace. The designs were simple, bold, and immediately recognizable: the yellow Stax, red Volt, dark blue and silver Chess, and black and yellow Specialty. There was the Sun rooster, Fortune harp, King crown, and the friendly red "HI" hugged on either side by blue sixteenth notes. Record-buying jags were like hog-wild rushes down supermarket aisles stocked with free beer and Cocoa Puffs. Black Flag singles on SST were in my bag with an Otis Clay 45 on Hi-Records; an Agent Orange album on Posh Boy with a Parliaments single on Revilot, and an LP on Homestead by the most obnoxiously wonderful noise band ever, the Happy Flowers, was bought at the same time as a George Jones Starday single. So much music, so many labels.

---

* Years later, I sheepishly introduced myself to Billy at a South by Southwest showcase, and with the vivacity of a game show host welcoming me to the stage, he pumped my hand and said/spat "Bloodshot! You got a cool label happenin'!" I was euphoric he had even heard of us, and I have never been more deeply satisfied by another label owner's praise.

Like indie punk labels, these older labels were the outgrowths of entrepreneurs and dreamers who were open to new ideas and believed passionately in often unpopular music. Since punk labels also operated outside the conventional marketplace, run by music geeks with a vision frequently incompatible with the norm, it appeared that they—a generation or two apart—had been cut from the same . . . *um* . . . vinyl. Outsiders hadn't begun to appear in my time, they'd always been here, hustling to achieve acclaim—no matter how meager and fleeting—on their own terms and in the face of an inattentive or fainthearted public. Some of their artists went on to fame, fortune, and household-name status. Some became cult heroes. Some vanished. Some labels blew up with unexpected hits, some settled into a groove or a niche, most tumbled into obscurity. And some became the shorthand for greatness: *Chess, Stax, Sun, Dischord.* The *real* history of American music was found in *their* grooves, not in boardrooms or Simon Cowell's circus rings.

These labels, these artists, comprised a web of sounds and styles and neurons and ambitions and hallucinations happening right beneath our noses. If you tugged one, you never knew how, when, or by whom it would be felt: string theory realized through music. It is a shared, if often unspoken, language that remains relevant only if we scrub the mushiness of sentimentality off it. Grab the Trashmen's "Surfin' Bird" out of the novelty section. You *think* you know it, you *think* you remember the aggression, the wildness, the *weird*ness, but listen to it with a fresh perspective. Do it now. Go ahead, I'll wait . . .*

Wow, right? What a mind-blower!

Dust off that Motown *Best of* collection you've forgotten about and cue up the Temptations' "The Way You Do the Things You Do." This isn't a stale hard candy in grandma's chicken-shaped glass bowl. Man, the harmonies, the production, the swing, the style, the *snap* still sound daring. Or "Rumble" b/w "The Swag," Link Wray's 1958 two-sided treatise on distortion and cool. How many days did I sit and listen to that on my headphones? That was the dark side of *my* moon, every strum of his guitar tickling a graviton three galaxies over, then, now, and forever. Forget the ten thousand times you've heard Booker T. & the MG's "Green Onions" as wallpaper. Put new ears on it, listen loud. Dig the chill of the cubes in the Naugahyde and faux chrome ice bucket. No matter how many times you think you've heard the song, you can't tell me with a straight face that it doesn't still simmer with an undeniable *coolness* that makes your day, *that* day, just a little bit better. This isn't nostalgia, this is alive. Don't remember these songs, listen to them. They shouldn't take us back; they should be with us now. It would be an unimaginable waste for songs and artists like these to be treated as sanctified relics or, worse, erased from

* If this book has interested you at all, the chances are reasonable you own a copy of this song.

our collective narrative altogether. These records meant something, even if they were, much of the time, unnoticed. They still mean something. When artists and fans (and fresh-faced label owners) come across these artifacts for the first time, they respond to them in their own ways, and then the songs take on another life. That restorative strength is indispensable; it is the fungal network beneath the soil keeping the forest healthy.

Did I seek such labels' advice or model ourselves specifically after any of them? No, but Bloodshot was an unconscious extension of what was already staring out at me from my record collection. So, when people told me in emails, letters, tweets, or gentle nudges of appreciation at a bar rail, "If I see the Bloodshot name on an album, I'm going to pick it up," it was a tip of the hat to the unacknowledged work and quirks and dedication of those who walked the path before us. Fans who were digging our artists likely didn't realize it, but they were also indirectly giving props to Jim Stewart and Estelle Axton at Stax, Ian MacKaye and Jeff Nelson at Dischord, Bob Koester at Delmark, Billy and Miriam at Norton, and so many others whose names I did know, and many more whose names I did not.

13

Riotous Overdrive

As the label was sputtering to life in the fall of 1994, another dry spell at R&B Painting and Carpentry drove my painting partners and me back to Mike's Old Town compound, this time for caulking and repainting the windows of a basement unit. Mike came downstairs ostensibly to check on our progress. He inquired as to what handsome working boys such as us were up to the coming weekend. We offered up nothing. We had learned. Undeterred, he showed us some washed-out Polaroids of a naked woman midair over a trampoline.

"She's a stewardess in town for the weekend. If you want, you can all sleep with her, but I get to watch."

Check, please!

Was Bloodshot anything other than a fool's errand at this point? Whatever it was, it had to be better than standing in a basement with a wearisome old man spinning wannabe *Penthouse Forum* vignettes. Music had gotten me out of darker rooms than this before. I had to trust that it would again.

Rather than quickly shuffle off to oblivion, another indie compilation on another indie label in another indie store cut-out bin, *For a Life of Sin* surprised us by finding an audience beyond Cook County. Chicago, apparently, didn't have a monopoly on people looking to classic country for the substance and excitement they used to find in punk. The promos we sent out or that I had dropped off while on tour had made their way into a growing national web of good-hearted loonies and subversives—writers, DJs, promoters, distributors, and store and club owners—willing to order a few copies or book the bands. Editors sent us *For a Life of Sin* reviews clipped from their weeklies ("Guaranteed to put your party into riotous overdrive"—*Detroit Metro Times*; "A raw and vital collection that will shake up any rocker's idea of what country is, and what it might become"—*St. Louis Riverfront Times*), asked for interviews, and made sure they were on the mailing list for future releases. (Future releases? What? *Yikes!*)

Locally, we worked for attention however we could. There was a local newspaper writer, a de facto historian of country music in Chicago, who we thought might appreciate the spirit, if not the form, of Bloodshot. So far, he'd been silent. Maybe he was simply dismissing us and the label as unwanted meddlers and treating the album as a lark. Legit responses. Maybe we were, maybe it was.

We knew he had a *cut him will he not bleed ink* old-school journalism romantic streak, full of nights late and bourbons neat. Eric and I got wind that he was to attend taverns on a particular route on a particular night. Our plan, in retrospect a bizarre and stalkery one, was to arrive *juuust* after him at each of his spots. At the first one, we sat on the other side of the bar, matched him drink for drink and didn't pay him any mind. On the second, we acknowledged him when we came in, a simple nod, and carried on to the corner of the room. By the stops at Weeds and Old Town Ale House, we had the bartender send a drink his way. He nodded, we nodded back. The night ended at the mother of journalists' watering holes: O'Rourke's on Halsted Street. Here, my notes got blurry. As he wrapped up his night, the writer walked past us and said, almost as an afterthought, "I like what you're doing. I'll write about it soon." While the next day felt like someone had been hitting my liver with a tube sock full of underripe oranges, one of the people we wanted to *get it* was *getting it* and might be willing to spread the word of this embryonic undertaking.

Two unexpected local media fans were Tom Thayer (#57) and Keith Van Horne (#78) from the 1985 Super Bowl–winning Bears.* They had a late-night radio show on AM powerhouse WGN and loved the hell out of what we were doing so they had us and the bands on their program several times for interviews and in-studio performances. Go figure. Tom and Keith would stride into shows at the Empty Bottle, man mountains amongst the reedy hipsters, and back-slap and drink-buy. Keith, with his unapologetic mullet, loud cowboy boots, and louder *I LOVE this stuff* made me feel like Chris Makepeace in *My Bodyguard*—I feared no man nor beast upon this earth with him near my side.

With a tentative confidence kindled by not immediately flopping, we quickly released seven-inch singles by two bands on the *For a Life of Sin* compilation: Moonshine Willy and Jon Langford's new *let's play for beer money* "hard country" band, the Waco Brothers. Their single's B-side was a double-time cover of reggae pioneer Jimmy Cliff's "The Harder They Come"—proving you could find the renegade spirit of country anywhere if you looked.

---

* A note for non-Chicagoans: the 1985 Bears cast an outsized shadow over the city's sport history, nay, the city's *any* history. Florence has DaVinci, and Ottumwa, Iowa, has Radar O'Reilly; Chicago has Payton, Perry, and McMahon.

We began getting letters at the "office" from fans around the country saying, *hey, we have a little scene going on here too and no one is paying any attention to it*. As these confederates pointed to *this* band from *their* town, we learned of unexpected underground country music hubs such as Phoenix, Kansas City, Detroit, San Francisco, and New York City. We were even pitched on bands from places that ostensibly *were* country music strongholds—Nashville, Austin, Dallas—but were being ignored for not being *proper* country bands. Since no one was yet clamoring to release this unmarketable music in these other towns, our next compilation emerged startlingly fast. While *For a Life of Sin* had taken months of planning and compiling, we didn't bring *Hell-Bent: Insurgent Country Volume 2* together so much as stay out of its way. Released in early 1995, the album jumbled rock, punk, bluegrass, stone-cold honky-tonk, dark folk, rockabilly, and woozy psychedelia into songs about bathtub suicides, snake oil salesmen, faded movie star suicides, climbing tools used by Lewis and Clark, small-town apprehension of floods, generational poverty, lying to God, and flawed love. You know, life.

And we kept working, figuring out what to do next, step by step. Starting as a hobby, as opposed to a business, accorded us the time to feel our way around in the dark. Rather than bend the world to us, we followed norms we liked and moved around or under ones we didn't. The mistakes were many, but the stakes weren't high. How best to build something around that, rather than bend the world to us, was the challenge.

With on-the-sly help from a friend at a major label promotions office in the Chicago suburbs, I carted off boxes of their promo cassettes and CDs. The cassettes, in time-honored DIY fashion, had their tab openings taped over and we dubbed *Hell-Bent* onto them (in real time, one at a time, like cavemen must have done). Everclear, Blind Melon, and Less Than Jake CDs and artwork were tossed and the cases repurposed as promos with our handwritten stickers. In the spring of 1995, the Gavin Radio report—"the most trusted name in radio"—conferred upon us a gratis registration for their annual convention in New Orleans.

Different kinds of country music were gaining traction around the country, and they were intrigued by this "insurgent" thing. Early discussions in chat rooms and on industry conference panels were thick with potential genre names vying to be "the one," to put the pin in the thorax of this unusual musical cricket so it could be displayed on a labeled square of mounting foam. New Country, Neo-Country, and the ungainly neologism Alterna-Country were given tryouts. Progressive Country sounded like a pithy description of Denmark. Twangcore, y'alternative, and other neo-bumpkin offerings were trotted out. Thrashabilly, punkabilly, garagabilly, grungabilly, and emo-billy all made regrettable appearances as people added "-billy" to everything, much as we plunk "-gate" at the end of any scandal. Consensus often settled around "Americana." In many ways, that was the least distressing, though it did put me in the mind of Lincoln's stovepipe hat and Fonzie's leather jacket.

With Mother's jambalaya stains from lunch on my shirt, I passed out *Hell-Bent* cassettes to any programmer I came across during a conference event at Tipitina's. I didn't think that "real" industry people might look at these ersatz packages and think us buffoons and trespassers. Some laughed in my face at the amateurishness of it. But I was armed with the earnest belief that this music would carry the day. Sure enough, Gavin's new "Americana" chart editor picked up *something* from us, and *Hell-Bent* got some solid play that spring on this yet-to-be-defined-to-death radio format. We were creeping in. Mission accomplished.

In June of 1995, after releasing Moonshine Willy's *Pecadores*—our first album by a single artist—and *Angels and Inbreds*, an EP by Phoenix's Grievous Angels, another *Hell-Bent* contributor, and a band whose solid country/rock alchemy was a couple years ahead of the times, we replicated the multi-band showcase model for the release shows. The cheekily named *Honky Skronk Weekend* at the Empty Bottle was an underground country murderer's row of talent. Ten bucks got you into both shows to hear compilation participants from around the country: the Grievous Angels, Moonshine Willy, Robbie Fulks, Kansas City's Starkweathers, New York's World Famous Blue Jays, and Detroit's Volebeats.

Headlining one of the nights was a four-piece outfit from Dallas, TX that had captured everybody's attention with their track "Por Favor:" the Old 97's. We'd first met singer/guitarist Rhett Miller and bassist Murray Hammond

Artwork by Mike Werner.

during their stint in Killbilly, and, at the second-ever Bloodshot showcase at the Double Door, asked their "real" band to open for Freakwater and Moonshine Willy. Seeing that first show of theirs was like watching a band arrive from the moon. A big, loud Texas moon. They were a fully formed gang: Ken Bethea's guitar a short-circuiting, post-punk Luther Perkins, Philip Peeples, the Ringo Starr of the train beat, Murray on bass and West Texas via Liverpool harmonies, and Rhett's manic energy, super-literate songwriting, and swoony charisma. They were *too* tight and *too* good and the songs *too* catchy, a perfect fusion of punk mettle and deep country soul.

During that summer of 1995, the Old 97's essentially moved to Chicago. They played the Beat Kitchen and Lounge Ax seemingly every other week to bigger and more enthusiastic crowds, and even did an acoustic set on a makeshift stage in the corner of Delilah's. People were singing along to *unreleased* songs. It was nuts. They recorded a single (the obsession going into ghastly overdrive "Eyes For You," b/w "W-I-F-E") and, in a callback to my DIY teenage years, I found myself stuffing them into folded sleeves in the back seat of a crappy Ford, rocketing past cheese and sausage emporia on our way to a release show in Madison, Wisconsin.

As the humidity thickened and the asphalt transformed into warm goo, the 97's set up in Attica Studios, so named because it was in an attic of a three-story frame house in Wicker Park, to record a full album. Days were spent sweating and recording in that smoky, stifling cauldron, and nights across the street rehydrating with cervezas frias or in my yard playing Jarts under R&B's painting lights.*

One afternoon Don Walser, the Pavarotti of the Plains, in town on tour, hobbled up the three narrow flights of stairs and walked around the attic whooping and clapping, looking for a spot of perfect natural reverb for his guest yodeling. The next day Jon Langford came by to yell ASSHOLE on their cover of "Over the Cliff," his song from the *For a Life of Sin* compilation. I may be remembering this wrong—but hey, never let the truth get in the way of a good story—Ken Bethea nailed his guitar solo in one take, but it took Langford three or four to get his ASSHOLE right. In and out in two weeks, Ramones-style, for $2,665. The album *Wreck Your Life* was born.

Since we had fall releases scheduled for *Wreck Your Life* and the Waco Brothers' debut, full-length album, . . . *To the Last Dead Cowboy*, we requested a showcase at the CMJ Music Marathon in New York City, then *the* industry event for indie radio, press, and distribution. They politely said no. Or maybe they just disregarded us. And why wouldn't they? Who the hell were we? No mind. *Fine*, we thought, *we'll go ahead and put on our own show*. During a well-established conference. With nothing but a handful of releases by unknown bands under our belt. In a city we'd never been to. Sounded perfectly reasonable.

Attica — OLD 97's
CD/Album
Studio
16 days @ 120.00/day 1920-
4 Reels Ampex 456 ½" 180-
5 cassettes (1.00/cs) 5-
2 60 mn. dats 20-
Studio Total 2125-
Lodging
18 days at 30.00/day -
Total - 540.00
grand Total = $2665.00
pd 7/13/95
ck #444

Old 97's "Wreck Your Life" budget.

With the help from allies at Brooklyn's Diesel Only label, we secured the stage at Brownie's, a cramped club on Avenue A between East Tenth and East Eleventh in the wilds of the Lower East Side. (At the time, the conference itself was in Midtown, and most of the venues were in the West Village and Union Square. The Lower East Side was a blank space on the map. And

* That's right—Jarts. *Real* Jarts. Pointy, steel-tipped, *When Jarts are outlawed, only outlaws have Jarts*, acquired via any garage sale, junk shop, or junk pile where we found them. No one got hurt.

Brooklyn? *Fuggetaboutit.*) And since we didn't want to compete with the "real" showcases at night, it would be a day party.

We made phone calls, sent out postcards, and slogged eight hundred miles east on I-80, not having any idea what to expect. We set up the backline, borrowed a Weber Smokey Joe to grill burgers in the prison yard–sized alley (in the time-honored assumption that if you offer free food, they will come), and opened the doors. A few people wandered in, some, probably, out of sheer habit. I went to the alley to char the *hackfleisch*, have a tall glass of drink, and pretend I was anywhere else as waves of anxiety crashed o'er me. I fumbled around my mental toolbox to recall the skills of achieving high school hallway invisibility. What *was* I doing here? I didn't belong here; I should be painting a closet somewhere.

After a while, somebody from the club told me I should come out front, that someone needed "help getting in." Help getting in? *Why . . . ?* I walked into the formerly empty room, now jammed solid, and jostled my way to the front door. A line stretched half a block south. *Hunh?* Waving at me was a man with black clunky glasses and wavy gray hair. It was Greil Marcus, critic and, to my mind, the early philosopher king of punk rock. In the books *Mystery Train: Images of America in Rock 'n' Roll Music, Lipstick Traces: A Secret History of the Twentieth Century,* and *Ranters & Crowd Pleasers,* which had been on my bookshelf, well worn, for years, Greil had lent legitimacy and heft to the premise I intuitively felt—but had a hard time articulating over Quincy's purple mohawk hysterics and chemistry teachers yelling at me because of a T-shirt: punk rock was more than poking people in the eye with a sharp stick; it was a deeper phenomenon that reverberated throughout our cultural landscape. It was a welcome affirmation for someone like me with chronic misfit-itis.*

I asked him to follow me and, with great trepidation, as if any second the wait, the *buzz*, would be revealed as a grand sham, the people in line would realize they were in the *Bloodshot line, what the hell is that*, and flee to the Cool Label show, I told the doorman, "Um, he's with me." And he let him in. And the club was still packed. Where did all those people come from? Was my dissatisfaction with the state of indie rock felt by others? By the time the charburgers were long gone and the Old 97's and the Waco Brothers had played, it was hard to breathe in Brownie's. The room felt alive. There was a jolt both new and old, familiar and yet wonderfully unknown.

Forty-eight hours later, I was back in Chicago. But now what? Were we a real label, whatever that meant? The club, gear rental, gas, and pastrami sandwiches from Katz's cost real money. So did stamps, envelopes, posters, typewriters (yes, you read that right), recording time, or the dozen new things that had started popping up every week. Shit. Time to pick up the brushes and roll out the tarps again.

* * *

House painting was hardly the usual passport into the enchanting world of music, but the money was good, even if the hours could be brutal. I didn't sit in an office cube, and I was my own boss. It also gave me the flexibility to go on popcorn shrimp benders at the Jazz and Heritage Festival in New Orleans, drive to Lafayette for *La Festival Acadiens*, or spend a week in Austin, Texas, for a burgeoning little shindig dubbed South by Southwest.

And it prepared me to expect the unexpected, to problem-solve on the fly, do what had to be done to complete the job, and move on. A swanky lakefront apartment had a shrine to hairspray-metal pinup Sebastian Bach, centered on a life-size framed poster and flanked by shelves with candles, signed photos, some with lipstick on them, and a silver belt buckle. I had a customer who sounded and dressed like someone who won a lot of Truman Capote look-alike contests, and each of his morbidly obese cats had their own bedroom and litterbox because *They don't like to share.* At an empty apartment we were rehabbing, cheering distance from the left-field bleachers of Wrigley, the only items left behind by the tenants, found on a back closet shelf, were a box of military-themed gay porn magazines, *Semper Fist*, and a not-unused enema bag. After having her mind blown on a trip to Sayulita or Cozumel, a woman hired us to paint her squat clapboard house and garage in the overwhelmingly Hispanic Little Village neighborhood. She was an older,

* Not to be confused with the much more insidious *Misfititis,* with its symptomology of Devil's locks, excessive weightlifting, and obsessions with zombies.

urban-pioneer-for-the-cause, frizzy-haired hippie dressed in flowing huipils and expensive-looking huaraches, and she wanted "Authentic Colors." After settling on a *¡Viva La México!* souvenir-postcard approximation of her reality, I was working on the garage door facing the alley when a wide-eyed, six-ish-year-old boy scuffled up to me and stared. His mother called him back and he impishly whispered to me, before turning and running home, "Fuck you, gringo." I smiled and waved.

We spent a month working on a faux-Edwardian mansion owned by a retired Carson Pirie Scott window dresser. His basement was stuffed with props, ephemera, holiday tableaux, and barrels of spare mannequin arms, legs, and heads; every trip down there to wash brushes or paint trays was one part *Pee-wee's Big Adventure* and one part Vincent Price's *House of Wax.* When all our tools were stolen out of their garage, the helpful Evanston police officer shrugged and suggested we go to Maxwell Street that weekend and buy them back. We worked for a scientist who peppered us with questions about our drinking habits after work—she was writing a book on the links between painters, alcoholism, and short lives. *Go team!* When necessary, I hired an Eastern European guy who started every day with a fresh pint of vodka in the back pocket of his overalls. When asked if he wanted lunch, he'd pat that pocket, *No, thanks, liquid potato.* By quitting time, it would be empty.*

While we were working in a Gold Coast high-rise, the elevator got stuck between floors. After a few minutes, the scene devolved into *The Open Boat*–level panic. I eventually pried the door open with my 5-in-1 tool and helped the others out. We were hired on retainer to refurbish a late-Victorian in Evanston. After the living room and library were finished, the owner threw a party for friends and colleagues and invited us as well. The grad students, professors, and North Shore social set gushed at our noble labors. *Raise ye goblets of cava to yon This Old House craftsmen/heroes!* The inadvertent condescension was alleviated by the non-cheap wine and fancy trays of what people kept calling canapés. Good thing we kept a cooler in the truck.

During a lunch break in the winter of early 1996, I was eating my forearm-sized burrito with my back against the radiator to keep warm in an apartment in the Edgewater neighborhood. It was a no-brainer landlord job: no fuss, no finesse, no filagree, no furniture moving, and no occupants. Fill the cracks, caulk the doors and windows, put on a fresh coat of inoffensive off-white, and be gone before the next tenants moved in. To pass the time, I sometimes read with a detached interest the warning labels on the products we worked with: "Prolonged and repeated inhalation, ingestion and/or skin absorption

* His carpentry skills were, as the woodworking joke goes, like lightning: his hammer never hit the same place twice. But he could sling paint well enough and did demolition work with a determined—if unnerving—efficiency.

may cause degeneration of the kidneys and liver." "Repeated and prolonged overexposure to solvents can cause neurological damage." "Contains Hexane, which can cause peripheral and central nerve damage." "Contains methylene glycol which has been shown to cause cancer in certain laboratory animals."

One day, I swiped a *Chicago Tribune* from the doormat of the apartment across the hall, to keep current on *da Bears*, blah blah blah, *da mayor*, blah blah blah, and *da wedder*, slush, cold, blah, blah, blah. And dere . . . I mean *there* . . . on the front page was a skyline blurb, "*Give it up, Garth: Insurgent music movement tries to bring country back to its roots.*" Riffling quickly to Arts & Entertainment, I found a full-color reproduction of the *Hell-Bent* cover—a garish Langford painting of Hank Williams riddled with arrows—and a full-page story about us by the paper's principal music writer. My eyes almost popped out of my head. At a time when such papers boasted enormous, generations-long readerships, here was a glowing endorsement coming from inside the establishment media gates. This writer had nothing to gain by writing about us: there was no *big scoop*, and it wasn't going to cause a *V-E Day!* rush on the newsstands or burnish his reputation as a critic. That it happened at all was another example of why Chicago was a special place for independent music.

I looked at my painting partner thinking it might be a methylene glycol-induced hallucination. I folded the paper back up, making sure there were no salsa or Linen White smudges on it, and returned to transforming the drab rental unit bathroom into a gleaming lavatorial palace.

Was Bloodshot trying to be the anti-Nashville?

There were frequent imputations in this *us vs. them* vein, but Bloodshot wasn't launched to be a thorn in the well-oiled saddle of Nashville's country music hegemony. Hell, I never even considered us a "country" label.

Early stories in the "alternative" press framed our Honky Skronk Weekend lineup as a showcase for "non-US99 country bands." (US99 was the station—every big city had one—that kept ratings high with playlists comprised of shiny belt buckle arena country. If it hadn't been in their name, I wouldn't have had any idea where the station was on the dial.) The *Chicago Tribune* article "Twang and Shout" and the 1995 *Chicago Reader* music section cover story "No Depression's Bull Market" posited that Chicago was an unlikely center of non-US99 country music, and that Bloodshot was an "antidote" to the Nashville assembly line, injecting some controversy into that otherwise bland world. We were? I thought we were an antidote to the Spin Doctors and Matchbox 20. I wanted to provoke indie rock, not stick my tongue out in Nashville's direction. Some regarded us as defiant, but it was more of an indifference.

Honestly, I was "anti-Nashville" the same way I was "anti-hippo attack"; both were objectively bad, but they had no impact on my daily life. Sure, if I fell out of a pirogue while on safari in South Africa's Kruger National Park, or if I was chained to a radiator during a song-pitch circle alongside a panel of major label A&R flacks at the Bluebird Café, it moved from the theoretical to the very real in short order, but otherwise . . . whatever. Mainstream country music just wasn't worth the effort to hate.

As South by Southwest 1996 approached, there were whispers that this *un-country* country music was "on the rise." On the cover of *Gavin* magazine, a radio trade mag published by the same people who had let us into their convention a year before, was a full-page, full-color picture of the Old 97's, a suave inset pic of me, and the suggestion that "through Bloodshot eyes" I would prognosticate the future of the "insurgent country movement" on college radio. Not bad for a label that had only sold about 8,000 records cumulatively to that point. Not bad, but also cause for suspicion . . .

Past the first dozen or so pages of announcements of promotions, mergers, expansions, FCC meetings, and other aspects of this world far removed from Bloodshot's day-to-day existence, and past the full-page ad for Lionel Ritchie's new album IMPACTING NOW at radio, was an *Olde West* mockup of a poster: *Wanted: Adventurous Radio Programmers for Twangy Insurrection.* After a quick history lesson on our founding, the rise of *No Depression* magazine, and a few "cowpunk" antecedents like X, the Blasters, Dwight Yoakam—music that combined a "punk 'tude with insistent twang"—Bloodshot was congratulated for putting a face to a faceless movement and, in the process, becoming an Important Indie Label. Without sourcing, sales numbers, or any evidence, really, to back it up, other than a need for a Next Big Thing™ and a feel-good little label that sort-of-could story, they asserted that "country-influenced punk and rock is being hailed as the savior of alternative rock." Furthermore, it had a chance to "become a commercial radio phenomenon." It was? It did? If so, where was my jetpack? Why was I working part-time in a low-ceilinged basement, sitting on an alley-picked chair held together by duct tape and habit, and painting bathrooms the rest of the time? Why were we being told at every turn that our bands were too country for rock clubs but not country enough for radio? Or was that vice versa? While I begged the reading audience of radio programmers not to fear music with country underpinnings,

Photo by Anthony Nguyen, used with permission.

or consign it to specialty show ghettos, I also pointed out the myriad reasons we didn't have a prayer of breaking into mainstream radio. For that, I was described as a "sober realist." Thanks, I guess. This industry boosterism was feeling a bit oppressive.

Major label dogs suddenly started sniffing around our bands' hydrants. Calls were made. *Let's meet up at the Four Seasons*—South by Southwest's base camp for executive schmoozing—*we love what you're doing*. The very same cabal of insiders that had descended upon Chicago a couple years earlier eager for alt-rock plunder was now turning their galleons in our direction, the smell of hypothetical riches on distant shores.

Given that the year before South by Southwest declined to invite our bands to play official showcases, and fortified by the experience of our guerrilla CMJ day party the previous fall, we had already made plans to attend whether we had "permission" to or not. We partnered with Yard Dog, a contemporary folk art gallery with a backyard on a rundown block in the wilderness south of the Congress Avenue bridge; it was far from the convention center, the expense-account hotels, and the gaudy Sixth Street entertainment zone, but close to the venerable Continental Club, numerous vintage stores, and the magical, tequila-based elixirs at Güero's Taco Bar. With a sound system powered by a generator on a pickup truck, an ad hoc stage set on milk crates, and two kegs of Lone Star beer, we invited one and all, no conference badge or festival wristband needed—an egalitarian approach we never wavered from—to enjoy an afternoon of free music. Knock on wood, some festival attendees might pry themselves away from gripping daytime convention panel discussions such as "Charles Whitman: How and Why Did it Happen?" and "Emerging Technologies" (with the ominous description *Are people* really *going to sit down at their computer when they want to hear music?*" Gee, I wonder.)

And pry themselves away they did—or about seventy-five people, anyway—to be entertained by distorted, poorly mixed, and thoroughly exhilarating sets by the Waco Brothers and the Old 97's. This was not a staid trade show gathering attended as a favor, an angle, or a foot in the door; it was a party. Deals weren't made, friends and fans were.

But, as it turned out, South by Southwest *did* invite the Waco Brothers and the Old 97's to perform that year. Furthermore, the festival assembled an entire showcase of "country-flavored alternative rock," "resonant rural roots-rock," and other word salads that appeared in the official descriptions. The program guide hyped our bands with "Bloodshot seems to be emerging as the Sub Pop of the alternative country camp," with "Sub Pop" meant to elicit a Pavlovian response to industry profiteers on the make.*

The showcase was at the Split Rail, a shabby roadhouse on Red River at the eastern edge of downtown. In addition to the Waco Brothers and Old 97's, there were bands that had either already been signed by major labels or were being aggressively courted: Mississippi's Blue Mountain, North Carolina's Whiskeytown, the criminally underappreciated Slobberbone from Dallas, and the Hangdogs of New York City. Going up against showcases like George Clinton & the P-Funk All-Stars,

* As a pre-internet/cell phone time-warp marker, the bulky program—which *no* festival attendee would have been caught without—also listed where registrants were staying so messages could be left for them at hotel front desks, and included a map to the public pay phones in the downtown area. Public pay phones! It was like we were smudging charcoal on the cave walls of Lascaux.

the Bad Livers, and Jason & the Scorchers at more prestigious venues, I was just concerned that there would be enough bodies in the room to keep the night from being an embarrassment. Sure, lots of people *said* they were coming, but I'd been around Music Industry Professionals long enough to know their word was good only until a free buffet or open bar came to their attention. Hell, I would have sneaked off to see those other shows if I could.

Again, a shock. I had anticipated many scenarios—roof collapses, power outages, or big, empty spaces—but a line down the block before the doors even opened hadn't been one of them. An hour later, I poked through the crowd in a curious fog of elation, greeting friends I'd made earlier in the day at Yard Dog and accepting proffered Shiner Bocks.

But something felt fishy. Though the show was sold out, I could walk around the front of the stage during the show comfortably. It didn't feel like Lounge Ax, Brownie's, or Empty Bottle shows, or even the Yard Dog earlier in the day, where fan responses were spontaneous, genuine, and *loud*. There was a reserve that gave me, to use a technical term, *the willies*. Here, the crowd was thick in the back, craning to see and be seen, eyes darting to names and company affiliations on badges to determine if someone was worth talking to. Throughout the night, I was asked to the back to chat and be told I was *on to something big*, and *hey, just between you and me* confidences like "if only the Waco Brothers were a few years younger" or "do you think Rhett is married to *this* band?" I was bathed in the gold-digger smiles of people paid for their cabbage-sniffing acumen. It took on the vibe of a livestock auction.

There is a scene in *Inside Llewyn Davis*, the 2013 Joel and Ethan Coen film, that takes place at an early 1960s recording session. Two folksingers, driven by monetary necessity, are recording a novelty number, "Please Mr. Kennedy," about a reluctant astronaut during the binary good/evil days of the Cold War. After practicing a bit, we hear a disembodied voice from the control booth say, *Ok, good, "Please Mr. Kennedy," take one, and rolling . . .*

It's awkward, stilted doggerel when they start. But the singers and song gel, we feel the spark and warmth as they bring a real dynamism to what should have been an insipid nothing, and the camera is right in the room with them. After a couple minutes, the sound gets echoey, distant, and cold, and the camera moves to the control room looking down on the performance space, giving it a terrarium feel. There we see a nondescript company man in a drab suit who doesn't have a name, we don't see him speak, and his power over everyone in the building is uncertain. With dead eyes, he arrhythmically bobs his head, possibly calculating the money soon to be made. When I saw that scene the first time, my brain instantly snapped back to the Split Rail and the music-biz clip-artists standing at the back of the room almost twenty years before.

Midway through the night, I had to get to the bathroom to puke. The stress was eating me up.* While I was on my knees in the stall-without-a-door—and nothing makes one feel more like a bigwig than being on a Texas bar's bathroom floor during one's sold-out label showcase—I wondered what I was working toward. Labels smaller than us—and we were still pretty dang small—had already parlayed a single album or artist into handsome payouts from bigger companies. They had "succeeded." But that didn't feel like a game I wanted to play or a *can't miss* circus cannon I wanted to be loaded into. I wasn't after streak-of-lightning cars and fancy clothes.

My free-floating distrust of power and popularity, honed by the Marx Brothers, Black Flag, and George Carlin, was flashing red. My intuition was to commit to the artists and the music in the present, not get seduced by gauzy and/or faithless hype. In short, I wanted to be with the fans up front and the musicians onstage, not with whoever was standing in the back. I was a fan. I was in the audience.

Some heady considerations for an otherwise aimless house painter and former stage manager who not too recently had disturbing photos of a naked stewardess on a trampoline shoved under his nose in an Old Town basement.

---

* Though it probably didn't help that the only vegetable I had eaten that week was salsa and the only fruit the limes in my margaritas.

14

A Pair of Brown Shoes

One night I was watching TV after a Lounge Ax show during the *I'll have just one more before bed* point of the early morning—perhaps a plate of Totino's pizza rolls at my disposal, never a bad decision—and I got caught up in an infomercial for a "Best of Johnny Carson" VHS/ DVD set.*

They showed a clip with George Gobel, a middle-tier '60s and '70s comic with a brush cut whom I had vague memories of from watching *The Hollywood Squares* with my grandma. On the couch with him were A-listers Bob Hope and Dean Martin. Everyone was smoking and boozing in that distinctly sweaty, beige, late-1960s way—Carson was even wearing a *cravat,* fer crying out loud. George looked around at the star power and said laconically, after squinting and taking a drag of flavor country, "Do you ever get the feeling that the world was a tuxedo, and you were a pair of brown shoes?" The whole panel fell apart laughing. He had 'em. On his terms. I could see the satisfaction in the glint in his eye as the laughter rang through the studio. He'd never be a Dino, Mr. Late Night, or Old Ski Nose; he knew who he was and where he fit in, and he was good with that.

In America, where the tenets of commerce boil down to *why do something when you can <u>overdo</u> something*—a civic ideal we should translate into Latin, make our national anthem, and print on our money and Big Gulp cups—we relentlessly pursue the trifecta of abundant, cheap, and convenient. We are bombarded by, and numbed to, signifiers, logos, mascots, and chummy slogans that aim to elicit a predictable reaction and the certitude of a specific satisfaction. People feel part of it, feel part of what everyone else is feeling a part of, and it thus circles back upon itself, a validation through manufactured

* I am easily sucked in by such things. I'll watch clips of monkeys biting Johnny, Foster Brooks's drunk act, or Andy Kaufman doing Latka doing Elvis all night long.

common experience. And while I was almost envious at times—*gawd,* it would be so much easier to *just fit in*—it never held much appeal for me.

In high school, when the packs of cool kids peeled out of the parking lot to go to Mickey D's, I was left on my own to hit the original Buddy's—the Mother Church of Detroit-style pizza—Athens Coney Island for two without onions, or the Chicken Shack Depot, formerly the Chicken Depot, formerly the Chicken Shack, its canvas awning a faded archive of its ups and downs—for a two-piece snack, slaw, and a roll. In these places, I learned that it wasn't only the world of underground music that offered opportunities for the strange and unique. There were communities of originality, clatter, and chaos swirling everywhere around me. I just had to pay attention. Again.

By the time I landed in Chicago, my preferences for those places that didn't cater to the stupid fools who stand in line were becoming conscious choices. I found comfort in musty taverns with incongruous seafaring crapola on the walls instead of televisions. When the bartender in a well-worn Superchunk T-shirt left my change for a $20 on the bar, there was the tacit, gentlemanly understanding that there would be another round *because a bird don't fly on one wing.* R&B Painting and Carpentry patronized neighborhood hardware stores staffed by grizzled clerks with hands like stump gnarls and who smelled faintly of Brylcreem and mineral spirits. They could explain, at length, the difference between two cotter pins, and what shelf they could be found on, as well as relate a quick anecdote about turn button fasteners if we gave them half a chance. Where else was I going to find the proper-sized torpedo level, or a table by the open front window of my neighborhood *bierstube* the Huettenbar, with its dark-wooded, maroon-stooled Bavarian chalet kitsch, snack sausages, and steins of Kutscher Alt? Less convenient, less organized, and less popular, these places provided a stark contrast to the orderly, standoffish offerings of liquor gun enterprises staffed by poor cogs wearing Kelly-green bowlers, and converted airplane hangars staffed by underpaid children in orange vests who weren't aware of much more than the general existence of saws and hammers but *could* tell me where the "sharing size" bags of Twizzlers were.

Road trips, too, were adventures. Rather than grimly surrender to a joyless trudge through an interminable and homogenizing landscape, *are we there yet?*, I looked past the off-ramp riot of predictable names, trademarks, signifiers, symbols, all clamoring for the attention of our wallets and gullets.*

My atlas was Jan and Michael Stern's *Roadfood,* the Stax or Slash Records of food guides. Before the one-click-away era of Yelp, TripAdvisor, and Instagram food porn, I never left the area code without my tattered copy in the glove box. (It's still there, *btw.*) It opened my mind to the importance of place and

---

* A girlfriend once marveled as we drove through New Jersey on the way to New York City one night, "The signs would be pretty if I didn't understand English."

opened my mouth to a panoply of Seuss-ishly named spiedies, muffalettas, snoots, fluff, étouffée, boudin, and burgoo. Before the internet, one could only wonder what these mysterious victuals could be—their ridiculous names on the stained menus revealing nothing. The book gave me the inside skinny on diners, crab shacks, BBQ huts, and pancake houses run by people who were iconoclasts, Luddites, and folk artists just as much as any indie musician or record store owner could be.

With its passion for exposing the strange and the wonderful, the book steered me to White Haven, an oasis in the endlessness of Pennsylvania, for scrapple at the Family Diner. I was lured to Gustafson's, a smoked lake fish dreamscape along Route 2 of Michigan's Upper Peninsula, and Gus's salsiccia-stuffed pretzels in St Louis. At Smitty's, a breakfast dive in Oxford, Mississippi, a half hour from the interstate to New Orleans, they had biscuits with three *(3!)* kinds of gravy. Who knew such extravagances existed?

Before internet and reality-TV fusspots fetishized every new barbeque trend moments after it appeared, *Roadfood* venerated the unpretentious artisans doing what they'd been doing for decades. BBQ mutton at the Moonlite in Owensboro, Kentucky, chopped pork at Ridgewood BBQ in Bluff City, Tennessee, and ribs at Leo's in Oklahoma City weren't mere foods one mechanically ingested on the way to somewhere else; one had to seek them out. Craig's BBQ, a low-slung white clapboard shed with smoke billowing out of the back, is on the south side of the two-lane highway paralleling I-40 in the flatlands between Little Rock and Memphis in DeValls Bluff, Arkansas. Their pig sandwiches are cheap, vinegary, smoky, and peppery, the dollop of creamy slaw on top a perfect compliment. Without an insider nudge, I would have driven by it a thousand times—presuming I would have ever found myself driving through DeValls Bluff in the first place—without stopping. Louis Mueller's, the Chartres Cathedral of Texas BBQ, is an hour off the highway to Austin in Taylor. The muddy yellow walls, patinaed by decades of smoky smoke, of this converted gymnasium are covered in local business cards, rodeo articles, and Stevie Ray Vaughn testimonials. When the all-business, *don't waste my time with small talk* carver throws me a little cube of peppered brisket while I make my order, time slows down. I feel like I'm approaching an event horizon. When it's good, it is impossibly good. When it's great, it is sublime. There is a complexity and depth of flavor in that brisket that speaks to history, to respect, to craftsmanship. To art.

These miraculous meals gave me the same rush as diving into a box of LPs at the back of a store. When I tucked into a *beef on weck* at Schwabl's in Buffalo, I felt the prick of adventure that I did when I heard the 1950s R&B punk of Don and Dewey on Specialty Records or Wire's "12XU" for the first time. Like Greil Marcus's writings and the suggestions by record store clerks or end-of-the-dial radio shows years before, the *idea* of road food offered the

Artwork by Melissa Swingle.

option of existing on the margins. Maybe it would have been "smart" business to do otherwise, but they weren't constitutionally suited to it. I could relate. *Roadfood* was another secret handshake that esteemed eccentricity and contrarianism and, as much as any indie label, was an aspirational template for Bloodshot.

I wasn't alone in this compulsion. As distinguished tour logistician Napoleon Bonaparte once noted, an army marches on its stomach; the same held for many of our artists. With a missionizing bent, we exchanged favorite hometown haunts and discoveries from our frequent travels. I was introduced to Kansas City's Arthur Bryant's by the Starkweathers, who mocked Chicago's sugary BBQ sauces, boasting that theirs was made of "vinegar and dirt." Ha Ha Tonka steered me to Joe Roger's Chili in Springfield, Missouri—a welcome tip on the I-44 corridor known more for gun stores, walnut bowls, and Jessie James hideouts. Trailer Bride made damn sure I got hush puppies and cobbler when they took me to Allen & Son BBQ on their home turf of Pittsboro, North Carolina. Alejandro Escovedo knew the best taquerias and cheap margaritas in East Austin and the intel was reciprocated whenever he played Chicago.

After a week of mixing a Kelly Hogan record in Athens, Georgia, she took me to her beloved Varsity for slaw dogs and shakes. Fans—the kind who got as carried away by the catfish and spicy rice at the White River Fish Market outside Tulsa, Oklahoma, as they did by side one of *Johnny Cash at San Quentin*—wrote letters and emails with suggestions of where to go if I came to their town. And if I asked eight people in the merch line at any club in Texas where I could find the best BBQ, I somehow got nine different answers. When bands came to the office, I wasn't going to let them go to a nearby Subway, I sent them to Rosded for Thai, Mr. Beef for a beef, or placed an order to Hot Doug's gourmet sausage emporium for a Marty "Hey Dere" Allen, a couple of Elvises, and maybe a Pete Shelley if there was a vegetarian in the van. (Fortunately, we never had to wait in line for the finest in encased meats; Doug was a fan, and we could call in our orders and skate, somewhat sheepishly, to the head of the ever-present line.) For years, any band coming to Chicago via Minneapolis was under standing orders to bring the office a pie from the Norske Nook in Osseo, Wisconsin.

On a short leg through the Midwest, I tagged along with Neko Case as the merch mule. A few miles outside Indianapolis, we stopped at the Hollyhock House, another *Roadfood* tip, for an early dinner. It was a grand old rococo house decorated by a grandma on an antiques bender after two shots of apple schnapps and famous for their family-style dinners. After a few days of featureless tour food, we tucked into the plates of Indiana fried chicken, biscuits with apple butter, and whipped potatoes with gusto. We showed up at the venue in pronounced food comas. After a couple of sluggish *too much gravy* opening songs, Neko apologized to the crowd, telling them where we had just eaten. The crowd murmured and laughed with *been there* recognition. For the rest of the night, people came to me at the merch booth with their own Hollyhock House stories and suggestions where we should go next time we came through. Moments like this create deeper bonds between musician and audience. Are these places easy to find right off an interstate exit? Not usually. Are there offbeat cooks and waitstaff, less than idyllic bathroom conditions, people not exactly like me the next table over, quirky ordering protocols that could lead to embarrassment, and unheard-of, easily mispronounced local specialties? Sometimes, certainly a possibility, quite likely, count on it, and God I hope so. It's the human carnival ride, get onboard.

Like the second-run movie houses, strange record stores, scruffy bookstores, and obscure labels where I had long found vitality, creativity, and interconnection, these enterprises felt comfortably peculiar, and peculiarly comfortable. They exuded locality and uniqueness—qualities that independent music fans regard as deeply felt parts of themselves. Mention Oxford, Mississippi, and I don't think first of Faulkner or Ole Miss, I think biscuits and gravy.* Say "scrapple" or "DeValls Bluff," and my mind instantly floods with a feeling of *connection*, the same way listening with friends to Booker T.

* Though the Confederate soldier statue in the town square with the chilling inscription "It was a just and noble cause" also comes to mind.

or the Knitters does. In their insistence to exist in the world on their terms, they were, well, punk rock. Try getting that from a value meal. Or a sponsored, algorithm-derived playlist.

If I may wander into territory some might promiscuously suggest is "philosophical," the kind of label I wanted Bloodshot to be would emulate those communities. Two batteries charging each other. Selling out to a bigger label at the first hint of good fortune did not mesh with that way of thinking. There were other, more important, intangible metrics to meet on our own terms. We were who we were. We were George Gobel in brown shoes. I was comfortable with that.

15

The Venal Snake Pit

In the spring of 1996, R&B Painting and Carpentry took a job at the apartment of a retired, depressive, chain-smoking chick-sexer (it's a thing, look it up . . .) in the then-sketchy Buena Park neighborhood north of Wrigley Field. The landlord—who *swore* his tenant was a star in the chick-sexer field back in the day—wanted to brighten up the dismal nicotine-yellow rooms. We set up our gear and laid out tarps that the tenant's asthmatic pug immediately treated as a canvas fire hydrant. I also brought a boombox and a cassette of Robbie Fulks's yet-to-be-released debut album, *Country Love Songs*.

Robbie, based on some nominal notoriety from his compilation appearances (especially *Hell-Bent's* "She Took a Lot of Pills (And Died)," a song that was something akin to Bloodshot's first "hit" single), had approached us with a modest proposal. In exchange for $3,000—an amount I doubt would have covered Garth Brooks's hat-blocking needs for a regional tour—he would deliver, and I quote: "*13 original country songs with an early '50s production aesthetic and arrangement, reviving certain types of songs (murder ballad, the xenophobic love song, the paean to food) long abandoned by mainstream country. Likewise, these songs will frequently violate current country songwriting trends which hold as taboo themes of negativism, forceful expression and stand resolutely against the poisonous tides of camp.*" And Steve Albini, in-demand engineer and agitating conscience of indie rock, would record it. Sounded punk as fuck to me.

Some days the tenant would bring a plastic lawn chair into the room we were painting, pug morosely in tow, and sit and smoke. And listen. He rarely spoke, but one day he said he liked the record. *And I* hate *country*, he rasped.

Hmm. If this guy, far outside my indie rock bubble, liked it, maybe there were others who didn't realize they were fans of atypical roots music, too. For someone to walk through a door, first there must be a doorway. Maybe Bloodshot could be that doorway.

* * *

As painting gigs kept coming and label work mushroomed—the more I did, the more I saw that could be done—there weren't enough hours in the day. The 3 a.m. Kinko's runs to copy flyers, mailers, and press releases had lost their renegade appeal. Sample color swatches for clients were getting mixed up with my lists of record stores in St. Louis or Louisville I had researched at the library, and a cramped studio control room was no place to reek of turpentine. Many was the night when my hair had streaks of Stonington Gray in it, or I left spackley handprints on the bar at Schubas because I'd come straight from a jobsite. If you patted me on the back, a puff of drywall dust was likely to rise off me à la the Peanuts' Pigpen.

It was getting harder to justify painting for over-mortgaged power couples, shut-ins, racists, and hoarders, no matter how good the money was. The father who yelled at his seven-year-old daughter when she wanted to show him a drawing of the friendly painters ("God, I can't stand the sound of your voice") gave me a head—and heart—ache that lasted for days. At one jobsite, a corpulent chain-smoker collapsed at the kitchen table while eating eggs Benedict and her husband, no thinner or less smoky than she, threw his van keys at me and said—with, thinking back, surprisingly little urgency—"Can you take her to the hospital? She's having a heart attack." We worked for a recently retired couple on their elegant house with ornately plastered ceilings in Lincoln Park. She was spending her retirement occasionally walking, often feeding, but rarely cleaning up after their three dogs that were in a perpetual state of incontinence, often on our drop cloths; he was spending his retirement in his "media room" watching two baseball games on two televisions, listening to another on the radio and drinking the whole day. He accosted us every day as we packed up with semi-intelligible rants on a broad range of subjects, from the damnable housekeeper to the neighbor with the damnable mulberry tree hanging over his fence to the differences between "good" Mexicans and the damnable bad ones.

A landlord had contacted us and, without elaborating, said *something's wrong with the bathroom floor*. We knocked on the door of a dilapidated shotgun house in Old Town, and a hobbling woman—she could have been eighty or a *hard* fifty—led us to the bathroom. The floor had cracked in the middle and sunk half a foot. When we opened the basement door to go down and determine what the underlying trouble was, a foul smell draped over us like strings of moist beads. A wan, bare bulb was at the bottom of the stairs. With bandanas tied over our noses and mouths, we turned on our flashlights. A rotted floor joist had cracked under the bathroom, but . . . the basement was full of rusty 55-gallon drums full of . . . dogshit? Against the hidden darkness of the back were cages filled with low, steady growls, white teeth, and eyes.

Empty dog food bags were stuffed under the stairs next to jugs of bleach. Praying fervently to the gods of cage-gate structural integrity, we backed up the stairs, told the lady we needed supplies, found the nearest pay phone, and called the ASPCA. We drove home, put the work clothes in the washer, and went to the Ten Cat to get as far from that basement as we could. It was time, again, to destroy the life neither safe nor happy before it was too late. It was time to see where this label thing might go.

* * *

When *Country Love Songs* was released in the summer of 1996, the resulting indifference, rapture, confusion, and hostility flowed over us like sweet, sweet party store wine. Fussy country purists hated him: Robbie didn't take Country Music "seriously." Folks raving about the current wave of retro bands like BR5-49 and the Derailers were peeved by his lack of vintage apparel and gear; he was like an Amish person using zippers! And the indie press dismissed him as too jokey, missing the depth and skill of his writing entirely. Some wondered if Steve Albini had lost his way.

But . . .

There wasn't a clam on the record, and anyone with half an ear primed for something original loved it. *Country Love Songs* zapped new life into time-honored tropes of country music, skewered them, turned them on their heads, and above all, honored and respected them. The lead track "Every Kind of Music but Country" (as in, *She likes* . . .), was instantly identifiable to any record nerd with a moderately catholic record collection, and the wordplay of "The Buck Starts Here" tied firearms to vinyl singles together in a way now so obvious it was hard to believe how inventive it was. "Let's Live Together" stuck it to moralistic blowhards as joyously and, I submit, as pointedly as the Dead Kennedys ever did, while "Rock Bottom" has a swing as sweet and supple as Al Kaline's.*

The album was truer to the spirit of the music than those who professed to be standard bearers of the One True Church. They couldn't hear it in Robbie because, after years anesthetized by the groovy country rock vibes of the Eagles and dizzied by the torrents of Billy Ray Cyrus cash, they had forgotten what it sounded like.

A few months later, the Waco Brothers' Jon Langford bulled into a booth with me at the Beat Kitchen with scrawled lyrics for a new song, "The Death of Country Music," that he *had to* show me. It was a wobbly, cartoonishly gory summation of how Nashville had left country music in a "deep black pool of neglect." Half glassy-eyed pub sing-along, half damning indictment, it is as

---

* I'm from Detroit; don't hold your breath if you're waiting for an Ernie Banks reference.

depressingly relevant today as it was when I first heard it. And it was just one of the three chords, truth, and amps turned to 11 salvos that became the *Cowboy in Flames* album.

Cowboy in Flames was the rowdiest and most succinct statement in the punk-tackles-country canon to date. Irreverent without veering to schtick and populist without being preachy, the Brothers were angry, jolly, and eager for another round. With the ghosts of Buck Owens and Bob Wills in the riffs, they played folk music about people getting shit on as well as the system doing the shitting. While their go-for-broke live personae could distract from the sharpness of their subject matter, shout-along polemics like "See Willy Fly By" and the title track were potent elixirs for times when reason and humor were at odds. The covers of *ur*-punks George Jones ("White Lightning"), Roy Acuff ("Wreck on the Highway") and Johnny Cash ("Big River") were pure country in one lane, pure punk in the other, and a blurry, faded yellow line separating them, no guardrails. The classic themes with updated intensity made for a perfect album to raise your glass and curse your boss.

Despite their open contrarianism, or perhaps because of it, these now-seminal releases gouged out a teeny foothold in a landscape dominated by Shania, Garth, Oasis, and Coolio. At first, it was our ardent supporters at the grassroots level who got the word out. Fanzines and free weeklies, primed by the earlier releases and compilations, got onboard quickly. Indie stores ordered, then reordered. The fanbase we were developing spread the word to their friends at shows and in primitive chatrooms. The vibrancy of a scene, slowly and steadily, was building.

This momentum, nominal as it was, brought more attention to the label. There was, it seemed to a growing segment of the industry directorate, something of a *there* there, and people didn't want to miss out. That was the only logical explanation I could think of when *Billboard* published a cover story about us. Why else would the "The International Newsweekly of Music, Video and Home Entertainment," committed to sales, sales, hits, and more sales, take notice of a label that hadn't sold as many albums in its entire existence as No Doubt's *Tragic Kingdom* had *last week*? The "Genre-Bustin' Rise of Insurgent Country" trotted out the *little label that could* feel-good narrative, gave a polite nod to my anti-everything rantings, and predicted a bright future for us in the warm bosom of the fraternity of Respectable Entertainment Enterprises. Other big-time magazines similarly predicted we were primed to make a quantum leap to bigger waters. The wisdom or necessity of doing so never questioned, the suggestion that we might not even want to, never considered. But *Rolling Stone* did coin "Cash meets Clash" for the Waco Brothers, which was pretty good. I'll give them that.

My reflexive high school vigilance kicked in again. Notoriety had come at us fast those first three years, before we had a chance to fully figure out what

THE INTERNATIONAL NEWSWEEKLY OF MUSIC, VIDEO AND HOME ENTERTAINMENT — DECEMBER 28, 1996

THE GENRE-BUSTIN' RISE OF INSURGENT COUNTRY

Acts Find Audience In Thriving Club Scenes

■ BY DEBORAH EVANS PRICE

NASHVILLE—Although the alternative country music scene gets some

radio airplay, the lifeblood of the movement is live performance. And while Austin and Nashville have long been known for their thriving club scenes, and Chicago is credited with sparking much of the current insurgent-country uprising, the scope of clubs tapping into

(Continued on page 74)

Movement Helps Broaden The Music's Base

■ BY CHET FLIPPO

NASHVILLE—There's a new musical tent under which are gathering all the performers the big top doesn't have room for these days. The big top shel-

WHISKEYTOWN BURCH

ters mainstream country music; the side tent is harboring those performers going by the name "alternative country," "insurgent country," or "progressive country," and it's starting to draw a crowd.

For years, it has been a critically important but commercially overlooked side of country music. Now, significantly, its appeal to a disenfranchised country audience and a curious pop and rock audience is beginning to make it a vital musical force and is drawing the attention of major labels.

It's a movement that has its own revered elders, its own magazine, its

SLOBBERBONE RIGBY

own nationwide circuit of clubs, its own Nashville live radio show, its own cookbook, its own string of gritty indie labels, its own young guns being supplanted by even younger guns, and even its own cruise.

KDHX St. Louis, KPFT Houston Among Radio Supporters . . . Pg. 81

Two recent musical events may illustrate and depict the movement's character and its appeal and musical diver-

(Continued on page 81)

Cutting-Edge Acts Find Home At Bloodshot

■ BY DEBORAH EVANS PRICE

NASHVILLE—Mention insurgent country music to aficionados, and

THE WACO BROTHERS FULKS

they'll tell you that the label on the cutting edge is Bloodshot Records, a Chicago outfit known not only for releasing albums by Windy City acts such as the Waco Brothers but for tapping into Nashville's alternative country music scene to produce "Nashville: The Other Side Of The Alley."

Bloodshot was formed in 1993 by publicist/club DJ Nan Warshaw, drummer/DJ Rob Miller, and Eric Babcock, who had worked at Flying Fish and

(Continued on page 79)

we wanted to do. I didn't want to buy into the hype, or listen to the back of the room back-slappers at showcases telling me *you're hot,* all with firm ideas, shackled to a particular industry rationale, of what we should do next. The biz was offering us a way in, but then what? What did Groucho used to say along the lines of not wanting to belong to any club that would have him as a member?

* * *

In early 1997, Bloodshot released *Straight Outta Boone County*, a compilation celebrating early independent label King Records and the *Boone County Jamboree*—a radio show that predated the Grand Ole Opry. With its powerful signal out of Cincinnati, the show was a staple of the airwaves throughout the Ohio Valley in the 1940s and 1950s, and the most influential proponent of hillbilly music north of Nashville. Through the label and show, millions of listeners were exposed to the music of the Stanley Brothers, Merle Travis, Hank Penny, Dolly Parton, Hawkshaw Hawkins, and Cowboy Copas, as well as lesser-knowns such as Zeb Turner and J. E. Mainer. While popular, the show and the label largely existed on the fringes of the "industry," which allowed for an autonomy and regionality that would have otherwise gotten homogenized in the broader marketplace. That was an immensely appealing, and relevant, idea.

For this collection, we thought it would be interesting for folks to cover something from the songbooks of these artists. Some contributors were well versed in the source material, some had a glancing knowledge of it, and some were listening to it for the first time. Tracks by Robbie Fulks, Slobberbone, Holler, Hazeldine, Whiskeytown, and others captured their charm, variety, and off-center inventiveness and reshaped them for a new audience, running the gamut from faithful revivals to complete overhauls filtered through the artists' own particular frames of reference. The reviews came in and our minor-league circle of media friends were smitten with it.

Then we heard the *New York Times*, the Gray Lady, was running a review. We never sought nor expected coverage from such august outlets. They had their world, we had ours, but still, we were excited for the nod from a media giant that typically ignored us. We bought a copy. The review was part of a larger story, another exegesis on the rise of a "new" and "more authentic" strain of country music, a "rebellion" against the mushy, radio-sanitized product that had taken over Music Row. After praising the paragons of this new *country-ness*—Travis Tritt, Clint Black, and Garth Brooks—for their critically sanctioned ascendancy, they dismissed *Straight Outta Boone County* as "pure butchery."

And here, friends, was where one decides what kind of label to be, where one wants to sit within the music industry pecking order, and how to respond, both internally and externally, to a review like that.

The choices were to accept the paradigms of "new country" that the industry was giving its imprimatur to. To acknowledge the elevation of artists with a veneer of novelty and a dash of daring to keep the coffers full and the image fresh, but not be so rash as to kill the goose laying golden country music egg. To tailor our future roster and releases to reflect tastes more convivial to these congealing templates. To try and move ourselves and our artists up some unspoken ladder to increase our cachet in convention halls, festivals, and media outlets.

Or we could lean into Pure Butchery. I could go to Kinko's, enlarge the words, cut and paste the *Times* masthead onto copier paper, and send faxes to all our retail accounts and distributors. We could use it as a tagline in advertisements in fanzines and in press releases to underground club owners where the bands were playing. I could take the same subversive delight in it I had with the Black Flag "As a parent, I found it an anti-parent record" sticker on their *Damaged* LP. We could wear it as a badge of honor.

The choice was clear.

To seal the deal, to ourselves and to the people whispering in our ears that if only we *did this*, or signed *them*, we would *make it*, we took the album to the belly of the beast, a music festival showcase in Nashville. At the venerable

Robert's Western World on Lower Broad, we put contributors the Volebeats, the Handsome Family, the Grievous Angels, and the Waco Brothers on stage in front of A&R professionals, tastemakers, and a few dozen rowdy drunks. As the show went on, I watched everyone except the rowdy drunks leave; they stayed and had a hell of a time. The others didn't see how to wring any dough out of this. Robert took me aside at the end of the night—in my memory he was seven feet tall and loomed over me menacingly—and said, "I don't want any of these bands playing my club ever again." Conforming to expectations and taking the easy road wasn't our strong suit.

* * *

Until this point, Bloodshot had been defined as much by what we were *against* as anything else, and it was easy to keep an ironic distance from the hoopla and magazine covers with a Gen X *yeah, whatever* smirk, but what did the label stand *for*?

I first felt the real significance of being a *label,* the responsibility of stewardship, the sheer weight of commitment to music—that which had already meant so much to me for so long—on March 22, 1998. For several years, the semiofficial and fully spiritual Sunday night closing event of South by Southwest had been Austin's adopted son Alejandro Escovedo headlining La Zona Rosa. This was the night when expense-account-purchased passions got on planes and went back to the office, and those who remained came together to be reminded why they loved music in the first place. It was also the night for locals and staffers, whose town had been swarmed by pale, Northern interlopers for the past week, to embrace their own and hoist a tankard for another festival completed, a celebration of the indie community.

A few months earlier, Alejandro had sent us a collection of live recordings, *More Miles Than Money*. Superlatively recorded at venues from Seattle to Paris (France, not Texas) and, with a focus on his Orchestra—think stirring cellos rubbing elbows with meaty guitars—songs from his previous solo albums glistened with intensity and deep soul. Plus there was a spectacular version of "I Wanna Be Your Dog," the one Stooges cover I acknowledge as necessary. I loved it. I *loved* it.

After his most recent record had failed to meet his label's sales expectations, they gave up on the album quickly and dropped him from their roster. Alejandro Escovedo was without a label, and he was asking *us* if we would we be interested in releasing his music. Here was someone I had loved since his days in Rank and File, whom I had seen devastate a room in Detroit as a duet, whom I'd seen in Chicago a few times put on shows of dizzying craftsmanship, audacious arrangements, and hard rock swagger, and he's coming to *us*? That the music industry couldn't find a place for someone like Alejandro said it all.

Looking back, a live record of material from an artist that larger labels had deserted was not, strictly speaking, something an "A" student in Music Biz

School would jump all over. But I was a fan. *Not* releasing it never crossed my mind. As South by Southwest rolled around, we were just a few weeks into the release and the record had already received positive reviews and was selling well. In interviews, he sounded positive about *the music* again. With us, he found a place where the expectations were simple: be Alejandro. Word had gotten out at the festival. "Anticipation hung in the air" is a tired thing to say about such nights, so I won't. But it did.

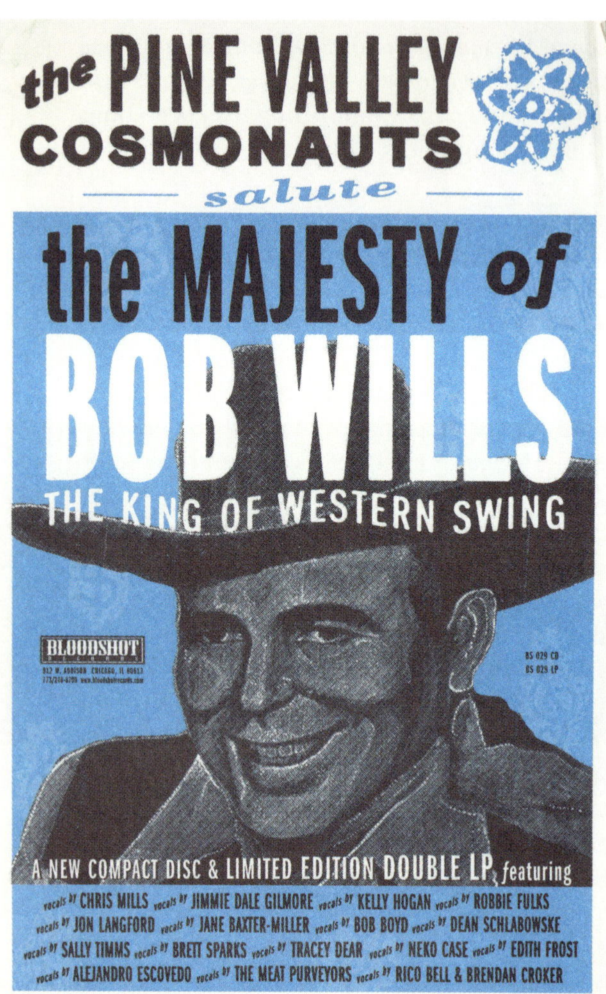

Artwork by Jon Langford, design by Markus Greiner.

The evening at La Zona Rosa opened with the release show for our album by The Pine Valley Cosmonauts collective: *The Pine Valley Cosmonauts Salute the Majesty of Bob Wills, The King of Western Swing*. With a crack backing band featuring members of the Waco Brothers, the Bottle Rockets, and the Poi Dog Pondering horn section, a powerhouse lineup of singers including Jimmie Dale Gilmore, Robbie Fulks, and Sundowner Bob Boyd paid homage to one of the titans of country music. Bob Wills had a streak of punk rock in him decades before Iggy smeared peanut butter on himself and Sheena got all hopped up and ready to go. He bristled at the genre orthodoxies of the time, freely pulling jazz, Dixieland, blues, and swing to country music, and sang about social injustices behind a glittering smile and irresistible beat. But as the decades went on, his image stagnated from *Bob Wills* to "Bob Wills," a sanitized caricature in white cowboy hat, boots, and neckerchief. His sound, so groundbreaking at the time, became untouchable and unchangeable in form and lost the innovation and excitement that made him *Bob Wills* to begin with. The Pine Valley Cosmonauts boldly sought to reclaim his music and return him to a rightful place of relevance.

Backstage before the show, some members of the band expressed worry that they might get run out of town for having the temerity to do a Bob Wills tribute deep in the heart of Texas. Given our *Straight Outta Boone County* debacle in Nashville a year earlier, it was a reasonable expectation. Texans have been known to be, um, *particular* about how their cultural touchstones are portrayed, and who is portraying them. A bunch of Chicago-based ding dongs promoting an album compiled by transplanted Welsh rowdy Jon Langford and telling *them* about Texas swing, on *their* turf? Visions of the Blues Brothers kicking into "Gimme Some Lovin'" at Bob's Country Bunker plagued my reptile brain and La Zona Rosa's stage offered no chicken-wire protection. But when Rosetta, Bob's daughter, came to the dressing room and told everyone that she was a fan of the record and said her dad would have been too, nerves were calmed. At least the family wouldn't be insulted by this.

We needn't have worried. From the opening instrumental, "Steel Guitar Rag," the band conjured the spirit of Wills, their tightness bouncing off their looseness, the looseness heightening the tightness, the improv balancing the crisp structures and the exuberance augmenting the musicality. Singers from the record, including Brett Sparks of the Handsome Family, Kelly Hogan, the Mekons' Sally Timms, and even Alejandro himself embraced passion over staid recitation. It was all there, on the stage, in the room; it wasn't in a labeled bottle on a shelf, or a diorama at a history museum. The music was alive.

Whew . . .

Later, before Alejandro's set started, I was sitting at a table stewing in a cocktail of trucker speed, tequila, exhaustion, and post-PVC-dodged-a-bullet rush with Neko Case, a then-unknown singer who had also performed the Bob Wills set and whose Canadian debut album we had rereleased in the United States a few weeks before. The room was now brimming with music industry insiders and lifers. The money, prestige, and experience they represented would have terrified me if I had presumed that I was part of the same world. It was only the year before that I had waited in line for two hours to find out the show was sold out and I couldn't get in.

Then the lights dimmed. The crowd roared. The announcer announced: *Ladies and Gentlemen, please welcome BLOODSHOT RECORDS recording artist ALEJANDRO ESCOVEDO!*

The roar got louder—some of it seemed to be coming from my head as well. The stress and pressure and strangeness of the past two and half years gave way to a sort of elation. I looked at Neko, tears starting, and, in that moment, I understood that the label was more than a knocking people's hats off goof. It was more than a trifling ploy to get into shows for free, to have some laughs.

Holy shit, the label space we'd built had become the home to an artist the caliber of Alejandro Escovedo.

And the show? It was epic. To his muscular and intuitive core band he added string and horn sections. Songs from his solo albums, as well as gems from his other projects the True Believers and Buick MacKane were constructed, deconstructed, reconstructed, refigured, and reinvented in ways that underlined his gifts as a writer *and* a bandleader. Songs I thought I knew inside and out were taken to places that filled me with wonder. There were gentle, mournful string-driven numbers that held the whole room in meditative thrall, greasy Texas glam and soul, full out rock and roll, and, of course, the uproarious "I Wanna Be Your Dog" that left the room swimming in sweat and smiles. To close the show out, he chose "Sway," a Rolling Stones cover on *More Miles Than Money*. On the record, it was a straightforward version. Live, in that room, on that night, with that ensemble, it rode the delicate line between melancholy and rapture. The song swelled and stretched, enriching the entire room, then it would shrink back coyly and beckon us to a corner to conspiratorially share a secret, just to surge ahead again with a euphoric buoyancy. As it went on, the musicians, one by one, took a bow and left the stage, leaving the others to play on, finally leaving only Alejandro and the string section, the pulse slowing, the evening already passing into memory, the knowledge that we had all just shared something very special not needing to be voiced.

It remains, if I could magically arrange it, the ten minutes I want playing in my brain in full sensory verisimilitude as I am pushed from shore during my Viking funeral.

At the end of the night, whenever that was, staying on a friend's couch somewhere past the HEB far south on Congress Avenue, I couldn't sleep.* I was being taken in again by the strong pull of the current of music. Here was an artist whose records I had in my own collection trusting us with his vision. It was a weighty proposition and a level of faith that commanded an equal or greater level of commitment and responsibility from me.

That night I saw that Bloodshot didn't have to be big to be valuable. We could have a seat at the table, or *a* table—preferably near the bar—on our terms. The indie communities I'd found growing up had been my guideposts on how to run the label all along. There was space for us to figure it out, to do it on a manageable scale in service of the fans and the artists. The music biz forces that had been nudging us to go in a particular direction, to exploit the hype, were missing what had gotten us to that evening in the first place. Millions of cars full of teenagers were never gonna ride through mansions of

---

* And not, for once, because of the ill-tempered, screeching, eagle-sized grackles that lurk outside every window in Austin in the spring.

glory blasting Alejandro, Robbie Fulks, or Moonshine Willy out of the rolled-down windows of their suicide machines, no matter how badly the industry wished it to be so. As noted by famed Strategic Growth Analyst "Dirty" Harry Callahan, *a man's got to know his limitations.* I liked pure butchery, brown shoes, and unpopular music too much to do anything else.

It was a long drive back to Chicago the next day and there was a lot of work to do.

* * *

Sitting in the back of that Detroit funeral home, all my *sneak in the side door and hope no one notices* teenaged self saw laid before me was a cheerless grind through a world that played by a set of rules I didn't understand, I hadn't agreed to, and I hadn't had any say in constructing. Moments of clarity in life are rare, but in a matter of minutes after I saw David Byrne's sly smile and heard that jumpy and subversive music, everything had changed. In remarkably short order, I went from listening to Rodney Dangerfield LPs alone in my room to yelling "Rise Above" into the microphone with Henry Rollins in a sweaty club surrounded by people as pissed off and confused as I was. I had never incorporated the accepted rock and roll canon. I didn't have an awkward "yeah, Genesis was cool" phase nor did I have a Loverboy bandana consigned to the back of the closet. To this day, ask me Music History 101 questions like "name a song on *Revolver*" or "which album is 'Whole Lotta Love' on," or "which guitarist played what on *Exile on Main Street*" and I'll give you a blank stare before running to Google. I'm not trying to play it too cool for school, but I really did not listen to music with anything other than a sad detachment until I picked up that first Devo record. I was like one of those Third World countries that never had landline telephones and went straight to cell phones, skipping whole decades of incremental technology and infrastructure.

It wasn't rebelling, it was surviving.

From this compressed and untutored scramble through the swirling, exciting mess of America's musical landscape, the love of what was between the genres and below the mainstream had seeped into my bones. Where most wanted slots and categories, for someone to tell them—arbitrarily it seemed to me—what was acceptable and what wasn't, I was drawn to bridges, interstices, and webs. I was suspicious of anyone trying to sell a happy, concise version of something; chances were if someone in charge didn't want you to know about something, it was worth looking into. The catalyzing precepts of underground music put the control into the hands and heads of artists, musicians, and fans. Where it belonged.

That openness lured some musicians into exploring the weirdness and beauty in our forgotten history and the designs and delusions of dreamers, decades past, that hung in the air whether we acknowledged it or not. As Faulkner said, "The past is never dead. It's not even past." It was all connected, it seemed obvious to me. No one has yet convinced me otherwise. That history and perspective was comforting as we negotiated our way through the turbulent label landscape and not cave to the pressures, the advice, to be *this* or *that*. Once I stopped wondering what I could have done better to fit in, I started looking ahead. Perhaps I would have found other opportunities to discover the possibilities out there in the world, but music, as surely as a file in a prison cake, was mine.

Was my odyssey to, and through, music unique? Maybe. Was it unusual? Definitely. And every leg of it unwittingly presaged what I wanted Bloodshot to be as a label. Not planned, but not an accident.

SIDE B

16

A Long Plastic Hallway

Several years ago, on the kind of pleasant late-summer day Chicagoans hold onto as a comfort memory during the demoralizing gloom of winter, I biked the lakefront path from Lawrence Avenue on the north side to the recently restored and repurposed South Shore Cultural Center—a magnificent turn-of-the-century, Mediterranean Revival-styled country club and duck hunting spot at Seventy-First Street. On the return trip, I swung over to Chinatown for to-go pot stickers and chicken fried rice from Three Happiness, back to the lakefront, and took a well-earned rest under a tree in DuSable Park, looking out at Lake Michigan. Chopsticks in hand, I watched the boats sail past and drank deeply the smell blowing in off the waters of the sixth largest freshwater lake, by volume, in the world.

A few trees over from me and closer to the walking/bike path was a nattily attired older Black man playing saxophone, his case open in front of him for tips. He was noodling through extended figures from Coltrane's *A Love Supreme*, the supple notes bouncing off the concrete wall abutting Lake Shore Drive behind me and filling this oddly intimate and momentarily private space with a wonderfully rich sound.

While denizens of Chicago neighborhoods will claim what lakefront we can further north and south for ourselves, downtown stretches are begrudgingly ceded to lobster-red tourists and suburbanites. You'd be no more likely to rub shoulders with rank-and-file Chicagoans here on a sunny weekend than you would if you sought out a New Yorker by standing in Times Square as a matinee performance of *Wicked* let out.

So it wasn't unexpected when my reverie was interrupted by a pack of knuckleheads wearing flip-flops, sleeveless Mark McGuire St. Louis Cardinals jerseys, and backwards shades à la Guy Fieri. Without missing a beat, the sax player about-faced from Coltrane to the unmistakable opening bleats of the *Sanford and Son* theme song. They went wild; the high fives and aggro *yeahs* flew faster than the Jet Skis on the lake. Coins, a couple of bills—Washingtons, not Lincolns or Hamiltons—hit the road case. He knew his crowd. A collective musical itch had been scratched. The organism rolled on to its next easily digestible delight down the trail and then, seamlessly, the Coltrane resumed.

If you asked that group, they would tell you they *love* music. And that's the push and pull of the independent label. Music is different things to people. There are those who naturally gravitate to the popular, and there is power in the common reference. Who doesn't dig that funky riff, the organ, and that fuzzed-out bass harmonica? It goes down easy. Who's in a bad mood after hearing it? Nobody. But, as an indie label geek, and then an indie label-owning geek, I wanted to stick around and hear what might happen after the crowd had walked on by. That was when things became interesting to me.

There's an adage, a particularly depressing American one, that a cause inevitably devolves into a racket. But was it inevitable? By the summer of 1998, success for the label was in the air, around the corner, and on the way. Or so we were told. Change came rapidly. Robbie Fulks and the Old 97's signed to major labels, and Neko Case—even the Waco Brothers—were receiving offers. Our partner Eric had left for another label the year before, and some higher-ups began to look at us as an industry "farm team." Times were . . . good? Due to these modest achievements—very, *very* modest by prevailing industry standards—I was invited to a luxuriously appointed hotel bar to meet with a major label Senior VP during a company party. I had never seen that much shrimp before. Good Lord, was that why albums cost so much? The Senior VP, with a conspicuously blasé demeanor, ordered two bottles of Dom Perignon for us.

"But we're closing soon," said the tuxedoed, *end-of-shift-tired* waitress.

He pulled out a hundred-dollar bill and winked with an unctuousness that made my skin crawl. "See what you can do." While we waited, small talk was made. What was I "digging" these days? Who was "blowing my mind" in the clubs? Questions about my background were asked while his eyes scanned the room and he gently nodded. *I'm from a village on American Samoa, where my family has fished for marlin for generations,* I could have said anything, he wasn't listening.

"Ah, look what we have here!" he said when the bottle arrived. "You know how to open one of these, sweetie?" he hammed to the waitress. A production was made of it, we stood, glasses were poured, toasts to the prosperity of The Company were made, then we retired to the high-backed, plush leather chairs near the cold, dead fireplace.

"How's the Dom?" asked the Senior VP (apparently only rubes feel the necessity to add "Perignon").

"Good, good, thanks." *Cloying. Didn't need more than one glass.* At $200 or whatever a bottle, I would have rather had ten cases of Old Style in my fridge, but sure, I'd play along. I still didn't have an idea of why I was here, and I felt like I was watching a poorly acted movie of what was happening to me. From the back row. Maybe it was an apparition brought on by the estuary of shrimp I had eaten earlier.

It was time to get "down to business." He word-saladed about concepting, matrices, ingesting new contents, monetizing emerging technologies—*quick wink to someone saying goodnight*—maximizing consumer engagement, co-branding, niche markets—*charismatic smile to a retail account manager while flawlessly skating through to*—genre integration. Tents needed to be poled, flags needed to be planted, looks needed to be better. He was a human version of a poetry magnet set you arrange on your fridge, except there was no poetry. The words "song," "music," and "art" were spoken the same exact number of times as "aardvark," "espontoon," and "honor."

He offered what were likely intended to be compliments. He commented on, without specifics of any kind, the work "your little label" had done. We had "hit" on something. I had "an ear." People he trusted said "good things about me." And, then, chillingly, "There's a place for you with us." Did I want to join the team?

He threw a salary number at me that I casually (I hoped) played off as intriguing. Given that my current salary was zero, and the label—still bankrolled in part by odd and infrequently lucrative painting gigs—dangled on the precipice of ruin during any given month, in my head I was jumping up and down and celebrating like Daffy Duck, *I'm rich! I'm rich!* Of course, there would be a competitive travel budget. *Competitive compared to what? No more staying at seedy motels with jockeying odors of mildew, bleach, and mistakes? I'm listening* . . . Expenses paid to conferences and festivals, and the chance to work with the "hottest" artists like . . . and then he said a name like it was some sort of jewel-encrusted carrot . . . Michael Bolton.*

I said I would think about it, but I knew my answer before he even started talking about an upcoming Christmas album that would "blow the doors off the market."

Friends of mine in the biz who had come up through the indie circles, who were of the *remake the industry from within* contingent, said I was an idiot to turn down this offer, that I'd be "on my way." But what "way" was that? For

* He didn't say "Michael Bolton." He said someone as execrable as Michael Bolton, but in the interests of protecting names of friends who got me into that room in the first place, I am using "Michael Bolton" to emblematically stand for the type of ultra-profitable industry cash cow who makes albums unfit to be used as drink coasters or skeet targets.

every indie rock darling these friends got to work with, they had to push the Bolton as well. They got flown around and stayed in nice hotels but had to hawk the Bolton. I wasn't that good of a liar. Fish-out-of-water bands may bring the street cred, some prestige, and even the occasional hit, but it was the Bolton that bought the Dom. Artists-as-interchangeable-commodities were ridden hard, pony express fashion, station to station, until they broke up, failed to deliver another hit, or dropped dead. Sustainable growth was ignored in favor of getting slopped at the cash trough; "Who Let the Dogs Out" over "Who Do You Love?"; Gangnam style over Gangnam substance. I knew when push came to shove which artists the guys with their winks and teeth whitened to a Vegas gleam would abandon without a second thought.

If this wasn't *the* way, where did I find *a* way? Beholden to only themselves, every independent label has had to face this question. The early years of Bloodshot had been a blur and a perpetual hustle, and that question had already been asked and answered with articulations of ingrained values over and above mere off-the-wall musical tastes. What came before and got me out of those long plastic hallways of high schools, malls, funeral homes, and dead-end jobs would be the guide to where and how we went forward. None of this decision-making seemed extraordinary to me at the time. In hindsight, it might not have even been a decision.

17

Son of a Jackal's Eyeball

How did the motley posse of unknowns, malcontents, longshots, no-shots, never-beens, and staunchly never-will-bes congregate under the leaky Bloodshot roof? Was there a coherent roadmap through the hoops and over the hurdles, around the minefields of whimsies and idiosyncrasies to unite them as a "roster" as eccentric as my record collection?

As if.

Like so many other aspects of the label, much of our roster "assembly" evolved intuitively. Before one could magically pull videos, sound files, and entire histories out of the ether with a few keystrokes, I relied on the same impulse of discovery and sabotage that I had had walking into the indie record store with the eyes-blacked-out Billy Joel poster in the window and something alluring on the turntable.

For each Bloodshot artist, there was a genesis story as varied as the artists themselves. Some were happenstance, some were mundane, some were no-brainers, and some were crimes of opportunity. It might have started with a show review in *No Depression* (Split Lip Rayfield, Trailer Bride) or a pitch from a publicist or writer favorably disposed to our cause (Luke Winslow-King, Ruby Boots); we may have heard about them from friends (Mark Pickerel, Firewater, Yayhoos, Rex Hobart & the Misery Boys, Jason Hawk Harris) or friends of friends (Vandoliers, the Silos, Maggie Björklund); we may have already been fans (Gore Gore Girls, Cordero, William Elliott Whitmore, J. C. Brooks & the Uptown Sound, Eddie Spaghetti); or they may have sent a demo that fortuitously didn't get overlooked, ignored, or accidentally kicked behind the jukebox (The Meat Purveyors, Ha Ha Tonka). At South by Southwest, I found the Yawpers playing on a deck in front of a sea of sozzled and sunburnt people and roller-skating waitresses with trays of Jell-O shots. When I heard Detroit's Deadstring Brothers through an old friend from my hometown, I didn't know a tough, exciting pub crawl between the territory of the Band's *Music from Big Pink* and the Kinks' *Muswell Hillbillies* that I'd been waiting for my whole life would hit me. Several artists—the Bottle Rockets, Murder by Death, Cory Branan, Wayne "The Train" Hancock—came to us after dispiriting experiences with larger labels. The one thing in common? The uncomplicated premise of us being fans. What would be the point otherwise? I may as well have been shift manager at the Ed McMahon junk mail factory or shilling the Bolton.

Then there were enviably surreal beginnings. As I ground away, eyes forward, never entirely sure if anyone outside our tight orbit was paying attention, people whose records had been on my shelves for years, if not decades, came looking for a home. Though they may not have had much impact on the broader music world, Rosie Flores, Charlie Pickett, Alejandro Escovedo, X's Exene Cervenka sure as shit had an outsized impact on me. These were *my* Beatles, Zeppelin, and Who. I tried not to giggle like the Pillsbury Doughboy when opportunities to work with them presented themselves.

Graham Parker, starting in the mid-1970s with his band the Rumour, coupled early punk's heat with a passion for American R&B and soul music. Despite being a darling of the critics and having a preternatural gift for crafting indelible hooks as well as an incendiary live act, he never achieved the ambiguous metric of industry "success" and was left in label purgatory.*

As luck and our intertwined circles would have it, the Rumour's drummer, Steve Goulding, had become a Waco Brother. For our fifth anniversary compilation, *Down to the Promised Land*, Steve lured Graham into covering a Wacos song. When the record surprised us by selling well, we sent him a few hundred dollars. I guess a label hadn't paid him in a long time and, before I could go home and blast his seminal *Squeezing Out Sparks* LP that was in my collection, we were talking about putting out his next album. He professed soft spots for the Band and Charlie Rich, but he'd never fully explored country-leaning ideas before in his recordings. The resulting *Your Country* went from Motown-warm to Nashville-melodic without missing a beat or admitting anything exceptional about the route. It made touchstones of Neil Young's "Harvest" and the Stones' "Dead Flowers" as easily as it did Tammy Wynette's "Stand by Your Man." It was the sort of masterful dismissal of genre constraints that had always intrigued me, and we had somehow made it possible.

Andre "Mr. Rhythm" Williams had been down, he'd been out, and he'd been down *and* out since his salad days whipping out cult R&B hits and misses. Coming up from Alabama in the '50s, he hit Detroit like a velvet chameleon,

* It has been alleged that Bruce Springsteen once said the only band he'd pay to see live was Graham Parker and the Rumour.

first with his doo-wop group the 5 Dollars, and then as writer, producer, hustler, survivor, and sinner for seminal labels such as Motown, Chess, and Fortune and artists like Ike Turner, Parliament/Funkadelic, the Contours, Mary Wells, Edwin Starr, and Stevie Wonder. He even wrote "Shake a Tail Feather." As the old song went, he'd been everywhere, man, a music biz *Zelig*. Finding his lascivious proto-rap grinds like "Bacon Fat" and "Jail Bait," I was stunned that someone made sides that wild back then. After a few hard years in obscurity, he stormed back in the late '90s with *Silky,* a record of smutty garage punk recorded with members of the Demolition Doll Rods and the Dirtbombs. Not long after, old friends from Detroit contacted me and said Andre had recorded some country material. Was Bloodshot interested? I explained to my partner who Andre was and why we should immediately say yes, and we said yes. Backed by the Two Star Tabernacle (featuring a boyish Jack White on piano), BS 041 was a couple of blasts of deep juke-joint garage country like I'd never heard before, his version of "Ramblin' Man" turning the Hank Williams bone-weary lament into a cacophonous, fevered confessional; he might have known he was heading down to the Ungood Place, but he wasn't going to apologize for it.

When Darren Blase, friend and owner of Cincinnati's renowned Shake It Records, asked if I would take a listen to a new album by Barrence Whitfield & the Savages as a favor, I was hesitant. When they blasted out of Boston in the early '80s with a force that shamed many hardcore bands, they became a gateway drug for me into another unknown world. Mixing primal soul, blues, and rockabilly with uninhibited fervor, and with Barrence as a vocal colossus standing astride the foundations of The R and The B, their repertoire brimmed with the anonymous, the overlooked, and the just plain cool. Songs credited to shadowy figures like Jimmy McCracklin, Bobby Hebb, Frankie Lee Sims, and "Pretty Boy" Don Covay had me scratching my head and quickening my pulse. *Who were these people? Where did they come from*? Hearing their version of Bobby Peterson's proto-punk "Mama Get the Hammer, There's a Fly on My Baby's Head"—that is one demented platter—I got dizzy thinking of the wonderlands of wild freakouts that were out there for me to find.

But I had been pitched dull albums by heroes past their prime before, though, and it could be painful. Before the first song on this demo was over, however, I gave our retail manager a look that he knew meant, "We're gonna put this record out." They hadn't lost a step. Soon, the Savages' master of the 1965 Gibson ES 125, Peter Greenberg, was on the phone discussing obscure sides on obscurer labels from long ago. What would be their Bloodshot debut, *Dig Thy Savage Soul,* burrowed deep into the frets between Chuck Berry and Fred "Sonic" Smith and laid down a groovy racket so thick and greasy I had to keep moist towelettes near the hi-fi. Occasionally, Barrence would call and tell me stories about blowing away headliners from the Damned to Bo Diddley to George Thorogood, but not until greeting me with hoodoo enthusiasms like *How are you, you son of a jackal's eyeball?*

* * *

In the summer of 1990, a dream job had come my way: stage managing the Cramps at the Latin Quarter. This shabby 1940s theater had hosted everyone from Duke Ellington to Marvin Gaye and was a couple blocks from the Motown Museum and GM world headquarters—bookends representing very different Detroit contributions to the world. And while it is often disappointing to meet your idols, the Cramps were, other than a tantrum by drummer Nick Knox over a squishy snare head, nothing but otherworldly cool. Afterwards, when Poison Ivy gently shook my hand and thanked me for the smooth night and promoting the gig on my radio show, I was in danger of floating away like the Underdog Thanksgiving Day parade balloon.

Given that my days started at 9 a.m. and often went until 3 a.m., "opening band time" customarily meant "nap time." I'd curl up in a back corridor and nod off.* But something about the preshow restless intensity of the guitarist/singer of the unknown opening band told me to stick around. The band was Flat Duo Jets, the guitarist Dex Romweber.

I was not disappointed. The band roared through a set of surf, proto-rockabilly, greasy denim hipster jive, and dark, vengeful blues. The show was fierce and anxious, unholy and soulful. Songs didn't just come out of Dex, they erupted. I cadged their self-titled LP, released on the tiny Athens, Georgia, label Dog Gone Records, from them after the show, and it quickly became a staple at home and on my radio show.

The album—another I have worn to unplayability—was a two-track smash and grab job at a possessed thrift store. Mixed in with their originals were super-charged nuggets otherwise consigned to oblivion, songs that sent me

* Insider tip: never, ever nap on a couch in a dressing room. It was usually more sanitary to doze off on the floor of a CTA bus after ten-cent beer day at Wrigley Field. Find a comfy road case instead.

on further deep-dive excursions. Benny Joy's juvie rocker "Wild Wild Lover" was a rarity I knew from a Norton Records reissue. Glenn Bland—now there's a name for the marquee—left "My Life, My Love" and "When My Baby Passes By" in the cosmos for Dex to tune into and blast out to another generation. The Jets' take on Gene Krupa's masterwork "Sing, Sing, Sing" was as unexpectedly punk as anything the New York Dolls ever bashed out. Who pulls apart a 1930s big band tune and reassembles it into a nitro funny car doing laps in a deep canyon? Was it genius? Madness? Or a marker for the danger and weirdness that has perpetually coursed through music? Yes, yes, and *yes*. From this bugged-out jukebox, Dex and his beat-up Silvertone guitar honed an extraordinarily idiomatic sound, a particular and readily identifiable *Jetness*. It was a sound that let the doorman size you up through the slit in the green door leading to rock and roll that was still real, *real* gone.

A few months later, my bosses at the promotions company booked Flat Duo Jets into Ann Arbor's Blind Pig. I wrote a story on them in the Detroit *Metro Times* and had Dex as a studio guest on my radio show. He rifled through my milk crates of records with a mania I was all too familiar with. *Man, check out this one by the Frantics Four. Play that Andre Williams tune. Play "I've Got a Rocket in My Pocket [and the fuse is lit]," ain't it wild?* It was a nerd conversation in what may as well have been Klingon to outsiders.

Fast-forward twenty years, Dex's manager sent me a demo out of the blue with a note asking if I might be interested in releasing an album, and so Dex improbably (or inevitably?) came to Bloodshot, bringing his undiminished gift for finding unmarked tombs behind the gaudy church of Rock and Roll with him. His first album for us, the *Ruins of Berlin*, featured *Dex-ified* versions of songs by Benny Joy, Billy Boy Arnold, Kitty Lester, and many others. The duets with Dex acolytes Neko Case, Cat Power, and Exene Cervenka, as well as Jack White chipping in praise to spread the gospel—"Dex Romweber was and is a huge influence on my music. I owned all of his records as a teenager. He is one of the best-kept secrets of the rock n roll underground"—got the attention of my partner and the staff who did not yet appreciate what Dex meant to those of us dedicated to the Dig.

On his second Bloodshot record, *Is That You in the Blue?*, he included a jumpy rendition of "Brazil," a song I'd first heard on the Tav Falco's Panther Burns 1981 Rough Trade release *Behind the Magnolia Curtain*—the seminal Memphis-based tangle of bordello blues and psychobilly sideshows. It was an album that turned me on to raw, sloppy, and inspired takes on Leadbelly, Johnny Burnette, and Sun Records second-teamer Ray Harris, among others. Panther Burns' version of "Brazil" sounded like a reverb-soaked bossa nova played in Kurt Weill's dungeon. I had subsequently tracked down the original by 1940s bandleader Xavier Cugat but was curious where Dex had heard it; maybe there was some other deranged version he could point me towards. “Man, I got that from a Tav Falco record,” he told me. Lineages intersected, worlds collided, rock and roll bees cross-pollinated. Travelling those independent-minded roads decades ago in high school, while liberating, was often lonely. But Dex and I were getting damaged by the same song from the same album, and we were now working together, in our own ways, to keep that cultural undercurrent flowing steadily and stealthily to ears willing or unsuspecting. We had already been tied together.

These artists had created lasting music in my record collection and became guides, lodestars, and lifeboats. My past musical worlds were meeting me in my present, heading to a future. To think of their shows I had seen, the incalculable hours I spent immersed in their music and scouring their liner notes, and to what and where those shows and records led, I wouldn’t be who I was without them. When they asked us to be a part of their expedition, it was like a bill coming due from rock and roll karma, and for me. There was an elementary imperative to simultaneously pay that back and pay it forward. A few years later, when I needed it most, Dex sent me a note: “Been wanting to tell you that you were 1 of the coolest if not the coolest record company guy I worked for. I mean that.” How could I not feel like I’d succeeded in some small measure by contributing to that continuum?

* * *

We also couldn’t resist the pull of intriguing one-off collaborations, thematic records, and bands who couldn’t tour more than three weeks a year. Working solely with artists who might “make it” had a joyless, mercenary tang to it, and these releases ultimately made up a distinct part of the soul of Bloodshot. I would not be deterred by what others saw (or heard) as foolishness. The Call of the Brown Shoes was too strong in me.

Could Austin’s the Meat Purveyors, the skunk tossed into the tent of stoic bluegrass revivalism, more Brothers Buzzcock than Brothers Stanley, more boots work than boots cowboy, ever break wider? Or Jim and Jennie & the Pinetops, who, behind Jennie’s voice—as fragile and powerful as a Walker Evans dustbowl photograph—wove Southern rock and bluegrass idioms into the universal dread and creak of Harry Smith’s *Anthology of American Folk Music?* Or North Carolina’s Trailer Bride, whose marrow-deep spookiness reminded me of a blind date with the Gun Club and Bobbie Gentry? Their languid vibe had the force equivalent of kudzu burying the rusting hulks of abandoned cars by the roadside, persistent and patient. Singer Melissa Swingle’s lyrics recalled ancient skirmishes with God, sex, and death fought in dark forests where *Apocalypse* was not just a word, but a living presence, and while she may have had a voice like blackberry syrup, one got the feeling she might have buried her last lover under the porch steps. What about Maggie Björklund? From a biz perspective, a solo record by an unknown, female Danish pedal steel guitarist did not check the boxes of a Prudent Label Executive. Her producer, an old friend, handed me her debut album at South by Southwest to see if we were interested. *Coming Home* had Calexico as her backing band and featured guest vocals by Mark Lanegan and Vizqueen's Rachel Flotard. Maggie's sound straddled delirium and ecstasy with its blend of country, indie rock, film scores, and psychedelia. It was the bead of condensation rolling down a beer glass in a dusty cantina, the sound *after* the gunfight when the vultures circling overhead look like doves. I could not get the album out of my head, I *had* to put it out, and, to me, those were the best records *to* put out.

Bloodshot was also in a city flush with talent. Need a twenty-feet-from-stardom backup singer? Nora O'Connor, Neko Case, Sally Timms, Kelly Hogan, and the Texas Rubies' Jane Baxter Miller were a phone call or an El stop away. If you were an inveterate liner notes reader like I was, you would have noticed a lot of the same names—Dave "Max" Crawford, John Rice, Deanna Varagona, John Forbes, Mike Hagler, Anna Fermin, Ken Sluiter, Edith Frost, Lawrence Peters, Harry and Dave Trumfio, Scott and Chris Ligon, Tom Ray, Dan Massey, Steve Rosen, Andrew Bird, and literally dozens of others—contributing their skills to multiple albums and artists throughout our catalog. Even if they weren't known outside the city limits, or even within them, this pool of creative and generous musicians enabled the scene to come, and stay and grow, together. While there might not have been a compelling *industry* reason to produce albums by in-our-own-backyard artists like Dollar Store, Devil in a Woodpile, Nora O'Connor, Al Scorch, or the Riptones, their releases elevated the whole scene around us. It was a pride in place, a desire to show the world our town, rather than a coherent business strategy.

In 2010, Jon Langford and I flew to Sydney, Australia, to finish a project he'd been working on with Roger Knox, a.k.a. the Koori King of Country. With crushing jet lag, we teetered through the Royal Botanical Gardens, beneath fruit bats the size of housecats and spiders the size of salad plates, stumbled into a van, and rode to the hinterlands of Tamworth (past, I was told by our driver, the prodigious ranch of AC/DC guitarist Malcolm Young). At the studio—which, if it wasn't in the *middle* of nowhere, was walking distance to it—we were greeted by trees full of colorful birds that screeched like car alarms and warnings about various spikey and bitey nature bits. At some point, Roger just . . . materialized . . . burned sage to cleanse us and the studio, and we got to work.

Stranger in My Land was a collection of songs written by indigenous Australian artists influenced by the American country music they heard via GIs in World War II. Without this album, some might have been lost forever. Behind Roger's honeyed bear hug of a voice, this was powerful material, heartbreaking and hilarious, downtrodden and uplifting, protest and celebration, suffused with longing, alienation, and resilience. This music from a largely unknown context possessed the urgency of an Alan Lomax field recording. It was an affirmation of the universality of music and the remarkable possibilities of cross-cultural pollination. Roger was closing the circle on a strange odyssey that took the stories of his people around the planet and back again to America. It was one of the most important records we ever released, but it was recorded in multiple studios, in multiple countries, on multiple continents; there were plane tickets to and from faraway places, musician fees, immigration hassles, and several other demands unique to the project. It cost a relative fortune, the appeal was negligible, there would be no more than a handful of tour dates, and there was no way I *wasn't* going to find a way to do it.

Did the job, family, or stylistic constraints that diminished the commercial prospects of these enticing projects and artists render them unworthy? I never thought so, and my long fascination with bygone indie labels, and the eccentricities they championed, taught me to not judge opportunities solely through an economic prism. Just as talking myself *into* a record because it might ring a few bells on the fickle *Hit-O-Rama Success Barometer* was bad, talking myself *out* of a record because of bothersome, non-music considerations was even worse; one could always find a reason to *not* do something. I remained open to what might blow through the windows and into my ears at any time, guided by that punkish spirit of *why not.*

18

One Never Knew

Wherever the artists or albums came from, I felt that spark, a sensation of possibility, connection, and yes, maybe even some feather-ruffling for good measure. Here are a few emblematic examples that made perfect sense to me at the time. They still do.

In the autumn of 1997, a writer and fan of our compilations from Toronto had sent us a local, independently released debut album he had flipped over, *The Virginian*, by a singer named Neko Case. Opening the office mail was recent Chicago via Atlanta transplant and Bloodshot's second paid employee, Kelly Hogan. (Our first, Steve Dubé, had come to us as a bushy-tailed volunteer. We punished his competency and eagerness by hiring him. $500 a month! Don't spend it all in one place!) Not unlike me, she had moved to Chicago to get away from music.

Hogan liked the cover photo and played the CD. Her pop-savvy sensibilities were tickled immediately by Neko's earwormy "Timber" and "High on Cruel," and the bubble gum twang on the Everly Brothers' "Bowling Green." She played the album not once, not twice, not thrice, but over and over and over. When she walked by my desk on her way to the bathroom, she was humming it; when she was on the phone on hold, she was absent-mindedly scatting it. I began to kinda hate the record.

One of my painting clients back then—since Bloodshot was still years away from providing me income for extravagances like food and rent—was the Chicago Children's Museum on Navy Pier. Galleries and exhibits with lots of bright, expensive colors changed every few months, and the head designer changed his mind not infrequently, telling us to redo rooms because they weren't "tangerine" enough. Since we were paid by the hour, change colors to your heart's content! My painting partner and I would show up early, tape off the gallery, and get to it. While rolling out some vibrant color one day, we noticed a clutch of children forsaking the thoroughly researched and thoughtfully laid out educational exhibits so they could watch the miracle that is paint-to-wall application. Hogan, whom I'd hired for the gig since she had paint-slinging experience of her own, stage whispered a warning to them, "Pay attention in school."

Our radio wasn't allowed when the museum was open, so to burn the hours, drown out the din of gleeful and distraught mobs of children, and distract ourselves from the powerful doses of birth control etched into the haggard faces of parents, we played word games, especially one that came to be known as "The City Game." One of us would say Paris, *par exemple,* and the next person would have to name a city that started with the last letter, an "S." Springfield. Detroit. Tokyo. Omaha. Amsterdam. On it went until someone got stumped and they were eliminated. As the obvious and famous hot spots were used up, the Georgia-born Hogan, whenever it seemed like she might be cornered, pulled a Kudzutown or Balls Ferry out of her spattered overalls. Her mind was packed with hamlets from deep in the swamps to obscure mountain passes. We couldn't call bullshit on her, it was pre-cell phone and internet, and she said them with such confidence they had to exist. After she'd won a few games in a row, we added rules like "a place a person possessing moderate geographical knowledge would have a reason to know about." She'd then toss out a Newnan with a stone-faced, *obviously it's the hometown of Atlanta Braves star and teenage heartthrob Dale Murphy*, or Tallapoosa, home of the famous Possum Drop. She couldn't be beat, but time was passed.

Once the museum closed and the crib lizards were herded elsewhere for naps or tantrums, though, our boombox came to life. And she had brought that damn Neko CD. I don't know, maybe it was the sweet, chemical fumes of Fiesta Pink and Pixie Green, or that she had ground down my will, but I did not object. When at some point I found I was humming the album in my head on bike rides or waiting for a bus, I knew I had been beat again. Neko's voice—with its depth, warmth, and *knowing*—finally set the hook in me. There was something waiting, something as yet unknown, lurking on the other side of this record. Phone calls were made, and a few weeks later Hogan and I were at CMJ in New York meeting Neko and her sister in corn, the endearingly loony and inexplicably under-known Carolyn Mark.* Plans were then hatched to rerelease the record in the United States early the next year.

The first time I met Toronto's polymathic Sadies, they had opened for and backed Neko at Lounge Ax on her album release tour. Their wigged-out surf, bluegrass, garage, punk, and country attack shrouded in cigarette smoke and shiny suits meant business. They were a quasi-psychedelic '70s work of string art, style-nails pounded into a board and connected by one long guitar string that spelled S-A-D-I-E-S. After the show, Neko and the band got to my apartment—they were crashing with me—and stayed up until dawn playing records, the bond between musician dorks and label dork sealed over Coasters and Tarheel Slim sides.

At some point that night, Neko pulled *Thrillsphere* (PopLlama Records) by Girl Trouble off my LP rack. They were a garage band out of Tacoma, Washington, that recorded early on for Sub Pop, but the Pacific Northwest industry feeding frenzy passed them

* "I'm midnight drunk, but it's only eight o'clock!"—Carolyn Mark, CMJ, New York, 1996.

over because they were more into the Sonics than Sabbath. Like many of my favorite bands, what they lacked in technical proficiency, they made up for with a shimmying preoccupation for what they did and who they extracted it from—the Wailers, Mr. Lucky & the Gamblers, and Don & the Goodtimes, anyone? I had seen them with eleven other people at Lounge Ax a couple years before and they turned the night into a lava lamp and cheap wine dance party in your weirdest friend's basement. Twelve people? It didn't matter. They were on a mission. Neko played a song from the album titled "Neko Loves Rock 'N' Roll" and danced/wobbled around my living room claiming the song was about her. As if this "Neko" was a real person. *No, really. That's me. I'm that Neko.* And so she was. Neko was "Neko." The circle will be unbroken. By the end of that summer, the Sadies recorded their debut album, *Precious Moments*, with Steve Albini, and we were on our way.

* * *

Deanna Varagona, baritone saxophonist for Bobby Bare, Jr. and Nashville alt-genre luminaries Lambchop, often stayed in my guest room for stretches while in Chicago for work. In the spring of 2007, she asked if a friend of hers coming to town to play a house concert could crash in the basement for a few days. Sure, my two-flat had become, to the consternation of the next door neighbors, something of a flop house for musicians anyway. Justin Townes Earle showed up one night, all denim, angles, and elbows. He carried a well-worn guitar case and a vintage suitcase out of a William Wyler film. I made pasta for the three of us. He ate like he might never get the chance again.

The next day when I got home from work, he was in my living room, my Meade Lux Lewis, Champion Jack Dupree, and Mance Lipscomb LPs scattered around him. We hung out and talked music, baseball (afflicted with Cubs Fever, the poor lad was), and Civil War historian Shelby Foote. I loaned him my copy of Ambrose Bierce short stories and pointed him to "An Occurrence at Owl Creek" in particular. Justin was both warm and deadly serious as he played my Sleepy John Estes and Pogues records and talked about their influence on him. He put on Mississippi John Hurt's "Make Me a Pallet on the Floor" and, as the side played, he rattled off licks and snippets that were mirages from other songs, other genres, other times, with a palpable intensity. The kid knew his shit. He asked if I was coming to the show that night. I hedged. While I was a fan of his dad, Steve Earle, I knew nothing of Justin's music and, as Pete Rose Jr. could attest—two base hits and a .143 lifetime batting average—past wasn't prologue. But weekday boredom and the prospect of novelty nudged me out of the house.

The concert was at a modestly grand North Shore manor. The thirty or so invited guests were mostly righteous old lefties who had done very well for themselves, the horseshoe shaped driveway filled with shiny SUVs. The cathedral-ceilinged living room was decorated at the height of Restoration

Hardware chic, with vases of willow branches and a neatly stacked pile of birch logs by the fireplace that would never be used. Guests came up to him one after another and told him how they loved his dad, when they had seen him last, and how great his dad's *Guitar Town* album was. He was the youngest person there by half. I made myself semi-invisible at the buffet in the artfully rustic dining room. The elegant cheese plate was not what I was used to in my family—as a rule, a choice between "white" or "orange"—and I was enamored by the charcuterie spread, before I was entirely sure what *charcuterie* meant. I found a chair in the back, and, with nonexistent expectations, waited for Justin to start playing in the space in front of the fireplace and the pyramid of never-to-be-burned logs. I thought how this show, and house concerts like it, shared the same pure-hearted, DIY motivation of the early punk shows I experienced, even if the surroundings and presentation were so very different. And with cheese.

Justin stepped through the crowd, bending his stork legs around chairs and end tables, said hi to the room, and immediately commanded the "stage." He stalked, he stomped, and he played his guitar like a percussion instrument. He seemed to be staring—or glaring—at something off in the middle distance the entire time, as if he were chasing something down or keeping something at bay; it was riveting. Halfway through the second song, the room and the audience melted away in a form of tunnel vision. I *knew* I had to be involved with the guy. The next morning in my dining room, we shook hands. He appreciated that I didn't give a shit who his dad was, that he wouldn't have any hometown pressure of being Steve Earle's son, and he could come to a Chicago label and just be himself.

* * *

The South by Southwest festival presents a particular show-going experience. A place of business, normally a restaurant, nail salon, or boot store becomes an Official Showcase Venue. Move a few tables, cram a Peavey PA into a corner, demark a "stage" on the floor with reflective tape, hire an exasperated, nicotine-tanned soundman with breath like a musty rug, and a dude with FTW knuckle tattoos to watch the door, and *presto*! It's a music venue! Now, wedge in as many lanyarded Music Industry Professionals as possible and serve margaritas the color of radiator fluid that are simultaneously too sweet and too acidic. Then present one band after another. Top of the hour. Every hour. All night. All week. Set up fast, play fast, break down fast. Factory work. For tourists, a blur of sound to regale those back home about the *crazy* Austin nightlife. For industry weasels, an expectation for the band to magically *get in the moment*, lay it out there and sell it, *em-effer*, sell it. *Make me love you. Go! You've got thirty minutes.**

---

* In reality, more like two songs.

This was the environment in which I first saw Lydia Loveless. Based on my appreciation of a brash, self-released CD we'd been sent by her manager, I swallowed my revulsion at the Spring Break with a Texas Twist gauntlet of Sixth Street, home to the similarly *gen-u-wine* cultural offerings offered on the streets Beale, Broad, and Bourbon, and wormed into her showcase. The venue was an "Irish" grill and bar. Guinness was available—though profanely served in plastic cups—so too were cross-cultural menu abominations like corned beef tacos. The diminutive Lydia disappeared in the crowd when people squeezed past, in front of, and around her. Behind her was a bassist who looked and played like he'd rather be in Anthrax and the poor drummer's ass practically hung out the window to Sixth Street from the hastily assembled riser next to the window.

Well, one never knew.

After a couple janky opening numbers due to shitty PA, shitty monitors, shitty nerves, or a dozen other plausible shitty reasons, Lydia and the band hit a stride . . . and fell out of it . . . and then found it again. It was rough, unvarnished, but . . . *but* there were moments when their grasp met their reach. The Bob Stinson/Pete Anderson mash-up guitarist and galloping bass were in the pocket, and her *voice*, so powerful, expressive, and urgent, cut through the clouds of bullshit swirling around me like pesky gnats, nerves transforming into *nerve*. Despite the unknowns—plans, goals, ability to tour, points of reference, musically or otherwise—I was in. No plate of O'Shaughnessy's tamales was going to get in the way of this.

* * *

Scott H. Biram, Austin's Dirty Old One Man Band, was in Chicago for a show at the Abbey Pub opening for Hank Williams III sideman Joe Buck when they burst into the office without warning. Scott talked fast and never stopped twitching, a street preacher high on his own supply of Jesus vs. Devil grudge match rocket fuel. "I know you don't sign metal bands, but I'm gonna be the first," he said and jammed his self-released CD in my hand and, just like that, he was gone. I looked around the office to make sure the staff had seen him as well, that I hadn't conjured the interaction out of whole cloth. Because I was somewhat frightened by him, I shelved the record. Then one day, just like that, I put it on. Maybe I was bored, maybe I was purging my backlog, maybe the Terry Gross *Fresh Air* interview that afternoon was about some showtune bullshit. I haven't stopped listening to Scott since.

It's been said that rock and roll came from the blues on the right hand and country on the left; Biram was the middle finger on both. With his '59 Gibson hollow body, mouth harp, and electrified stomp board, he played a potent brew of blues, classic country, bluegrass, rock and roll, punk, and heavy metal with *intent*. In Biram, I heard the tortured urgency of Hank alongside the gravelly wildness of Lemmy. I felt the rawness of Hasil Adkins, R. L. Burnside's Mississippi Hill Country blues drone, and the high and lonesome—emphasis on high—of bluegrassers like Jimmy Martin. This was revival tent fierceness sung with feet already half-way in the fires.

But did Biram *fit* Bloodshot? There were a hundred one-trick, one-man bands out there pummeling audiences with abrasive punk blues and wearing buckets on their heads. As I listened more and more, I tried to talk myself out of it. It wasn't country enough. It was too punk, it was too blues, it was too . . . *Shut up, brain.* Like staring at waterfalls or demolition derbies, it was best to let my vision blur a bit, let my ears go places that might not make linear sense, let detail slide away, let the chaos and beauty sharpen. And while Scott's persona often screamed head-banging and mosh pits, there was a song on the album with a true, beating country heart, "Wreck My Car," a jukebox hit at the honky-tonk behind the looking glass of CBGB. It was sad, sweet, and funny, like the best country songs are, and its quiet, resonance song took Scott beyond charges of witless gimmickry. And so, I gave in and bathed in the burning waters of Biram. As he growled on his classic song, "Blood, Sweat & Murder," from the CD he handed me that day in the office, *it might be baptism / or it might be a murder*. Either way, I had seen the light.

* * *

By the one a.m. slot on the Saturday night of any music festival/conference, pleasure has given way to survival. It is no longer about finding deep, meaningful connections through music, but managing dwindling stores of energy. Gin-soaked zombies plod heavily up hills only they can see between venues, and hollow-eyed writers sway like sea anemone at the back of the room, yearning for one last kick before returning to the real world of family, cubicle, and deadline. I was doing that same cadaver shuffle during the 2016 Americana Music Festival in Nashville, but I was *not* going to miss North Carolina's Sarah Shook & the Disarmers, who had been punished with that unenviable set time.

A couple of months earlier, our lead publicist had received their self-released album from a writer frustrated that this band was going unnoticed while many lesser talents were getting loads of coverage. He passed it on to me with an insistent "listen to this." I put it in a stack with other CDs to review on the way to the festival and drove to Nashville.*

I didn't get past their record. *Sidelong* played on repeat the better part of the trip. The band had a magnetism, both lean and edgy, sorely lacking in much of the often staid Americana realm. Sarah wrote with a startling bluntness. I was hearing what she'd seen: world wise, lessons learned—or not. Her sly turns of phrase were smart, funny, mean, and above all, uncompromising. From "Dwight Yoakam" was a country song couplet for the ages: "I'm drinkin' water tonight / 'Cause I drank all the whiskey this morning." The tune "Fuck Up" clinched it for me. Anyone can find a rhyme for "fuck up," but profanity without purpose was the difference between Sarah Silverman and Andrew Dice Clay. There was so much more to the song, a subversion of expectations, a heaviness and weariness, the hangdog lyrics kindling Saturday night regret and Sunday morning repent. The anger was as confrontational as it was concise and the humor as wry and resigned as a park bench prophet. They weren't playing for laughs. I couldn't wait to see them.

About a dozen people made it to a room that held three hundred for the final show of the day and the festival. The night was winding down, glasses were being cleaned and chairs getting stacked, and somewhere in a back office the week's monies were being tallied. Everyone was ready to go home. Looking out at that mostly empty space, instead of playing like they had nothing to gain, they played like they had nothing to lose. Sarah stalked the line between vulnerable and menacing, her voice strong *and* uneasy, country classic but with contemporary tension, and the Disarmers hit the sweet spots from Bakersfield to Alphabet City, as simple and muscular as the Buckaroos' Don Rich, and as downtown shady as Johnny Thunders. It was a spin in the

* *Of course* I drove. If I flew, how could I stop at Shirley Mae's Café in Louisville for so-tender-you-don't-need-teeth spareribs and banana pudding luscious enough to weep over?

suicide seat of a '77 Olds without seat belts: half joy ride and half escape. I was sold.

Talking to me beforehand, Sarah was blunt that, as a single mom, she had considerable touring limitations. Day jobs, bills, and responsibilities precluded the *let's put out a record and hit the road forever* scenario of so many rock bio pics. There were plenty of reasons not to do it from a business standpoint, but I knew there would be a way.

* * *

And back to Kelly Hogan. She kept opening the Bloodshot mail, calling radio stations and writers, and chatting endlessly. One night she said her friend, honky-tonk absolutist Dale Watson, was in town at Schubas, did I want to go? At some point during the set, Dale asked her on stage. *She sings?* I thought. They duetted on the Conway Twitty and Loretta Lynn chestnut "After the Fire Is Gone," and the room lost its collective mind. *What the everlasting fuck is this person doing working other people's music* . . . After the show, I fired her. Sort of. She kept working the phones, but her musical itch needed scratching again. She recorded compilation tracks, singles, sang on records by the Sadies, Alejandro Escovedo, Pine Valley Cosmonauts, Decemberists, Jakob Dylan, Mavis Staples, and more, ultimately releasing her own solo albums and rising, according to Andrew Bird—with whom I will not disagree—to the level of "a national treasure." Like mine, her move to Chicago to escape music was not very effective.

That was my A&R "strategy." If I had stuck to a plan, a checklist, I would have missed the invigorating *oddnesses* that lurk away from the easy or the inevitable, the musical equivalents of Craig's BBQ in DeVall's Bluff, Arkansas. Sure, I referred to a road map now and then, but I never lost the thrill of stuffing it under the seat whenever a sign pointed to something curious.

Were you bothered when bands left for larger labels after you discovered them?

Regarding the idea of "discovering" artists, I'm sure the Wampanoag people were surprised to learn that they had been "discovered" by the settlers of the Plymouth colony. I was uncomfortable to take that sort of credit. I'd accept "early advocating," though.

But to the question: I thought it was a victory when a band moved on to a bigger label, and I did what I could to help them find a beneficial fit. Was the bigger label's interest genuine, or based on a perceived trend, or a "that label has a band like this, so we need one" scenario. I walked people through offers, making sure they knew what would be expected of them, and left the decision to them. When Neko Case was living in my coach house for a few weeks after the release of her second album, *Furnace Room Lullaby*, she started getting courted. The phone would ring, I'd pick up, and so and so from Major Label Records would ask to speak to her. While she covered the mouthpiece, I'd whisper to her, "Make sure you keep your masters, ask for complete creative control," etc. That it was done while she was in her pajamas on the couch while we watched *Night Court* reruns made it even more anti-glamorous and, well, insurgent.

Did you try to convince them to stay?

It wasn't a matter of convincing, it was usually the right time. We all understood the label's inherent—often self-imposed—limitations. We couldn't provide enormous recording budgets or tour buses, nor were we keen to operate in the unseemlier realms of the industry that one often found themselves in in the race to get ahead. The lifespan of a band can be so short I never faulted anyone for "going for it." We would have been doing them a disservice if they stayed.

Was it hard to say goodbye when they moved on?

It was bittersweet, and some folks left more gracefully than others, but ultimately, the goal was to get an artist I believed in heard by more people. If going up that ladder was the best way, then it was best not to stand in the way. I never wanted anyone on the label who didn't want to be there. And, regardless, we never stopped working on their behalf. Years after they left the label, we still promoted new releases and shows by the Old 97's, Neko Case, and others. We had Alejandro Escovedo and Justin Townes Earle participate

in parties and showcases. Robbie Fulks went to a major after his second album, *South Mouth*—a stone-cold masterpiece from beginning to end—but our work went on: advocating for his two Bloodshot records and growing his name and body of work wherever we could. These weren't *our* artists, or *our* records. They belonged to the community.

19

So You Want to Be a Rock 'n' Roll Star?

In 1999, on my way to the CMJ Music Marathon in New York City, I stopped to see my grandmother at her small farm in Utahville, Pennsylvania. (Draw a straight line between Altoona and Punxsutawney, and somewhere in the middle you'd be close.) While I was there, her sister, my great aunt, died, and I took Grandma to the funeral chapel the next hollow over for the service. The chapel stood hard against the two-lane route that was the sole way in or out of town for any coal truck, lumber truck, or pickup truck with a failing exhaust system, and a graveyard sloped up to a gothic tree line. The sky was ash gray and the exposed slate ridges above town were slate gray. An autumn storm had settled in for a week and the leaves were too miserable and colorless to be bothered to fall off the trees yet. I was not out of place in my work boots and denim jacket. The only tie in the building was on the preacher.

After the service, I was recruited as a pallbearer. I'd seen pallbearers in action on TV: dignitaries and mourners in matching suits fluently rolling a casket on a brass bier to a waiting hearse polished to a high shine. Here, pallbearer was not an honorary position. Six different-sized-and-aged men awkwardly held a casket with the very real weight of a body in it. We were to go outside to the slanting rain, and up a sodden hill to an un-tented hole where a Bobcat and two men in rain slickers waited. This was not ceremony, this was function, a literal burden that needed bearing.

As we girded ourselves to the waiting weather, the preacher, standing at the foot of the casket, said some final words about the departed sister, the flock less one. Then he looked at me and said, "You're Ellen's grandson. She tells me you're in the country record business. My daughter sings the gospel music. Can I give you a tape?"

My brain melted as my eyebrows arched. I felt as if the whole chapel were staring at me and thinking *there's got to be a better time for this.* Even as we stood there, there was a VFW hall up the road, with people beginning to gather for the communal rituals of mourning, bearing casseroles, trays of baked chicken, ham with pineapple slices from a can, a dozen macaroni and Jell-O salads, Styrofoam cups of unnaturally red fruit drink, and urns of coffee. And pies. Sweet Mother of the Lardy Crust, the *pies*! *How about we wait until then?* I pled with my eyes. He put his Bible *on* the casket and gave himself a full two-handed frisk. Why did he even have a cassette on him in the first place? Did Grandma set me up?

The other pallbearers expressed either curiosity or annoyance. Or complete disinterest. I couldn't tell. I was in no position to politely explain the context of our tiny label's impractical adventures in merging punk rock muscle with the tropes of classic country music, that the worlds of *American Idol*, Grammys, and *The Masked Singer* were as far away from me as Tyson Chicken Niblets were from the Platonic ideal of a chicken fried steak at Stroud's in KCMO. In this faded mining outpost whose heyday—such as it ever was—was at least two generations past, I was simply "the music guy from the city." He found the cassette and handed it to me. The doors opened, and the pre-autumnal wind hit us and out we went, trying not to slip in the mud.

* * *

As I said, I was heading to CMJ, where hundreds of bands went every year to get discovered and make it "big." Or at least get wasted on vodka and Red Bulls, take selfies in CBGB's bathroom, and act like a rock star in the Big Apple for a long weekend. With so much music, what, bands asked, did I listen for? Could I distill that process to a sentence?

Anything I had to say on the matter was wildly subjective. I didn't consult pie charts, Venn diagrams, or feasibility studies to build a roster. I didn't have to worry about growth agendas, shareholders, broadening our portfolio into diversified sectors, or keeping up on the payments for the infinity pool at the CFO's Aruba getaway. So, to the potential signee looking for guidance, some of what I have to say might be hard to take, just like your demo.

Zing! I'll be here all week.

First, let's flip the question for a few minutes. Before asking *How* to convince someone to commit brains, hearts, and wallets to your music, it is only fair that you first ask *Why?* Answer with brutal honesty. What are your goals and expectations? To make a living as a musician? To hit the road, see the world (or at least the greater Midwest) every few months, have some laughs, and possibly meet comely personages of the opposite/same/undetermined sex on a somewhat regular basis? Is it a bucket list item to be checked off, or a *before we have kids* last hurrah? Or does your message burn with the heat of a thousand volcanos and it must be shared with the world?

Is the goal to make a record? Again, why? To document this time and place, this group of friends playing together? Because you sell out the local dive bar every month and go home with a warm fuzzy in your soul? Because hi-fivey, shot-buying guy told you that *you rule and you're better than 90 percent of that fuckin' shit on the radio, you should make a record*? Are you the band with the cool record store clerk on guitar—every town has one—who has 1,300 LPs, espouses the merits of Let's Active and Roky Erickson, and effortlessly writes hooks that light up the club? That's great. Really. These are totally legit reasons for you and your buddies to pool some dough and knock out a record. It *is* fun, it *is* rewarding, and bands like these are the beating heart of every local, indie social circle.

But making a living in music is dirty work that takes time, focus, and incessant effort. "Getting signed" will not, in and of itself, move you from playing for tips on Half-Price Pitcher night at the Dew Drop Inn to the Bonnaroo farm any more than putting greasepaint under your nose makes you Groucho Marx or going to church makes you a Christian. You need ambition, courage, and arrogance to overcome the unceasing obstacles that *will* be thrown in your path, to carry on in the face of seeming futility. Even then, there are no guarantees. Many a great band or powerful song has been shunted aside in favor of some telegenic, endorsement-friendly, flavor-of-the-month pap.* The septic-tank metaphor—that only the big chunks rise to the top—is depressingly apropos too much of the time.

So, if you already have a career that involves schedules, sensible shoes, and 401Ks, if there are familial responsibilities, mortgages, or an alpaca farm to tend to, if that hook-smart record store dork—in between rants about how the Surfaris weren't fit to carry the Ventures' Mosrites—can't tour, it's best for everyone to leave a label out of it. You would be quite insane to throw away your stable source of income, ready access to clean sheets, fresh fruits and vegetables, and a bathroom that hadn't been recently used by Taco Bell–eating bandmates, to chase a long shot wrapped in an improbability and deep fried in an unlikelihood. Put the record out on your own and be content, and proud, to sell a few hundred to local fans, stores, and friends. You might even make a few bucks at the end of the day. Keep a realistic perspective and you will enjoy the experience immeasurably more. We can't take your career more seriously than you. A record deal should not be the goal; it can be a means to the goal, but that leads right back to defining what that goal is.

OK, you've answered questions and defined goals, and yes, you still want to run into this tunnel of crazy. Now, you wonder, who to approach?

- Before sending anyone anything, do basic research about what a company does. Bloodshot was a label, that was it. We were not an

---

* When asked his opinion about a friend of mine's band, a major label executive told her manager that "her ass was too big, and she needs a nose job." The music was, at best, a secondary consideration.

entertainment or management conglomerate, nor an employment referral service for songwriters, drummers, tour managers, or session guitarists. We would not pitch your songs to artists, even ones we received about Barack Obama (pro and con) and Princess Di (also, weirdly, pro and con). And while we certainly didn't need a polished album for our purposes, sending a "developing project" with the kicker that "We will finish the songs once we have an agreement" missed the point. Asking me to finish your song was like asking the maître-d at standout Chicago restaurant Girl & the Goat to cook your food.

I was also not interested when the four-time National Beard & Moustache Champion contacted us for representation, or the stylist/image consultant sent us a "demo" and an offer to "remake" one of our artists for free. (How *dare* they! Our artists were perfect just the way they were!) A professional juggler looking to move to "the next level" (more chainsaws?) sent us a packet with an 8×10 glossy photo showcasing his impressive mullet, spangled vest, and various objects—bowling pins, daggers, colored balls—hanging in air, being juggled, testimonials from satisfied club owners but no DVD or VHS cassette to confirm his talents. My all-time favorite was a CD from a ventriloquist. Let that sink in. A CD. From a ventriloquist. I don't mean to brag, but on CD I am also a brilliant ventriloquist.

- Make a list of bands who track well with what you do, of artists you admire or have been influenced by. Are there labels that tie them together? If so, follow the leads and dig into their catalogs. While appreciation of twee pop, hip-hop, hardcore, noisecore, emo, and techno varied from person to person in the office, they didn't fit our roster. (Based solely on the Bloodshot name, we attracted a lot of confused Death Metal and Gangster Rap interest). A Casio keyboard synth-pop country single, "hotforyou.com," addressed the tribulations of courting in the computer age, and it was pretty damn catchy (twenty years on, I can still hum it), but its cheese factor was next-level cheddar. We received a proposal from someone looking to transition out of his current career as a porn actor and into his first love: music. He sent a filmography and links to performances on stage and, um, elsewhere, but it was his painful alt-folk that did him in.*

I've heard rooms go wild over someone belting it from the Mariah Carey School of Soulful Over-Singing that was technically impressive, but . . . *wait, oh Christ, is this a song about sparrows?* . . . left me clammy. You don't internet-date without seeing pictures or pertinent details first, so, for everyone's sake, put at least as much forethought into a potential artistic partnership as you would in finding a hangout for the 4:15 p.m. set on the Saturday Green Stage at Pitchfork. Don't

* Judging by his *curriculum vitae*, baby face, and diminutive stature, he plied his trade in the MILF/horny, inexperienced stepson genre, if you were wondering.

think "yeah, we will be the exception." We filled dumpsters with the demo packages of such exceptions.

- Read about the label to understand where they fit within the broader label terrain. A lot can be learned by what they consider a score, how they handle it, and what *their* goals are. Do they balance "big" artists and "cult-ish" ones? Do they have long-standing relationships with artists who are not, in eyes of The Industry, big sellers? If something doesn't "hit," what happens next? Do they have a "one-straitjacket-fits-all" approach to marketing, using the same coterie of highly placed (and priced) publicity and promotions companies? Do they have partnerships with sponsors or bigger labels that might influence both roster *and* content? In short, are they an independent that acts like, or wishes it were, a major? And, to go back to the beginning, how does this information relate to the assessment of *your* goals and expectations?
- Respect policies on unsolicited demos; ignoring them will vex the recipients. Do not blindly contact every label in a database you got your eager paws on; blanket submissions addressed to Alligator Records, ZTT Records, and everyone in between assures that your inbox will fill up with anatomically inventive suggestions as to where to stick your album.

Following these simple suggestions will save you time, money, and the embarrassment of ending up on a Wall of Shame. (See appendix D.)

After winnowing labels down to a manageable list to intelligently approach, the question becomes: *What should I send*?

- Follow the time-honored adage of KISS: *Keep It Simple, Stupid*: send the best you've got and be concise. Indie label folks are overworked, underpaid, jaded, cynical, and snarky, and we've seen all the tricks to spark our interest. Don't send shirts, baseball caps, or silk-screened posters from your residency at a bar we'd never heard of or been to; save them to sell to your fans. We received demos with samples of locally distilled potables, one even came with a pizza, and while such accompaniments were welcome, the music was typically not; no amount of your bestie's moonshine or cornmeal-dusted artisanal dough topped with arugula and prosciutto and fired in a *forno bravo* made a bad demo good.
- Don't stuff your package with press clippings from the *Traverse City Nurses College Gazette* or endorsements from the door guy at Cooter's Bar. Spare the good label people Xeroxed pages of lyrics and radio charts showing that your self-released album reached #178 on a station in Halden, Norway. Fancy vellum cover sheets sent by law offices with imposing letterheads representing artists who were "a perfect fit for Bloodshot" got quickly shuffled to the bottom of the pile; vellum

reminded me of college term papers, and you did *not* want me thinking about my twenty-six page masterpiece, "The Development of the Flying Buttress in Medieval Church Architecture," when I should have been paying attention to your demo.*

- Skip the name-dropping: listing artists who used the same studio/producer/mixing console/engineer/dog walking service that you did would not elevate my opinion of your music. Just as standing in a garage doesn't make you a 1968 candy-apple-red Dodge Charger R/T, neither does recording a demo at Electric Lady Studios make you Hendrix. Given my weakness for rattily recorded old punk, blues, and rockabilly, I never put a premium on pristine anyway. Nor did we pay attention to lists of bands you've "shared the stage with." We knew what that meant: you *opened* for them; you were the first band on a six-band bill; "sharing" was not involved.
- If directing someone to video content, it better not be a YouTube link of a show recorded on your buddy's iPhone as he's being jostled in the crowd or trying to hit on the woman next to him; *yeah, I'm working with the band, can I buy you a White Claw?* Four minutes of tuning and banter isn't charming or funny. If I clicked on something and the band didn't jump right into an engaging performance, you'd already lost me.

In short, submit a few songs that get to the heart of what you do and directions to a website or a local show where I can learn more if interested. As my Italian barber I used to go to in Roscoe Village (whose name was, no joke, Sal Mineo) would say with a great flourish when he finished, "basta con la pasta." As in, *that's it.*

What if you didn't have a demo yet, due to lack of funds, connections, or know-how? Then prepare thyself to impress The Label at a frightful "showcase"—such as those filling every conceivable nook and cranny of CMJ and South by Southwest—that held the potential of every snag being magnified, and no one feeling good about it when it was over. All kinds of things could go wrong. Maybe you didn't get a soundcheck and couldn't hear the guitar until the next-to-last song; your drummer had a stomach flu, and the bassist was still pissed at the singer for buying a gas station burrito; the soundperson repeatedly interrupted your set to fix the kick drum mic, giving the crowd extended flashes of ass crack; the temperamental PA system made you sound like Limp Bizkit, and not in, *er,* a good way. From the stage you hear drinks being ordered and mixed, the soda gun, the scoop in the ice bin, the pint glass washer, the Ms. Pacman game in the corner, and the barback thoughtlessly

* Handy homeowner tip: unwanted demo CDs, which is to say most of them, can be hung in sheds, barns, garages, or under eaves, where they will deter hornets, wasps, and birds from nesting. You're welcome.

dragging a garbage can by the stage. Cell phones go off and people cheer the touchdown on the big-screen TV during the moving ballad about your mother dying. Techno throbs from the club below and some numbnut yells "Free Bird," opening the floodgates of stupid to more ironic requests. God help you if there is a pool table in the room. And you are likely the opening band—we know the cruel indifference they encounter.

On my end, perhaps I was exhausted from seeing fourteen bands a day for a week at the festival, and during your set I was daydreaming about bonfires made of guitars. Maybe I had come from seeing a forgettable band whose joyless energy—*the songs rhymed, and they played them in time*—would have been put to better use digging wells. Or I saw a band that had a '70s saxophone sound so cheesy I couldn't stop thinking about cheap Chianti and lime-green shag carpeting. Maybe I was being ensorcelled by the bartender in a flowery sundress who made the perfect Negroni or distracted by the Tamale Guy at the Hideout. I might have even been hungover (it's happened), or my humors otherwise out of balance. I once missed out on a great band whose manager was imploring me to sign because I was paralyzed by a clinical depression at the time; Ike and Tina Turner circa 1963 could have been on stage that night and I wouldn't have cared, so deep was I in a gummy muddle. You just never know.

Tune out that tangential horseshit you can't control. Don't crumple under the chimera of the *big show*. This isn't the movies. The dream of label meets demo, band meets label, and they skip happily to the main stage at Coachella is the exception, not the rule. If a label wouldn't sign you because the doorperson forgot to put them on the list, there was some errant feedback during a solo, or someone pissed on their loafers in the cramped, mephitic men's room, then you didn't want them to anyway. I didn't carry a sheaf of contracts with me and wasn't going to rush up to you after the show, shoving aside groupies and hangers-on, to tell you, *baby, you've got it!* So don't play for me, a label, or a scout; play to your *fans*, even if there are only forty-four of them out there, and the other 1,956 are in your head. Go out there and *play it like you mean it*. That you *can* control.*

* Personally, for these and many more reasons, I hated putting bands in this situation: someone they'd never met standing in the back and coolly analyzing a performance (with, possibly, a cell to their ear, only half paying attention) while expecting them to *kill it* in thirty minutes or less. I never asked to be on the guest list for a band that I was "scouting"; it set up an expectation of quid pro quo. I was happy to support an up-and-coming band coming through town free from the added or implied industry smarminess. If I hated the show, I could sneak out guiltlessly without having to explain that I thought, "on a scale of 1 to 10, it was not so good," or ask, "Is that the way you intend to sound?" Nobody should lose a ticket sale for the "privilege" of my "judgement."

Totally straightforward now? But wait! Remember, independent labels are, by their very nature, products of their owner's idiosyncrasies; there *will* be hyper-specific pet peeves that could inexplicably doom *or* anoint your chances. (See appendix E.)

But, truthfully, even if one followed (or knew about) these guidelines with great diligence, it was still a crapshoot if the demo would get listened to. It may sit in a box for two years, or it might get noticed solely because of a glancing *Raising Arizona* reference in the bio. One day I opened an envelope with nothing in it except a CD and a handwritten note on a torn scrap of paper that said "Rocks" and a website address. I was seduced by mystery. Turned out it was doom metal from Iowa, but still, I listened. The endearing vagaries of the indie world.

* * *

What, then, is an artist looking for a good home to do in the face of this maddeningly imprecise advice? Carry on. Don't wait for me, don't wait for anyone. Don't let any label's reaction or non-reaction get you down. Learn something from every step, every night. Get on the bill with other bands on the labels you like when they come to your town and grab the room by the metaphorical throat. Develop a network that, regardless of whether you get signed or not, will benefit your career. Walk that thin line between persistence and irritation. You never know how and when you'll catch the ear of someone. If I didn't like what you were doing, and you thought that made me full of shit, then you were exactly right. Hold out for a partner who loves what you do. They are out there.

One day the office was startled when a wiry dude with long black hair and a stringy beard barged in with an acoustic guitar. He announced that he was fresh out of prison and had some songs he wanted to sing for us. Wow! What a find! What a story! *Play, good sir, play!* Alas, he was atonal, arhythmic, and more than a little scary. Still . . . he might have been amazing.

Returning to that chapel in Pennsylvania at the beginning of this chapter: yes, I did listen to the preacher's daughter's gospel tape and, no, it wasn't good. Her voice was thin and wavered around notes rather than landing on them. The music was a tinny keyboard with a flat, damp cardboard drum sound. But her dad was proud of it, and I'm sure she was too. Maybe she never made another tape, maybe she only sang in church or the shower.

But the thing was, I listened. I had to. I never know when or where I would find that particular needle in a haystack of needles. Putting faith in a checklist, reading the charts, or following the socials of industry pundits wouldn't, if I was true to my ears and my passions, lead me to it.

As for all the rules, tips, and guidelines I have thoughtfully laid out and backed with sober reasoning? I have ignored every last one of them, and would again without hesitation, if I heard *it*. I regretted the handful of times I went against that instinct.*

So what did I listen for? I sought guidance in the spirit of Supreme Court Justice and unwitting doyen of music criticism Potter Stewart who, when asked in 1964 how he defined pornography, replied, "I know it when I see it."

Hey, it turned out I *could* distill my process to a sentence after all! Heart over brains. Madness over market share. Conviction over caution. It's what makes independent music so great.

---

* I will take those names with me to the grave.

20

Rod & the Shades Walked into a Studio . . .

On a summer day in 1997, members of the Grievous Angels, the Volebeats, my former Wood Butcher bandmate Phil, producer Jim Diamond, and I were mucking about in Ghetto Recorders, the converted chicken slaughterhouse that served as a nerve center for Detroit's garage rock explosion. Beer was had. Someone had the bright idea to go to Tiger Stadium for some matinee baseball. More beer was had. From behind home plate—tickets bought from a guy on the Fisher Freeway bridge who kept them under his porkpie hat—we watched Justin Thompson pitch a masterful game for a Tigers win. Man, his curve was snapping that day. We adjourned to the studio where, perhaps, more beer was had. Noodling ensued. Tape rolled. And, by accident or mystical conjuring, Funkadelic's instrumental psychedelic freakout "Maggot Brain" started to emerge.

The Volebeats, as much myth as institution in the Motor City, who ask and answer the musical question "What would it sound like if Brian Wilson took Gram Parsons surfing, and Gram Parsons took Brian Wilson on a peyote safari?" provided the foundation. The Grievous Angels' pedal steel player summoned both neon-lit honky-tonks and black light–lit pot leaf posters with his woozy licks, and Phil's guitar took to flight and soared, his love of Eddie Hazel and Ennio Morricone transporting the session into a beery afternoon groove. When it was over, we weren't sure what had happened, and when it was time to press it up as a 7-inch single, it didn't fit on one side and so it spilled over to the B side. For the cover, we buried the good-natured Delilah's bartender Mary up to her neck—*can you brush that bug off my face?*—to recreate the iconic album cover. It was the most spontaneous single with zero commercial potential Bloodshot ever released. And I cherish it.

People regularly asked how involved the label was with the recording process. Was there a well-thought-out map from Point A to Album B? Did I roll into the studio on the first day of recording at the crack of four in the afternoon, roll up sleeves, turn amps to 11, stand over the console, aim my finger guns, and say, "Hit it?" While, yes, it may have been tempting to possess the despotic power of a Motown's Berry Gordy, to prosper in the environment we were creating of the uncertain and the uncharted, there had to be mutual trust, the recording process another element of our ongoing collaboration so vital to independent communities. When an artist said, "I'm going to try this . . .," I knew they wouldn't fly in the USC marching band or turn in an album of goth, or whatever the hell bro-country was, and they knew we wouldn't make them do things they didn't want to do to make them into something they were not.

As with our genesis stories—*who* to work with—the same individualized, intuitive approach informed *how* we worked with them. My years of house painting and stage and production managing had instilled the flexibility to be ready in whatever capacity I could. For input on logistics, recording, mixing, mastering, or sequencing, I would chip in for all of it, parts of it, or none of it. They could ask for advice, take advice, pretend they would take advice and then ignore it entirely, or not ever ask. Whatever they wanted.

When Kelly Hogan wanted me to help mix her *Because It Feel Good* album, I drove to Athens, Georgia (stopping at the Smith House in Dahlonega, Georgia, on the way for platters of fried chicken, turnip greens, and peach pie, served family style. Elbow to elbow with a friendly-to-the-point-of-creepy family, they asked if the music I was working on was godly or not. *Boy, this chicken's good, isn't it?* I deflected, *please pass the fried okra . . .*) One night in the studio, Hogan and I had what could be characterized as a spirited disagreement over a particular song. I went outside to the back of the parking lot and sat on a grassy knoll to let tempers cool, undoubtedly thinking, *when will she realize how right I am?*

A few minutes after returning to the control room to tackle the issue from another angle, I felt a burning sensation on my neck. Then my leg. Then my shoulder. Then my other leg. "Fire ants!" Hogan pointed. Before you could say *What manner of hellscape is Georgia*? I stripped to my boxers and Sun Records T-shirt right there in front of the console as I brushed them off me. I quickly began to feel not so well. Back at the house where we were staying, liberal amounts of lotions and ointments were applied and Advil consumed. Whether I won the argument, or it was conceded out of pity, I don't remember, but the resulting sublime torch songs for the dismayed sung by a haunted Dusty Springfield on a Staples Singers jag spoke for themselves. What was a few agonizing welts and a feverish night of half sleep? Anything for the team.

I went to Memphis for the Grievous Angels' *Miles on the Rail* mastering session, Payne's BBQ, and meat and threes at the Four Way. Feeling guilty about spending money on an indulgence like a hotel room near the studio, I found a cheap two-story, horseshoe-shaped motel in a less than desirable part

Artwork by Kathleen Judge.

of town, its marquee promising *Clean ro ms, A/C, Colo TV in ev ry room.* The band dropped me off and I inquired through the bulletproof lazy Susan about a room.* The clerk told me the rates and I gave him my credit card, catching a quick, mouthwatering waft of curry when he spun the Susan. Hanging out in the spartan lobby was a spindly, squirrelly guy in a cream-colored Rayon shirt. He asked me if I wanted any weed. *No, I'm fine.* Then he offered me coke, *sniff, sniffing* to, I suppose, clarify what he meant. *Uh, no. Thanks.* Did I want "a lady to lay with?" *What?* The clerk returned, told the guy to get out, asked if I *really* wanted to stay there as he handed me the key, a real old-school number with a bulky, rubberized handle of unknown origin as the fob. Off to my room I went, thinking, boy, the money I'm saving . . .

The TV didn't work one bit, and the AC worked even less. Before I shoved my bag under the bed for an illusion of security, I gave a quick scan with my Maglite. It looked like a mushroom garden, except they weren't mushrooms, they were used condoms. My bag spent the night next to me. I went to bed but did not sleep. I never took my shoes off. The next night, I slept serenely, and guiltlessly, under the mixing console.

To afford Eric "Roscoe" Ambel's production services for the debut album from local cabaret punks the Blacks, titled *Dolly Horrorshow,* he stayed at my apartment for a week. He got my room; I took the couch. Most nights after the session, we'd hang out on the back porch overlooking the alley, me with a beer and him with a joint, and talk about the record—a wild fusion of glam and rock, with X and Roscoe Holcomb as chimerical way stations. One night,

* Being from Detroit, I am not unaccustomed to conducting business through bulletproof glass, so it didn't immediately register as a red flag.

in the window of the coach house on the other side of the alley, we saw odd shapes shifting and contorting, the lamplight weaving and wobbling. It was a dude getting it on with his blow-up doll. We didn't stick around. We were not going to poison our eyeballs any further in the name of keeping costs low.

During the 1999 New Year's Day blizzard, I brought Andre Williams and the Sadies together in pre-renaissance Detroit's Ghetto Recorders to record.*

The streets went unplowed for days, and the mayor was imploring people over the radio to come shovel downtown sidewalks. There wasn't anything open nearby, no groceries, no party stores, no nothing. I had to walk eight blocks through knee-high snow in my Chuck Taylors to a liquor store to meet Andre's Captain Morgan needs. There were snowdrifts in the corner of the studio, we warmed our hands over tube amps and effects racks, survived on rice and beer, and went quite mad. We may as well have been on Hoth.

The results were as far out as they were unexpected. From the opening couplet of the lead track, "Hey Truckers," *Hey Truckers / Bad mother . . .* well, you can fill in the rest, what would become the *Red Dirt* album slathered country-soul smokers with Andre's gravelly *how da doin' ladies* growl while the Sadies Pollocked a slinky, spaghetti western garage-rock backdrop. Covers of Lefty Frizzell, Harlan Howard, a tormented version of Leon Payne's bizarro tale of tragedy and murder "Psycho" (brought to my attention years earlier by Australia's Beasts of Bourbon), and a Katy-bar-the-door take on Johnny Paycheck's "Pardon Me, I've Got Someone to Kill"—sung like he meant it—thrust Andre's tail feather right at unsuspecting underground country fans. And if I had a recording of the stories Andre told in the studio between takes, it would be a document of early rock and roll so outrageous that it would have to be true, even if (*especially* if?) it wasn't.

I had been a fan of the Detroit Cobras since I reviewed their first 7-inch single for a fanzine years before they landed at Bloodshot. Unearthing and reinvigorating the hits, near hits and sometimes total misses from the deep

* For the entire weeklong session, he called me "Rod" and the Sadies "the Shades." It was Andre Williams; he could call us whatever he wanted.

and groovy history of soul, and making them their own, the Cobras were *the* go-to party band for those in the know, recording albums that played like mix tapes for leather-jacketed romantics. Mary Ramirez's riffs powered ass-shaking anthems to good times, wild times, and the high and lows of L-U-V, doing justice to the legacies of both Motown and Detroit Rock City. Rachel Nagy's formidable voice seduced listeners from the pulpit of the Church of the Immaculate Irma Thomas, reaching all the way from the back pews to the barstool next to you. For their newest record, they were stretching out in the studio, trying new sounds, new approaches, fuller instrumentation, and they were a little unsure of the results. Did it still have that mojo, that *Cobra-ness*? Mary asked me to come to Detroit for a listen.

Sitting in Mary's car outside Slows BBQ in the shadow of what used to be the Michigan Central Train Station in the winter of 2007, she played me the rough mixes for their *Tied and True* album. This time around, the Cobras were putting their raw soul and punk stamp on obscurities like Gino Washington's Correc-Tone disc "Puppet on a String," Irma Thomas's Imperial release "Hurt's All Gone," and the Cookies' Dimension single "Only to Other People." Then the tape got to their take on Little Willie John's 1959 King Records romp, "Leave My Kitten Alone," a song I had been wild about for years. Detroiter Little Willie was best known, to the extent he was known at all, for "Fever," the torch song classic covered by both Peggy Lee and the Cramps (now *there's* a double bill . . .). I'd first heard his name via the Blasters' version of his song "I'm Shakin'" from their self-titled album released on Slash Records.* "Leave My Kitten Alone" was tough and feisty and had a background vocal groove that still floors me, and the Cobras had done up that song, all the songs, *right*.

After the tape played, I was quiet.

What do you think?

Here I was, listening to a killer new album, one that took some gutsy chances but remained true to the songs and to the band, in a mid-1970s Buick Riviera on Michigan Avenue with the guitarist from a band I had loved for years that was now on my label. My brain stumbled around like a crappy old computer with a faulty processing unit, thinking of what to say, how to frame my thoughts, what nuances to use, trying to be helpful.

She was getting kinda pissed.

You got nothing to say?

And here was a time where my experience, my know-how, my input, consisted solely of looking at her and saying, "That was fucking awesome."

---

* Jack White laid out that song for another generation on his *Blunderbuss* album. A member of his touring band, the Peacocks, and performing in the video for that song was Bloodshot solo artist and pedal steel guitarist Maggie Björklund. So many strands tying so much of the strange and wonderful fabric of underground music together.

* * *

Often our appeal was not what we did, but what we did not. Artists who had already clawed up a few rungs, carved out their own niche, and had little interest in doing laps in the septic tank again were attracted by our willingness to stay completely out of their way. *You mean I can turn in a record and not have it re-mixed, re-sequenced, re-mastered, or shelved indefinitely without my input or consent?* Robbie Fulks would walk into the office, make awkward small talk—something we both excelled at—hand me a finished recording, and walk back out. For Graham Parker, advice was neither asked for nor offered. Did Howard Cosell tell Muhammad Ali how to box? Methinks not. And what to do with someone like Wayne "the Train" Hancock, the Ramones of juke joint swing, so intractable and unmoving as to be subversive? In his elixir of western swing, blues, Texas rockabilly and big band, was a defiance that he wore like a chain mail Nudie suit. Suggesting that he alter his sound or approach would be like asking Louie Mueller's to serve White Castle sliders. After recording their *Whine de Lune* album, Trailer Bride's Melissa Swingle sent the tapes and sheepishly told me she had bought a banjo before the session and tried playing it on some of the new songs. *Oh brother,* I thought, no band on a budget should buy a banjo (or a harpsichord, or a sitar, or whatever) and use the studio to learn how to play it, but her accidental joyful noise added an element of hillbilly goth to their already uneasy sound. Against all reason, it just . . . worked. I told her she had captured the clunky and primitive vibe of Dock Boggs, the 1920s Virginia clawhammer cult figure who disappeared for decades until the folk music revival of the 1960s; a few raw recordings can be found on the *Harry Smith Anthology of American Folk Music.* It's thrilling, magical stuff. She answered, "Who?"

So who was I to tell artists what to do and what not to do when they often weren't aware what they were capable of, what they might channel, dig up, or pull out of the air? I had my job, the artists had theirs, and at the end of the day it was their music. They wanted to be left alone to create, their way, without interference. As I did. That meant mistakes might be made, but it was the inspired tension between reward and peril.

Sometimes it was my job to disregard buttinskies and shield artists from their "helpful" gobbets of wisdom. If the Old 97's would do this, if Robbie Fulks would be a hair less acerbic, if Lydia Loveless could write more songs like this and fewer like that, and if we stopped wasting our time with certain artists, side projects, and compilations. Trained in the dark arts of A&R and marketing, these wise counselors made determined cases to us regarding albums and artists they saw as inherently flawed. *If only you'd listen, you could make a buck, and fast.*

But some artists came to us in need of patience and space to tune into their own elusive frequencies. In 2001, after barely surviving a couple major label dog and pony shows, the Bottle Rockets were wrung out. Even with an enviable run that included their self-titled debut album, *The Brooklyn Side*, and *24 Hours a Day*, it was depressingly obvious that the world would never be quite sure what to do with their Crazy Horse stomp and songwriting that looked at the faces in dying backwater towns and crafted populist anthems with the sympathetic eye of Woody Guthrie. It was tenacious folk music sporting more beards and biker wallets than most were comfortable with.

Looking for, perhaps, a breather or career palate cleanser, they approached us with an album of Doug Sahm songs, and when a band of the Bottle Rockets' caliber asked me to do something, I found a way to say yes. Though he was hardly a household name, from the Sir Douglas Quintet's British Invasion twisting and shouting with American proto-garage rock, to redneck psychedelia kindled by time served in Haight-Ashbury, to Tejano roadhouse ravers in the Texas Tornadoes, few figures cut as varied and influential a path as "the Cosmic Cowboy." While *Songs of Sahm*, a collection of covers of a relatively obscure figure, might not have been a logical career or business move, it transcended mere tribute; they found his groove and let their freak flags fly for a rowdy, reverent invocation of his ingenuity, infusing his songs with their brawny American soul. In the process, the Rockets were finding *their* groove again. Without *Songs of Sahm*, I wonder if their late-career resurgence on albums *Zoysia*, *Lean Forward*, and *South Broadway Athletic Club* would have happened.

When we signed Justin Townes Earle, there were real pressures on him to be "Steve Earle, Jr." His first two albums, *The Good Life* and *Midnight at the Movies*, were glimpses of an artist zeroing in on a sound and a voice of his own; I could hear it around the edges, even if I wasn't yet sure what *it* was. The albums were solid reflections of his influences—Guthrie, classic Nashville honky-tonk, and Delta country blues—but every review began, invariably, with some variation of "Son of Steve. . . ." We brushed them off and let him take his time. Then his third full-length album, *Harlem River Blues*, a dazzling prism of emotion and detail that continues to surprise me, arrived at the office. He had moved to New York the year before and the album revealed a next-level gift for writing with an intense sense of place, and he sounded, remarkably, as if he had lived there his whole life. It was both inward-looking and expansive, and lyrically as sharp as a lover's tongue as she walked out the door after emptying his wallet. Attending that house concert of his years before, there was an immense talent I could not have imagined but somehow felt might be there. It just needed the space. On that album, he went from "Son of Steve" to "Justin." Full stop.

Art by Roberto Valadez. Screenprint by Steve Walters.

Alejandro Escovedo was, by many fusty industry standards, "washed up." Few minds were changed after we released the *More Miles than Money* live record, followed by 1999's *Bourbonitis Blues*, an odds and sods collection of live-in-the-studio new songs, covers of the Gun Club, Velvet Underground, and Ian Hunter, and a loose *and* tight spirit showcasing Alejandro's immense versatility. But those albums were merely prelude. In the fall of 2000, Alejandro convened his telepathic core band and guests from the Backsliders, Whiskeytown, Superchunk, and the Squirrel Nut Zippers in the Chapel Hill, North Carolina, studio of Chris Stamey, from the roots-leaning power pop legends the dB's. After recording was completed, Alejandro asked for my thoughts on the sequence, and I listened to the mixes on a plane to Portland, Oregon, with my snazzy new Discman.*

As I soared over the Plains and the Rockies, I wanted to plug the record into the PA so everyone else on the plane could hear what I was hearing. *A Man Under the Influence* was a trip through the terrain of love, loss, and redemption. In times of manufactured drama and cheap emotions, it was easy enough to talk of such things, but Alejandro crawled

* A sidenote for the youth: the Discman was an ancient, portable CD-playing device. It had recently replaced my Walkman, a Reagan-era device that . . . oh never mind.

inside these themes and meditated on them with unflinching honesty. He squared his shoulders and faced what life offered, for better and for worse, as a cinematic whole. The opening tracks, "Wave" and "Rosalie," told the epic story of separated lovers writing letters to each other for seven years before reuniting and marrying, while "Velvet Guitar" was as sweeping as any John Ford western. Over the years, we received a score of fan letters telling us they used "Wedding Day" as "their" song. And a foxy, nameless, arhythmic castanet player acted as muse for the three minutes and thirty seconds of rock and roll perfection that was "Castanets." This exquisite blend of orchestral grandeur and glam rock strut is as captivating now as it was when it was released, maybe more so. The true sign of a classic, what *makes* a classic, is its timelessness, its ability to give something new as one's own life passes. *A Man Under the Influence* is a classic, but it took three albums to get there.

A shitty, condescending subset of the outside advice I received was reserved for female artists. Lydia Loveless's first Bloodshot album, *Indestructible Machine,* took our narrow world by storm, its cocky, punk rock candor fused onto country classicism. Soon, writers and distributors, all men, sent me emails, made calls, or buttonholed me at shows suggesting to *me* what I should I tell *her* what would be "best" for her next record. *She's young,* I'd say, *let her figure it out on her own,* knowing full well what I would have done at that age if someone tried to tell me what I could or couldn't do. And what to do with reptilian industry lackeys telling me, you know, *for her own good,* that Sarah Shook would be "prettier if she smiled more" and she might get better coverage if she "dressed the part" better?

On her debut, *The Virginian,* Neko Case got pegged as a neo-Patsy Cline siren with a gorgeous gift of a voice. Combined with the retro album art, she fit very nicely into many referees of taste and commerce's narrow view of the rising "alt-country" scene. They were eager for more of the same from her second record, and I was asked by people who could "help her out" for assurances that we/she weren't going to alter this *winning formula.* Was she going to "play along," or not? I shrugged them off and waited for her to finish *her* album. When I received a cassette of un-sequenced mixes, I popped it in my car's player as I was running errands—to the poster printer, a store that needed play copies, Andersonville's Middle Eastern Bakery for hummus and spinach pies, wherever. I had to pull over.

The Virginian 2.0, it was not. Whereas that album was full of raw talent, it was unfocused and a bit unsure of itself. It leaned *back* for the ride. *Furnace Room Lullaby* was a quantum leap in confidence and execution. She was writing her own songs and exploring a broader range of sounds and possibilities in the studio. It crackled with sharp lyrics and had a keen ear for dynamics and mood. The haunting Middle Eastern–inflected title track *still* makes the hairs on my neck stand up. I wasn't sure if the people who had been pleasantly surprised by "Honky-Tonk Hiccups" from the first record, who wanted her to remain, oxymoronically, *classic alt-country,* were going to come along on this album, but I didn't much care. She was learning to lean *into* the ride, marking the start of her path as artist rather than an interpreter in a circumscribed field. The album augured the torch country noir she put an ethereal edge on with the tour de force that followed, *Blacklisted.*

These releases didn't happen thanks to brilliant, six-dimensional chess tactics, and they look like no-brainers only with the benefit of 20/20 hindsight. Rather, they were an outgrowth of our trust in independent artists. Many of the younger ones were still searching for their voice, which is a process, and many of the more established ones habitually challenged themselves and expectations, also a process. Let them be. The trouble was an industry that wasn't necessarily keen on "process"; it mostly preferred "processed." If a first (or second, or third) record didn't do well, it was our job to figure out how to work it better next time. The conversation was never "change what you do." Hopefully, we made that creativity easier to get at, and I also got to tag along on unforeseen sonic road trips where plans often meant limitations. How awesome was that? Did this mean that, in a way, the lunatics ran the asylum or that we were herding cats? Maybe, at times, but it led to . . . the unexpected. And it was a reminder of the Split Rail showcase and my decision not to work for those standing in the back, but for those in front of, and on, the stage.

What is your office like? Is it as fun as I imagine?

People's interest in our day-to-day office life was always oddly touching. It reflected the idealism of independent art and community, that, in a sense, yes, a label that released the music they enjoyed was a merry workshop, immune from the quotidian banalities of a "normal" business. They fancied lots of snappy banter, the designer draping mock-ups of album covers over drafting tables, Big Red Pencil wielded with dramatic flourish, "No, no, *no,* this will *never* do"; musicians wandering in and out with their horns and axes or scribbling lyrics in the corner. *Why look, isn't that Bobby Bare Jr. sleeping under that desk? Is that Rosie Flores mixing drinks and Andre Williams drinking them? Is Kelly Hogan giving haircuts?!* (Full disclosure: Kelly Hogan used to cut my hair in the office.)

The original Bloodshot office occupied the basement of a six flat close enough to Wrigley Field that I could hear Harry Caray slurring the seventh-inning stretch and the rising din as Kerry Wood struck out a record-tying 20 Astros on May 6, 1998. (I had free tickets to that game. I didn't go because, I don't know, there was work to do. I was an idiot.

Photo by Anthony Nguyen, used with permission.

I don't want to talk about it. Other Cubs-related bits: I taped a schedule to my dashboard, so I knew the days not to drive to work; we occasionally had to roust Sammy Sosa enthusiasts pissing in our alleyway; a college friend who was a beat writer covering the New York Mets would bring players by before games. Six-foot-two Al Leiter had to duck under the ceiling fans lest he get the Vic Morrow treatment, and Ricky Henderson referred to himself in the third person, as in, "Where can Ricky get a glass of water?")

The lack of natural light and *Das Boot* vibe gave Kelly Hogan panic attacks. When we needed a chair or desk lamp, we haunted the alleys. Our $4 thrift store microwave dimmed the office lights when reheating leftover burritos as big as our heads. We called people on corded telephones and *talked* to them. We had one phone line and one modem for the entire office: if someone had to go someplace known as "online," they yelled at everyone else to hang up. When we needed edits for our Website 1.0, we'd compile a list of changes and fax them to our "programmer" every two weeks or so. From where I sit now, it feels so distantly primitive, like I was Fred Flintstone using a woodpecker as a phonograph needle.

When we outgrew that space, we moved to a place neither clean nor well-lighted on a cheerless stretch of Irving Park Road. It was a storefront sandwiched between an Ecuadorian restaurant that never had any customers and a dodgy Serbian market that never had any produce; all I ever saw through their smeared window were three or four old guys wearing icy stares and soiled white T-shirts, the sole indication of commerce a bushel basket of humorless root vegetables. The one consistent business on the block was the corner drugstore, where there was routinely a line of people getting their sadness prescriptions refilled.

Our office had previously been a semi-operational junk shop, which, I suppose, was semi-appropriate. The dank basement was full of shelves and shelves and *shelves* of ceramic anthropomorphized pumpkin and ghost figurines. Creepy on its own but coupled with the neighborhood scuttlebutt that the building had been serial killer John Wayne Gacy's lawyer's office in the '80s, one did not tarry there. During the first office Christmas party, the swaybacked tarpaper roof drooped noticeably under the weight of the snow that fell that morning. I wedged a stepladder underneath to prop it up, wrapped it in tinsel and lights, and trusted it would hold it for the night. It did, but the rotten roof settled *around* the ladder as the room full of oblivious people, including the couple who conceived a child in the one and only bathroom—much to the consternation of those waiting in line—made merry below it.

I felt bad for visiting fans who came from all over the world, cameras in hand, often bearing hometown gifts, expecting an indie label version of Universal Studios. We had no Bruce the Shark. We had postage meters and occasional rat infestations. There were bills to be paid, payrolls to meet, writers to cajole, Belgian distributors to strong-arm for payment, metadata to prepare for DSP ingestion—whatever that meant—shipments to prep, data to enter, and mail orders to fill. All happening every day. Every month. Though visitors might chance upon a band lined up to use the bathroom after a long van ride, dashing in for merch, or filming a video in the front room—there were even times when Neko Case, Kelly Hogan, and Sally Timms worked the phones as undercover publicists—the office was a determined hive of music lovers doing their level best to spread the Bloodshot gospel inch by data-crunched inch. Following the decentralizing lead of punk, it was as far as could be from Nashville's Music Row or the Capitol Records tower in Hollywood. It was part of the neighborhood, as it should have been.

21

Shut Up and Play

As for lyrical content, it never occurred to me to tell artists to shy away from prickly subjects. Ever since I started paying attention to music, politics have been present. Listening to the Electrifying Mojo and *Radios in Motion*, discovering records on Frontier and Fortune, or considering the possibilities that Vietnam was a lie, Reagan and his cronies were corrupt clowns, and there was something deeply malevolent about the murder of Vincent Chin, I found in music a vital tool for showing me *the way things were* in a different light. I saw the personal in the political, and the political in the personal, and was never threatened by being entertained and asked to think at the same time. As I kept learning about the world around me, it often felt like a charnel house where truth and justice were fungible tools in the hands of the powerful.*

This "hands-off" approach was evident from Bloodshot's earliest releases. On their first single, "Bad Times Are Comin' Round Again" (BS 003), the Waco Brothers poked those within power and voiced outrage on behalf of those without. With amped-up roadhouse bluster and Newt Gingrich in his open casket label art, it cheekily recounted the USA's 1994 embrace of nitwit ideologues (who seem rather pedestrian these days). Lyrics about white men in Klan hoods running for office played like over-the-top laugh lines to the denizens of Gunther Murphy's and Jimmy and Tai's Wrigleyville Tap. Thirty years on, *sigh*, they're not as funny anymore.

The Bloodshot catalog was filled with songs like these, moments big and small, sly and in your face, real stories from living in this world. Politics, in the guise of humanist storytelling, shaped the work of the Bottle Rockets, Robbie Fulks, Roger Knox, Justin Townes Earle, and many others, but didn't define them. Theirs were songs taking place in systems rigged against the

---

* When will that feeling go away?

marginalized and the bullied, not doctrinal screeds. Moonshine Willy wrote about sexual assault, Cory Branan about police violence, Ha Ha Tonka about small town cronyism, Trailer Bride about working moms with hungry children, the Grievous Angels about religious hypocrisy, and Graham Parker about the bungled Iraq war. The Meat Purveyors' pro-weed "Go Out Smokin'" was both fist-raising political statement and set-closing funtime. Neko Case's chilling "Deep Red Bells," from her *Blacklisted* album, was a song about the gnawing terror of growing up with the shadowy horrors of the Green River Killer. Were these bands and songs "political"? While they didn't bludgeon with polemics the same way as the Dead Kennedys' "Blow it out your ass, Jerry Falwell" or the Circle Jerks' "I don't wanna die in a nuclear war" did, "politics" were unquestionably a piece of their creative toolkit. As George Carlin once said, "Art is politics."

Some wouldn't have it, though, and let us know it at shows and online. *There's no room for politics in music* the "Shut Up and Play" crowd—a small-minded, inbred stepbrother of the "Shut Up and Dribble" contingent of fans, pundits, and performative outrage-mongers—sputtered. *I want to listen to music not preaching.* But how can music be a meaningful reflection of reality if we insisted artists cold-shoulder so much of what permeates our lives? To ignore the struggles and inequities that slosh around us, or worse, force them to be ignored because they make some uncomfortable, would open a gaping void in the dialog between musician and listener.

Since I'd always listened to music with strong viewpoints, I was jarred when fans—presumably on a similar wavelength about music and culture as I—gave us shit about releases. Alejandro Escovedo's lustrous "Wave," from *A Man Under the Influence*, sang of the simple dignity and romance of a trans-border family. Did I think it "political" when I first heard it? No, I thought it noble; the writers of the anti-immigrant and *taking our jobs* comments we received thought otherwise. (I can't imagine the vitriol we'd have gotten in today's world.) In 2002, we released the Pine Valley Cosmonauts' *The Executioner's Last Songs*, a collection assembled by Jon Langford (*a foreigner!!!*) that saluted/lamented America's fascination with crime and vengeance and raised money and awareness for the Illinois Death Penalty Moratorium Project. And oh, how the hate mail tumbled in via the post, the phone, and the internet . . . *How dare he,* many venomously opined, *if he detests America so much, he should leave.* "Pro-criminal," "anti-victim" charges were levelled at us; I was asked "what if your (fill-in-the-blank family member) was murdered, how would you feel then?" We got it all, in voluminous and profane spades. The wrath for having *the nerve* to stain the traditions of country music was doubly ironic, since most of the songs were covers of "accepted" members of canon like the Louvin Brothers, Hank Williams, Charley Pride, Merle Haggard, and Bill Monroe.

Some were so quick to take offence at the slightest indications of a "stand"—we were too anti this, too pro that, too questioning of the other—I became genuinely curious what their record collection might consist of. Examples of artists whose bodies of work would be diminished and Disneyfied if their "political" songs were erased swirl around us every minute of every day on the radio and in sports bars, airports, Home Depots, and Pizza Huts. Buffalo Springfield, Nirvana, U2, the Doors, Prince, Creedence Clearwater Revival, Hendrix—I could play this game for a month of Sundays and not run out of examples. Is "All You Need Is Love" political? If not, why not? Does McCartney get a pass, but not Lennon because "Give Peace a Chance" and "Imagine" sound a little too woke? In the high school halls, all I knew of Bob Dylan was the spark-it-up anthem "Rainy Day Women Nos. 12 & 35," "The Times They Are A-Changin'" and "A Hard Rain's A-Gonna Fall," long forgotten. Don't think of the garage punk anthem "Louie, Louie" as political? The FBI did when they investigated it, and the Indiana governor did when he banned it. And Bob Marley trustafarian cosplayers over at the frat house would have a rude awakening if they listened to his music for something deeper than ganja references.

Or are these songs and artists OK now because they have become so decontextualized as to be meaningless? Since no one actually *listens* anymore, they've been diminished to opiating shots of the good old days? "Four dead in Ohio," "Rape, murder, it's just a shot away," and "Never gonna give you up / Never gonna let you down" are interchangeably inoffensive lyrics to sing along with while sinking the 7 ball in the corner pocket at O'Flanagan's Good Tyme Pub.

I can't fathom navigating the minefields of indignation that the virtual entirety of blues, soul, rap, folk, and gospel present for the easily affronted. Are their hip-hop collections limited to "Bust a Move" and "Baby Got Back," and they retire to the fainting couch when "The Revolution Will Not Be Televised" or "Welcome to the Terrordome" darken their earways? Did I think of John Lee Hooker as a political figure when he played "Boom Boom" in *The Blues Brothers*? No, but it was unavoidable when years later I heard "The Motor City Is Burning," his song about the Detroit race riots. What "Change Is Gonna Come" did they think Sam Cooke was singing about? Aretha's "R-E-S-P-E-C-T" was not a spelling lesson and listening to Little Richard's version of "Long Tall Sally" instead of Pat Boone's was a political act, even if the white kids awkwardly doing the hand jive on *American Bandstand* didn't savvy it.

What about offended punk rock fans? Weren't politics part of its foundational makeup, or were they a phase long past, the faded Ramones' "Bonzo Goes to Bitburg" T-shirt worn only when washing the car? The mosh pits with your bros at a Rage Against the Machine concert back in the day were fun, but now, *jeez, I don't know, that shit's edgy*. What machine did they think the band was raging against? A Cuisinart with a faulty "pulse" function? On the flipside of Flipper's 1982 "Ha Ha Ha" single—a hilarious, peak-Neanderthal dirge made even better if Whip-its were involved—was "Love Canal," a tortured yowl about the toxic waste disaster outside Niagara Falls:

We are / dying
Our common grave / is the Love Canal

Literally, two sides of music. Does one take a penknife to that side because it confronts us with seething outrage at entrenched power? Disgust at a horrifying reality?

Even a cursory perusal of country music history makes it plain that it was long the music of the voiceless and the shafted and carried a social justice perspective that tied it directly to punk. So, were the *Shut Up and Play'ers* fans of Dolly Parton's "I Will Always Love You," Loretta Lynn's "I'm a Honky Tonk Girl," and Johnny Cash's "A Boy Named Sue?," but if they heard "Just Because I'm a Woman," "The Pill," or "Man in Black," they'd fire up their Dixie Chick CD crushers? Again, I could go on for days; there are more examples of "political" country songs by "non-political" artists than there are rhinestones on a David Allan Coe jumpsuit.

In the end, what gets cast as being too "political?" The song, the album, the entire catalog? Some of it? All of it? And who decides? Does it depend on the subject matter? Does one keep updated lists of grievances? Are streaming service filters adjusted to reflect the freshest outrages? Does one pretend that Black Sabbath's "War Pigs" and Merle Haggard's "They're Tearing the Labor

Camps Down" don't exist and queue up "Iron Man" and "The Bottle Let Me Down" instead? Do they sing along to the choruses of "Born in the U.S.A" and Neil Young's "Rockin' in the Free World," but plug their ears for the rest? It is a theoretical playpen constructed of very thin skin.

If the flaccid *Shut Up and Play* argument was played out *reductio ad absurdum,* we wouldn't be left with much more than variations of that piña colada song. It'd be a soundtrack of voguing and shrugging towards Bethlehem, a crystal cavern of neutered sentimentality. One thing is for certain, if a Shut-upper stays true to this ideal, that's one boring record collection. If their party playlist opts for Stevie Wonder's "I Just Called to Say I Love You" instead of "Master Blaster (Jammin')" and the Clash's "Should I Stay or Should I Go," not "This is Radio Clash," I'm gonna be a hard pass for their next BBQ.

Does all music have to be political? Of course not. Is all music with politics good? Don't be absurd (I'm looking at you, Billy Joel's "Allentown" and Frankie Goes to Hollywood's "Two Tribes," to just get warmed up). But to suggest, sometimes pugnaciously, "there's no room for politics in music" *is* political. Not being political is a political act; not to choose is, at the end of the day, a choice. Music reflects life and life is political, and those telling people to *Shut Up and Play* likely benefit from our inaction.

Additionally, while I didn't start a label so I could think about economics, the dismal science that makes my eyes water with boredom and my soul darken with despair, one thing became indisputable as Bloodshot went on: if you are a fan of indie artists, and an active participant in local businesses, then almost every purchase you make is already political. I learned, and saw firsthand, the value of a local store versus a chain, how much of the money spent in the neighborhood stays in the neighborhood, how it recirculates, supports others, and nourishes the cycle. For all of us. The choices we make day by day can directly support these independent ventures, or they can line the pockets of faraway people who do not care about genial notions of neighborhood. If you want the eccentric bookstore in your neck of the woods to stay open, go there; don't give into the false comforts of convenience by having an oligarch's underpaid minion bring it to your door the next day. If you want your local diner that serves up an incomparable dagwood to thrive, don't let it get muscled out by the cheap, gaudy bliss of the Bloomin' Onion at Outback. If you want to keep the clerk with the Mountain Goats and Chaka Khan fetish employed, give that record store your business rather than an impersonal purveyor of Everything Ever Recorded at a Discount. This is an ongoing commitment, not an occasional lark. It is an effort, yes, and might cost a little more in the short term, but it pales in relation to what we lose in the long term. While these choices don't seem to involve politics, they cannot be separated from them.

Did I discourage the artists from "politics"? No. What if I didn't "approve" of what they were saying? Ultimately, as with so much about the label, I trusted them. Just as I was confident that they wouldn't take a turn toward bro-country—whatever the hell that was—I knew they wouldn't hand in albums titled *Skrewdriver Sings in the Key of Country* or *Shut Up and Get Back in the Kitchen: Songs for My Wife.*

Did I insist on political material? Of course not. To the extent I possessed any control over content, I'd have been more apt to forbid them to write about man sandals, beets (the worst vegetable), or Steely Dan than anything broadly deemed "political." They were going to write about what was going on around them. Why get in the way of that?

Did major labels offer to buy you out?

By 1998, a few majors (or their boutique "indie" imprints) were eyeing us the way a crocodile drools over a chubby terrier at the water's edge. Just as it is easier to trot out a prequel, origin story, multiverse mishmash, or *Fast and Furious XXI* than come up with a fresh movie idea, they offered us "development deals"; that is, we do all the work, they use our street cred, send us a little dough, and if it was a hit, take it for themselves—leaving us with an ugly hickey, a bad taste in our mouth, and no ride home. We had watched as a few of our peers went this route: artists losing control, labels getting saddled with unmanageable debts in a grow, grow, grow doom spiral, bands breaking up, albums delayed, retooled, or shelved entirely, and the thrill, freedom, and creativity vanishing in a cloud of corporate rapacity. I was not favorably inclined to follow suit.

After calling one morning to see if we were available for a meeting that afternoon, the VP of a new company financed by a major label flew into Chicago from Nashville within three hours. We convened in what one might have generously referred to as our conference room. One might have also called it the room where broken office chairs, boxes of paid invoices, and outdated iMacs ended up stacked next to my 1979 Bally Supersonic pinball machine. He and his mute assistant sat on our alley-picked brown couch. Water and Mr. Coffee coffee were offered and declined. Pleasantries about the flight and traffic and upcoming projects that "excited" us were made. After fifteen minutes, the mute assistant took a sheet of paper out of her portfolio and handed it to the boss. He clicked his pen, wrote something, folded the paper, slid it across our thrift store coffee table, and said flatly, "I think this is good number." *Wait, this sort of thing really happens?* I tried not to laugh. It was more parody than drama. I looked at the slip of paper and said, "I do have a number" (as I thought of the bonuses and support I would give the staff and the lesser-known artists they were most certainly *not* interested in), "but this isn't it." I slid it back across the table. He handed it to his assistant. There were a few more minutes of stilted chitchat. He looked at his watch and said, "We need to get going." And going they got. Back in the limo, back to the airport, back on a plane, and back from whence they came, never to contact us again.

They were out of business within five years.

22

Get Offa My Lawn

Jumping into the murky "insurgent/alt-country" waters, I underestimated, or tuned out, the inherent difficulties of existing between genres. As our roster and catalog grew, I could no longer brush people off with *country meets punk, Cash meets Clash* in interviews and quickly get on with my day. The need to pin down the music and our artists became a persistent bête noire as industry people wondered, *Where do I file this, where does it fit, who,* in short, *will buy it?* I was even asked, with a straight face, in a 2002 interview, "Do you prefer the Bloodshot sound described as country-infused punk, or punk-infused country?" Others wanted answers to questions I never really thought about: what was it, what wasn't it, what couldn't it be, and who was entitled to play it, everything measured by foggy metrics of "authenticity."

Mired in their binary ruts, the country and punk camps questioned the very idea of *insurgent country.* I mean, could two genres be more incompatible? How could one inform the other, or vice versa? Did that mean Henry Rollins in buckskin? Dwight Yoakam covering Wire?* Mohawks. Confederate flags. And never the twain shall meet.

At the time, it was easy and acceptable in rock circles to dismiss country out of hand. Baby, bathwater. "I hate country, *all* country," said critics and indie fusspots as they enumerated the Garths, Kennys, Rebas, and Travises littering the airwaves and halftime shows with their bland arena ballads. I got it, I didn't like what I heard, either, but reflexively condemning an entire genre based on a few really bad apples was no different than saying, "I hate Styx"—a reasonable perspective, to be sure—and thus by the transitive property, "I hate all rock music." Carl Perkins? *Puh-leese.* The Stooges? *Bleh.* Sleater-Kinney?

* Which, obviously, I would buy in a second.

Gag. Consigning "She got a TV Eye" to the same dustbin as "Domo Arigato, Mr. Roboto" was as stupid as treating "I took a shot of cocaine and shot my woman down" the same as "You got to know when to hold 'em, know when to fold 'em."

Many mainstream critics hyperventilated as if country didn't already permeate every corner of Rock 'n' Roll. Cobo Hall tailgaters taking fierce tokes off their pal Digger's bong yelled, after all, "I like to ROCK," not "I like to Country-Rock!" or "Let's Rock 'n' Roll with rockabilly-country-blues undertones informing the structure and thematic content! *Dude!*" To bridge a gulf that need not exist, I tried to destigmatize the premise in interviews by rattling off obvious examples of shared ancestry in the classic rock canon: the Byrds, the Band, Rolling Stones, even the odious Eagles.

And listen closely, dear skeptical listener, with unbiased ears, to Bruce Springsteen's *Nebraska*, the comforting populism of John Cougar/Mellencamp, the Beatles covering Buck Owens, and that crazy earworm lap steel in Stealers Wheel's "Stuck in The Middle with You" from the *Reservoir Dogs* soundtrack the kids were going crazy over. It was right under your noses in Janis Joplin's "Me and Bobby McGee" and Sheryl Crow's "All I Wanna Do Is Have Some Fun." Hear the mandolin on R.E.M.'s "Losing My Religion"? Even Led Zeppelin dusted off a banjo and pedal steel guitar on a few songs, and did they not hop atop rock's Mount Misty? If released today, should Neil Young's *Harvest* or the Allman Brothers Band's *At Fillmore East* be banished to alt-country playlists? The genetic material of Lynryd Skynryd was woven into the denim jackets of the Bottle Rockets, the Beatles' harmonies in the Old 97's, the flannel and work boots soul of the Replacements in Justin Townes Earle, the anarchy of early Who in the Waco Brothers, and Mountain's massive, sweaty, wall of crunch in Bobby Bare Jr. Where, I'd pose, did "country" begin and "rock" end? What tipped it? There was no reason to be hostile to it, it was already there.

The *you got chocolate in my peanut butter* mindset was even stronger within country music. The very idea that *their* venerable cultural treasure could manifest itself in fishy, undisciplined new ways agitated the bellyaching sticklers. There shall be no desecration of the masters! The objections came in many forms. Our artists sang about degenerate topics unbefitting the music's legacy—the Old 97's getting castigated for singing about Percodan on the *Wreck Your Life* album, to cite one example—as if pharmacological dalliances were unheard of on Lower Broad. Our artists couldn't play like real country musicians, forgetting that Luther Perkins—Johnny Cash's guitar player—was mocked by a lot of accomplished session players; his simple, now instantly recognizable, *boom-chicka-boom* licks weren't examples of studied minimalism opposing the prevailing trends of frippery, he simply couldn't play very well. Our artists weren't *country* enough to be in the genre, as if there was a geographical line of acceptable "Southernness," defined, inevitably, by wherever the ax-grinder wanted it to be. Even though many of the tropes of country music had been first worked out in a bog, a moor, or after some Highlands clan bloodbath, Brits like Graham Parker and Jon Langford weren't seen as legitimate representatives. Neko Case was suspicious for being erroneously believed to be Canadian—Neil Young, k.d. lang, Joni Mitchell, and Hank Snow notwithstanding—and her cover of Ernest Tubb's "Thanks a Lot" on her debut *The Virginian* was cancelled out on the judgement ledger by her cover of Queen's "Misfire." Many took umbrage that *Chicagoans* were telling *us* about country music. I also heard more than enough confidential, vile suggestions that Alejandro Escovedo and Andre Williams weren't, *wink, wink*, "country material." With *there are barbarians at the gates* side-eye, they pronounced that what we were doing was "Not Country."

But, hey, it wasn't me who had chloroformed the legacies Hank and Patsy, relegated Johnny and Loretta to midweek county fair stages, and championed bubblegum country with Top 40 production aesthetics. That was done by those who disappeared inconvenient crime scenes and biographies with the skill of top-level mob cleaners. These people and their suffocating notions of purity could go fuck themselves.

Because here was the thing: the more I explored the fascinating jumble that was country music, the more I heard music that questioned (or ignored) their hegemony. The more I listened to those artists now accepted by polite society as titans of the genre, the more I unearthed rebellious streaks stretching back to western swing master Bob Wills telling the Opry to stuff it when they wouldn't let him bring drums onstage, Loretta Lynn getting banned on radio for singing about birth control, and Johnny Cash and Hank Williams being booted off the Opry. Before their histories had been sanitized, they were anti-establishment in their time and made music that, in spirit at least, was not far from the tenets of punk.

Some of the country's greatest music exists despite, not because of, the accepted nostrums of wizened industry brainiacs. Take 1969's "Homecoming" by Tom T. Hall, writer of "That's How I Got to Memphis," "I Like Beer," and dozens of other astonishing songs.* This remarkable song is a one-sided conversation that takes the listener, in exquisite, economical detail, on a trip of regret and loss. The nonchalant last line, "And by the way, if you see Barbara

* Alas, also the writer of "I Love," a side of Grade A schmaltz my mother turned up on the clunky, push-button AM Radio in the family's Chrysler New Yorker land yacht. TTH's pre-internet listicle of things he loved, like little baby ducks, pickup trucks, birds of the world, and fuzzy pups, was way too syrupy-sweet even for me, and I was practically snorting Pixy Stix in those days. This lachrymose tune unfortunately tarnished my view of him for decades until I learned better.

Walker / Tell her I said hello," cuts to the fundamental ache of *what could have been*. A four-hundred-page novel lurks in its three-plus minutes, but it was a hit factory marketer's nightmare: there is no chorus and no verses, and the title is not in the lyrics. They wanted another hit like his "Harper Valley PTA" out of him, not this. Regardless of these "flaws," it went to the Top Ten, and Tom T. Hall wound up in the Country Music Hall of Fame.

Through 1974 and into 1975, the country music charts had been repeatedly topped by releases from the genre's *fresh new voices* John Denver, Olivia Newton-John, and Donny & Marie Osmond. Then, that spring, Willie Nelson released *Red Headed Stranger*, the best goddamn country record of the '70s. Recorded outside of Nashville, both physically and sonically, for his new label, it was a concept album the bosses mistook for a demo because of its spartan production, interspersed story vignettes, and short instrumentals. Mozartian in precision, but also pure punk in execution, the album's sparseness made it both grander and more personal. It is timeless. It is *out* of time. Its eventual hit, "Blue Eyes Crying in the Rain," is a perfect country song, a perfect *song*. It is a song I am hesitant to breathe during, as it seems so fragile. But who did this pigtailed apostate in his marijuana leaf T-shirts think he was? Country stars didn't look this way! Cue rhinestone-clutching, the Nashville equivalent of pearl-clutching. It blew a big cloud of herbal smoke square in the face of what the establishment thought made money and it will outlast us all.

This history was new to me as I plugged along with the label. Many interviewers assumed I had an extensive, pre-existing grasp of it when we started, but I couldn't have discussed the relative merits between Olivia Newton-John and Waylon Jennings any more than I could have proffered an opinion about *Rubber Soul* vs. *Revolver*. Finding out that many of the figures carved into Mt. Opry granite were, at one time, outsiders themselves, that they were shunned before they were embraced, I didn't find the entrenched interests to be reliable authorities on the matter of what *was* and what *wasn't* "country." It was no coincidence that Loretta Lynn and Johnny Cash's careers were resuscitated by labels and producers known outside country (Loretta's *Van Lear Rose* on Interscope, 2004, produced by Jack White; Johnny's *American Recordings* on American Recordings, 1994, produced by Rick Rubin). With the snobbery of any top-down institution, these "experts" were frequently wrong but never in doubt.

Since I hadn't gotten into this racket to rile the hidebound country music overlords anyway, I wasn't really bothered by what those fundamentalists thought, fundamentalists of any stripe being a tiresome bunch. It was to be expected. So, yes, in many regards, we were indeed "Not Country." Thank you, I took that as a compliment.

What bummed me out were when the calls came from within the house, from our own burgeoning scene. It wasn't like we had invented anything.

Long before Bloodshot had sent its first release into the world, I had shelves of records by artists who had discovered a timeless, untapped (or neglected) *something* in country music to point to as antecedents. I assumed most of our fans were versed in some of those early punk-roots bands and were open to our evolving, messy idea.

While "insurgent" had been coined out of necessity early in our existence, it quickly became something of a millstone as people with *TweedyRules* and *hankisgod* handles in Internet 1.0 chatrooms ascribed their own biases to it. With rulebooks and do/don't lists crammed into their OshKosh B'Gosh overalls, they engaged in discussions about what was and what was not "alt" enough that took on the silliness of John vs. Paul feuds, Wilco vs. Son Volt fan spats, and Detroit-area Lafayette Coney Island vs. American Coney Island squabbles. Writers asked me to re-evaluate other music within the context of what we were doing. (Once I was even given a yes/no list—would these artists in the country music canon be considered "alt/insurgent" now?—which led back down snoozy rabbit holes about what the canon was and who decided it.)*

Self-appointed sourpuss arbiters of authenticity quickly sought to codify what the "Bloodshot sound" *couldn't* be, and, remarkably, began telling us what the term meant and who could claim it. The first time I read that a Bloodshot release didn't *sound* like a Bloodshot release was regarding Robbie Fulks's *Country Love Songs* in 1996, our eleventh release. Without the overt punk rock proclivities that bands like Old 97's, Moonshine Willy, and Waco Brothers displayed in abundance, fans and media just beginning to get their heads around the whole *punk meets country* argot couldn't see how he "fit." *This isn't Insurgent Country,* they asserted. *This doesn't sound like the Old 97's,* they pointed out. Of course, it didn't sound like the Old 97's! You know who *did* sound like the Old 97's? The Old 97's, and that was good enough. We'd been in business for two years at that point and minds were being made up about what the limits of "insurgent" were, as if our sound was already encased in amber, as if we should release *Wreck Your Life* ad infinitum. I felt the same dull ache in the back of my skull that the claustrophobic horseshit in the punk and hardcore scenes had given me. I understood that people wanted a sense of ownership of the music, *we were here before you, this is special, this is our thing,* and to keep it away from the dilettantes and bandwagon-jumpers, but I wasn't keen to trade one orthodoxy for another, This Land Is Your Land curdling into Get Offa My Lawn.

---

* On the other hand, if tagging Willie Nelson and Dolly Parton as "alt/insurgent" kept them from being worshipped as ossuary pieces, then, hell yes, I'd claim them as "alt" and take them down from the mantle so they remained revered *and* relevant.

Ultimately, such inclinations to exclude smack of control, and the constipated, you-are-not-allowed-to-play-this thinking tugged my mood between tedium and rage. During some downtime in the studio while recording the *Red Dirt* album with the Sadies, Andre Williams was telling me why he liked one Hank Snow song more than another. "Andre," I asked, surprised at his detailed comments, "How'd you get to know so much about country music?" Now, Andre was an old-school music business character, who regaled the room with tales large and small, some true and some unabashed bullshit, but told in an unmistakable manner Kelly Hogan had dubbed *Andre-ance*. But as he answered, "Andre Williams" melted away and only Andre remained. He told me that when he was a kid working in the fields in Alabama, the "man on the horse" always had three things: mirrored sunglasses, a shotgun, and a transistor radio. He hated the man behind the sunglasses, he hated his shotgun, but he loved the country and western songs that played all day on his radio. I will never, *ever* forget that. He had experienced a time and a place completely beyond my comprehension, yet here he was with a devoted fan/label poindexter and a band from Toronto, using his life experience to connect us through music. It was as improbable as it was humbling and underscored the richness of possibility in music. I wouldn't trade that unique viewpoint and what came of it for anything. That was the sort of perspective that should never be lost or suppressed based on a shadowy "they" deciding what stories would be told, and by whom, by what was deemed "authentic" and what was not.

Courtesy of Pravda Records, used by permission.

Music, indeed any art, is more interesting when it embraces the unfamiliar, not when it is endlessly regurgitated. Sometimes outsiders, those who don't "belong," who don't "know better," are the only ones willing to do that. Mating with your own kind to the exclusion of everything else achieves what? An ever-diluting pop-culture ouroboros? A weak-chinned, slow-witted royal family? "We Built This City" and "Red Solo Cup"?

When some punk rock naïf picks up a Hank Williams LP for a buck at a thrift store and starts a band, it's going to reshape the music. Is that transformation less authentic because they weren't fully versed in everything about him or his context? The Ramones wanted to be the Beach Boys, but they couldn't play that well, and we ended up with the Ramones, which is an objectively good deal all the way around. The Mekons dismantled Hank's classic "Lost Highway" with grand and daring ineptitude on their *Fear and Whiskey* LP and showed that one can be respectful of the genre but not constrained by it. There were a lot of highways to get lost on, I didn't want anyone telling me how or which one. To paraphrase noted food critic Anton Ego, not everyone can make great music, but great music can come from anywhere.

So, what and who is authentic? Steve Earle didn't serve two tours in Vietnam, John Fogerty wasn't born on the bayou, Johnny Rotten wasn't the anti-Christ, and Johnny Cash never shot a man in Reno just to watch him die. Pat Hare, Muddy Waters's guitarist, released a single on Chess Records in 1954 titled "I'm Gonna Murder My Baby." In 1963, he did just that. If we demanded a Pat Hare–level of authenticity from our art, the HQs of entertainment conglomerates would look like the elevator door opening scene in *The Shining*—a torrent of blood. Take a Bàhn mi sandwich (but don't take mine . . .): Is it authentic? It ain't French, it ain't Vietnamese, yet it's somehow both *and* its own thing. If someone's going to turn up their nose at a ginger pork Bàhn mi out of some warped sense of purity, well, good, that leaves more for me. If someone's going to turn their ears off to music played by someone who fails to meet some amorphous standards of authenticity, fine, then they won't be standing next to me at a show bothering me with their opinions.

After a few years of persistence, our idea that punk and country could bounce around one another stopped being so exotic. If the tagline "Insurgent Country" accomplished anything, it might be that people are, at least in indie circles, less reflexively resistant to the idea that "country" is more than one thing, that it can insinuate itself into unexpected and exciting places, that it is a living musical form, always growing and always evolving.

Now that I am out of the trenches and no longer need to soothe and coax with gentle, reassuring analogies, I can answer the *What is alt/insurgent country?* question with the candor I'd forever wanted: It's whatever I say it is. It's whatever you say it is. It's whatever that weirdo at the end of the bar wearing a Slobberbone trucker cap and lime-green Chuck Taylors nursing their third ranch water cocktail says it is. Alt-country is not one thing. It can never be one thing because the "alt" is defined by my perspective, your perspective, that weirdo's perspective, and the perspective of any artist moved by the almost infinite possibilities these fertile musical grounds offer. Who cares what it is? It *is*. Just listen. You'll know it when you hear it.

23

For a Few Dollars Less

When numbly cruising the interstates, have you ever been walloped by the distinctive funk of manure through the AC vents, then noticed gargantuan, low-slung compounds set faraway enough from the road to avoid undue attention? Out back are shiny railcars or row upon row of semitrucks. No signage anywhere or on anything. That's where the proverbial sausage is made: endless cans of commodity meat churned out for buckets of wing dings and belly-busting burgers, and the proprietors aren't keen to advertise the unspeakable things being done to pigs, cows, chickens, the environment, workers' physical and mental health, and, ultimately, the tastebuds of their consumers. Some people might see efficiency, low cost, and high profits; I've read *The Jungle*, no thanks.

It's not hard to draw a metaphor (meataphor?) for the potential hazards of growth within the Music Industrial Complex. From our first whispers of viability came pressures to scale up, to supersize. That was the goal, right? America wants more, and to behave otherwise invites suspicion. On the occasions we found ourselves with a decently selling title, distributors were quickly on the phone or in the office suggesting we raise our prices, press more records, release any unreleased material—no matter how unreleasable we or the artists felt it was—and rush out another album. Build rationally for the future? Bosh! CDs are cheap to make! Strike while the iron is hot! Find more artists like this, and *fast*. Then we'd be able to move to a luxe office in Fulton Market with sleek, pan-ethnic, way-out-of-my-league receptionists wearing earpieces and offering visitors espressi from our brass Victoria Arduino Venus semiautomatic.*

---

* It goes without saying that the volumetric dosing and soft infusion systems are without parallel.

Was it tempting? Sure.

Success, though, doesn't necessarily beget success; success will, if one lets it, beget the stress and necessity of finding more success. As anarcho-environmentalist Edward Abbey preachified, "Growth for the sake of growth is the ideology of the cancer cell." Going big was an invitation to hop on the fearsome Hamster Wheel of Debasement and Compromised Principles suspended over a lava pit where the wheel only got bigger, and the lava only hotter. It could be easy to lose perspective, to forget what we were trying to do. *How* to engage—or not—was the ongoing question. How could a smaller label use the beneficial nuts and bolts of often hostile (or indifferent) media and retail machines and their propositions to "succeed" without being swallowed by them?

Persuading glossy magazines or daily newspapers to cover us, even in an era when indie music was ascendant, wasn't a sensible use of our time and resources. Many started leaning into fluff pieces about how great Courtney Love thought Stevie Nicks was and how ironically rebellious it was when Urge Overkill trashed hotel rooms in the kind of proudly dim-witted rock star excesses that made punk so indispensable in the first place. We were a nano blip on a radar built to be tickled by the mega. Add to that, shrinking budgets and gutted staffs + more music to cover = underpaid and overwhelmed writers working under unblinking deadlines. They could be forgiven for parroting the dead-hearted promotional babble sent to them by office tower publicity firms instead of crafting thoughtful critical appraisals. It had to be hard to muster a spirited advocacy for something novel when they had that two-thousand-word review of the New Kids On The Block's "Magic Summer" tour hanging over their head that the editor insisted be done two days ago. On the infrequent occasions when our releases intersected with the zeitgeist, and folks higher up the ladder suddenly "discovered" us, one could set their watch by the reactive "cutting-edge" "trend" pieces and *look at the artist we found first* angles hyping "whiskey-soaked, twang-tastic punks" with "Stetsons full of attitude" that would appear. To make it easier for overworked writers, I tried to shape the story *for* them in such a way that they could seem like the clever messenger. Our press releases were easy copy for the incurious, the lazy, or the desperately behind. In the brave new cut-and-paste world, the narrative hooks I scribbled in my notebook before, during, and after shows and polished in the office the next day appeared under other writers' bylines thousands of times, increasing the chances that words crafted from *our* perspective became the content. Better to have them crib from me than pass on the release due to time constraints, or, worse, write something boring, rote, or completely off base.

For an early Waco Brothers magazine cover story, I was asked about the incongruity of a "country" band being so political, the skepticism of the very idea palpable, suggesting it was mere schtick. I gave the writer a thumbnail sketch of the history of politics in music, from Bob Wills thru the MC5 to Steve Earle, and went on that the Wacos were simply tying into threads that were already abundantly woven through music, threads that, in these trying times, were routinely shied away from. Then, to wrap up, I jokingly threw in, "Besides, they're just a bunch of fucking limey socialists." And that, my friends, was the only quotation from me used in the piece, to the great annoyance of myself and the band. They didn't have the room for the rest. I would sooner get eloquent negative reviews over reductive rubbish like this.*

Additionally, by the late 1990s, music retail was mirroring the offramp culinary environment as independent stores were getting crushed by chain retailers attracted to (cue tractor pull/mattress sale reverb voice) *Volume, Volume, Volume*. Enterprising local scenes were no match for soulless spreadsheets and sales histories spitting out of dot matrix printers in centralized command centers with all the human warmth of decommissioned missile silos deep beneath the Dakota plains. Navigating this persistently opaque distribution network that, pre-internet, was the primary mechanism to spread albums around the country to be sold, lost, or returned, was a nightmare. All the great publicity in the world meant nothing if a potential fan couldn't find the album in a nearby store.

Even with our comparatively paltry sales numbers, we were encouraged to pony up at their high stakes marketing table and play with the seasoned card counters. *Pay for pricey retail promotions at Enormo-Mart or they won't stock the record*, even though that was not where Robbie Fulks and Andre Williams fans shopped; no amount of money was going to change that. Their customers came in, bought what they heard on *American Idol* or the Hit Radio Station, and were out. Tens of thousands of times over, every week. *Roll out the dough for displays at Nondescript Twelve-Store Midwestern Chain for prime placement and in-store play.* Wall displays of the Scott H. Biram album were not going to convert anyone looking for the hot new disc by Matchbox 20. Confuse? Sure. Offend? Possibly. Convince to buy? That was rich. Paying a chain store to stock 1,000 CDs unthoughtfully in racks next to the latest Shania Twain smash just to have 987 of them returned was blithely considered "the cost of doing business."**

Commercial radio—country and rock—had frozen out the challenging and the interesting long ago. Gone were regionality, personality, and choice.

---

* See "pure butchery," *New York Times*.

** In our early days, many a Saturday afternoon was spent driving to big-box retailers in Chicago and moving Old 97's and Alejandro Escovedo CDs out of the "country" sections, where they were carelessly filed into "rock," to where they stood a better chance of selling. Guerrilla warfare!

The airwaves had become the aural equivalent of a Panda Express in Topeka, Kansas: you could be anywhere, you could be nowhere, the same few songs a hundred times in a hundred different cities churned out between the same electronic burping, burbling promo bits and bumpers. Alternative Rock radio playlists, after a brief lark of broadmindedness in the wake of Nirvana's *Nevermind,* coagulated into a *lollapa-looting* snoozefest as bubble-grunge bands sprouted from the same boardrooms and demographic sales charts like disco and hair metal bands had in times before. The same old hit machine—but in flannel shirts instead of lamé jumpsuits—offered up a profitable earwash of Goo Goo Dolls, Gin Blossoms, and the Dave Matthews Band.

As for the once glorious concept of free-form FM radio, it had been drawing from the same tired well for decades. Did anyone need to hear "Satisfaction" ever again? That opening riff, once so revolutionary (or so I was told) and dangerous (or so I was told), had been shrunk to . . . that riff; the station could stop the song after a minute, and the listener could somnambulantly fill in the rest. Jefferson Airplane were psychedelic, hard rock groundbreakers (or so I was told), but what was being crammed down my ears by that point was Jefferson Starship, who sucked so hard they may as well have been called Jefferson Vacuum Cleaner. If it was Monday, here's BTO's "Takin' Care of Business." Two-fer-Tuesdays and the prospect of *two* Journey songs in a row! All praises be to Marconi! Wednesday Hump Day, and Loverboy's "Working for the Weekend" was already queued up. *Get the Led Out,* Beatle Breaks, 5 o'clock Traffic Jams, '80s at 8, '70s at 7. Be the fourth caller to score Kansas tickets at the casino or get backstage passes for the *latest* Final Who Tour. These decrepit embodiments of rock 'n' roll have been pounded so relentlessly into us that they are both meaningless and inescapable. Survivor's "Eye of the Tiger" isn't part of my musical DNA because I want it to be, any more than I chose to have flat feet and tree nut allergies. *I hope I get old before I die. . . .*

Country radio was even more iron-fisted as twangy Bryan Adams and Nickelback soundalikes ruled the airwaves. Music once packed with resonance had been hammered into rustic tchotchkes at a Cracker Barrel gift shop, the edginess and rebellious appeals sanded to a comfortable background hum while I ate my Cajun burger with pulled-pork tots. *I slapped a man in Reno, just to watch him cry.*

Our artists weren't trying to be a Billy Ray, or Reba, any more than they were trying to find a slot on a playlist between Bon Jovi and Counting Crows. The issue wasn't *if* corporate radio would play ball with us, it was that they played an entirely different game with an entirely differently shaped ball.

And streaming platforms? Theirs was a phantasm of unlimited choice wrapped in a classic catch-22: a song or an artist needed more plays to nudge the algorithms to get onto more popular playlists, but they needed to be on more popular playlists to affect the algorithms and get more plays. One does not argue with an algorithm. One does not cajole an algorithm with a guest list spot and a Tito's and soda. One does not seek favor from an algorithm based on innovation, or quality. Algorithms do not stand in front of a stage and have their minds blown by a new band.

I was a late-addition guest on NPR's "Talk of the Nation" in 2001 for a segment on the rise of this "new kind of country" that was becoming popular-ish and the difficulties of getting commercial radio to embrace it. The other panelists were a consultant for a media conglomerate and a big market DJ. The conversation was thick with demographics, market share, and listener engagement, as well as the inevitable "what *is* this music?" enigma. My mind wandered and I stayed largely mute, none of the conversation having much to do with me or our business. Then the consultant, with *righteous fight fought well* in his voice, recounted how, after much lobbying on behalf of the "alternative country" cause, his program director added the Eagles to some playlists. The DJ concurred that this was "a step in the right direction" for the future of the genre. I thought to myself, *More Eagles? More Eagles was never the solution to any problem. This is the stagnant thinking that makes me want to take a mallet to my radio.* And by "I thought to myself," I meant "it came out of my mouth into the live mic." For a beat or two, the only sound I heard was the hooting and laughing of the staff who were listening down the hall on the office radio. The host quickly ended the segment with a "well, we'll have to leave this discussion here for now." And . . . wrap. It pretty well summed up what we were up against.

These were not battles Bloodshot could fight, but, more fundamentally, they were not battles we needed to fight. These were closed systems. The goal was not to make the unreasonable happen but to make the possible happen, even if that simply meant selling enough to record another album. Maggie Björklund and Neko Case, Trailer Bride and Graham Parker, Roger Knox and Justin Townes Earle: all may have been equally irresistible to me, but they could not, should not, be fed the same way into a system with a historically low tolerance for chance-taking. That would have been a grand folly. If we would do anything to get our foot in the door, who was to say they wouldn't someday come for the rest of the body? They would not respond to our releases unless it suited *their* needs. We accepted that and searched for strategies that worked on our terms. Once again, the road led back to Crass: *If you don't like the rules they make, refuse to play their game.*

But what were the alternatives to their game?

They already existed. I had been surrounded by them since I first stepped into Sam's Jams to buy Devo and Flatt & Scruggs records, noticed the SST logo on an album bought out of the back of a van after a show, picked up a *Metro Times* at the theater running a Charlton Heston festival (*Planet of the Apes*,

The Omega Man, Soylent Green!!!), or heard Pere Ubu for the first time on *Radios in Motion* decades before. In short, we would, as any grizzled politico will tell you, *dance with the ones that brung ya.*

Instead of chasing tastemaker publications to tell the world it was OK to like us or our artists, we focused our efforts on where the music *fans* browsed, where I browsed: in the coverage found in local weeklies, fanzines, and DIY newsletters. There, critics wrote about whatever they wanted, without concern for circulation or wide appeal, wearing their passions on their inky sleeves. It was a symbiotic voyage of exploration for reader and writer, the line between the two wonderfully blurred. No one article had the figurative juice people thought it did anyway, and at best it would be a piece of the ongoing, larger puzzle. If I may invoke the buttoned-down world of golf for a quick metaphor: a glowing feature-length rave put another club in our bag but, in and of itself, didn't get the ball into the clown's mouth or past the windmill.

Similarly, we worked with the retail shops run by people with an incurable mania for discovery, not impersonal unit movers, the neighborhood anchors I had been haunting myself for decades as I thumbed through albums in unhurried reveries. They were far more important allies than a superstore that might sell a few copies but quickly move on when the next pallet of *Cracked Rear View* CDs arrived at the loading dock. They played records they liked on the store PA, taped handwritten reviews to the jackets, and provided flesh and blood, algorithm-free, RIYL suggestions at the cash register. We weren't appealing to cogs who couldn't tell Alan Parsons from Gram Parsons from Graham Parker; we wanted the ear of the diehard clerks who could dispense unprompted rants about who was 1) worthless, 2) worthwhile, and 3) brilliant.* They *advocated*, without prodding or guile. They could be counted on to follow our artists and take good-faith chances because they were in it for the same reasons I was. It was not a coincidence that one of the first questions we asked fans when our steam-powered website first launched was "Where do you buy your music?"

That it was a given that only a few low-wattage, left-of-the-dial oases would ever touch the likes of the Knitters, Girl Trouble, Minutemen—or us—never felt like a limitation. I knew from personal experience the outsized impact a few dedicated DJs and their idiosyncratic radio shows could have through their wild dives into subgenres, sub-subgenres, and places marked "unknown" on the maps, catering to people quite comfortable with their unpopular tastes. Their shows were rec rooms where you and some friends got together with stacks of albums and had a stereo party. You listened, you learned, you shared, you grew, you made formidable, long-lasting relationships. They weren't hemmed

* 1. Alan Parsons 2. Gram Parsons 3. Graham Parker, if you're keeping track.

in by fixed ideas of what was *this*, or what was *that*. (I bet if you asked other indie label owners, most could cite several offbeat conduits that helped steer them away from the main highway and onto the dusty, bumpy, curvy side roads at impressionable points in their lives.) I never forgot that care package Norton Records sent me when I was a college DJ, so I never ignored their shows when we heard about them or when they contacted us. Finding sincere advocates was worth far more than any expensive radio report generated by a hired promotions company telling me we had seven spins last week in the Tulsa Market *and, by golly, that took some doing*.

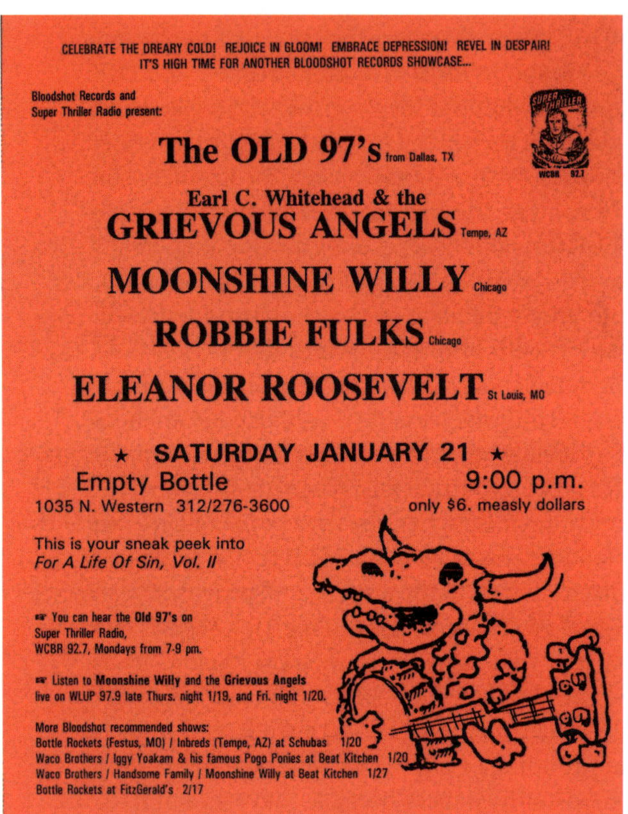

Early Bloodshot mailer/flyer.

Above all, the fundamentals of grassroots networking, directly influenced by early punk labels and sharpened by a very necessary frugality, were our go-to stone tools: crude and cheap, yes; flashy, no, but self-sustaining and effective. Much of it may seem like piffling stuff, almost comically so, but it wasn't. We wrote to the DJs, writers, and store owners from my lists compiled over days slouched in the library room. We sent CDs and posters and invited them to a show. Did a band get a good crowd in an out-of-the-way town? Then send another there! Better still, we'd organize a showcase with three or four bands on the label and have a party; if people didn't dig one of the bands, there would be another artist for them to latch onto. We fanatically gathered snail mail addresses (before it was called snail mail, we just called it mail . . .) at showcases, from touring bands, from mail orders, and from the steady trickle of fan mail, to reach out to the committed and the curious.

Through this grunt work, we connected to scenes percolating in the unlikeliest of places—Lincoln, Madison, Lexington, Champaign, East Lansing,

Springfield, Oxford, Denton, Raleigh, Knoxville, Des Moines, Wichita, Arcata, Bozeman—that were often passed over because established wisdom deemed the markets "inconsequential." Tell that to the outcasts with offbeat tastes in music living in them. *Retail is detail*, as my friend who owns the Chicago vintage shop *Strange Cargo* says. It was a process. Keep moving, fan by fan, and fan to fan, to build a dedicated community.

In this way, a victory for one became a victory for everyone, the releases and artists interlaced. A rising tide lifting all boats. If we garnered some attention with a compilation, we used that to hype contributors like the Grievous Angels or the Blacks. The Old 97's' *Wreck Your Life* got us the funds for Robbie Fulks's *Country Love Songs*; Alejandro Escovedo's *A Man Under the Influence* strengthened Neko Case, which in turn made Trailer Bride records workable; Ryan Adams's *Heartbreaker* bankrolled the Pine Valley Cosmonauts' *The Executioner's Last Songs;* Wayne Hancock's consistency provided a cushion for Lydia Loveless's debut; and the ascendency of Justin Townes Earle defrayed the Roger Knox losses. With that trust between label and fan, we could nudge folks to take chances on new or offbeat projects and expose artists to a wider, preexisting base without jeopardizing our entire undertaking. Starry-eyed, expensive failures and misfires didn't help them, didn't help us, and didn't help the other artists on the label.

In 2002, when the *O Brother, Where Art Thou?* soundtrack buck danced up the Billboard charts to #1 past the likes of J-Lo and Creed and carried home baskets of Grammys, the industry came down with a potent dose of rural fever. It felt familiar. Queasily so. A non-Journey wheel in the sky was turning back around on us.

During the first Roots Rock Scare of the mid-to-late '90s, as we were finding our way as a label and the post-grunge music biz was willing this New Thing to be the Next Big Thing™, we almost didn't make it. Much like in the days of Big Muff distortion pedals, bands were getting signed as soon as they unpacked their dobros or fiddles onstage. Flannel shirts gave way to overalls and John Deere gimme caps, and anyone looking like a hillbilly J. Mascis fresh from a possum hunt got a contract offer. Bands we wanted to work with suddenly didn't have time for us because a major label rep was promising to fly in. "Hey, I like Hank Williams, too," they schmoozed. Why, then, sign with an indie? Some, in a misguided bid to please these distant, inscrutable sultans, stopped being themselves and, eventually, lost themselves. It was a relief when this frenzy subsided.

Nevertheless, here they were a few years later with a fresh directive to find more *O Brothery* music, to seek gold in them patched denim and straw hat mines. Bigger labels started calling me again, looking for something "genuine" to buy out and claim as their own. Kansas's Split Lip Rayfield's name kept getting mentioned, as if A&R folks had done a word search for "bluegrass" on our website, and a reference to them, however oblique, came up. *How about them? Would they succeed?*

Well, success was in the eye of the beholder.

- One of the most exhilarating live bands I have ever seen? *Check.*
- Minds blown by prairie winds and the spaces that were both wide open and dead ends? *Check.*
- Songwriting with time-honored themes of bad cars, bad jobs, bad women, loss, and longing, updated for those who didn't have shitty farming or mining jobs but did have shitty Walmart or Home Depot jobs? *Check.*
- Took the spirit and musical inventiveness of the Stanley Brothers, Slayer, John Zorn, hell, even Rush, and came up with something definitively "Split Lip Rayfield"? *Check and double check.*

Was this what they had in mind? Could they overlook both Split Lip Rayfield's appearance and pugnacious live shows? Would they turn a blind eye to the schtick—a homemade bass, the "Stitchgiver," fashioned from the gas tank of a 1978 Mercury Grand Marquis, and its one string from a weedwhacker that bloodied hands and caused set delays so the bassist could wrap his fingers in duct tape—and give the band the credit they deserved for their musicianship

The Stitchgiver; photo by Jeff Eaton, used with permission.

and songwriting? It boiled down to this: if you didn't *love* Split Lip Rayfield, you hated them. If you didn't get their logo tattooed on your arm, neck, and/or upper thigh the day after seeing them, you wouldn't be able to get to the store fast enough to return the record. Their pull, and their push, was that strong.

But since they had a banjo and a mandolin, the mania for neo-hayseed riches provided all the incentive they needed to chase figments of pipe dream rainbows, and the growth would be rapid, foolproof, and, without a doubt, never-ending. The voices from on high urged me to get onboard or get out of the way, greed is good, shit or get off the pot. I was unconvinced. In due time, equilibrium would return, brand-new dulcimers would get dusty on their handcrafted maple stands next to the hi-fi, coupon books of music lessons would go unredeemed, and another thing people couldn't believe they'd lived without for so long would soon come along. Some rolling the old-timey dice might clean up in the short term, but most others would be left limping behind in the long term as the possibility of the big time fizzled out. Whatever. *Next!*

Split Lip Rayfield was just one example, and I didn't look at them, or anyone, as dice to be rolled in the reflexive quest for the grail of growth. We worked with artists looking for sustainable ways to build a career doing something they loved. If we only cared about artists and releases that we thought would lead to *more*, then the mentality of "keep growing, keep growing" would likely succeed in killing us.

If we were seduced by a boom mentality, then the inevitable busts would follow. If stakes and expectations were continuously pushed upward, then the label would become drudge work, recalling my ruts in stage/production managing and junk mail and plastics factories. We aspired to a scale that was manageable and flexible, to build a loyal fanbase and weather these spasms of mercenary interest that routinely ended in disappointment, or worse, and never put ourselves in a position that we needed a "hit" to survive.*

Stretching back to the early days of punk, I had questioned the very notion of "largeness." Pottering into a bewildering landscape armed with a *gee whiz, let's do this thing* credulity pitted against immense forces of mass media promising stardom and suitcases of money if we played along, many liked to frame our story as one of slinging stones from the brook to bring the giants to their knees. But I never looked at it that way. Instead, I thought of us as scurrying from rock to cave to hollow, avoiding entrancing promotional tar pits. We had to be nimble, turning disadvantages into advantages, and avoid chasing the dragon. Did not "going big or going home" evince a lack of conviction in our artists or their music? Or was it a rational assessment of playing in

* I was told once by an interviewer that this was the most "Chicago" attitude ever.

a game that was dealing us in on a deck of fifty-one? A lot of people in the professions of promotion were paid handsomely to tell labels and artists they could be "big" if the rules of "hitmaking" were uncritically applied to them. A few, perhaps, even believed it. But it was a dead-end street if people only came to our website or a show looking for one song, one artist, one hit, one star. Having clear-eyed expectations, unique to each artist and release, was an existential requirement for a label like us, an acknowledgement of practical reality that I never looked at as defeatist. It made possible the organic, manageable growth for artists like Justin Townes Earle and Neko Case, but it also kept a place for the odd, on-the-margins-of-the-margins Trailer Brides and the Maggie Björklunds.

It is wise to only gamble as much as you can afford to lose. It was a deep allegiance to the artists, and the ever-lurking specter of financial cataclysm, that kept me at the nickel slots with like-minded schemers, trying to charm another complimentary Screwdriver out of the waitress, not at the Baccarat table with a bottle of 1982 Chateau Mouton Rothschild. And while the rare opportunities were to be seized when they arose, we had to use them wisely and not get used to them, lest we get used *by* them.

We didn't invent this grassroots wheel, but it felt like, in the wake of the mad alt-rock cash grab and ill-considered scramble for the gravy train, such outreach had been forgotten in the name of *going big*. But it was legitimate currency in the circles I frequented, as a fan and as an embryonic label owner. We were operating in a time—and such times are fleeting—when our earnestness in the name of a shared purpose was taken at face value. (See appendix F.)

How did Yard Dog contribute to Bloodshot's success?

> "I want you to know this is against my better judgment."
> —Yard Dog owner Randy Franklin after a tequila shot at the noon start of our party.

From our first events at Lounge Ax and the Empty Bottle, the value of a showcase was clear. It wasn't just a show, it was a narrative thread running through the day, bringing people together in a communal setting, band connected to label connected to audience, and vice versa.

That ethos carried into our annual South by Southwest shindig at the Yard Dog Art Gallery. Every March, I'd shed my Woolrich jacket, make sure my sunglasses and copy of *Roadfood* were in the glove compartment, pack some sunblock to protect my fishbelly white pastiness, and drive to Austin, Texas. And in the ungodly morning hours every festival Friday, we'd set up a stage and PA in the hemmed-in-on-three-sides parking lot behind the gallery. After allowing myself a panic attack or two, noon rolled around and . . . people came. Since our party's humblest of beginnings, it steadily grew into something more anticipated, more crowded, and more fun every year.

Maybe you've been to South by Southwest before. Maybe you've been going long enough to notice as it shifted from a gathering of independent labels, artists, writers, venues, and promoters committed to increasing awareness of the whole underground network to an aggressively manufactured, "organic," experiential happening telling us what we wanted. As parties outside the purview of the official festival proliferated from breakfast until the wee hours every day, music spewed from any available storefront, courtyard, and rooftop, and, as all light becomes white light, all noise becomes white noise, negating any meaning or nuance it might contain. In time, lucrative offers to move to bigger and "better" spaces were made to us. They would provide us with a "more important clientele," trendier sponsors to please, and greater opportunities to pursue that elusive but essential *something bigger*. Blerg.

Over the decades I attended South by Southwest, there were few sadder sights than a vast parking lot hosting a party or showcase put together for the sake of credentialed industry insiders. Entry was overseen by bouncers built like Russian MMA B-Teamers with scowls and earpieces, and clutches of invitees huddled joylessly near the back with some provocatively dressed marketing reps giving out shots of a new acai berry vodka. A band with a stage filled with virgin gear played to an expanse of asphalt while sponsors' banners flapped limply in a moist breeze and *Bladerunner*-ish ads were projected onto any vertical surface. It looked unbearably somber for everyone involved.

Was it "smart" business to stay at the Yard Dog? It was a financial and logistical nightmare, and there were always significantly more fans than industry badges attending, but I'd rather be in that cramped, sweaty tent off an alley pulsing with energy. For fans, packed to the front, they were as much a part of the event as what was happening onstage. For bands that, the night before, or the thirty nights before, might have played to forty or fifty semi-interested patrons—or maybe they only played a handful of shows a year—they were *stars* that day. People who'd never seen or, in many cases pre-internet, even heard of these artists, accepted them, and intensity and love bounced around that space so thick and fast it was as intoxicating as the tequila someone always brought me. It connected to a larger picture, to the powerful and animating benefits of community.

What was borne out of necessity in not having our bands accepted by the festival we turned into an advantage, and I looked at the day as a yearly gathering of friends, not a gathering of assets. I never considered moving to a bigger place. (See appendix G.)

24

Beware the Wrath of Eyjafjallajökull

We, the fans, have it pretty good. We go hear live music once a week, maybe more, probably less. We partake in a fantasy that we share this stand-alone night with the artist, that they have saved the best for *this* show and will pour themselves into the music as if it is both the first and most awesomest time. We let ourselves believe that every joke is fresh, every segue unique, every set list tailored to our desires, and that their joy in the moment is genuine. And the next day we are safely back at our lives, having dinner with friends or family, sleeping in our own beds, using our own bathrooms, and eating a fresh piece of fruit without having to fight the drummer for it.

If we could peek behind the scenes, we'd like to imagine the musician walking into the office with a new song. After listening to it on our vintage Bang & Olufsen stereo setup, I exclaim, with cartoon $$$ circling my head, "It's a hit!" Fast-forward to the Record-Being-Made montage set to Raymond Scott's "Powerhouse," the reels of tapes, the pressing plant, the delivery trucks, the teens mobbing the store for the hot new platter, the spinning trade papers announcing the surprise smash of the summer. Act Two opens with the band floating from town to town on the gossamer wings of adoration and easy money from the comfort of a luxe bus, sweet, sweet Connies hanging on every word of every song and erupting in jubilation at the end of every show in every town. A million faces seen, all rocked. Fast-forward some more to the artist showing up at the office with a shiny new car and custom-made, monogrammed, ostrich-skin cowboy boots and treating the staff to a bacchanal at a downtown restaurant the likes of us aren't usually allowed into. Then comes the string of hits, the sold-out concerts, boutique mezcal añejo co-brands, and emceeing the Sugar Bowl parade with Kelly Clarkson. Then there's the requisite downfall, the guileless star tested by wine, women, and wrong, the hasty, ill-advised marriage to an Instagram influencer or lesser

Kardashian, the wrecked sportscar/speedboat/hang glider because he was high on booze/pills/scientology after a sleepless week at Bonnaroo/Burning Man/Mar-a-Lago—a bona fide Mad Libs of rock star crash-and-burn cliches. It wraps up with the newly chastened and humbled artist releasing a poignant redemption song, and then—*cue the soft-focus cutaway shot*—finding a spiritual fulfillment more powerful than any crank-bender or torrid, pan-sexual threesome on Ibiza could ever bring. I know, I'd seen the movies. *Ray, I Walk the Line, Bohemian Rhapsody, Glitter*. After all, how hard can it be to drive a few hours and play a show for forty-five minutes?

Ha! Bullshit!

Making a living in music is a mercilessly tough, rarely cinematic free-for-all, and artists need all the help they can get. Creation, dedication to one's art, is hard work that never stops, and bands must go out there again with the same pizazz to meet the same expectations the next day, the next week, the next month, in a different city, on a different stage. To do that takes a level of fortitude, nerve, and determination that we cannot imagine. Most don't know, and maybe don't want to know—we all have shit to take care of, too, you know—what it takes just to *get* to that show.

To some degree, though, I did have some idea how hard it was. I could put myself in the artists' shoes—not the vintage platforms or stylish green suede creepers they've got onstage, mind you—but the threadbare sneakers they wore the rest of the time, when the formidable, unglamorous, and *necessary* grunt work got done. My time as a stage, production, and tour manager—along with the DJ gigs, fanzine writing, and my pitiful stint as a drummer when I crumpled under the barely discernible pressure of playing in front of sixty people—provided the empathy and perspective needed to appreciate that distractions, fuck-ups, and meltdowns didn't happen in a vacuum. Much as I had a thousand things to worry about in the office, unnoticed and largely unappreciated, so did the artists as they navigated the music business.

I knew that touring was not traveling, or a vacation, or an *anything's possible* grand excursion. There were the stresses of separation from home, family, and dogs.* The elemental need of getting from one town to another quickly and efficiently was often a disheartening endurance test. Accommodations were chosen by brute economics. What murdery, off-brand hotels lacked in sheets with high thread counts, they made up for with smelly heating/cooling units, door hinges that have never known lubrication, and stain-hiding, patterned, poly-fiber bedspreads both greasy and highly flammable. Morning buffets may hit the magic price point of *free,* but they left one feeling empty, even after filling up on dehydrated eggs, suspicious-looking sausage pucks, and vitamin pancake.

* I guess people missed cats, too.

And a highway is a highway is a highway, be it in England, Ohio, Germany, or Georgia. They neuter and numb the countryside, erasing all traces of culture and temporal grounding. There is precious little charm in the trudge from Seattle to Sacramento or Denver to Minneapolis and rarely time for detours to a national park or the World's Largest Ball of Twine. Boredom builds as bands put four hours behind them with four hundred miles in front of them. They swim upstream against time and distance, passing "200 miles to Boise" signs, only to whiz past another an hour later that says it is now somehow "275 miles to Boise." There might be the novelty of a moose dolefully eyeing the van from the side of the road on the way to Uppsala, Sweden, or the sophomoric kick of exits for Climax, Michigan, *let's get off here, heh heh*, but it's generally a smudge of green mile markers, white line fever, the highway stare, getting lost on frontage road mazes of Red Lobsters and Mattress Kings to get gas, coffee, or an electric blue energy drink—anything to get *there*, wherever *there* is, on time. They need to make that radio interview in Columbia, Missouri, before five, the headliner requires the opener's soundcheck must be finished by six, and an overturned semi carrying bottled dish soap on I-70 was blocking two lanes with suds. This is faced through punishing heat, demoralizing cold, ferocious crosswinds, torrential downpours, in a van sardined with gear, duffels, musicians, and the last remaining Arby's beef 'n cheddar under a seat somewhere, all marinating for fourteen hours and the clock is ticking. It can be tempting to surrender to the alluring pull of a concrete bridge abutment.

Once at the club, the indignities continue to pile up for our weary road warriors. The "green room" might be the murky basement with a stained couch, prison lighting, and funkier than a James Brown concert, perfumed by bleach, bad weed, and sour beer. With the temperature of a meat locker or a sauna, it could make a body feel like it is coming down with TB. For hospitality, expect a finer vintage Kentucky wine, a bottle of Blind Ivan vodka, a tub of off-brand three-layer dip, a few rubbery celery sticks and some . . . grapes? They look like grapes, they must be grapes, right? If there's a restaurant attached, perhaps there's a band menu with a tempting array of offerings from the "brown" food group. Forget about the luxury to throw tantrums about M&M colors and foldable lunchmeats.

If the band is running late, there is no time at the club to get their bearings, let the road giggles melt away, eat, poop, adjust the wristband the doorman put on with strangulating zeal, or *let's get our hands in the circle and yay team* psyching up. It is straight to a line check and *go*!

Conversely, if there is an abundance of nowhere time before showtime, the temptation to kill boredom by having drinks for dinner is a powerful one; carnival ADMIT ONE tickets for the band are good for well drinks and Whatever We Can't Sell Lager—even though the club might have thirty-two delicious local craft beers on tap. Avert your eyes, plebes, from the top-shelf goods!

As for the show itself, remember the matrices of humiliation in chapter 19? Those don't magically go away. Maybe the vaguely hostile, baked, or inexperienced (or all three) soundperson makes the monitors sound like a burlap sack of hammers being thrown onto a rusty fire escape, there's enough feedback to loosen dental fillings a quarter mile away, and the stage lights are both melty and blindy. Under these conditions, it's hard to hit the stage with *let's do this* focus.

But hey, the travel, logistics, gear-humping, food-choking, and watery whiskey headaches are behind them now. It is the golden time for the band, their music, and the audience, right? Except . . . it's Tuesday. The gainfully employed and the be-childrened are already looking at their watches. Or it's a dead crowd that needs cajoling, *C'mon [city we're in], are you are ready to have a good time*, to breach the unbreachable barrier between the edge of the crowd and the front of the stage. The smell of *stiff* hangs heavy in the air, an encore is neither wanted nor proffered. After the last song, the applause hasn't even stopped and house music and lights come up. *Goodnight, [city we're in]!*

After the crappy show on a split door deal with three other bands and nineteen paid plus five albums and four T-shirts sold, the band might be $80 richer. Eating a complimentary lukewarm pizza off a paper towel on the bar from Tony's or Vinnie's or wherever was still open at that hour, they learn the bassist needs new strings, the drummer needs new heads, and did anyone else notice a worrisome rattling under the van's passenger-side front panel? That $80 windfall turns into a $400 shortfall faster than one can say, "And how much for the *used* tire?" Fans and friends, perhaps the band's sole attachment to a recognizable reality, have already been unceremoniously badgered out the door by the doorman, *you don't have to go home, but you can't stay here*. The evening is over. Load out. Move, move, move. No time to bask in the glory—to the extent there was any. With a sliver of low-grade pepperoni still hanging on an incisor, they're out on the curb, it's dark, it's thirty-seven degrees and drizzling, and, shit, to keep expenses down, the hotel is ninety minutes away.

At the end of the tour, they return home sluggish, a few pounds heavier with a colon swinging between under- and overactive, grayish skin with a 40W Valvoline sheen, and a dull, imprecise ache that may be presaging organ failure. The tolls of intra-band fights, fits of self-loathing after a bad set, waves of self-doubt after a bad turnout, and the omnipresent fears of financial insolvency are tallied up. Driving five hundred miles to play to fifty people—a gallon of gas and ten miles for each person—was a more horrid fiscal model than trickle-down economics.

To the fan, music is effortless. For the creators, it is not. Considering what they suffer through—the traffic jams, the pickled bar sausages, the mildewy hotel rooms, or the cough the singer just noticed—and what they are expected to deliver in the crucible of live music, it is a marvel that they don't hit the stage in a suit of armor. What they do, every night, is, quite simply, an act of bravery.

* * *

Bloodshot's ongoing responsibility, as I saw it, was to answer that bravery with effort. Every release and tour meant juggling dozens of details and reacting to a smörgasbord of surprises. From the office or home—most artists had my number—I was travel agent, logistician, shipping coordinator, therapist, law resource, advisor, provider of an ear to listen or an outlet to vent. We had to contend with border troubles, wiring bail money to small towns for bullshit infractions, buying plane tickets for the replacement drummers, and tour vans that had broken down, been broken into, ticketed, towed, or stolen. Justin Townes Earle missed a valuable in-store performance in Louisville because a jumper on a bridge over the Dan Ryan Expressway in Chicago halted traffic for hours. During an Andre Williams & the Sadies European tour, we started hearing stories from promoters that Andre was, how shall I say, enjoying his newfound popularity to an alarming degree: late arrivals, a broad menu of substance use, a few shoddy performances, and growing frustration on the Sadies' part. Then the Sadies called—overseas rates, from a telephone box in the Netherlands—and said they'd *had it*. The breaking point? The sartorially resplendent Andre had a hat box that took up too much space in the van.

Figure it out and move on.

If I went on the road with a band, for a day, a festival, a month, whatever, I did all that and more: tour manager, driver, merch loader, merch seller, settler with promoters, loud-talker shusher, and procurer of food/drink/parking/guitar strings/weed/and/or accommodations. I rousted green room lizards, moochers, hangers on, and the *how'd he get back here* guys, smooth-talked sound people into putting a little more effort into it, and cadged extra guest list spots. I pacified a cowboy built like a Croatian power forward with a couple slugs of tequila at a St. Louis club after the Meat Purveyors' singer got mouthy with him. I patiently explained—without seething hostility, I hoped—basic financial realities to fans who would say to their buddy, right in front of me at the merch table, "I've already got that album, I'll burn it for you." At a Waco Brothers/Sadies gig in Edinburgh, Scotland, I surreptitiously loaded out the merch and gear cases to the van before the show ended and ran interference on the speed-freak bouncers with frayed tams and blurry knuckle tattoos, who were intent on beating the bands into puddles for some undetermined slight. When they caught onto to the bug-out plan, they unplugged the PA to drive the Wacos off the stage. After a rousing, PA-less rendition of "Do You Think about Me?"—the pub crowd singing along—they grabbed their instruments and made a run for it as the scene degenerated into a wee bit of the old ultra-violence. As we drove away, the bouncers swarmed the van, pounding on the windows with their mallety fists, and shouting frothy Scottish unpleasantries that I assume meant we shouldn't return any time soon. All in a day's work.

Adding to these headwinds were circumstances when artists were their own worst enemies. Every show was an opportunity, and to watch them missed was to watch them lost. Drunk shows, indifferent shows, noodling, unfocused shows; showing up late, too long a set, too long between sets, too long between songs; shows when the artist seemed mad at somebody or something and the audience was going to pay for it; new albums nobody knew yet played in order; working out new, untested material to a showcase crowd; the Waco Brothers going a beer too far, from charming to cringey. Wayne Hancock often compulsively played until no one was left in the room. Bobby Bare Jr. played a sold-out show with his country music star father at the Old Town School of Folk Music, a very classy venue with an older, more upscale clientele. Bobby Jr. came out and did his full-on *punk-rock motherfucker* set and drove the kindly concert goers out the door. The next night, at a sold-out show at the not-so-classy Empty Bottle with a younger, indie-rock crowd, Bobby played an acoustic set showcasing his fantastic songwriting and drove the less kindly concert goers out the door. Switch the shows, as would seem blindingly obvious, and it would have been a killer weekend. Instead, not.

We had recently released Rex Hobart & the Misery Boys' latest album and secured them a plum opening spot for the Blasters' original lineup reunion show at FitzGerald's in Berwyn. The joint was packed, and everyone was ripe for a killer show. Rex and the Boys, whose reputation as an energetic, play it in the Key of Bakersfield honky-tonk band was growing, came out and did what became known around the office as the "Promise to be Honest" set—so named after the slow, somber song from the new album they opened with and which set the tone for the night. Rex's demeanor, a suave *let's dance and have a beer to deal with the pain* appeal, was ponderous and restrained. I thought, as I watched the crowd get restless and turn from fans-to-be into clock-watchers and drink-getters, *OK, any minute now*. That minute never came and the polite golf-claps at the end were the deafening sound of what was missed.*

Bands blew off radio appearances at influential college radio stations to have home-cooked breakfasts at friends' houses. They missed interviews, photo

* Sidenote to the evening: I found myself in the doorway to the dressing room engaged in a lengthy fanboy discussion with George Wendt regarding our mutual love of the Blasters. Patrons walked by and continuously yelled, "NORM!" I asked if it bothered him. "That? I don't even hear it anymore."

shoots, and forgot or couldn't be bothered to set up merch. One artist skipped an NPR "Morning Edition" interview and performance just . . . cuz. "I'll do it the next time," he told me later that day, after I'd gotten an earful from the staffers who busted a hump to secure this opportunity. Buddy, there won't *be* a next time, don't you get that? Bands went on hiatus after recording. Bands didn't want to do release tours. Bands broke up after recording and before release date. Bands broke up after the first week of a release tour, before any momentum could be built. Bands broke up during the last week of a release tour, now that there was momentum. The always volatile Blacks broke up during the encore of their sold-out reunion show. Shakespearian deaths by a thousand small cuts. It was enough to drive this fella to drink until I was done.

Adding to the steady thrum of mayhem was the intertwining of label and life that was as unconscious as it was necessary for me, with the former often overwhelming the latter. When my apartment was the de facto way station for touring bands, books, CDs, LPs, warm gloves, toothpaste, ramen, and bottles of booze disappeared. Complete strangers groggily greeted me from my couch in the morning with the blanket absolution *It's cool, I'm with the band, can I take a shower?* I was left with barfed-in sinks and barf-soaked towels from forlorn attempts to clean said sinks. A Trailer Bride guitarist invited a dude he'd just bought drugs from in the alley behind my house to come in and split a can of soup. Justin Townes Earle hit the road suddenly, leaving my bathroom in a non-functioning state that could be characterized as "third-world bus station." My old apartment had a gas stove that had to be lit by a match, but the Meat Purveyors' bass player wasn't wise to that when she threw a frozen pizza in the oven and promptly took a nap. When I got home an hour later, I was lucky I didn't have pet canaries and that no one smoked; explosions and suffocations were avoided only because the house was so poorly sealed. I've been locked out of my own house and had to break into the garage to get a box cutter and ladder, cut out a screen, and climb in a back window. When I drove Bobby Bare Jr. and the band home after a show at 3 a.m., he hopped out of the van in the middle of Western Avenue to see if the Popeye's was still open. The police took notice and followed us home. As I stood in the alley, calmly explaining that everything was fine, a nightstick testily poking my chest, the whiskey-blind drummer loudly demanded bread from my backyard, an episode for which one neighbor hates me to this day.*

I was hounded by stress dreams about setting up merch tables and no one showing up, being directed to dressing rooms that were taped off, being

* Though, tbh, she's always carried herself with a demeanor suggesting a cat that had eaten a sour mouse.

onstage playing bass and hoping no one noticed I couldn't play, gluing projects together and the glue not working, and being surrounded by hippies and some Jim Morrison-ish skeezy pied piper in a public square.

And sometimes, what should be a grand fanboy moment goes terribly wrong. X's John Doe had played the Old Town School of Folk Music a few blocks from my house. Maggie Björklund, the Danish pedal steel player, was in his touring band, and, as any band at that level wanted to keep expenses down, I offered my guest room to her.

In the morning, the rest of the band came to pick her up and head to the next city. Also in the touring band was longtime friend and perpetual optimist Dead Rock West's Cindy Wasserman—frequently, and rightfully, cited as one of the most pleasant people you will ever meet in the music biz. She wanted a quick tour. While Maggie finished packing her gear and I showed Cindy around my place, which had an aesthetic one might charitably call Rustic Garage Sale, the others wandered in. *Wow. John Doe in my house. Be cool. Ignore my inner nerd. Don't run upstairs and tell the neighbors, don't pull out the X/Knitters/solo LPs for him to sign. Act like I've been in the end zone before. Small talk. Congeniality.*

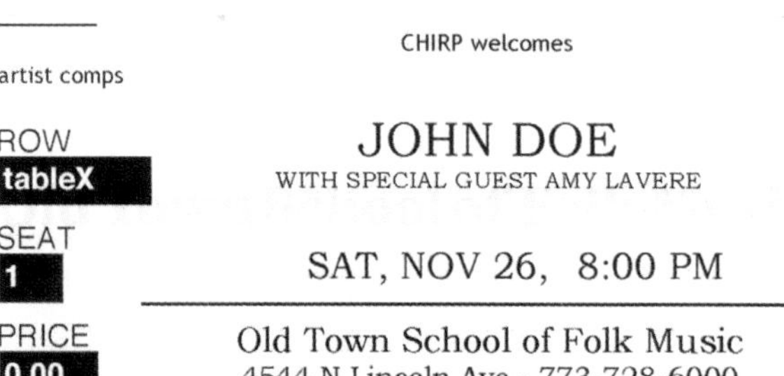
artist comps
ROW
tableX
SEAT
1
PRICE
0.00
CHIRP welcomes
JOHN DOE
WITH SPECIAL GUEST AMY LAVERE
SAT, NOV 26, 8:00 PM
Old Town School of Folk Music
4544 N Lincoln Ave - 773-728-6000

And then.

In the living room, John sniffed and said, "I smell dog shit." I didn't have a dog. We looked around and someone had indeed tracked dog shit all over the apartment. Everyone started checking their shoes. John looked at his boot and it was him. Noticing the time on my wall clock, he remembered the Central Time Zone hour lost and said in a rush, "Fuck, we gotta go." After a quick hug or two and an *oops, sorry,* the whole lot was out the door in a Road Runner-like cloud.

As I spent the next two hours scrubbing dog shit off throw rugs, hardwood floors, linoleum, and carpeted foyer stairs, I brooded, *Well, I never would have imagined this encounter back when I saw this punk rock idol up there on the big screen in* Urgh! A Music War. The glamor metaphor writes itself.

It was tough not to judge the musicians based on one night, one encounter, one set, one befouled bathroom, and none of us wants to be remembered when we are at our worst. These are often flawed people in an unusually tumultuous, judgmental environment. On any given night, a show can go sideways in countless ways by obstacles, for the most part, unseen by the audience.

Compounding this strain is, in the internet age, knowing that any foul mood, dustup, or assertion of dignity to a rude promoter/writer/fan has the potential to reverberate beyond that moment. A throwaway line of sarcastic stage banter, a clammed song, a slammed down guitar/bottle/cup/shitty tub of dip backstage, onstage, or in the alley due to the frustration of a bad show, or just being tired of the road might go viral. Now an isolated event becomes a far-reaching forever, and it can shatter that special fan–artist connection. But it was tough to watch an audience get disappointed. I was out there too; I was a fan. People pay money to be entertained, to make a connection with the music, and fair or not—I leaned toward not—a bad show could tear down more than a good show could build up. Call it the Yelp factor: ten good plates of *gai pad kra pow* at the neighborhood Thai restaurant go unremarked upon, but get one foul ball and the scathing reviews fly. As a restaurant is not permitted to serve a bad meal, a musician is not permitted a bad night. When you or I have a bad day at work, when we mess up, or miss something because of wave after wave of distractions, there isn't a crowd watching it happen in real time on a stage with nowhere to hide.

Then there were times when the world tossed us full-on *fuck yous*. One sunny autumn Saturday, there were three of us in the office doing whatever nondescript drudgery we had to catch up on when I noticed that the sunlight disappeared from the 6' × 6' air shaft that served as my view of the world. I saw . . . stuff . . . falling . . . and then embers. I went to the window, looked up, and saw the building next door was fully ablaze. Quickly, the flames jumped to our roof and the apartment upstairs started burning. I told the others to unplug computers and take them outside. The office was already noticeably hotter, and I felt the air being sucked out when the fire department arrived and yelled at me to get out *now*. I *yoinked* my desktop from the wall and ran out the door. Standing on the street, watching windows blowing out from the heat, I assumed everything was about to be destroyed: stock, masters, artwork, files, my stadium seats salvaged from Tiger Stadium, every box of accumulated history. After a few hours of thoroughly impressive containment and extinguishing, I was let back inside. The ceiling in one section had collapsed from the weight of the water, and the main office was a sooty, soggy, and, in places, charred mess. I worked until dark, moving anything of import to safe, dry areas. When I got home that night, smelling like burning, I collapsed from stress and exhaustion. Next day, we were back at it. The one hundred things that needed doing on any given day still needed doing; there were just more buckets, mops, trash bags, plywood, Murphy's oil soap, and industrial fans around than usual.

The second Bloodshot album by Chicago's chamber pop-punk folk collective the Scotland Yard Gospel Choir . . . *and the horse you rode in on*—exuberant yet steeped in romantic tragedy, equal measures mope and merriment—had come out the week before. Following their knockout album release performance at our fifteenth anniversary festival at the Hideout Block Party, they had that radiant glow of a band possessing the inscrutable ripple of *buzz*.

A few days later, it was over. On the way to their CMJ showcase, one of their tires disintegrated at high speed on I-80, sending the tour van rolling down an embankment. Everyone was injured, some critically, and for several days we were unsure if the bass player would survive. In the end, they all recovered, but the band—and their incipient career—was essentially finished. It was another reminder of the inherent dangers of a profession and a passion that insist on so much roadwork, and how quickly hard work and dreams can disappear. The prospect of accidents remained a diffuse terror in the back of my head whenever a band was late to check in at an event.

After three years and two albums, an EP, several singles, and intensive touring, Justin Townes Earle achieved a place of critical and commercial acclaim that most artists never come near. The hype had built beautifully as the release tour for his latest album, *Harlem River Blues,* began. But a few dates in, Justin's hard-fought addictions resurfaced, leading to an ugly incident at a venue. The next night at the sold-out Lincoln Hall in Chicago, I felt I was watching a friend slipping into a fast-moving, black river. I left the venue with a deep sense of foreboding. The next morning the rest of the tour was cancelled, and we helped Justin enter rehab. I was heartsick that his work, the momentum that was building, might be lost forever.

In 2010, on the heels of the Dex Romweber Duo's *Ruins of Berlin* album, the band was offered a European tour with lucrative anchor dates. It wasn't a tour that was going to make him a pop star—Dex would never be a pop star, *could* never be a pop star, that's part of what made Dex so Dexy—but it might open doors to the festival circuit, bump his career up a notch, and provide some vital steady income. These were the opportunities a label our size, for artists our size, had to seize and maximize their impact.

To that end, we checked the usual to-do checklist, some items needing to happen months in advance:

Publicity and promotion: work press, social media, emails, local promoters, and existing allies.
Distribution: posters to stores, albums in stores, ads, in-store performances planned.
Driver/transportation/accommodations/gear arranged.
Visas and assorted bureaucratic irritations addressed. In triplicate.
Merchandise to sell at venues sent to an arranged pickup point, numerous shipping and paperwork labyrinths involved.
Etc. Always *Etc.*

Everything was in order, dies cast, wheels set in motion. However, far below the surface of Iceland, the planet's crust moved and warped, and, one day, unconcerned with our puny human efforts to orchestrate a simple tour, a swarm of microquakes started a chain reaction between expanding magma chambers, triggering a series of explosions beneath Eyjafjallajökull.*

An enormous amount of ash—there were a *lot* of zeros when measured in terms of cubic meters—spewed into the upper levels of the atmosphere and paralyzed transatlantic air travel for weeks. The tour was cancelled. Alas, we had forgotten to anticipate contingencies for the eruption of a two-centuries-dormant volcano.

Geopolitical and macroeconomic horrors intruded as well. During the 2008 financial collapse, our sales didn't slow, they stopped. Panic and uncertainty were rampant. We had released a record that week and had *one* online sale. The other partner and I stopped paying ourselves so we could keep staff on payroll as we held on for dear life. I even wrote a "thanks for everything" press release in anticipation of our doors closing. Collateralized debt obligations, mortgage derivatives, credit default swaps, *what the everlasting fuck?* Let me make records. That everything I'd worked for might evaporate because of some morally bankrupt Wall Street lummoxes, seemingly so far removed from my world, was as sobering as it was infuriating.

On the morning of September 11, 2001, I was readying to drive to New York City for CMJ. We had our annual party at Brownie's in three days and bands playing their own showcases throughout the weekend. I had my duffel in the Dodge Neon when my upstairs neighbor told me to come up to see the news on TV. Like everyone else, we watched in horror as the second tower was hit.**

I went to the office immediately, and we quickly became an ad hoc clearinghouse for artists and fans frantically looking for information. I was on the phone and sending emails to bands and friends, pleading them to check in when they could or telling them to cancel travel plans and watching the ten-inch Sony I'd had since college when the South Tower collapsed. I stared at the set until the North Tower followed. The phones went quiet. It was as if everyone in our circles was frozen silent. One of my ongoing duties was

---

* It's pronounced exactly like it's spelled.

** I didn't know it until three weeks later, but a college friend was on that plane, someone who saw in me a kindred nutter when I first arrived on campus, gave me brush cuts in the dorm, introduced me to some of the cool kids, had me babysit her pet rat, and loaned me Jonathan Richman and D.O.A. albums. Her name was Jane Simpkin.

compiling and maintaining our fan mailing list. In the days before widespread email usage, nine people had signed up using an address in the World Trade Center. Numbly, I highlighted the names and deleted them, and the tangible onset of loss started. In the coming weeks, I would learn that at least two of those fans died.

Find any of that shit on some preparatory checklist. Everything about this endeavor was walking a tightrope. No, it was walking an invisible tightrope while both ends were being shaken by monkeys hopped up on Jägerbombs. It was a great recipe for madness.

What to do in the face of this? Accept that there will be chaos. Don't buy into the highs, and don't get beaten down by the lows. Manage what I could, let go what I could not. Try our best to mitigate the burdens, known and unknown, so the artist's focus could remain on performing, creating, and seeking that elusive, profound space where the music forges a bond between artist and audience. When the maddening vicissitudes of the music industry ground the soul on that frosty March in a mostly empty room, when it was hard to see to see the point, let alone progress, find light in the dark night. Remember why I was here in the first place, to find any edge or opening, however slight and however fleeting, for the artist.

Because, even on the shittiest of nights, one never knew if there might be some unassuming knucklehead in the corner who loved the show and will bring five friends to the next one, who chats up the record and plays it on their radio show or podcast, who books festivals, who works at a TV or movie studio, who evangelizes in a dozen other intensely personal ways, or who might be driven to do something completely absurd like start their own label to lend a hand to a band like yours. How, I always thought, could I help?

During a festival at a semi-derelict "holiday camp" in southeastern England, I volunteered to be Mark Pickerel's merch person. Mark, the Screaming Trees' original drummer, had caught our attention a couple years earlier when he came through Chicago in Neko Case's band and told us he had a solo album. *Oh good*, said no one ever, *the drummer's got an album,* but I was quickly seduced by his sly baritone, equally inviting and troubling, a reincarnation of Lee Marvin's warm whiskey breath on a cold winter's night. His album of deep canyon soul flitted over a staticky radio spectrum like a trail of mileposts in the rearview mirror.

He was on the side stage set up in a "Four Years Old and Up" play area. The space was filled with murals of smiling crocodiles, enormous rabbits, and happy, happy tulips. Think Bob Ross on mushrooms. The painfully British opening act engaged in Hammer Dulcimers of the Gods twee folk and hobbity mysticism. The female singer, who looked like a cross between Jacob Marley and Iggy Pop and dressed from the Stevie Nicks Collection clearance bin, kept asking the crowd if they felt "the mystery of the magic of the rush." It was not where anyone driven to create and perform their own music would ever have chosen to be at that, or any, stage of their careers. It was nobody's rock and roll fantasy as they fell asleep with Keith Richards's *Life* on their chest, a yellowed Hot Lips logo poster taped above the bed, and *Let It Bleed* playing through shitty headphones.

Yet there Mark was, and the show must go *something something something*. If he could stand on stage and muster the conviction to play in that moment to a sparse but possibly, hopefully, receptive crowd, I could stand beneath a vaguely nightmarish mural of Andy the Aardvark holding an iced lolly asking *What's your favourite flavour?* to sell merch, keep a mailing list, champion his latest release to anyone who'd listen, and plot the next steps, however small.

The journey of a thousand miles, as they say . . .

25

In Praise of the Flip Phone

Hand in hand with the chaos, the only other certainty in the label racket was change. During my tenure at Bloodshot, it never stopped. Some of the changes we encountered were subtle, and some seismic. The trick was to never let change, *the how*, lead away from *the why*.

There were technological advances that made life easier. I did not lament giving up late-night trips to Kinko's, driving downtown every time I had to approve artwork film proofs, Fed-Exing ad copy, or waiting at a mastering studio while the engineer burned a reference CD in . . . *ooh . . . think of it!* . . . 2x real speed. I did not mourn the passing of once-ubiquitous phone cards needed to set up interviews on the road, making sure an artist called at a precise time from a gas station eighty miles outside of Bozeman, Montana. Don't forget the different time zone! Never again would shouts of *do we have another roll of fax paper?* ring through the office. The magic of email meant that I didn't have to block out a half hour for the well-meaning, but long-winded, old hippie arts editor in Norman, Oklahoma (yes, I've heard of the Pure Prairie League, no I don't want to talk about Phish), or the old-school *wink and a nudge, I'm just kidding* racist regional sales rep. And I definitely did not miss the phone book room at the Harold Washington Library—that guy next to me has a cough that sounds serious. And contagious. Thanks, Netscape . . . I mean, Google!

But keeping up with new technologies could feel like holding on to a rope of sand. New formats appeared that radically changed how fans consumed music. When Bloodshot started, CDs were the polycarbonate plastic and atomized aluminum discs that would never grow old, and LPs were relegated to curiosity status, à la Bakelite dial phones and three-camera sitcoms. The future is now! Portable, pristine sound that never wore out! It will never get better than this! But in the absence of any alternative to the CD, album prices soared, and people were compelled to shell out $18.98 to have "Macarena" or that Chumbawumba song. Old records were remixed, remastered, repackaged, and reissued, then they were enhanced and expanded, then they were Deluxe, Super Audio, and, inevitably, Super Deluxe Audio. To offer a veneer of value, albums bloated to seventy-four minutes of alternate takes, bonus tracks, live tracks, and hidden tracks because they could, though no one asked if they should.*

After having their pockets dipped into time and time again with "new" and "better" CD ploys, it was little wonder that customers quickly horse-and-buggy-ed them when Napster and P2P file sharing became the new best thing. The creative expression known as music was now rendered in incomprehensible 1s and 0s by free technologies that rendered the basic physical product of the business—the album—a fetish object at best, a relic at worst, that most wouldn't pay for.

The hemorrhaging of paying consumers only accelerated when labels started suing fans and millionaire fossils like Don Henley went to Congress to plea for justice. (I mean, yes, illegal downloading was theft, but if Don Henley was against something, the punk contrarian in me was kinda for it.) Evincing little capacity for self-reflection, innovation, or moderation, they scolded others for the collapse of their business models. Classic. They didn't teach me much commerce theory in my university creative writing department, but it struck me as imbecilic to treat one's customers as the enemy.

To fill the revenue vacuum created by the CD gravy train running off the tracks, labels scrambled for gimmicks. Ringtones, thumb drives, posters, postcards, and pieces of art with digital download codes, concert DVDs, enhanced CDs, kids' records, box sets, and other "collectibles" were *the answer*. Christ, some even tried to bring back cassettes; *Hey, they sound like shit, but at least they're inconvenient!* Let's try licensing, yeah, that's the ticket: pitch songs to *Guitar Hero*, *Rock Band*, and *Grand Theft Auto*, pray for a placement on *Gray's Anatomy* or *America's Got Talent*, it's free money! At every South by Southwest, cryptically named startups prowled showcases and day parties with their latest schemes . . . *Invest now! Can't miss!* . . . offering solutions when they didn't fully understand the problem.

Then digital downloads had their moment in the sun. eMusic, iTunes, iPods, and internet jukeboxes were the future, we were told, Catalog was King, they said, the Long Tail of the Internet, they termed it.

Then came the shadowy algorithms. Algorithms? The shit that bored me to insensibility in high school math? *Those* algorithms? A shorthand, dummy definition of an algorithm (as this dummy understands it) is a predictable,

* See: Park, Jurassic.

rule-bound process that draws on historical data to solve problems. In terms of music, streaming services commanded by algorithms provide an anaesthetizing lullaby of incremental or adjacent suggestions tarted up in a bogus promise of unlimited choice. Streaming services popped up like so many (non-delicious, non-psychedelic) mushrooms promising access to every note of recorded music for pennies a day. Why "own" a song when it can be "accessed"? What a miracle! What a time to be alive!

As a result, we build—or have built *for* us—a music library that is, to paraphrase the depressingly relevant George Orwell, like putting together a jigsaw puzzle and calling it a painting.

But it is precisely the unpredictable, odd-shaped pieces of the puzzle that don't seem to fit that remained so thrilling to me. In music, in art, in food, in my neighborhood. An algorithm and its orderly, systemic principles do not have the capacity to strike like lightning and change you; it reinforces what is already there, a bland, cloud-based mahout offering a substitute for an actual safari, gentle prodding masked as revelation.

Nothing in my history hinted that I would be floored hearing my first blast of Elmore James's guitar, or listening with my broken heart to a twenty-eight-year-old Hank Williams sounding as timeless as the Permian Period sedimentary belts of the Appalachians. Nothing in my background suggested I would never be the same after simple-mindedly walking into a 1982 Bad Brains gig at Detroit's Clutch Cargo's or a ferocious 1984 Jason & the Scorchers show at Saint Andrew's Hall. With AM radio's saturation airplay of "Georgia on My Mind," I thought I had Ray Charles figured out, that he wasn't for me. Then I heard his frenzied 1953 Atlantic single "Mess Around." Shit, these were two very different Rays; I'm glad I didn't give up on him. Before I basked in the unrestrained joy radiating from the Chicago Theater stage and settling into the aisles filled with spontaneous dancing, Ibrahim Ferrer and Rubén González were merely names of Cuban musicians I had read about but had never heard. I fancied I had a grip on the intensity of punk, then I slapped on a Sister Rosetta Tharpe album that I had bought because the cover looked boss, and I realized I didn't know shit. If I had followed—or been led by—algorithms, I might never have heard the three chords, *strum . . . strum . . . STRUM . . .* at the beginning of the Cramps' "Sunglasses After Dark," a sun peeking over the horizon in *2001: A Space Odyssey*, a *Thus Spake Poison Ivy*–level epiphany. These weren't incremental nudges; these were incitements. Anyone who loves music lives for these moments. Late-night, left-of-the-dial radio shows, fellow outcast bandmates, friends with enormous record collections, small labels I loved and trusted, and record store clerks, those had been my algorithms.

What awaits us beyond algorithms? I suppose, not too long from now, songs will be directly implanted into our brains by some company with fewer scruples than a Spotify owned by someone with worse tastes than a Musk; "I can't get that song out of my head" will take on a frighteningly literal meaning.

* * *

Until very recently, one of my charming eccentricities was my battered flip phone. In an industry of ubiquitous smart phones, my ancient black Nokia provided plugged-in staff, artists, and people at shows with a great deal of amusement as it took several minutes of intense concentration for me to clunk out a six-word text.

It was a cold Tuesday in late March. Not freezing, mind you, but the stiff wind off the lake restrained any hint of spring from nudging into the city, and the graupel signaled that winter wasn't done with Chicago just yet. The North Face and fleeced populace plunged into a black mood. My expectations for the night's Cory Branan show at Schubas were low.

Fast-forward four hours: the show had been a near sell-out, the room filled with love for Cory's wild energy and songs that could be smart, cutting, and wholly hangdog romantic—often at the same time. It was one of *those* nights when I remembered why I did this, when struggles were forgotten, and all was right with the world. The label staff and Cory were on cloud nine, and I stayed two or three (possibly four) celebratory drinks longer than I had anticipated. Around one in the morning, as I was getting ready to leave, Cory handed me a roll of twenties, a $2,000 payment for his merch. I zipped it up in the breast pocket of my jacket and, at a level 2 wobble, went out into the night.*

---

* Wobbling scale: 0 = no wobbling, 4 = falling over and not getting up.

The Southport El stop was four blocks away through a neighborhood commonly swarming with sozzled brogrammers and trixies spilling out of sports bars. Tonight, the street was empty, except for that giant dude in the baggy khaki jacket jaywalking straight for me.

Uh-oh, I thought, resigned, *here it comes*.

He was half a foot taller than me, with a big head and a blocky build that crossed the slow-witted Badger from *Breaking Bad* and the animated Dire Straits' "Money for Nothing" video guy. An aura of dumb, sudden violence hung over him.

He leaned into me. *Wallet and phone*.

Since he hadn't said anything along the lines of "empty your pockets," I did not feel obligated to hip him to the fact that his nose was eighteen inches away from a hefty score. The obnoxious literalist in me might pay off for once.

I took out my phone and, as I assumed I'd be filling out a police report shortly, looked at its clock—yes, this marvel of modern communications had a clock among its many features—and noted the time. He looked at this ancient gizmo, as distant to him as a UHF dial on a console TV, and said in a flat tone, *You've got to be fucking kidding*. I reached for my wallet, but he was already disappearing down a dark side street. Maybe he assumed that, instead of a wallet, I carried a tattered leather coin purse with two buffalo head nickels and a Jewel coupon for 75 cents off a jar of Vicks VapoRub. Whatever the reason, he didn't hang around. Poor guy. He had mustered the nerve to mug someone in an area normally ripe with targets, and instead got me and my ten-year-old paperweight.

The point here being, every innovation might provide a quick boost, more efficiency, more convenience, but then what? Building a creative endeavor reliant on, or reacting to, a particular red-hot, bee's knees, cutting-est of cutting edge technology will be a dead end, because tomorrow there will be something else. Whatever gadgets or new platforms are *must have* as I write this are probably already obsolete. Carping about or trying to stop technological advances has never worked; vaudeville houses bemoaned the advent of player pianos, nightclubs shook their fists at the rise of radio, Don Henley was outraged he couldn't buy another island because of file sharing, and just as I figured out how to program the proper time on my VCR, I had to toss it in favor of a DVD player that . . . wait . . . which closet is that in now? Change *will* come.

Many of the astounding (and sometimes contentious) tech transformations I experienced seem so distant and trifling now. I was one righteous dude strutting the high school hallways as I filled my skull with X-Ray Spex on my Sony Walkman. What could be better? Now it would feel like carrying a shoebox. Recordable CDs were a boon, then a bane. iPods were miraculous; now they are something else in that drawer with tangles of cords and chargers.

Napster was the end. Or was it the beginning? As a stage/production manager, a frequent duty was making sure no one was photographing or recording the shows. Imagine that now. In the early days of YouTube, many hands were wrung at conferences about the best way to keep content off the site. *It's ours,* they insisted. Now everything is there and, indeed, almost everywhere, moments after it happens. At the end of the day, if the music, the effort, the creativity, was not valued, no new format or technology would save us. Those battles had been decided already, so any indie label looking to hold on could never lose sight of their center: believing in the musicians and their art.

To that end, we had to do our best to educate people on the impacts these changes would have. We had to trust the fans would be willing to join us in assuming a level of responsibility in supporting the communities they loved—otherwise they might disappear.

Tech wasn't the answer; it was a tool, an ever-changing tool. But as a Vitamix 5200 blender can mix a killer pitcher of blood orange margaritas, it can also chop off your fingertips if you're not careful. Putting all the proverbial eggs in an untested basket, in the name of distant mirages of opulence . . . well, it was better to approach any new saviors with a cautious eye, stay focused on the basics, and sometimes hold on to the flip phone.

What is the future of labels?

Amid the upheaval brought on by the abandonment of physical formats and the transition to streaming, the very necessity of "the label" was called into question. Since anyone could put their music out themselves via countless avenues, why bother signing to a label anymore? What was the benefit?

While the hold of monolithic gatekeepers has been greatly, and rightly, curtailed by the rise of independents and the internet, news of the death of labels had been overblown. For the fan, with tens of thousands of songs being released every day, with millions already out there, the miracle and the curse of having every one of them at our fingertips could be paralyzing. Navigating this enormity was like staring into the Matrix while sailing the Charlie and the Chocolate Factory Wonka-tania around the warehouse at the end of *The Raiders of the Lost Ark* after spending the afternoon at the all-you-can-eat Super Happy China Buffet. For the artists, in the absence of filtering or limiting mechanisms, how would they find fans and supporters over the din of everyone screaming "look at me" at once? What set their music apart?

That was where a label could help. We offered artists a conduit to fans, and fans a conduit to artists, one that, I hoped, had been built on trust. Good indie labels, like the curated record store or trusted radio show, reduced the sheer volume of music into manageable portions. Good indie labels passionately fought to raise the artists above the widespread mediocrity that was easier than ever to disseminate.

There were not enough hours in the day for a working musician to take care of the business of music on their own. Over twenty-five years, we had built a network of fans, promoters, writers, radio people, and retailers that an artist would have had a hard time developing on their own. They needed a supporting crew to take the panoply of niggling organizational bits off their plate, maximize opportunities, and stay on top of the expanding hodgepodge of multiple income dribbles. They should not have to be burdened with the time-sucking and infuriating (yet very necessary) minutiae of promotion and distribution. If they were, they wouldn't have any brain space left to write songs. And, let's face it, many with the—*how shall we say?*—"artistic temperament" did not often possess the logistical flair to make this machine run. No one asked me to write a catchy melody, craft meaningful lyrics delving into the human condition, or deliver a stirring live show. No one should ask an artist to make sure digital service providers are given the proper metadata, coordinate an ad campaign over multiple platforms, or set up an in-store performance in Fort Collins, Colorado. We were there to free them to do what they did best: make music.

It was true that the idea that a label doing one thing—selling records—was an old-fashioned one. In that sense, then, yes, the "label" was dead. But I thought of Bloodshot as one component of an artist's "team." Perhaps that was the more relevant term now. For me, though, it was always so.

26

A Philosophical Inquiry into the Origin of Our Ideas of Music and the Sublime, Or, Music as Dumpster Pizza

When I was in college, there was a pizza place that threw away unclaimed pies after closing. Being in the prime years of stick-it-to-the-man, Raskolnikov-lite poverty, we'd stake out the dimly lit alley by the dumpster and claim our spoils. Toppings? Size? Square? Round? Who cared! Slices missing? Gloppy ovals that had slid to one side of the box? Pshaw! Bags of doughy, oily bread sticks? Bonus!

Word spread, and soon, like a growing army of Morlocks, a horde joined us seeking their rightful repast. Eventually, complaints about noise and concerns over health, safety, and liability led the place to chain the dumpster shut. How dare they!

Far from being discouraged, the rabble of the night moved on to the next pizza joint. Brand loyalty? Hah! Free pizza is free pizza. Furthermore, since the alluring patina of OUTLAW had been attached to these raids, the pepperoni was that much spicier, the bland sauce *saucier*, and the rubbery cheese more *crema della bell'italia*. Soon, no restaurant was spared as our horizons spread beyond merely pizza. Hell, it didn't even matter if we were hungry; it was the *free* that mattered.

Sound familiar?

* * *

In light of our persistent, if not unlikely, survival in a notoriously fickle and difficult line of work, it was inevitable that a measure of . . . um . . . *expertise* was conferred upon me, and I was often asked to gaze into the crystal ball: *what does the future hold for music?*

What people were really asking, even if they didn't know it, was what is the future of the music *business?* What will provide musicians with ways to keep creating while earning a living, to keep the symbiotic relationship between fans and artists alive?

In recent years, there has been a welcome growth in appreciation for locality and craftsmanship. People are aware of, and eager to support, non-corporate local breweries, craft distilleries, farm-to-table restaurants, bakeries, butcher shops, ethically sourced clothing, and small-batch anythings. Their choices reflect personal beliefs and honor effort, commitment, and ingenuity.

For whatever reason, this appreciation has not necessarily carried over to music. The staff and I watched in frustration as many self-proclaimed independent-minded fans blithely chose to purchase (or access) music for farcically microscopic amounts—or nothing at all—and spur the massive growth of faithless corporate behemoths that have never themselves created a note of music.*

As the whole point of punk and independent music was to demolish the top-down hierarchy, so too, the world wide web, at first, was a great leveler. It gave someone living in a faraway town who couldn't visit a cool record shop the opportunity to hear our music. Indie labels with limited budgets could put music and information right next to the conglomerates and let democracy reign. Sadly, and perhaps unavoidably, the internet has become no more democratic than, say, a dysfunctional oligarchy that rewards the already wealthy. The United States of America, for example, pops into mind.

Now, this same person never has to seek out a store or a label, or come face to face with an artist; the entirety of music is laid before them on a velvety pillow of petabytes. This consequential shift in technologies had a profound effect on listeners' relationship to music and how they valued it. With every innovation, music became cheaper and more convenient, something to be gotten with little effort and even less cost. This is a very real issue of livelihood for musicians, and we appealed to fans to recognize that their decisions didn't happen in a vacuum and carried consequences. At the level most indie artists exist, we're not talking about upgrading the Gulfstream jet; every lost sale hurts. It's that much less money for gas in the tank to get from Little Rock to Louisville, that much less time off from day jobs to go on tour in the name of exciting music that existed on the fringes. They won't be able to come back. Period. There are no winners.

When I pressed people (gently, I hope) about this dissociation between thought and action, many replied with variations of *I didn't buy the record,*

* Maybe Jeff Bezos has released an amazing folk-rap album, but I haven't heard it.

but I posted a video on TikTok or *I'll get a T-shirt at the next show.* Well-intentioned but lost-the-big-picture friends once told me, "We're against Spotify, but we use it." These same people would never walk out of a cocktail lounge after drinking a $20 basil-tini sweetened by honey from a beehive on the roof without paying and justify it with *I'll post on Instagram later about how amazing it was.* To treat art as a "take one, they're free" kiosk hurts labels, artists, writers, filmmakers, photographers, and anyone else in the creative fields. A memorable album that connects to you, that connects you to others, that becomes part of who you are, should be worth at least as much as that drink that will, one way or another, be out of your system in a few hours.

And not to be the "I labored five miles uphill—both ways!—in a snowstorm wearing boots with holes in the soles to the record store to buy the Mono Men's *Wrecker*" guy, but before the internet, if you heard a song or a saw a band that piqued your interest, you had to *find* the music. There was value in that effort. Does something sink in and become a part of you if the extent of the effort to get it was entering a keystroke or two and—*bango!*—it's on a server or, even more mystifyingly, the cloud? Yeah, it's uncomplicated and often without a noticeable cost, but it has all the soul of the food court in O'Hare's Terminal 3. It makes music feel . . . frivolous.

The fan, unaware or unbothered by the underlying intentions—*I want the lowest price, end of story*—submits to the perfidious convenience hidden in the algorithms of a few companies. I first noticed their subtle, disquieting manipulations after a grisly hiking accident on Colorado's Mt. Princeton. I needed a cane for a few months, and, since I couldn't very well walk on over to Al's House of Fancy Walking Sticks, I ordered one from Amazon. Previously, the only items I'd ordered from them were obscure rockabilly Christmas collections for DJing purposes and a DVD set featuring Johnny Rotten, Iggy Pop, and the Clash on the *Tomorrow with Tom Snyder* show. After the cane, the algorithms took over. Gone were recommendations for punk rock box sets or turntable accessories, now they tried to seduce me with offers for suction-cup shower stall bars and bulk rates on Depends. I've been wary ever since.

On our way to South by Southwest one year, a couple staffers and I were in the middle of the nowhere between Champaign and Cairo on I-57 in downstate Illinois. It was getting late, we were hungry, and expectations were low; dinner would be no more than, as Bukowski put it, *fuel for the machine.* We came to an interstate clump with a UN of cuisines—we could travel the Silk Road at Panda Express, go Down Under at the Outback, *viaggio in Italia* at Olive Garden, *viajar a Mexico* at Qdoba or Chipotle—where centuries of global culinary refinement were reduced to fried sticks and balls accompanied by specimen cups of dipping sauces. There was even, I kid you not, something (someone?) called Carlos O'Kelly's that had a banner heralding/threatening, again, I'm not kidding, "The Best Margaritas and Fish & Chips."

We homed in on what looked like a regional chain with a low-key family restaurant vibe. It was only seventy-five yards away but took fifteen minutes and a mile and a half of infuriating Access Road Navigation to get there. Inside, the restaurant was pastels, brass, and ferns: we've all been there a hundred times, different cities, different times, different names, but the same place. The menu was *aggro-American*, pushing regionally themed menu options like the "Wisconsin" cheeseburger, "Cincinnati" pork chop, and "Brooklyn" ziti. Every dish, accompanied by a lurid photograph that failed to heighten its appeal, pledged to take me on a "culinary joyride." I surrendered to the "ultimate" grilled cheese—a hard order to mangle—and added, for a bit of "Southern Flare [*sic*]," fried okra. It was fine. And by fine, I mean I left with a rock in my stomach, a weariness in my soul, and a fine film of *ick* on my face and hands. But I was no longer "hungry." With the excess of choice, with, indeed, the *perception* of limitless options, that the menu—as well as the entire multitude of chains that tentacled in every direction—seductively proposed, one would think that gratification would be easily attained. But in its everythingness, it achieved nothingness, or worse, emptiness (despite the roiling ball now in my stomach). There was only *food* like all the other *foods* at all the other food places.

One could—and so I will—compare it to the consumer's relationship with music in the era of limitless choices. When one has access to everything, how does anything stand out or sink in? Is it realistic to approach a musical oneness through the everythingness available in the streaming world, or does it become just another plate of half-eaten deep fried mac and cheese brisket bites that leaves one full but unsatisfied?

As the actual music becomes less and less "valuable," artists are driven by necessity to participate in festivals to make up for lost revenue, thus the festivals become bigger, thus the festivals—not the artists or the music, they are almost incidental to the event—become the story, and thus more money flows upward into fewer and fewer greasy mitts. The rest are left to scramble for the leftovers, to find a way to break through the flashing lights and shiny bits of tin foil in the gutters. Do we really prefer the spectacle of the pricey, colossal festival, the extravagant karaoke music heard on a faraway stage as we head to the henna tattoo booth or to buy a bowl of the latest craze in Taiwanese noodles after tweeting a set list in real time? The event displacing the music? Do we passively accept the sanitizing and euthanizing forces that treat community as commodity again?

I think not. I hope not.

These are choices that esteem ease of use and the paths of least resistance, but they come at a cost. If we value convenience over conscientiousness, we will be awash in the fatuous and the trivial, and art becomes a slurry of indistinguishable novelties. When someone stands in a crowd and views the show through their smartphone screen, or is distracted by a meme-tastic sideshow, and is craftily told what it means, knotted into what David Foster Wallace called "the management of spontaneous moments," do we assimilate anything to help us connect to the art, to others, on a deeper level? Or, will it disappear as quickly as today's Instagram recipe for a hibiscus donut ice cream sandwich to die for?

Many look to social media for meaningful connection, but this is a river that's often a mile wide and an inch deep. Personally, I don't care what artists think about fidget spinners or bitcoin investing, or if they consider themselves Monicas or Joeys. I wasn't interested in what cereal the Cramps liked, nor did I care if they even ate cereal. A shared love of Cocoa Puffs was not the steadying hand in an unsteady world I craved. I wanted to create the wider context and meaning of their art for myself. To do otherwise willingly (or lazily) cedes that autonomy for the superficial sake of likes, retweets, and followers. But clicks are not community.

Several years ago, I was at Schubas for the album release show of a Chicago-based singer-songwriter. In the weeks before, there were print media features, previews, and rave reviews. Several online outlets ran free song/album-of-the-day promotions. There were interviews on radio and local TV. It was an enviable buildup. The show sold out and the audience loved it, but at the end, no one bought anything: no CDs, no LPs, no T-shirts. The moment was over, the crowd filed out past the merch booth. Again, cue Bugs Bunny at the end of "The Rabbit of Seville": "Next."

But what do I know?

None of the media or promotion empires are going broke investing in mega-funhouse festivals with eye-test promo posters listing scores of bands. Streaming behemoths' grip continues to tighten as fans rationalize their use with "I'm paying something so I'm not committing piracy," as if the micro-pennies trickling their way to artists were meaningful income. In 2022, the Goldman Sachs CEO DJ'd a set at Lollapalooza; if that doesn't give you an ice water enema chill, then you're gonna love the first Grammy handed out to a song "written" by ChatGPT. If it is a "freeconomy" we inattentively end up with, where people have all the choice but none of the responsibility, where music is without inherent value, then the whole indie galaxy that was so formative to me—and to so many others—might gradually melt away. We will be left with the Bolton. It is a quick slide to masked singers, dead artist hologram tours, and songwriters who garner millions of plays but still need to keep that gig slinging pumpkin spice lattes to make rent.

In a world of hot takes and sugar-high attention spans, the kind of community building that Bloodshot engaged in might not be possible anymore. As CD sales diminished and streaming ascended, a dampening effect on the compilations, one-off collaborations, and releases by niche local artists that I loved to do had already crept in. Some of the less commercially minded artists could only afford to do shorter tours, fewer tours, no tours, or just . . . give up. It was painful to think about the music not getting released, not being supported, or, worst of all, not even being made.

We must treat the artists as partners, not assets, their art as materially important in and of itself, not a gimme or an add-on, and we need to ask ourselves what responsibility we are willing to assume to help sustain them. Similarly, we need to acknowledge the value of the businesses in our neighborhoods. We can't internalize the distorted expectations of immediacy that technology has enabled; free overnight shipping is not free (or necessary). We need to do the work and show up at the clubs. These might not be events, but as corporate media sucks up the lion's share of the oxygen covering the massive shows, it is more important than ever to go the indie venues where creation and refinement take place, where inventiveness is cherished. Without that support, clubs will, out of financial necessity, devolve into feedlots of unchallenging nostalgia, forsaking original music for Byrning Down the House—the music of the Talking Heads, an evening of Radiohead with Perry Noid & the Androids, or Too Live Crüe—the finest in dirty rap and shitty metal.* We are left with a well unable to refill itself.

In college, when my friend Jim and I were doing the *Friday Night Fish Fry* radio show, there were some big blues-nerd Yugoslavian exchange students who frequently phoned in requests. Coming from a time and place where the very ability to *possess* records was not a given, they told us about a game they developed in their record collecting circles back home. One person would

* I made up these names. I apologize if they in fact exist.

play a song from another's collection. That person would then have to know the song, the artist, the album, the year, the label, and, get this, the running time, or he would forfeit the record.

We take so much for granted.

* * *

So, what is the future of music? Well, if I knew that, I would have written this book in my guest villa overlooking the turquoise waters at Richard Branson's Moskito Island resort in the British Virgin Islands with a tumbler of sixty-four-year-old Macallan in my hand. But whatever it is, it's in our hands. And our ears. Together.

If we love something, we shouldn't kill it by accident or apathy. We need to be mindful of what kind of culture we want and make informed, *conscious* decisions that embody those beliefs. It won't be easy or one size fits all, and sustainability will be an endlessly moving target, but we must be persistent and stay invested. If we don't care where or how music (or art, or film, or literature, or . . .) is made, only that it's cheap and plentiful and we can have it any time we want, then The Walmartization of culture will continue unabated, and it might look a lot like a dumpster full of discarded pizza.

Will vinyl LPs save indie labels?

The reemergence of the vinyl LP is an objective good. Not only do LPs sound more real, more human, more present, they provide something beyond recorded sound: they are totemic artifacts of one's fandom, the ritual of playing them carrying an essential, though intangible, value. With their pops, skips, creased jackets, liner notes, and smells (when I moved to Chicago, my albums bore a bouquet of Marlboro Lights thanks to my smoker girlfriend), a beloved LP collection is suffused with markers of one's musical voyage in ways that no digital file can achieve. Price stickers on jackets take me back to the jumbled stacks of those stores where they were purchased with bottle deposit returns, plastics factory paychecks, or painting earnings. $3.99 at Wazoo for Hound Dog Taylor and the HouseRockers' *Natural Boogie* introduced me to the world of Alligator Records; $4 at Off The Record for the Ramones' *End of the Century*, with its soaring "Do You Remember Rock 'n' Roll Radio," the closest thing punk has to an opera; a trek to Car City Records on the far east side of Detroit and finding the MC5's *Back in the USA* for $4.72 made the trip a good investment. I had heard *of* them, but I hadn't heard them; now was my chance.

I bought the Bad Livers' *Delusions of Banjer* on Quarterstick Records from the band after their show at Lounge Ax, my ears ringing from the volume and disbelief of what I had just heard. When I play it, my brain calls up other bands I saw there as I was finding a sense of *place* in my new city.

Holding my *12 Cajun Hits, Volume 3* compilation on Swallow Records, I'm transported to Ville Platte, Louisiana, and the store where I picked it up, whose hand-painted sign read *Hardware/Hunt/Fish/Records/Tapes.* Featuring the Cajun National Anthem—Belton Richard's "La Jole Blonde"—and "The Back Door" by "the Cajun Hank Williams" D. L. Menard & the Louisiana Aces, the album, in turn, takes me to the cafe toward the square. They only spoke Cajun and the one word I understood the waitress say was "gumbo," which was a half chicken served in a tureen of broth so ambrosial I could have drank it by the quart.

When I was writing reviews for fanzines, I grabbed the Detroit Cobras' first 7" single "Village of Love" b/w "Maria Christina" on Human Fly Records out of a promo pile because they had "Detroit" in their name, not knowing it was the first step on a path that led to my label releasing their albums years later.

In a merch tent at the New Orleans Jazz and Heritage Festival, I blew some of my étouffée money on a record by Irma Thomas, the Soul Queen of New Orleans. With the LP in hand, I went to a show later that night at her club, the Lion's Den. After her first set played to maybe forty people, I asked her to sign the album. The cover was a twenty-five-year-old photo of her in a racy sequined dress. "Aw, I wish I still looked like that," she said as she signed it. "Um," I mumbled, I was in awe, I thought she was incandescent, "you look the same to me." Her eyebrows shot up; she hugged me and told the bartender, "You get this boy a big bowl of rice and beans." During her second set, while I was holding on to my barstool, trying not to float away, she dedicated "Time Is on My Side" to me. Pulling that record off my shelf and listening to it was a reminder to keep my eyes and ears open, because sometimes, in out-of-the-way clubs, out of the spotlight, giants still walk among us.

I believe every music *lover* has these LPs in their collection, ones that revive cherished moments but do not exist in the mindless puddles of sentimentality. They reach back but also look forward. They tap into an active web of context and autobiography. The thrill of discovery and comfort of community that I hear, that I feel, on these records doesn't fade away, and they remained instincts informing my approach to the label. To paraphrase Johnny Thunders, you can't put your arms around an MP3. Besides, if you are listening to an LP, you need to get up every twenty minutes to flip it over, which is a perfect opportunity to freshen up your drink. It also counts as exercise.

But vinyl LPs will not be a panacea for labels. Vinyl is more temperamental, time-consuming, and expensive to make, distribute, and replace, and it is subject to long turn times, backlogs, and delays at swamped pressing plants. As a bonus, LPs take up a lot of space, bulky memento mori I could feel judging me when I walked by an unsold box in the warehouse. Hopefully, there will always be a place for vinyl, but if hipsters from Silver Lake to Gowanus to Avondale stop buying it when they decide LPs aren't worth the pain in the ass to move to another apartment, labels that believed them to be the latest savior will be disappointed. No amount of special, limited editions with different weights, colors, or covers will change that.

27

The Gospel According to Joe

On September 12, 2009, we threw a block party for our fifteenth anniversary in front of the Hideout, the venerable Chicago club out by the Streets and Sanitation Fleet Management garages. We'd spent the past several months fighting for our survival in the wake of the Great Recession. With *may as well go out with a bang* aplomb and money from a well-timed beer sponsorship, we had assembled a dozen celebratory showcases that summer and fall around the country, and now we were coming home. Thanks to mulish determination and the fierce dedication of the staff, it felt like our efforts might pay off and we'd live to fight another year.*

After months of planning, the gates opened, and for the next fourteen hours I never stopped moving. Four thousand people from twenty-eight states and four countries showed up for a full, sunny day of belt sander races, a drunken spelling bee, a kids tent, Honky Tonk BBQ, and a Yard Dog exhibition.

And music.

With the Chicago skyline in the background, reminding me of the view at that long-ago Blues Festival, friends and allies old and new soaked in the Scotland Yard Gospel Choir, Bobby Bare Jr., Deadstring Brothers, Rico Bell, and the Waco Brothers; they saw joyful reunion sets by the Blacks and Moonshine Willy; thousands of like-minded loonies yelled *Chicken*! along with Scott H. Biram; and Alejandro Escovedo's "Castanets" rang out past Elston Avenue, over the Kennedy Expressway to . . . well . . . it's probably still out there, heading to that luminous black leather palace where all perfect rock and roll goes.

---

* At the Philadelphia showcase, Graham Parker, ever the team player, posed for photos with the beer sponsors and their product. Afterwards, he turned to me and said, "OK, I've had a Rolling Rock, now can I get a beer?"

Around midnight, after we paid the bands, the security and ticket staff, and the sound, stage, and light crews, and made our donations to the organizations we had partnered with, I was pleased to find that we were $29 in the black for the night. I took my half and bought a margarita the size of a fishbowl, left the rest as a tip, and fell asleep at a picnic table drinking it. First one in, last one out, and no $14.50 payday was ever so sweet.

Was this the *best* night of our mad journey that eventually spanned over twenty-five years, three hundred releases—some selling tens of thousands and some only tens of dozens—thousands of concerts, parties, and showcases, from CMJ in New York, starting at Brownie's in the Lower East Side, and then moving to Union Pool in Williamsburg, the Groove in East Nashville during AmericanaFest, and the mother of all South by Southwest day parties at the Yard Dog Gallery in Austin, not to mention the untold number of events in Chicago clubs and on stages at distilleries and breweries, galleries and LP vinyl pressing plants, street fairs and the Taste of Chicago, all extensions of the belief in inclusion, exploration, and, you know, *fun*?

Was it the singular moment, that one show, that one event, that sticks out to me?

No, because there was no end to the list of "best" nights. They come at me in impressionistic flashes, some already scattered throughout this book, and stretch from the beginning to the end. From Moonshine Willy hyping their upcoming song on *Bloodshot Records* from the Beat Kitchen stage, the first public mention of our name; the feeling of exhausted accomplishment and shock as I sat on the Western Avenue curb outside the Empty Bottle—wait, what's that a puddle of?—after the Old 97's *Wreck Your Life* release show; listening to a thrilling version of Alejandro Escovedo's "I Wanna Be Your Dog" echo through the downtown concrete canyon when he opened for Patti Smith at a WXRT festival in the plaza in the shadow of the Tribune Tower; the subversive joy of watching crowds full of little kids shouting the chorus of Robbie Fulks' "She Took a Lot Of Pills (and

Died)" at street fairs in Andersonville and Lincoln Park; Cordero's *En Este Momento* album release party at the Empty Bottle, when their Puerto Rican slinky garage punk meshed perfectly with headliner Dengue Fever's Cambodian psychedelic surf vibe—this was a night of country music, who cared *which* country? It was a party; the look of transcendence on Rosie Flores's face when she was deep into one of her solos . . . *Jeezus, the Rockabilly Filly is on my label . . .;* Neko Case and Kelly Hogan doing a perfect and absurd version of Heart's "Crazy on You" on Halloween at the Hideout (in full costume, naturally); my mind boggling at the sheer improbability of Barrence Whitfield, Andre Williams, and Dex Romweber—so many of their records on my shelves—showing up at the office at the same time one day. Split Lip Rayfield's Kirk Rundstrom diving into the crowd from the second-story Yard Dog balcony, and then, a few years later, displaying courage incarnate as he was dying of cancer on his last tour, leading the hoarse and tearful packed Empty Bottle with the exhortation from their song "San Antone:" "If you want to die with me, *let's go*."

At the end of the *Stranger in My Land* session in Australia, Roger Knox gave me a bear hug of indescribable warmth, and, chuckling a deep, resonate chuckle, told me I was alright "for a white fella." I can still feel the drums in my chest when Bobby Bare Jr. used My Morning Jacket as his band for the 2006 South by Southwest showcase promoting his upcoming *The Longest Meow* album. Justin Townes Earle's appearance on *Late Show with David Letterman,* a triumphant return to performing after a very public struggle with personal demons. I watched him knock "Harlem River Blues" (with Jason Isbell on guitar) out of the park on a TV at Delilah's with a dozen or so other folks and, afterwards, stood outside on Lincoln Avenue and wept with relief; Wanda "The Queen of Rockabilly" Jackson pushing some label weasels out of the way at a conference to smack a lipsticky kiss on my cheek and call me "doll"; Kelly Hogan whipping the Abbey Pub fruit roll-up crowd into a "Señor Don Gato" *meow, meow, meow* singalong during the matinee release party for our kids record, *The Bottle Let Me Down.* Every year at South by Southwest, with the crowds and momentum building throughout the day, the way the Yard Dog tent would vibrate when the Waco Brothers' Deano sang "I get *murdered* in Texas every time" during "Red Brick Wall."

Partly instigated by our 1999 tribute album, *Poor Little Knitter in the Road,* the Knitters reunited for a West Coast tour in December, and I flew out to see the show at the Aladdin Theater in Portland. Halfway through the set, Exene, worrying about the show, leaned over the edge of the stage to ask me if it sounded OK. Tamping down the Ren & Stimpy *Happy Happy Joy Joy* feelings in my head during my dream concert, I calmly (I hoped) assured her that everything was cool, super cool. I can still feel the looks of people around me in the crowd wondering, *Who the fuck is* this *guy?*

During a sleepy, midweek night at the Hideout, Dex Romweber was playing a sloppy solo set to seventeen people. At some point, he abruptly sat down on the stage and talked. To us, to himself, to nobody, unspooling dark thoughts and obviously struggling. *This is . . . bad*, I thought, *very bad*. Then he got up, strapped his guitar back on, and played a transfixing twenty-minute instrumental that soared—loud, quiet, urgent, intense—it was like a Beethoven movement on a Silvertone. In the middle of it, a smile crept onto his face. He was gone, man, real, real *gone*, getting lost and getting found. The ten or twelve of us paying attention were beaming at the end with the privilege of having experienced it. I'm still not sure what happened; talking to him afterwards in the alley out back, neither was he. It was as unforgettable as it was unrepeatable. And all the way to what turned out to be our last party, in November 2019, the release show for our twenty-fifth anniversary compilation—*Too Late to Pray*, where we revisited the idea that Chicago was a special place for roots music—when ROOKIE blew hundreds of minds as they hit the stage at Smashed Plastic Record Pressing with their cocky, hillbilly update of Deep Purple's crunching boogie.

But these were only moments, and not necessarily "successes," in a strict business sense. While it is easy to point to the biggest sellers or the highest profiles, the real success was watching artists grow in confidence as writers and performers and creating bodies of work that could mean so many different things for so many different people.

As an unreformable music geek, I loved that Bloodshot rewarded other geeks who liked to dig and explore. There were melancholic moods when Jim & Jennie and the Pinetops' "Mt. St. Helens" was a soothing quilt, times when the fat punk soul of Andre Williams's "Never Had a Problem" was needed to blow the cobwebs from the day, or shitty drives in unmoving traffic when I needed to roll down the windows and let the raunchy glam roots of the Blacks' "Dolly" annoy the guy stuck in the car next to me. Artists like Graham Parker, Lydia Loveless, Cory Branan, and Robbie Fulks, among others, had so many layers to their writing that I found something new in practically every listen. There were opportunities to reassess songs through different lenses or find

25th anniversary party at Smashed Plastic. Photo by Anthony Nguyen, used with permission.

something new to treasure or old friends to revisit. If the listener was willing, and I unfailingly was, the catalog was never static or fixed, it kept revealing hidden sparks, it kept giving.

Every multiple-of-five anniversary—five, ten, fifteen, etc.—I got *Did I expect the label to last this long* questions. Never. Not in my wildest hallucinations. In many ways, by advocating for frustratingly between-the-genres roots music in a city known for anything but, Bloodshot was set up to fail. Furthermore, given that the lifespan of indie labels in general can be as fleeting as the tenure of a Spinal Tap drummer or the greasy euphoria of a late-night KFC Double Down, I knew our continued existence was never assumed or assured. The work was Sisyphean, weeks, sometimes months, would go by without a paycheck, and complications were omnipresent and constantly shape-shifting. There were artists and albums that I thought *surely the broader public will recognize how objectively awesome this is* and they would catch on. Then they didn't. And if they did, standing back for a moment to marvel *We've made it* invited complacence, missed opportunities, or Icelandic volcano eruptions. Don't jinx it. Keep working.

One fine summer day when I was in a generally upbeat mood, our label manager and I visited our primary distributor in suburban Bensonhurst, out by the airplane hangars and the warehouses the size of airplane hangars. In addition to a tour of the facility, we'd be taken for lunch and drinks afterwards at a Hemingway-themed seafood restaurant. Complimentary food and booze! The sun shone brightly.

As we walked around the gargantuan facility, I became slightly depressed by the untold rows of shelves stretching to the skylights, filled with millions of CDs from thousands of bands on hundreds of labels, and tried not to get run down by unsmiling order-pickers zipping past us on roller skates and push scooters.*

Then we got to the Crusher: an imposing, sharp-toothed, blackhearted gizmo that ground unsold and returned CDs into an undignified pulp. In this maelstrom of glinty plastic and shredded paper, my eye caught a few Bloodshot titles. Watching it churn and crunch, I pondered how small we were in the scheme of the industry. It was a potent dose of perspective, "a little too much fucking perspective," as Spinal Tap's David St. Hubbins would say, that left my Old Man and the Seafood platter and watery Papa Doble with a sobering aftertaste of futility.

And was it all worth it? Hell yes, it was worth it. I never punched a clock, I don't know how to tie a tie, I never had a boss to hate, I walked into a crazy hive of activity where I never had to fear succumbing to suburban desk rot, every day was different, I got to work with music every day and many late nights, and I believed in what I did. Not everyone can say that. I was a lifelong music fan who was lucky enough to put out one album—a record geek's wet dream—and went on to create an entire collection. It was an amazing job that wasn't even a job in many ways, it was a cause.

It was so much goddamn *fun* to be a part of an audience as it was unexpectedly floored, to feel the sublime electricity when it was brought into the moment, and to have the privilege of having a part in making it happen. And no, it never got boring or annoying to stand near someone singing along at a show, seeing a Bloodshot T-shirt in the crowd or a Bloodshot bumpersticker on a well-beaten Toyota tooling around town, and hearing an artist say "Bloodshot" from the stage always, always caused a ripple of pride in me.

It's always been impossible for me to pick *one* highlight, *one* album, or *one* song— because it means looking back, and I tried to never do that. Finding unexpected amalgams of time, place, and influence in the constant, churning motion and reinvention of music—for that, one needed to keep eyes and ears forward. I moved ahead, looking for that thrill I had when I saw the unknown Old 97's open one of our early showcases, or Ruby Boots slay her debut Yard Dog appearance. I wanted that elusive and seductive feeling of hearing Howlin' Wolf, X, or the Yawpers for the first time again. Onward!!

---

* The "pickers" were all middle-aged Korean women; our guide told us that they stole the least.

During those thousands of shows, on those hundreds of albums, I was always able to find a moment, a song, an interaction, an entire evening, that spoke to the essential purpose of the label. And when it all came together, the promise, the hype, the material, the effort, the sales leading to something greater than the parts, there was nothing like it. The ongoing kick, what drove me to plug away in a rearranging-deck-chairs-on-the-Titanic industry was hearing something I believed in finding a connection. The best album would be the *next* one. The best moments could happen any night. Maybe tonight. In the process, in the work. And *even better* was always on the way.

Every year the label found a way to stay in business was a gift and a surprise. As I saw the thousand ways labels could blow up, fall apart, stray from their principles, or get pulverized by forces beyond their control, my appreciation grew for our resilience, our tenacity, and the longer I was involved with artists navigating the paths less worn, despite formidable obstacles, the braver what they did became, the drive more noble, and the results, when they went right, more mysterious and gratifying.

* * *

Bloodshot began as a side hustle—hustle meant not as a negative or a dance, but an energy, a mindset, a *get away with something until someone tells you to stop* spirit. Chicago is a city of side hustles, it's like it invented them. It was a place where the lessons and ideals I had osmosed through the years could be put to good use. Existing outside the industry, we could be ourselves—unburdened by history or convention or the meddling of outsiders—on our own scale. No one was looking over our shoulders telling us how to do things—and if they did, they were far away, and we could ignore them. With a solid bedrock of club owners who took chances on our bands early on and became advocates, media that cared and wrote about what was happening at the street level, record stores and left-of-the-dial radio lending encouragement, as well as exceptionally tolerant and curious fans, it was an exciting and productive place for artists to be. Not everywhere had such a supportive infrastructure; I never took it for granted. For these reasons, among many others, talents like Kelly Hogan, Neko Case, Jon Langford, etc., moved here and found fertile grounds. Alejandro Escovedo chose Chicago for a four-night stand in the city (at four different clubs) for the *Man Under the Influence* release, bands frequently had the best nights of their tours here, and several considered it a second home.

While many cite Nelson Algren's famous comparison of our particular patch to loving a woman with a broken nose, I imagined it as a woman who, on a first date, insisted on going for an Italian beef at a favorite spot. She knew her sweet versus hot, dipped versus not, and was hip enough to know to sit by the napkin dispenser; she rolled up her sleeves, tied her hair back, and, like a pro, dug in. Practical and fearless, sloppy and determined. That was Chicago to me. It is unthinkable that Bloodshot could have existed anywhere else.

What prepared me for these indie rock trenches? Everything and nothing. In 2017, I attended the Grammys with Robbie Fulks, whose stellar *Upland Stories* had been nominated for Best Folk Album. While he walked the red carpet, I took up a spot on the side, watching the other nominees file past—like watching cars go through a car wash—and the only artists I recognized were John Doe and comedian Patton Oswalt. But perhaps this was my advantage.

While naïve, I also believed that a balance between commerce and outside-the-mainstream art could be struck. It was through the nurturing of an innovative community that independence would thrive, and vice versa. One does not exist without the other. Finally, I never doubted that long-term personal change was possible through music, and that personal change could encourage broader social and community change. Maybe not through a particular song, or a specific concert, that's a little too Hallmark Channel-ish, but the certainty that songs, artists, and scenes could reshape how one orients to the world.

What was remarkable about our decision to start a label was how *un*-remarkable it was, and, as improbable as this endeavor was, there was something strangely inevitable about it. And by doing it, I was stepping into a continuum. Everything that followed from that first *For a Life of Sin* release took me to tangled, exciting terras incognita where extraordinary discoveries—like tree bark that will cure hypertension, dropsy, or male pattern baldness—or unpredictable dangers—like dead ends, cliffs, or first contact with tribes that knew not of syphilis or "Free Bird"—awaited.

In 1983, after slugging it out in grotty Detroit clubs like the Freezer Theater and Clutch Cargo's, the Misfits booked a gig at a more "respectable" venue: Henry Ford Community College in Dearborn. *Cool, whatever, a show's a show,* I thought. Not being well versed in the indelicate shenanigans of exotic "punk" shows, when this 110-pound hi-top sneakered dingbat stage-dove, the students below me stepped aside in alarm and I hit the hardwood floor *hard.* As I lay there, with the wind knocked out of me, faces stared down as if pondering, "This primitive expression of rebellion would make a fascinating 3-to-5-page paper for my Sociology 101 class." Oh well, sometimes people will catch you. You never knew. But I never thought *not* to jump. Once I jumped into the label, I wasn't bothered by not knowing how or where I'd land. People would catch on. Or not. Who knew?

Bloodshot endured many cycles. In the beginning, we thrived because of the gift of low expectations. Then, alt-country was *it.* And just as fast, it wasn't *it.* Wait a bit, then, again, it was hot. A year later, when no artist broke "big," "death of roots rock" pieces were written. So . . . not hot. Again. Then it was back. Rinse. Repeat. Throughout it all, I kept doing the work, because alt-country, insurgent country—or whatever it will be called next time—like a strange, colorful, and possibly poisonous toad that lies dormant in the mud of an Amazonian rain forest, will re-emerge when it is necessary.

If I had known how hard it was going to be, I doubt I would have put down the paint brush and even started. Ignorance had been a mighty shield. I didn't know what to do and followed an intuition based on preexisting forces I may not have been aware of. Who knows what sort of label Bloodshot might have been if the guy that barfed on me at the Alice Cooper show had been slumped over in a different row, or three seats down, or had one less room-temperature Stroh's out of the trunk of his Chevy Malibu in the parking lot? Or if the counter dude at Sam's Jams had laughed at me when I asked about the Ramones? I might have resigned myself to spending the remainder of high school desperately trying to find meaning and identity from a twenty-five-minute drum solo on a Zeppelin bootleg album. *Hey man, pass Bongzilla over here.*

While I ran around every year at our South by Southwest Yard Dog party, saucer-eyed with stress, excitement, and the racking fear that I was missing some detail or opportunity, few moments could compare to people thanking me with that *look* in their eye—the joy of discovery—that look that I had so many times, for introducing them to a new artist. Something had resonated with them. Something I had helped to make possible.

But them thanking *me*? Much appreciated, but they had it exactly backwards. All the showcases and parties were my way of thanking them, as well as carrying a responsibility to what had come before me, what had gotten me there, and gotten me out of where and what I was heading for. They were attempts to create spaces where I would have felt comfortable, places where simpatico people could come together and share their passion for music and everything that came with it. What I helped put into the continuum pales compared to what I took out of it. It was payback and pay forward. I like to think that eventually we were thought of as a *community* label, something more than a spreadsheet of titles and sales figures, an asset in a city that had provided me with a unique environment for experimentation and acceptance.

On an otherwise unremarkable Wednesday night at Delilah's several years ago, owner Mike Miller was entertaining a few friends from high school or something. While I nursed some powerful and obscure libation he had put in front of me, I watched him work the room. The bar wasn't crowded, there was no special promotion going on, the staff had everything well in hand. Almost unconsciously, and while still talking to his company, he walked from table to table and cleaned up tamale wrappers, straightened stools, and wiped tables, his eyes on the details, to make someone's moment in his domain a little bit better. I could relate. Achieving a level of success was a matter of never stopping caring, trying to do the right thing even if, *especially if*, no one was looking.

And being grateful, because, well, remember the Crusher.

Maybe there's something to learn from what Bloodshot did. Maybe there is more to learn from what Bloodshot did *not* do. And on it goes.

* * *

In the end, what did it all mean? Maybe nothing. While I was in the middle of it, I never had the time or the inclination to look back and dissect it. There was always another record, another artist, another showcase, the drive to move ahead. Besides, as eminent music journalist Nick Tosches wrote, "Meaning is the biggest sucker's racket of all."

Or maybe it meant everything.

In the spring of 2002, I tagged along with Trailer Bride on their first European tour, selling merch, doing media interviews about the label, meeting promoters—the long list of the behind-the-curtain things that needed doing to advance an enterprise such as ours. On a Tuesday, after two ferry rides and lots of pre-GPS navigating through the Dutch countryside in a top-heavy van we had nicknamed "Tippy," we pulled into Terneuzen, a wheel of cheese's throw from the Belgian border.

Terneuzen? I had never heard of Terneuzen. (*Het spijt me*, Terneuzen!) The two-hundred-or-so-capacity club was accessed via a narrow staircase cobbled together in the 1640s, before math, standard rises, and right angles had been invented. None of this put us in a good mood. How could there be a good show here, tonight, for an unknown band from North Carolina? We met the local promoter, and he took us to the dressing room. Behold! Platters of local meats, cheeses, and breads laid out in an aesthetically pleasing spread worthy of the still lifes we'd seen in Amsterdam's Rijksmuseum a couple days earlier. A bartender brought in an impressive selection of bottled and draft local beers and explained, in better English than a couple of the North Carolinians spoke, the flavor profile of each. Our eyes boggled. Our livers clicked their heels. In hundreds of clubs all over the United States, every night, every week, every month, every band has seen enough seasick-gray turkey slices and spreadable tubs of alarmingly orange cheese on a card table next to a Styrofoam cooler filled with Busch to last a lifetime. This was . . . unexpected.

The promoter, watching us pounce on the table like hyenas on an impala, let us know that this was for the soundcheck, don't eat too much, our *meal* would be served later. When I expressed my amazement at this bounty, at the kind effort to make us feel welcome, especially on a weeknight in a little town, he looked at me quizzically and said in his adorably clipped Dutch accent with a sincerity that almost made me burst into tears of gratitude: *But you are bringing us the music.*

And there it was.

In the office, I often felt like I was screaming into the void. The struggles, the indifference, the long hours, the low pay—many were the days when I wanted to walk to the corner payphone, call a coupla guys to burn the place down and "make it look like an accident." Late one February afternoon, after several hours of mushifying my eyes/brain in front of Excel spreadsheets, I schlepped down the office gangway to the sidewalk in the shockingly early darkness of winter. A stiff wind blew an empty Flamin' Hot Doritos bag smack into my face just as the #80 bus lumbered past and splashed me with meltwater the color of dogshit, as if to say, *Good night, Rob! See you tomorrow!*

Why . . . did . . . I . . . keep . . . doing . . . this . . .?

But you are bringing us the music.

It was a reminder of the essential lessons absorbed and instincts sharpened in funeral homes, high school hallways, and soul-deadening shopping complexes. It was, whether I consciously meant it or not, a nod to the Dead Kennedys, the clerk at Schoolkids Records in Ann Arbor who pointed me to the Chess Records collection, the open-minded owners of Lounge Ax who gave us a chance, the Flat Duo Jets handing me their record, Lux Interior screaming "Reality" to *me* from a hundred-foot-tall pillar of fire (or was it a four-foot stage?) during "Beautiful Gardens," Drivin' Sideways' boozy seminars on country music, *Radios in Motion*, the Electrifying Mojo, Brad for asking me to be in the band, Ms. Taras calling truth to power, the windowless college radio studio with miles of LP shelves, and that heavenly little freebie of brisket bark from the Louie Mueller's counterman. It was, to paraphrase Joe Strummer, an admonition to search out the good stuff, go underground, and don't buy what's shoved in front of you. It was an exhortation to hold onto the outsider feeling with both hands as if everything depended on it, because it just might. *Just keep going*, because I never knew who was out there hearing this band for the first time, who might hear this latest album and find an echo, a whisper, or an intriguing suggestion of something that might accidentally change their life.

And yes, Terneuzen could, in fact, bring it on a Tuesday night. The room was packed, the crowd had a hell of a time, and the band glowed afterwards in that inexplicable bonding spirit of music. We were all in it. We were always all in it. It can be easy to forget. It can be even harder to remember.

Epilogue

In March of 2020, the staff and I were prepping for our annual South by Southwest mischief and two sold-out Murder by Death shows at Thalia Hall. Also, the local band ROOKIE had a sold-out album release show at the Empty Bottle that weekend and was experiencing a level of buzz for a new act we hadn't seen in a while. In short, we were busy, that good kind of *really, really busy*. Which was welcome because the previous year had been tough. My business partner had left under very dark personal and professional clouds that cast shadows over what I thought were shared commitments to the values of the label. That year, the accumulated trust and goodwill that had been freely conferred upon her by the staff, the artists, and the community were treated with shocking disregard. Over the years, questions of a *What was your worst mistake, what was your biggest regret?* nature were regularly asked. For twenty-four-and-a-half years, these were difficult to answer. Cool bands had been overlooked, opportunities blown, decisions made or not made at the right or wrong time, but there was nuance, context, and hindsight to consider with any assessments of *biggest* this or *worst* that. These good-faith mistakes paled in comparison to the one that made the question regrettably all too easy to answer now. I believed we had been united in a purpose: to create a label that championed and respected artists and their work. In this, it now appeared, I was mistaken. We were stunned, and it had taken its toll. We were so tired.

But we were also hopeful. We still sincerely believed that what had taken so long to build up would not be so thoughtlessly torn down; the staff was more committed than ever and bursting with ideas to expand on the principles they had fought for so intensely over the past months; we had a roster—a mix of artists establishing themselves, veterans, and new blood—we were wholly excited about; we had over a year's worth of releases being readied, including a series of reissues that, for the first time, looked back through the catalog to introduce it to new audiences. We were as confident in the future as we'd been in some time.

Then one day, SARS-CoV-2 arrived. South by Southwest and the shows were, one by one, cancelled. On Friday the 13th, we had a staff meeting and divvied up office schedules and responsibilities, then I said, "See you in a couple of weeks." And we went home and washed our hands, coughed into our elbows, sprayed our groceries with Lysol, and binged *30 Rock*.

The couple weeks turned into a month. Then six. Then a year. In that time, our fans stepped up and mail-ordered like crazy. Our frightened, stressed hearts were warmed and humbled by their support and their notes of encouragement. They added tips. They rounded their sales totals up. It was community at its best. We worked like mad, each of us taking solo turns in the warehouse for a week at a time to fill orders. Stressed and frightened artists called me throughout the summer, as some couldn't make rent or mortgage payments, some were getting gear and vans repossessed, and some couldn't afford their medications. And all of them were separated from the audiences that energized them. I did what I could to get as much money out to the artists as quickly as I could. It was an agonizing time.

As the months went on and we learned more about the Greek alphabet than we could have ever thought necessary, incalculable damage was being wrought on every aspect of the independent music ecosystem. Listening to records home alone and watching online performances from makeshift basement "stages" was some comfort, but I acutely felt the absence of in-person interactions and adventures with fellow dedicated fans. It was a harsh reminder of how fragile it was, how years of organic, local, sustainable work and growth could vanish with astonishing speed. Nothing would ever be the same.

Eventually, due to circumstances simultaneously both well and inadequately documented, the label was forced into a sale, an outcome that neither I, the staff, nor the artists desired. And that, as they say, was that. Through all the adversities we faced, all the tribulations we overcame, that everything I believed in and built up might be taken down by a squalid internal rot never entered my mind. At any rate, the answer to *What does the future look like for Bloodshot?* is worlds different than it was when I started this project. Maybe that tour manager a long time ago in a venue far, far away was right: the music business is no place for a music fan to be.

So it goes.

I began this project in 2018 as a way to answer a host of seemingly simple questions, explore the challenges and triumphs that an independent label experiences, and reflect on the thousands of micro-decisions that made us who we were. I could also speak to the changes I've gone through personally, such as how the pill bottles on my desk that once used to be trucker speed and aspirin gave way to fish oil and Advil, or how my feelings toward bands like Steely Dan have achieved something faintly recognizable as maturity, from "I hate it—you suck, you're stupid, and you have bad taste" to "It's simply not for me, thanks." But what started as a merry romp through Bloodshot's implausible durability also ended up being something of an obituary and a farewell to the city.

This was certainly not how I imagined my time in the trenches to wind up, but few get to plan their own endings. Owning an independent label was never what I expected, but then, music was never what I expected. It was always more. Writing this book helped me remember that.

When Bloodshot started, Chicago was one of those special places in time for indie music like Athens, Georgia, Minneapolis, and Seattle had been before. Springing from the unpredictable confluences of many elements, such scenes are rare, and they come with equally unpredictable expiration dates. Since our inauspicious beginning, Chicago has changed, as it always will. Affordable, quirky diners are disappearing faster than *Zimne Pivo* signs hanging in front of bars, I get disoriented in neighborhoods where I used to know every secret-squirrel unmetered parking space and which taco joint had the best asada, and the developments around Wrigley Field have transformed the area into a bland entertainment district. Shows at long-shuttered Chicago watering holes like the Clearwater Saloon, Jimmy and Tai's Wrigleyville Tap, and the Double Door feel like crazy fever dreams from another time. Since Lounge Ax closed, it has been a revolving door of shitty frat boy hangouts, the Augenblick turned into a floral shop, and Quencher's a kids' dentist office. COVID-19 ravaged many of my neighborhood's gems. Rosded, my beloved Thai hole in the wall, couldn't hold on, and I'll be having no more late-night grilled cheese at Jeri's Grill. The eccentric and inviting Huettenbar is now a nondescript bar place, its homey Bavarian murals and chalet scrollwork replaced by half a dozen flat-screen TVs showing the latest sports games.

Just as cities change, bands and labels rise and fall, elements of scenes ossify into cliques, stores, and venues open and close, so many things we hold dear in our creative and social spheres feel dismayingly fragile. Despair not, though: fresh and passionate crusaders will emerge to reinvent and reinvigorate out-of-the-mainstream, not-quite-normal ideas in continually surprising ways. We won't have to wait long because it never stops. In fact, it already happened. Yesterday. Last week. Two months ago. Tomorrow.

And since music is so powerful, and the need for the working band in the neighborhood remains, there will be someone stupid enough, brave enough, and obstinate enough to start a label so it can be heard. Even though I always answered "Don't" to the question "What advice can you give to someone who wants to start a label?" it's gonna be rough, but get to it. Time's a-wasting. Over the years, I was asked lots of questions, but the question I asked myself the most was "How can I help?" So, how can you help?

In the fall of 2022, the Banditos played a gig at Chicago's Golden Dagger and asked some of the former staff and me to come. When they brought the band to my attention at South by Southwest a few years earlier, I was quickly taken with them and their music. They were an endearing bunch of rowdy friends from Alabama with big hearts and great potential in their meat-and-three platter of Southern rock gusto, Muscle Shoals hipshake, and populist choogle that recalled many but sounded like nobody but themselves. We saw a solid future for them, especially after they took imposing Metro stage as unknowns during our twentieth-anniversary show in 2014 and immediately made a thousand converts.

Now here they were, in a much smaller club, without a team behind them, and, between COVID-19 and the chaos engendered by one of their former label owners, their window to "make it" had likely closed. Hanging out before the show, some band members were surprisingly sanguine about the situation. They weren't making any money at this, they had day jobs, some now had families, but they still loved performing, traveling, and the camaraderie. It was different, and it wasn't where they thought they would be, but they still felt a joy, a value, in doing it.

During the encore, there was some muted onstage discussion about what to do next.

I picked up "Should we do it?"

"Rob will love it."

A repeated four-note riff, tense, edgy . . . instantly recognizable . . . on a lone guitar. A *something* rushed through the room. Without really being aware of it, I floated to the front of the stage as thirty seconds later (or was it thirty years before?) the whole band tore into a redneck soul version of Television's proto-punk masterpiece, "Marquee Moon."

Everything outside that building, everything I'd been dragged through the previous couple of years—and would endure for another couple more—melted away. It was transporting. It was eight minutes that echoed everything that had gotten me to the front of that stage in the first place, as well as a suggestion of what *might be* . . .

It is impossible to describe the privilege and gratitude I felt in that moment.

Acknowledgments

Thanks to:

The fans: You came early, and you stayed late. I thought of you in everything I did because I always remained one of you. I apologize for all the awkward exchanges at clubs over the years; I'm awkward. I once asked a bartender during a chaotic show of ours how the crowd was treating her, and she said, "Your shows are fine. Your fans are polite, sloppy, and good tippers." I am all these things and proud to be associated with such a lot; it's a crowd I want to hang with.

The last staff: If you were a boss, you wanted them on your team. If you were a band, you wanted them on your side. If you were a fan, you knew that they were, too. Hannah Douglas, Mike Smith (if that's his real name), Nina Stiener, and Josh Zanger: loyal, resolute, and possessing unshakable moral cores. Like no others, they knew what we were fighting for and what we were up against, especially at the end. I am forever in your debt.

Every band that played their guts out on a night that it didn't matter except to a few people: I was one of those few. It did matter.

The Bloodshot artists: That you allowed me to be a part of the bodies of work you created was an expression of faith that never stopped being humbling and that I never took lightly.

The fans, allies, and artists—you know who you are—who took the effort to reach out with small kindnesses and simple expressions of friendship and support during the dismal times after my departure from the label; you'll never know how much they meant.

Copy editor Natalie Reitano, for her "light dusting," and project manager Tad Ringo for his patience—their fingerprints are all over this book and it is so much the better because of it; the whole team at the University of Illinois Press; and most of all, Martha Bayne: During a Job-level sequence of

The Bloodshot staff at Delilah's, 2019: Josh, Hannah, Nina, and Mike. Photo by Anthony Nguyen, used with permission.

personal travails, she gave her time and her talents to be an early champion of this project, pulling me out of my own darkness. As an editor and friend, her patience and encouragement made the result immeasurably better. She even helped make me a bit better.

Also, to Anthony Nguyen for his photography and unflagging good nature, Lisa Christensen, JP Pfäfflin for buying me that flip phone, Joe Swank for the endless joy his velour saxophone pants brought the office, all former staff and interns who honored me and the artists with their time and talents, Figgy Pudding (if you know, you know), the Garage Mahal crew and Roy Kent (he's here, he's there . . .), the Fernet Boys and the Pretzel Gang, Melissa Hellstern, Sharon Woodhouse of Conspire Creative, Jeff Nelson and Neko Case for their thoughtful last-minute suggestions, Mike and Sally Miller (no relation, probably) for owning Delilah's and providing Bloodshot with an early clubhouse, Ramesh Soekhoe for the Dutch translation help, the ghost of Heywood Broun, the breweries of southwest Michigan, WRHC-FM Radio Harbor Country for letting me spin weird records from my collection, and the libraries of Bridgman, Stevensville, Three Oaks, and St. Joseph, Michigan, and Chicago's Sulzer Regional Library. As America once again embraces harassment of librarians, book-banning, and book-purging, I am freshly appreciative of the free and unfettered access to ideas public libraries provide.

Bloodshot 15th anniversary at the Hideout Block Party. Photo by Marty Perez, used with permission.

What an irreplaceable resource they are and should forever remain. Public libraries: Don't Fear Them!

Special thanks to Gromit aka Grom-Grom aka Lord of the Sniff aka Count Sniffington aka Sir Sniffs-A-Lot, for the long, ponderous walks when I needed them, and profound gratitude to Diana Maldonado for being there when we returned.

APPENDIX A

A Way There Always Is

Tour Manager Words of Wisdom

I constantly Skywalkered expertise from the parade of grizzled tour manager Yodas who came through town. Their wisdom went beyond tips on conjuring good monitor sound out of a shitty system, how to make a lighting rig look better than it really was, or when to push the crew and when to let them find their rhythm; it was an almanac of accumulated lore and *there once was a band that*... teachings.

On navigating the show:

- Never give your duct tape to anyone. Follow them and get it back.
- Steal every Sharpie you can. You'll always need one more.
- Never let the band crack a bottle of the good stuff after the set. It's just a waste.
- Jameson's is more controllable than vodka. Never let the band go onstage with vodka.
- Never refuse clean towels.
- Re: Intervening between an aggro, drunk fan and a bouncer: It's unwise to get between a fool and his folly.
- Re: Setting up gear that requires precision after a heated disagreement: Never shave angry.
- Re: Be wary of chatty, charming promoters: They've got endless stories. All of them pointless and most of them lies.
- Beware of club owners who overpromise and under-deliver.

An introduction to the Buddhist fatalism and gallows humor casserole everyone dines upon when a night goes wrong:

- You can't make lemonade out of shit.
- When Jesus closes a door, he opens a window, but he never pushes the right son of a bitch out of it.

- Life isn't a kung fu movie, where problems come at you one at a time.
- Re: Tour managing a band he hates, both personally and musically: If being a glutton for punishment made me fat, they'd have to load me on the bus with a crane.
- The best part of the show is when he says, "Thank you and good night."

On navigating after the show:

- NO ONE misses bus call at the hotel. I don't care if your name is on the marquee, 8 a.m. means 8 a.m.
- After doing an idiot check of the hotel room, have another idiot check it.
- Make sure the correct number of bodies are on the bus when you leave the truck stop. People wander off. Especially drummers.
- If you're driving the van, make sure your piss bottle is screwed tightly shut. You spill, you clean.
- Take any apparel offered at any radio station or record store where you appear. You don't want to mop your sweat or soak up a spilled beer in the van with a shirt you care about.
- Never leave anything to eat or drink behind; that hospitality plate banana or generic hummus might not look good before, during, or after the show, but a hundred miles from nowhere at four in the morning, it'll look like a T-bone steak.
- Never get BBQ in Texas from a place that needs a billboard to advertise it.
- If you can, avoid Indiana.
- GET THE MONEY.

APPENDIX B

Delilah's Country Night Playlist

Playlist of cassette recordings from a couple of nights circa 1997:

Dwight Yoakam	"Little Sister"
Jerry Jeff Walker	"Up Against the Wall, Redneck Mother"
Roger Miller	"Dang Me"
Kitty Wells	"It Wasn't God Who Made Honky Tonk Angels"
Jason & the Scorchers	"Absolutely Sweet Marie"
Buck Owens	"My Heart Skips a Beat"
Bodeco	"Hill and Gully Rider"
Tammy Wynette	"Stand By Your Man"
John Doe	"Dyin' to Get Home"
Tennessee Ernie Ford	"16 Tons"
Mojo Nixon	"Chug-A-Lug"
Johnny Cash & June Carter Cash	"Jackson"
Marty Robbins	"El Paso"
Dolly Parton	"Puppy Love"
John Anderson	"Swingin'"
Rolling Stones	"Country Honk"
Loretta Lynn	"Fist City"
Minutemen	"Corona"
Michelle Shocked	"(Making the Run to) Gladewater"
Meat Puppets	"Comin' Down"
Red Sovine	"East of West Berlin"
Pogues	"Boys From the County Hell"
Ronnie Dawson	"Up Jumped the Devil"
Ray Price	"Heartaches by the Number"
The Texas Rubies	"Hank Drank"

Southern Culture on the Skids	"Daddy Was a Preacher but Mama Was a Go-Go Girl"
Suicide Kings	"Even Hookers Say Goodbye"
BR5-49	"One Long Saturday Night"
Dale Watson	"Nashville Rash"
Ray Charles	"Busted"
Nine Pound Hammer	"Run Fat Boy Run"
Junior Brown	"Highway Patrol"
The Reverend Horton Heat	"You Can't Get Away from Me"
Charley Pride	"Is Anybody Going to San Antone?"
Johnny Horton	"Honky Tonk Man"
Mudhoney & Jimmie Dale Gilmore	"Buckskin Stallion Blues"
Elvis Presley	"That's Alright Mama"
George Jones & Tammy Wynette	"(We're Not) the Jet Set"
The Mekons	"Hole in the Ground"
Lefty Frizzell	"Saginaw, Michigan"
Texas Tornados	"Is Anybody Goin' to San Antone"
The Flatlanders	"Dallas"
The Gun Club	"Bad Indian"
Dave Dudley	"Six Days on the Road"
World Famous Blue Jays	"Do It for Hank"
Beasts of Bourbon	"Ten Wheels for Jesus"
Wayne Hancock	"Thunderstorms and Neon Signs"
The Red Devils	"Tearin' My Hair Out"
Wanda Jackson	"Riot Cell Block #9"
Link Wray	"Fatback"
Johnny Burnette & the Rock and Roll Trio	"Tear It Up"
Tex Williams	"Smoke, Smoke, Smoke That Cigarette"
Jon Wayne	"Texas Wine"
Evan Johns and the H-Bombs	"My Baby She Left Me"
Bad Livers	"Lust for Life"
Speedy West & Jimmy Bryant	"Stratosphere Boogie"
Flat Duo Jets	"My Life, My Love"
Osborne Brothers	"Rocky Top"
David Allan Coe	"Longhaired Redneck"
Bill Kirchen	'Tombstone Every Mile"
The Beat Farmers	"Gun Sale at the Church"
X	"Beyond and Back"
The Pontiac Brothers	"Straight and Narrow"
George Thorogood	"Move It On Over"
The Flying Burrito Brothers	"Sin City"

Merle Haggard	"Mama Tried"
Jerry Lee Lewis	"Breathless"
Charlie Rich	"Lonely Weekends"
Al Caiola	"The Magnificent Seven"
Ennio Morricone	"The Good, the Bad and the Ugly"

APPENDIX C

The Unhappy Hour

From 1 a.m. until closing, I'd pull out the dark stuff for what I called *The Unhappy Hour.*

George Jones	"He Stopped Loving Her Today"
Patsy Cline	"She's Got You"
Tammy Wynette	"Apartment #9"
Lefty Frizzell	"Long Black Veil"
Johnny Paycheck	"Pardon Me, I've Got Someone to Kill"
Hank Williams	"Ramblin' Man"
k.d. lang	"Crying"
The Handsome Family	"Drunk by Noon"
The Louvin Brothers	"In the Pines"
Iris Dement	"Big City"
Willie Nelson	"Blue Eyes Cryin' in the Rain"
Tom T. Hall	"The Homecoming"
Roy Orbison	"Love Hurts"
Bobby Bare	"Detroit City"
Charlie Pickett & the Eggs	"Liked It a Lot"
The Blasters	"Little Honey"
Thin White Rope	"Bartender's Rag"
The Knitters	"Trail of Time"
Webb Pierce	"There Stands the Glass"
Ry Cooder	"I Knew These People" (from the *Paris, Texas* soundtrack)
The Gun Club	"Mother of Earth"
Jim Reeves	"He'll Have to Go"

Commander Cody	"Daddy's Drinking Up Our Christmas" (a staple of the Holiday Unhappy Hours!)
Freakwater	"Out of This World"
Freddy Fender	"Wasted Days and Wasted Nights"
The Cramps	"Lonesome Town"
Hawkshaw Hawkins	"Barbara Allen"
Johnny Cash	"The Man Who Couldn't Cry"

APPENDIX D

It's Genuis!

Greatest Hits from the Demo Wall of Shame

I'm not sure who first taped a sad/funny/ridiculous bit from a demo package to the bathroom wall at the office, but as the years went on, the tired, brown tilework got covered by a rotating collage of foul-ball proposals, lyric sheets, and head shots. Visiting bands lingered in the bathroom, the laughter and *wows* audible from all the way in the front room; when we had events at the office, fans stood in the doorway and took photos.

For me, the Wall of Shame was two things. One, yes, it was objectively funny. But two, it was a reminder to show humility. As screwy as they were, they were trying. To see these efforts every day was to know there was so much going on beyond our walls, and that mine was but one opinion. They weren't for us, but someone might love them. *One man's trash*, as they say. And, for all I knew, somewhere out there was another wall of shame with half our bands' demos on it.

With that caveat, I give you some of the classics. Names and song titles have been redacted to protect the misguided. Emphases are mine.

> "I'm a *freshman in high school*, who has been working *my entire life* in music. I recently just did a show and was told that I should try and get signed. I'm very much into indie rock and the alternative selection. Here is a sample of my last night's performance, please excuse the tiny child throwing a fit."

> "I just think my songs are REALLY good, even better than the ones on TV. I also think I'm good looking, which completes the package."

> "I can sing. Signed [X]"
> (*Kudos for getting to the point.*)

> "I am currently looking for a label. The format is alternative country and it's a very good album. I am not computer oriented and do not have an e-mail. Please drop me a line and I will forward the CD to you."

"Hi, my name is [X]. I have in my possession about *1000 songs* that I've written. How would I go about doing this and getting compensated?"

No idea who we were or what we did:

"We are *a groove metal band* that features former guitarist from XXX. May we send you some information on the band?

"We are a *5 piece metal band* from Pittsburgh. *We have studied up on Bloodshot Records* and determined that working with you would help take us in the direction of our goals."

"We write humorous lyrics that combines *Tenacious D with '60s rock.*"
(*Tell me more!*)

"Wondering if you would be interested in working together. *I am a comedic rapper*. People say I sound like a combination of Weird Al and Eminem."
(*How could we not be?*)

"Our group is called XXX. We are an *evangelistic musical group* with the sole purpose of evangelizing God's word to a world that so desperately needs to know our Lord and Savior."

"My name is XXX. I am a Junior Communications major. I have a passion to serve the Lord and make His name famous by having His Word known."
(*As a communications major, he gets an A+ for identifying his target label.*)

"I am XXX and I'm a solo singer and a rapper and I can sing the voice of Akon, Mark Antony, Justin Bieber, Pitbull, Akcent, One Direction, Zayn and many more. I can sing better than all of them. I want a record contract from you. So what do you say?"
(*The answer has to be yes, yes, YES!*)

Buttering us up never hurt:

"I am sending you my demo because I have heard you were professional and serious."

"Your company rocks. We have performed our research on your label company & would be honored to collaborate with your label on XXX's adventure into outstanding progression. We are eager to tour & to have BLOODSHOT RECORDS backing us into THE FUTURE. Our goal is to have BLOODSHOT RECORDS as our label and gain as many endorsements and sponsors to collaborate with for progression into a successful future as top artists."
(*Your word salad intrigues me.*)

The hard sell:

"I suck at mixing. Attached are [*sic*] some stuff I recorded on my phone and some songs that still need work."

> "The demo was poorly recorded and over-processed . . . A few of our tracks (the better ones) are available on our website."

> "I received your name from a person of influence in the music industry. We have hooks, bridges and LYRICS!"

> "I have 16 originals and 10 covers. All memorized!"
> (*Show-off!*)

> "If you happen to listen, I screwed up the track listing as well. The second half is really better. XXX and YYY really kind of stink. Who knows? My friends like XXX. No one likes YYY. Oh well."

> "Dear Sir/Madam: I'm deeply sorry about the vocal recording on this track, I'm not a singer."

> "I don't mind showing my boobs in a video if it gets me more views."

Finally, I don't claim to be perfect, nor do I believe that many of my musical heroes weren't barely literate and no less brilliant because of it, so I couldn't help but be charmed by sloppily written demo pitches:

> "I want to get *singed* quickly."

> "Music has been a *hugh* influence on my life"

> "A radio station programmer referred to me as a *genuis*."

> "We didn't want to *right* a long bio . . ."

Don't get me started on misuse of the possessive . . .

> "I won't make a speech, I'll let my *song's* speak for me."

> "After two self-released *album's*, we think we are ready for the next step."

> "The Bottle *Rocket's* is one of our favorite bands, so we are sending this demo to you."

> "We've gone on three national *tour's* with much success."

And a ***chef's kiss*** for getting our name wrong, a misspelling, and misusing the possessive:

> "The band *agree's* that *Blood Shoot* Records will be a great fit for our *carreer*."

APPENDIX E

Random Things I Hated

About those pet peeves . . .

- Once social media became a thing, I was not concerned with your number of followers when considering a demo. I once heard a major label flack at South by Southwest bark authoritatively into his cell that he didn't even *listen* to a band unless they met very specific thresholds. Then he rattled off these sacred numbers, as if music was a goddamn mathematics equation. I should also mention this happened while he was standing next to me at a urinal. Volume should not be confused with virtue. All sorts of terrible people have lots of followers.
- People who tried to sell me on their "rural" credentials. Working in and around a genre of music that many people had a narrow belief about where it came from and who could perform it, I was regaled with Rockwellian vignettes of growing up without running water, roping calves, repairing the clutch pressure plate on a 1949 Farm-All Cub, and relatives smeared with coal dust, even if they had to go back three generations to find one. Rebuilding my grandma's outhouse or helping her render hog fat didn't imbue me with the powers of song, subset country.
- Don't look bored on stage; if *you* didn't care about your music, why should I? If music was to be more than Muzak, it had to be played with conviction. Moxie trumped technical prowess for me every time.
- The "music as cocktail recipe" description: Bands that described their sound as "Add one part punk to two parts classic country and a dash of yacht rock" made me one part hostile plus two parts leery. With a twist of eyeroll.
- Prolific output boasting was a flapping red flag signaling issues with focus. I wasn't aflutter when somebody had five more records "ready to go," was in four other bands, and had written three hundred "really

good" songs. Know who else has written three hundred really good songs? No one.

- Mistaking unsigned and ungood for underground and edgy. If a demo submitter couldn't get a major label deal, well then, by God, that must mean they were "insurgent" and thus perfect for us. They googled "independent" and "country" and maybe our name popped up, so they sent us their slick mainstream-wannabe songs about *drivin' 'round this old town*, with sepia-toned photos of a burly guy in cowboy hat and boots walking along the train tracks with a guitar slung over his shoulder. It was like One Direction reaching out to Sub Pop.
- Bands who looked at the rich, indelible history of humor in country music, who cited Bloodshot artists like the Waco Brothers, Robbie Fulks, Bottle Rockets, and Split Lip Rayfield, and equated them with hayseed shtick. The Dadgummits, the Corn Likker Boys, or the WhiskeyBillies, who described themselves as country-fried, beer-swillin', hog-tossin', yee-haw hellraisers, smacked of a shallow appreciation of both the wittiness *and* the seriousness of country, as if "The Streak" was interchangeable with "Long Black Veil." (To the best of my knowledge, I made these band names up. I apologize if they in fact exist.)
- Accordingly, promo photos with hay bales, pitchforks, shotguns, or heads resting on a bar with an empty bottle in hand should have been tossed in a bonfire, not sent to us.
- Dress-up folk singers with a well-cultivated, neo-Depression rumple and Woody Guthrie affectations, and hard-luck country artists in pristine vintage Wrangler pearl-snap shirts who looked and sang like they had never been beaten up or hungover. Come back after living and losing a bit more. Certain music demands some scar tissue.
- After we released albums by Justin Townes Earle and Bobby Bare Jr., sons of Nashville royalty, submissions highlighting prospective artists' genealogical *bona fides* started arriving. *Greetings, I am writing on behalf of Little Jimmy Dickens's cousin's niece. You probably know the work of my aunt, Lynn Anderson. My uncle is a Statler Brother.* While it probably seemed like a good tactic to slow me down as I speed-read through yet another bio, perhaps we could discuss its effectiveness over drinks while we listen to my favorite Chet Hanks raps and Frank Sinatra Jr. albums.
- Genre opportunists: Several known and semi-known rap-rock, goth, punk, and metal artists, as well as a few TV and movie B- and C-listers, who had hit a creative or commercial wall heard that "this country stuff" was a "desirable sound." Since they were "country at heart," they coopted trendy aesthetics for a "fresh" and "unconventional" sound, which was neither. In a way the idea was tempting; they would have certainly gotten media attention and possibly even been financially beneficial, but the music was . . . unimpressive. And, after my stage-managing experiences, I wasn't prone to being wooed by

fame, anyway. The one time I have been genuinely starstruck—other than whenever I was in proximity to a member of X—was on a family trip to Universal Studios. We were in the commissary line when my mother pointed to the man behind us. It was Alan Hale Jr., the m'f'n *Skipper* from *Gilligan's Island*! In full costume! (They were filming the made-for-TV masterpiece *Harlem Globetrotters on Gilligan's Island*.) Wiping aside a look that I would later recognize as a Thoreauian "life of quiet desperation," he gamely summoned a "Hey there, little buddy." Magical, I tell you.

- If the percussionist wore harem pants crafted in Chiang Mai and thanked everyone at the yoga center, they were barking, or chanting, up the wrong tree by sending a demo to me.
- Finally, if the band photo contained more than zero (0) dudes wearing sandals, they should put their demo in an iron box and toss that iron box into the Mariana Trench.

Again, these were my eccentricities. Perhaps others shared them; perhaps not. For all I knew, other labels might *insist* on seeing hairy hammer toes in promo photos.

APPENDIX F

A Box Full of Letters

We got a lot of mail. Remember mail? Tactile, real-world mail? We got drawings of bands, Polaroids of Bloodshot stickers on gear at the tops of mountains or on the bumpers of '87 Cutlasses, boxes of candy, home-cured meats, and letters.

Notes came on crumpled paper, torn half sheets of paper, flyers, backs of receipts, grocery bags, bar coasters, a Wendy's bag, even parking tickets. They were written in pen, pencil, Sharpie, crayon, or on a typewriter with lots of XXX crossed-out words. There were cursive scrawls that wandered all over the page and around the margins—a possibly alarming look into a person's life in that moment—and neat, orderly, blocky print, the occasional heart substituting for the dot on an "i." I could smell cigarette smoke or booze on many of them. Some were stained with coffee rings.

We received compliments and condemnations, unintelligible nonsense, and long, thoughtful stories of how a particular artist or album connected with them. There was late-night gallows humor—I imagined them blasting the music while they sat in their favorite threadbare chair, surrounded by empty beer cans and a pizza slice on the speaker—and simple expressions of gratitude for our efforts. There were show reviews, album reviews, suggestions for local bands, banana pudding recipes, and some felt like old friends just checking in on us. But they took the *time* to write, find an envelope, buy a stamp, and groggily wander down the street in their robes to a mailbox to *mail* them. That sort of commitment commands respect and admiration in this day of anonymous and instantaneous communication.

Receiving them was a real connection, a human exchange between fan and label. They felt comfortable, welcome, and involved enough—perhaps even obligated—to tell us what was on their minds. You don't feel that in a tweet.

Doodle accompanying a fan letter.

Here is a tiny sampling of my favorite correspondence over the years, a cross-section of the highs and lows, both praise and scorn, both sweet and demented, and quite often profane. Emphases are mine.

Arcata, CA:

> "Your label is kick ass. I thank god for you every day, and I'm a professional theologian, so it means something."

Jamaica Plains, MA:

> "I am Irish. Sick of fuckin *Riverdance*. Rather hear Mexicans sing with their hands in the air than watch Irish dance with their hands by their side. What the Celtic scene has turned into has become embarrassing. What Bloodshot is doing should receive the Nobel Prize for shit kicking music. As for that fucker Michael Flatley!! I'd like to take that tin whistle of his and stick it up the royal arse of the Lord of the Dance."

Eureka Springs, AR:

Send me another copy of the Blacks' *Dolly Horrorshow* CD ASAP. My kids took my cassette copy and lost it in the quagmire of their bedroom—it was their favorite lullaby they used to play in their Fisher-Price cassette player (creepy, huh?). I am having the DTs."

(*Yes, all kinds of creepy for all kinds of reasons.*)

Spokane, WA:

"Heard one of your CDs at Tiger Tattoo shop while watching my son get his back done. Thanks for your efforts, keep the circle unbroken."

Round Rock, TX:

"Not that you care or anything, but I'm getting divorced and ex took almost all of the CDs. Thanks for helping me get some of my favorites back."

(*We DID care!!! If it weren't for marital disintegration, where would country music be?*)

Sonoma, CA, re: Robbie Fulks:

"I may be 60, but I can still appreciate a 'talent' when I hear one. Hope he has a LONG and successful career."

(*The use of the quotation marks around "talent" could be a mistake or could rise to a level of snark that Robbie would appreciate.*)

Colfax, KS:

"'She Took a Lot of Pills (and Died)' is now my official favorite song of all time. I played it 10 times in a row last night and my girlfriend swore she would leave if I played it one more time. I got the headphones out and poured her a drink. She stayed."

Evansville, IN:

"Fave Bloodshot bands? Unfair. That's like asking me which testicle I would rather have crushed. But I guess I would say Bobby Bare Jr. and Waco Brothers."

Asheville, NC:

"I saw the Waco Bros two years ago. It changed my life. I saw Split Lip Rayfield six months ago & I met the devil. Nice guy, just has a real problem with authority figures. Could you ask Sally Timms or Melissa Swingle [*ed.:* from Trailer Bride] to marry me? Please let me know which one answers yes first."

Carbondale, IL:

> "Dear Bloodshot Folks: Now that I have my '83 Ford Ranger running again I need some more Waco Brothers, since they're one of the outfits that sound good over my cheap speakers and the rattling of the truck."
>
> (*I cannot think of a finer compliment!*)

Los Angeles, CA:

> "I think that either God or the Devil must've whispered Neko's name in my ear and said, 'Buy this.' Whichever it was, bless them."

San Francisco, CA:

> "After seeing Rico Bell, I now have a new standard for COOL. Henceforth, cool shall be judged on the Rico Bell scale with a person's coolness expressed as a fraction of a 'Rico Bell.' For example, an extremely cool person would be a '*.9 Rico Bell.*'"

Washington, DC:

> "You just mention Sally Timms to some people and they soil their pants."

Cambridge, MA:

> "To whom it may concern: What can you do to get the Yayhoos to release some more music? My seven and eight year old daughters recently received blank stares from their fellow classmates when they ID'd them as their favorite singers, and my youngest started singing the 'Bottle and the Bible' at their Catholic school. Got a phone call from the priest in charge and had to do some explaining."
>
> (*This is A+ parenting.*)

Browning, MT, re: a free sampler CD we included in a mail order:

> "I put the CD on and BAM the Yawpers came on. I am including some cold, hard cash I earned cleaning shitters at church (yeah, their shit stinks too) for their albums. It should be enough to cover shipping and if there is still anything left throw that shit in a hat being passed around at a Yawpers show or take [Scott H.] Biram out to eat or buy him some new guitar strings since he breaks so many."

Haleiwa, HI, re: the purchase of the *Down to the Promised Land* compilation:

> "I like the kind of country music that sounds like it's made by people who get drunk a lot, have nasty sex all night long in cheap motels & wake up with severe hangovers & I can't stomach all the Nashville pretty boy shit. I was

hoping this album would be something special. WOW! It was everything I hoped for & MORE. I've been playing the discs non-stop for the last couple of days & friends look at me a little funny, but then I play them some of the songs & they start singing along with me. I'm enclosing $150 for more. Send me what you think I'll like. If it goes over, bill me. I'm good for it. If it's too much, buy yourself some beers on me."

(*You don't conjure brand loyalty like this out of thin air.*)

Denton, TX, re: Scott H. Biram:

"I'm going to get naked and drink whiskey to this shit. Just so you know."

Tempe, AZ, when answering the question "How did you hear about this artist?" on the reply card in a Scott H. Biram CD:

"I heard about him while I was getting naked with a friend. How's that for honesty?"

(*A little TOO honest, actually.*)

Kirkwood, MO, re: her purchase of Scott H. Biram stickers:

"I love me some Biram, and I'm going to put these bumper stickers on my boobies."

Austin, TX:

"Scott H. Biram makes me shit my pants with pleasurepain and the Meat Purveyors make me not care that I'm sitting in my own shit."

(*Apparently, they retain writing privileges at the institutions for profane coprophiliacs that house many of Scott's fans.*)

Lancaster, PA:

"I saw the Deadstring Brothers at the Chameleon with Shooter [Jennings] last week. My wife threw her bra on stage. I approve of this behavior."

Norcross, GA:

Fave Bloodshot artists: Nora O'Connor/Neko Case
How did you hear about them: "Friend of the family who was fucking my wife behind my back."

Springfield, MO:

How did you hear about Neko Case: "The guy my wife has been fucking behind my back."

(*Dang, early Neko brought out the adultery in people . . .*)

Brighton, MA:

> "If I die in some freak accident before the next Neko Case album comes out, my spirit will haunt your office for all of eternity."

Austin, TX:

> "Bought *Blacklisted* the day after seeing Neko. Excellent! Two days later, some fish head broke into my house while I was in church and stole my CD player and .38 special revolver. They missed the CD, though . . . and it plays in my truck."

Lawrence, KS, re: the purchase of a Bloodshot work shirt with a random name patch:

> "The shirt is great, I like the color and the sleeves, and the patches . . . except for one. The name patch is, ummm, sort of a problem. What are the odds of the name being my ex's? I have hung the shirt in my closet and keep looking at it, but I can't bring myself to wear it—let alone have my boyfriend wear it. Is the shirt exchangeable?"
>
> (*Of course! And I was impressed one of our fans hung their clothes up!*)

Columbus, IN:

> Please send free catalog. I am mostly interested in *KARAOKE* music.
>
> (*Who isn't?*)

Idaho Falls, ID:

> "I love Ryan Adams because I hate *everything* else. I don't even eat breakfast because I hate it. And I hate bowling shoes. So I wouldn't eat breakfast in a bowling alley."
>
> (*Admirable usage of the transitive property.*)

Denver, CO:

> "I saw Jon Langford and Sally Timms here on Friday. They were not pleased with the sound. SALLY is a world class cusser."
>
> (*I couldn't fucking agree more.*)

You can't have fan mail without hate mail:

Ft. Worth, TX:

> "My favorite BS artist: None, you guys have no music that I'm into & don't showcase bands like mine!!!"

Pittsburgh, PA:

"Please do not send me anything related to Ryan Adams. I have been to well over 1000 shows of artists and he is the most unprofessional, cry baby drunkard in the industry."

Evanston, IL:

"I saw Sally Timms on Friday and I have to say I haven't seen that much of an unpleasant person performing on stage in a long, long time. She really pushed the envelope as far as being rude and just an all-around sour person. I am surprised Bloodshot would promote such an incredible bitch. I didn't realize Bloodshot signed Divas."

Clarkdale, AZ:

"The *Furnace Room Lullaby* cover is horrible. Is Neko trying her best to stay unheard of?"

Cathedral City, CA:

"I sent back the Yayhoos CD. I don't want it because it contained vulgarities. The cover of the CD did not have an advisory sticker. This is outrageous. I'm serious. Please return my money immediately."

(*Geez, if we returned everything with vulgarities. . . .*)

Eden Prairie, MN:

"I just purchased Kelly Hogan's *Because It Feel Good* CD. The plastic thing that sticks to the upper edge of the CD is ruining my life and breaking my heart. PLEASE STOP USING THOSE THINGS. THEY FUCKING SUCK."

(*If this is your biggest problem, perhaps you have a life worth ruining and a heart in need of breaking. . . .*)

We received a fair number of remarkably frank catalog requests from jail/prison/state hospitals:

"Punker needs help getting music in a mental hospital."

"I'm a true country fan in NE TN, I am currently serving time for drug possession. I would be grateful for a catalog."

"Please send me a catalog and any free promo stuff. It sucks here in drug rehab. It's so boring and I'm a big time rock n roller."

Finally, two letters on opposite sides of the spectrum, both touching in their own way:

Mundelein, IL, from a seventh-grader:

> "My favorite bands are Split Lip Rayfield, Scroat Belly, and Scott H. Biram. I have to write a letter for a school project, and I need a point of contact for them."
>
> (*This was in 2008. So this kid is now either a super cool programmer on the cutting edges of space/nano-technologies . . . or doing hard time.*)

Return address unreadable:

> "Do I get a gift if I'm on acid?" [Came with a drawing of a shaggy outlaw cowboy smoking an outsized doobie.]
>
> (*Nice try. As the Great Gretzky said, "You miss 100% of the shots you don't take."*)

If there is any point to these, it is this: if you are a supporter of independent businesses, show your love, however simply. They will appreciate it. It gets lonely fighting the good fight. It was always good to know that there were people with us.

APPENDIX G

Bloodshot's Yard Dog Party Lineups during South by Southwest

NEVER AN INVITATION, WRISTBAND, OR BADGE NEEDED:
FRIDAY STARTING AT NOON
NO COVER
FREE BEER

Photo by Anthony Nguyen, used with permission.

1996

Old 97's
Moonshine Willy
Waco Brothers

1997

Whiskeytown
Lonesome Bob
Hazeldine
Jon Langford's Skull Orchard
The Volebeats
Moonshine Willy
Grievous Angels
Waco Brothers

1998

Moonshine Willy
The Riptones
Neko Case & the Sadies
Grievous Angels
Split Lip Rayfield
Trailer Bride
Calexico w/Howe Gelb & Lisa Germano
Alejandro Escovedo
The Meat Purveyors
Waco Brothers

1999

Devil in a Woodpile
The Blacks
Neko Case
Grievous Angels
The Handsome Family
Trailer Bride
Split Lip Rayfield
The Meat Purveyors
The Sadies
Waco Brothers

2000

The Riptones
Calexico w/ Alejandro Escovedo
Kelly Hogan & the Pine Valley Cosmonauts
The Blacks
Devil in a Woodpile
Rico Bell & the Snakehandlers
Split Lip Rayfield
Rex Hobart & the Misery Boys
Waco Brothers w/Sally Timms

2001

Split Lip Rayfield
The Blacks
Caitlin Cary
Rico Bell & the Snakehandlers
The Meat Purveyors
Sally Timms
The Riptones
Rex Hobart & the Misery Boys
Four Killer Flats
Paul Burch & the WPA Ballclub
Waco Brothers

2002

Jim & Jennie and the Pinetops
Rex Hobart & the Misery Boys
Kelly Hogan
Bobby Bare Jr.
Split Lip Rayfield
The Yayhoos
The Meat Purveyors

2003

Jon Rauhouse & Calexico
Rex Hobart & the Misery Boys
The Legendary Shack Shakers
Trailer Bride
Kelly Hogan & Jon Rauhouse

Wayne Hancock
The Meat Purveyors
Dollar Store
Bobby Bare Jr.
Waco Brothers

2004

Rex Hobart & the Misery Boys
Dollar Store
Bobby Bare Jr.
Jon Rauhouse w/Kelly Hogan & Sally Timms
Graham Parker
Trailer Bride
Paul Burch
Split Lip Rayfield
The Meat Purveyors
The Yayhoos

2005

Devil in a Woodpile
Pat Todd & the Rank Outsiders
Sally Timms & Johnny Dowd
Jon Langford & the Sexy
Dollar Store
The Meat Purveyors
Nora O'Connor
Rex Hobart & the Misery Boys
Jim & Jennie and the Pinetops
Scott H. Biram
Waco Brothers

2006

Carolyn Mark
Devil in a Woodpile
Matt Mays & El Torpedo
Bobby Bare Jr. and Sr.
Bottle Rockets
Deadstring Brothers
Scott H. Biram
Mark Pickerel
The Meat Purveyors
Cordero
Waco Brothers

2007

Danbert Nobacon
Carolyn Mark
Ha Ha Tonka
Deadstring Brothers
Mark Pickerel
Jon Rauhouse
Graham Parker
The Silos
Gore Gore Girls
Clem Snide
Waco Brothers

2008

Firewater
Carolyn Mark
Bobby Bare Jr.
The Scotland Yard Gospel Choir
Ha Ha Tonka
Justin Townes Earle
Deadstring Brothers
Mark Pickerel
The Silos (a tribute to Drew Glackin)
Andre Williams
Waco Brothers

2009

Walter Salas-Humara
I'm Not Jim
Charlie Pickett
Dex Romweber Duo
Ha Ha Tonka
Exene Cervenka
Andre Williams
Deadstring Brothers
The Meat Purveyors
Justin Townes Earle

Artwork by Pete Klockau.

The Scotland Yard Gospel Choir
Waco Brothers w/ Rosie Flores

2010

The Silos
Whitey Morgan & the 78s
Ben Weaver
Ha Ha Tonka
Rosie Flores
Justin Townes Earle
Exene Cervenka
Deadstring Brothers
Waco Brothers

2011

Carolyn Mark w/ the Jack Grace Band
Maggie Björklund w/ Cobirds Unite
Lydia Loveless
Exene Cervenka
Whitey Morgan & the 78s
Freakwater
Eddie Spaghetti
Ha Ha Tonka
Waco Brothers

2012

Southeast Engine
Valerie June
Cory Branan
Deadstring Brothers
Wayne Hancock
Lydia Loveless
Rosie Flores
JC Brooks & the Uptown Sound
Waco Brothers & Paul Burch w/Bill Kirchen

Artwork by Pete Klockau.

2013

Lydia Loveless
Deadstring Brothers
Luke Winslow-King
Bobby Bare Jr.
JC Brooks & the Uptown Sound
Murder by Death
Rosie Flores
Waco Brothers

2014

Lydia Loveless
The Deslondes
Luke Winslow-King
Robbie Fulks
Bobby Bare Jr.
Rosie Flores
Ha Ha Tonka
Barrence Whitfield and the Savages
Waco Brothers

2015

Water Liars
Rosie Flores
Banditos
Luke Winslow-King
Bobby Bare Jr.
JC Brooks & the Uptown Sound
Waco Brothers

2016

Possessed By Paul James
Rosie Flores
Banditos
Luke Winslow-King
Lydia Loveless
Robbie Fulks
The Yawpers
Al Scorch
Waco Brothers

2017

Zach Schmidt
Sarah Shook & the Disarmers
The Yawpers
Banditos
Cory Branan
Ha Ha Tonka
Waco Brothers

2018

Joe Purdy
Vandoliers
Jon Langford's Four Lost Souls
Sarah Shook & the Disarmers

Ruby Boots
Waco Brothers

2019

Jason Hawk Harris
Sarah Shook & the Disarmers
William Elliott Whitmore
Banditos
Robbie Fulks & Linda Gail Lewis
Vandoliers
The Yawpers
Laura Jane Grace & the Devouring Mothers
Waco Brothers

Index

ROB MILLER is the co-founder and former co-owner of Bloodshot Records. His website is robmillerwriting.com.

The University of Illinois Press
is a founding member of the
Association of University Presses.

Text designed by Jim Proefrock
Composed in 10.25/13 Miller Text
with Steak display
at the University of Illinois Press
Manufactured by Versa Press, Inc.

University of Illinois Press
1325 South Oak Street
Champaign, IL 61820-6903
www.press.uillinois.edu

CMJ
MUSIC
OB MILLER
RECORDS
9, 1995
Tully Hall
Lincoln Center
Blind Pig
k.d. lang
★ AND ★
BARRENCE
WHITFIELD
and The
SAVAGES!
MAYNE STAGE
328 W. MORSE AVE. CHICAGO, ILL.
FRIDAY NITE, OCT 3RD, 2014
TO BE BROADCAST NATIONALLY ON PBS STATIONS
DETAILS AND UPDATES AT BLOODSHOTRECORDS.COM
XRT
SOUTHERN CULTURE ON THE
WITH WOGGLES
AND SPLIT LIP RAYFIELD
CH1103
BALC3R
FRONT BALCONY
A
28.00
CAPA PRESENTS
BUENA VISTA SOCIAL CLUB
$1.50 RESTORATION FEE INCL
CNT 42X
A 306
4031150
A28JUN9
14050 GRATIOT S. OF 7 MILE
372 2320
Friday
Feb.22
$6
SCREAM
FROM D.C.
FROM TEXAS
M.O.R.
RECORDS
Rob
Miller
Bloodshot Records
GAVIN
to THE KNITTERS
KELLY HOGAN & THE
CATHERINE IRWIN
NORA O'CONN
JOHN DOE
THE HANDSOME
FEB.21
THE